Adi Shankara: The Jagad Guru

His Life and Philosophy

Dedicated to

My brother S. N. Nagji (Etta)

And my sisters

Radha Devidas (Omanchi) and

Indira Prabhakaran (Innachi)

ADI SHANKARA
The Jagad Guru

(*His Life and Philosophy*)

Shantha N. Nair

GLOBAL VISION PUBLISHING HOUSE
20, Ansari Road, Daryaganj, New Delhi-110002 (INDIA)

GLOBAL VISION PUBLISHING HOUSE
F-4, 1st Floor, 'Hari Sadan' 20, Ansari Road,
Daryaganj, New Delhi-110002 (INDIA)
Tel.: 011-64691271, 23261581, 23276291
E-mail: nsingh_2004@vsnl.net; info@globalvisionpub.com
Website: globalvisionpub.com

Adi Shankara: The Jagad Guru

First Edition, 2010

ISBN: 978-81-8220-306-8

PRINTED IN INDIA

Published by Dr. N.K. Singh for Global Vision Publishing House, New Delhi-2 and *Printed at* Balaji Offset, Naveen Shahdara, Delhi-32

Acknowledgement

I am highly indebted to all the authors of various articles, and books on Adi Shankara and the scholars and spiritual leaders who translated the *Upanishads*, *Brahma Sutras*, *Bhagavad Gita* and the stotras and *Prakarana Granthas* of Adi Shankara from the original Sanskrit version in to English. All these have helped me immensely in writing this book.

I am grateful to my husband K.C.N. Nair for all his valuable help through out. I appreciate the interest shown by my son Uday Gowri Shankar and my daughter in law Roopa Shankar in helping me at every step. I cannot forget the interest and enthusiasm shown by our nephew Vishwajit who accompanied my husband and me to Kaladi, the birthplace of Adi Shankara and his friend Santhosh for all his help at Kaladi. I am highly thankful for their co-operation. This book is my gift to my grand children Pranav Shankar and Gayathri Shankar.

Preface

This book is about the life, works and philosophy of Adi Shankara, who was a remarkable genius and a spiritual giant. Adi Shankara emerged on the Indian scene at a time when moral and religious chaos was reigning supreme in the holy land of India. Adi Shankara's advent had a great impact on the religious, cultural and spiritual history of India.

Shankara's childhood was marked by extraordinary happenings. When he grew up and became a monk he showed a remarkable combination of the qualities of a staunch devotee and a poet. Shankara during his lifetime as a wandering monk also proved to be a real *Karma yogi* or a man of action. The incidents during this period in his life as a wandering monk and religious reformer are standing testimony of his keen intelligence, sharp logic and reasoning power and rational analysis together with his ability to silence his opponents in debate and in philosophical arguments. He also proved himself to be a great commentator of many of the scriptures the most important being the *Prasthana Traya* that contained ten of the principal Upanishads, *Brahma Sutras* and *Bhagavad Gita.* His commentary on the *Prasthana Traya* especially is considered as the masterpiece of all works of Shankara. His works also included many hymns in which Shankara placed himself as a *Bhakta* and philosophical treatises that explain in detail about his philosophy of Kevala Advaitha Vedantha. Shankara's divine mission on earth was to bring back the lost glory of *Vedic Dharma* that forms the basis of *Sanathana Dharma* or the universal *Dharma* or code of conduct or the Hindu religion. Shankara could not have achieved his life's mission had he remained in *Nirvikalpa Samadhi* in which nothing but Brahman is experienced. It is also said that Shankara had learnt all Vedas and other Hindu scriptures including the *Smritis* and mastered the philosophical doctrines of other sects and religions found in India during his time, and had mastery over Hatha Yoga, Raja Yoga and so on at a very early age. The knowledge of these gave him enormous psychic powers like clairvoyance, telepathy and so on. To spread the message and teachings of the Vedas, particularly Advaitha Vedantha he toured throughout the country bare foot. With this purpose he also established four Mutts in the four corners of India, the Sringeri Mutt in the South, the Govardhana Mutt in the East, the Dwaraka Mutt in the west and the Joshi Mutt in the north of India. These Mutts were headed by four chief disciples of Adi Shankara.

Shankara based his philosophical arguments on the four Vedas namely, the *Rig*, *Sama*, *Yajur* and *Atharva Vedas*. He propagated his teachings in all the nook and corner of India and succeeded in establishing the superiority of the doctrine of Advaitha Vedantha. As a Bhakta or devotee he wrote several hymns in praise of several Gods and Goddesses, some of which have the undercurrents of his philosophy of Advaitha Vedantha. He also wrote several philosophical treatises known as *Prakarana Granthas* that explained his Kevala Advaitha Philosophy. Shankara also set aside all misconceptions, misinterpretation and confusion about the great and ancient Vedic Dharma that forms the basis of *Sanathana Dharma* or the universal code of conduct or Hinduism, and re-established the true Vedic path. In this process he proved himself to be a great Bhakta or a devotee, a real *Karma Yogi* or a man of action and a remarkable *Gnana Yogi* who followed the path of wisdom. To him Devotion or *Bhakti* and action or *Karma* led to *Gnana* or wisdom in the realization of the ultimate truth- the knowledge of *Parabrahman* that is the same as *Paramatma* or the Universal soul that is not different from the *Jeevatma* or the individual soul. After fulfilling his divine mission he bade good-bye to the world. He lived nearly 2515 years ago and lived only for 32 years. Still, India and the world feels his impact in resurrecting the lost glory of the real Vedic path and Vedic Dharma.

This book is divided in to seven chapters. The first chapter introduces one to Adi Shankara, the remarkable genius and the spiritual giant the world had ever produced. It gives a glimpse of Adi Shankara the genius, the Indian scene during the advent of Adi

Shankara, an outline of the religions other than Hinduism and the traditional doctrines that are based on Vedas but are opposed to Vedantha that were found during his time, Shankara's life and mission, and finally mentions the names of records titled as Shankara Vijayamas' that give an account of Shankara's life. The second chapter gives a short sketch of his biography. It gives a brief account of Shankara's birth, his remarkable childhood, his life as a Brahmachari, Shankara embracing *Sanyasa*, his journey towards his teacher or Guru, his Digvijaya or tour through out the country as a wandering monk and as a *Karma Yogi*, the incidents during his travel, about his disciples, the establishment of Mutts by Shankara, his ascent to *Sarvajana Peetam* or the Throne of eminence, and his last days. A brief account of Shankara's works that include mainly his commentaries on the ten principal Upanishads, the *Brahama Sutras* and *Bhagavadgita* that form the *Prasthana Traya*, the names of popular hymns that he composed and his philosophical works that are known as the *Prakarana Granths* are included in the third chapter. A glimpse of Shankara the *Bhakta* or devotee and an excellent poet as seen through the summary of 28 of his very touching, poetic and devotional stotras that he composed is given in the fourth chapter. The fifth chapter shows Shankara as a devotee and a philosopher at the same time. The gist of 12 hymns that has devotion and the undercurrents of Advaitha philosophy are presented here. A brief summary of 23 hymns and philosophical treatises put together that give the essence of the Kevala Advaitha Vedantha philosophy of Shankara forms the sixth chapter. The concluding seventh chapter gives a brief outline of Advaitha Vedantha particularly the Kevala Advaitha Vedantha philosophy of Adi Shankara. It starts with a brief account of the importance of Advaitha Vedantha, its basis, its tradition, and then goes on with an account of Advaitha Vedantha as seen in *Upanishads* and in the writings of Goudapada who was Shankara's *Parama Guru* or teacher's teacher, the Parampara or the lineage of Shankara in Advaitha Vedantha philosophy, the Kevala Advaitha Vedantha of Shankara, his Vivartha Vada, the place of *Jnana* or wisdom in this doctrine, Mayavada of Shankara, the notions regarding world, three levels of reality, *Maya* or illusion, Iswara or God, *Jeevatman* or the individual soul, Paramatman or the universal soul, *Moksha* or liberation in Shankara's philosophy, about Shankara the reformist, Shankara and Buddhism, misconceptions about Shankara's philosophy, and concludes by giving a glimpse of the terms connected with Advaitha Vedantha, Advaitha Vedantha in modern Science and relevance of Advaitha Vedantha in the modern world. A few concepts that frequently appear in spiritual knowledge, particularly in the philosophy of Advaita Vedantha are taken up here just for sharing the views of the author with the readers.

This book is meant for young minds and common people who are eager to know about Adi Shankara's life, works and his interpretation of Advaitha Vedantha that is termed as Kevala Advaitha Vedantha and to benefit from it. It is a fact that the young minds today are filled with the knowledge of scientific and technological advancement that has enhanced the material well being of man. These are to be welcomed as they have benefited the human society greatly by raising people's standard of living. But at the same time one cannot ignore their negative impacts especially when the material knowledge that is acquired is being misused for the degradation and destruction of man and this has become a matter of great concern for the entire world today. Not only that. We do find instances where the inventions that were meant for greater human welfare have actually brought about severe damage to health and happiness of man. This is because ethics and spirituality are relegated to the background to day and religions that is meant to lead to spiritual knowledge and teach ethical code of conduct and a life in accordance with the cosmic laws that govern the universe are being misinterpreted, misunderstood and are confined to mere rituals and worship. Nodoubt, rituals and worship to the chosen deity of one give a lot of mental satisfaction and peace of mind and happiness as long as one concentrates on the idols that represent the cosmic power, and also there is nothing wrong in seeking material happiness from the divine, the Almighty, the creator that is the supreme energy and power that is the cause of the entire universe. Afterall, idols that are worshipped are only manifestation of that supreme energy. As long as it is not possible for one to turn inwards and understand that this supreme power or energy, that is the cause of all creation is right inside one's own heart, there is nothing wrong in seeking the divine guidance and blessings for material and non material welfare by performing rituals and by praying and concentrating on the idols that are external to oneself, if one believes in them and has experienced the efficacy of prayers and has faith in them as faith can do miracles. Sincere and honest devotion to the chosen deity whom one considers as the Supreme power and on whom one has faith gives immense support to man especially in times of misfortunes. Material well being is also important as long as one lives in the material world and when one leads a normal life unlike that of a *sanyasin* who has forsaken all attachments to the world. But one must also understand that one should go beyond such seekings atleast gradually as age advances. Instead of seeking material things and material happiness that is only temporary one should seek the ultimate wisdom for ultimate happiness, firstly because one's life is the outcome of one's own good and bad Karmas of the past and one cannot escape from their effects and also lasting happiness can be got only by going beyond material happiness derived from the senses and mind, as denoted in the scriptures and in the teachings of the *Seers* and saints of ancient India. Also while there is no harm in rituals and worships accompanied with rituals, one must try to understand their real inherent principles underlying these rituals to elevate one's mind to get everlasting happiness and peace. Such knowledge also will make man to face the challenges of life in a calm manner without being disheartened or shattered when he comes face to face with adverse situations or misfortunes in life. Lasting happiness and welfare of mankind can be achieved only through elevating one's mind spiritually. While the lower mind craves for material happiness the higher mind seeks spiritual upliftment. For everlasting happiness it is necessary for man to know that material happiness is not everything in life as it cannot be lasting because of the ever craving nature of the mind. So it is essential that while one tries to fulfill the craving of his senses and mind, should at the same time realize that it is impossible for him to satisfy all such cravings permanently since the wants and desires continue to crop up one after the other and also because the happiness derived by satisfying the wants and desires of body and mind last only for a while because later after some time they cease to provide any happiness and also, in some cases they even turn to give unhappiness to man. Running after material happiness continuously can bring about negative qualities and hence negative energy in man ultimately. The knowledge and Understanding of that energy that is located in the core of one's heart, definitely, would lead to jnana or wisdom that give permanent peace and bliss. So, even while living in the relative world one should try to know that supreme energy that is right inside one's heart and derive happiness that is imperishable and everlasting and realize the fact that one can hope to achieve permanent happiness only by training his mind to accept and at the same time reject all material happiness with a sense of equanimity. While leading a life in the world it is necessary that he involves himself in many things but he should take care to see that he does not get entangled in them. It is a wrong notion to think that spirituality is concerned with the liberation of the soul only. Even the Vedas, that are considered as the basis of Indian thinking and ethos are supposed to satisfy all the four types of human aspirations, namely, Dharma, *Artha, Karma* and *Moksha*.

According to the ancient seers who have realized the ultimate truth through their introspection at their Supra conscious, meditative state, the one who has realized the eternal truth will have equanimity in which one sees one in all, (as all beings are the same in their subtle form although they seem to appear differently physically at the gross level) and enjoys even mindedness in which one accepts and receives all fortunes and misfortunes of life in an equal manner without giving any importance to them. Such virtues would eliminate all negative qualities like hatred, violence, jealousy and so on and in its place one can find love, kindness, charity, selflessness and so on that would bring about a happy state of well being and at the same time pave the way for the upliftment of the soul spiritually that culminates in the liberation of the soul in which one goes beyond the cycle of repeated births and deaths.

A knowledge about the great ancient Indian scriptures and the biographies of great teachers and their teachings the principles of which that are to be included in a value based education that is to be made as a part of formal education in schools and colleges can go a long way in bringing about the necessary change for better that is required to day especially in the mind set of children and young people. The parents also have an equal responsibility in inculcating the great values and virtues in the minds of their children as this will make the future citizens of any country tolerant, loving, caring, compassionate and so on and that would help in creating a harmonious society, in which all humans lead a life in contentment, happiness and peace and with a live and let live attitude. The older generation too would benefit immensely from such knowledge as it would help them to lead the twilight period of their life in a happy, peaceful, understanding and tolerant manner by uplifting their mind as revealed by the sages of ancient India, especially as this is the period of failing physical health, emotional, physical and sometimes even financial dependence. It is also a period when they (unless they have elevated their mind spiritually) are faced with a feeling of lack of attention and due importance to them and a loss of authority. It is usually said that in old age people become intolerant, complaining and full of self pity. But one must understand that mind has no age and even in old age one can, if he wants to, train his mind to uplift itself. A person who has uplifted his mind with the knowledge of body, self and the world, physical problems and sufferings due to old age need not cause mental sorrows as they are the creations of mind. The gross physical body that is the product of the five elements is bound to follow the natural process of growth, decline and decay. But it need not depress a person. We all know that physical suffering is not felt by a person whose mind is dormant. For example, one does not feel the pain of surgery, when one is under anaesthesia. So, it is the mind that creates sorrows and happiness for man. The feeling that one is being neglected and becomes unwanted and burdensome in old age is mainly because of too much of mental dependence and attachment to worldly things and also because of the sense of ego and the unnecessary feeling that one has become old and hence useless. The remedy for this lies in developing a sense of detachment by gaining the required spiritual understanding. A healthy mind does not bother much about an unhealthy body. But an unhealthy mind creates problems even for a healthy body. An unhealthy body creates mental agony only for those who lack the necessary higher knowledge. It is a fact that man desires only peace and happiness but not lack of peace and sorrows. Contentment that leads to Peace of mind and Happiness can be achieved in any period of one's life only by elevating one's mind. Both heaven and hell are in the world only. The one whose thoughts, words, and deeds are positive has positive energy in him and he also spreads positive energy everywhere around him and there by creates heaven for himself and for the others. On the other hand the one whose thoughts, words and deeds are negative not only suffers from negative energy but also spreads negative energy all around him and there by creates hell for himself as well as for others. The knowledge that would elevate one's mind can be got by self analysis through continuous meditation and self awareness without taking the guidance of scriptures and teachers, which is usually possible only for the great sages, or by people who are spiritually advanced since such a knowledge is not attained easily as it requires a lot of physical and mental discipline. It is like reaching a destination without any knowledge of the route. Sometimes it is like groping in the dark as there is every possibility that one who tries this method, if he is not competent enough to tread this path, would end in a wrong place or will have to remain in the same place or returns to the same place from where he started. In this method one does not believe unless one gets the experience by himself. In the other method, one takes the guidance of scriptures and teachers. It is like taking the routemap for reaching an unknown destination. Such a person learns the spiritual truths from the study of scriptures, and without belief or disbelief, that is, without accepting or rejecting them, but by understanding the fact that the great knowledge as told in the scriptures and by the teachers are the results of their subjective experience, analyses the contents and their teachings, ponders over them and then comes to understand the truth by himself through self analysis. Whichever method one follows this knowledge of the ultimate truth alone would help in creating happiness in the individuals, family, society, nation, and in the world as a whole.

The intention of the author in writing this book is to give a taste of some of the great Indian thinking as seen through the findings of the great seers of ancient India through this book on Adi Shankara's life, works and philosophy to benefit youngsters, parents, educators and people who are advanced in age. It is also an effort to give an idea about the great Advaitha teacher Adi Shankara to people who have no knowledge of this great genius and spiritual giant about whom our country should really be proud of. Finally it is an effort to induce the young minds and the general readers to go deep in to the philosophy of Advaitha Vedantha after going through this book on Adi Shankara- the *Jagad Guru*-the world teacher.

Contents

1
Adi Shankara: The Genius

Adi Shankara or the first Shankaracharya, the *Jagad Guru*, the world teacher, who is also popularly known as Shankaracharya, Shankara the teacher, and also as Shankara Bhagavad Padacharya, meaning the teacher at the feet of the Lord, emerged on the Indian scene at a time when moral and religious chaos and confusion were reigning supreme in the sacred land of India which was once the happiest, glorious, and peaceful land of the greatest of *rishis* and sages. The advent of Shankara had a great impact on the religious, cultural and spiritual history of India. He was unique in the sense that he combined all the attributes of an extraordinary child, great mystic, practical and comprehensive philosopher, a Yogi and a *Jnani*, a staunch devotee, an illumined sage of the highest order, a gifted poet, a stupendous writer, supreme religious reformer and a theologian, a wonderful teacher, an unparalleled preacher and debater, a great ascetic, an intellectual giant, a remarkable exponent of Advaita Vedanta and a stupendous spiritual force. He was also a giant metaphysician. He was a marvelous and a super human genius with mastery over logic. As Dr. Radhakrishnan has put it "The life of Shankara makes a strong impression of contraries. He is a philosopher and a poet, a savant and a saint, a mystic and a religious reformer. Such diverse gifts did he possess that different images present themselves, if we try to recall his personality. One sees him in youth on fire with intellectual ambition, a stiff and intrepid debator;

another regards him as a shrewd political genius (rather a patriot) attempting to impress on the people a sense of unity, for a third, he is a calm philosopher engaged in the single effort to expose the contradictions of life and thought with an unmatched inciveness; for a fourth, he is the mystic who declares that we are all greater than we know. There have been few minds more universal than this". The English philosopher Douglas Grant Ainslie described Adi Shankara as the "mightiest mind that ever dwelt in human body". Swami Vivekananda said, "He who declared "I will come whenever virtue subsides" came again, and this time the manifestation was in the south, and up rose that young Brahmin boy of whom it has been declared that at the age of sixteen he had completed all his writings; the marvellous boy Shankara arose. The writings of this boy of sixteen are the wonders of the modern world, and so was the boy".

Shankara's childhood was marked by extraordinary happenings. Later when he grew up and became a monk, he showed a remarkable combination of the qualities of a staunch devotee and a poet, and poured forth his inner most carvings, to his chosen Deities with form or *Saguna Brahman* that was to him a manifestation of *Nirguna Brahman*. He also visited many temples that were neglected and revived worship in all those temples. Shankara's divine Mission of his life would not have been accomplished if he had remained in *Nirvikala Samadhi*, in which nothing but Brahman is experienced. The incidents during his lifetime as a wandering monk and religious reformer are standing testimony of his keen intelligence, sharp logic and reasoning power and rational analysis coupled with his remarkable capacity to make his opponents agree with his philosophical arguments. He also proved himself to be a great commentator through all his great commentaries particularly the commentaries on the Prasthana Thraya. It is said that Shankara had learnt all the *Vedas*, *Upanishads* and all other ancient Hindu scriptures and completed *Sadhanas*, and mastered the philosophical systems of *Nyaya, Sankhya, Mimamsa, Yoga sutras* of *Patanjali*, the Buddhist philosophical systems like *Sautantrika, Yogacharya, Madhyamika, Vaibhasika* and so on, the jain philosophy and also that of Charvakas by the time he was eight years old. He also learnt *Hatha Yoga*, and *Raja Yoga*, the science of disciplining the mind. The knowledge of these subjects gave him the gift of psychic powers like telepathy, clairvoyance, moving in space unseen, and so on. In the third year of his study under his *Guru*, Govinda, Shankara mastered *Jnana Yoga*. By sixteen, he wrote Bhashyas and commentaries on the principal Upanishads, Brahma Sutras and *Bhagavad Gita*. In fact he was one of the very few gifted geniuses that the world had ever produced. He was a *jeevanmukta* who got liberated even while living in this world although he continued to live in this world, for all practical purposes, like lotus in water, totally detached. He also wrote a number of devotional hymns and philosophical treatises. He lived nearly 2515 years ago and lived only for 32 years 6 months and 10 days and still India and the entire world even today feels the impact of the life, writings and the philosophy of this unparallel, unique and extraordinary spiritual giant and Genius and his impact has remained unfaded even to this day.

Shankara's life was very short but highly eventful. He was the greatest exponent of Advaita Vedanta and he was the first one to consolidate the philosophy of Advaita Vedanta. He is appropriately called as the pillar of Advaita Vedanta. Single-handed, with in a very short span he overpowered the numerous powerful forces opposed to Vedic Sanathana Dharma and restored Vedanta in the form of Advaita Vedanta. Through his rare analytical power and unique argumentative ability he preached Advaita Vedanta with fullness and clarity and convinced one and all who belonged to the opposing philosophies. He walked barefoot through out India and defeated his opponents. He condemned human and animal sacrifices and foolish rituals in the name of religion. Even as a monk he performed the funeral rights for his mother that was against the tradition of monks and that was vehemently opposed by the whole Brahmin community of his native place.

Establishment of Mutts

Shankara founded Mutts or monasteries in the four corners of India to strengthen, sustain and foster Vedic Hindu Dharma. He established the Sringeri Mutt in the south in Karnataka, Dwaraka Mutt also known as Kalika Mutt in the western part of India in Gujarat, the Puri Mutt in the eastern part of India in Orissa, and Joshimutt in the northern part of India in Uttarkhand. His disciples Padmapada, Hastamalaka, Totaka and Sureshwaracharya were made the heads of Mutts at Dwaraka, Puri, Joshimutt and Sringeri.

The Sharada Peetam at Sringeri was associated with the mantra 'Aham Brahmasmi' found in the Yajur Veda that means 'I am Brahman'. The Govardhana Mutt at Puri was associated with the mantra' Prajnanam Brahman' found in the Rig Veda, that means, Brahman is knowledge, the Dwaraka Peeth at Dwaraka was associated with the Mantra '*Tat Tvam Asi*' found in the *Sama Veda*, that means, 'That thou art' and the Joshi Mutt was associated with the *Mantra 'Ayam Atma Brahman*' found in the Atharva Veda that means, 'This Atman is Brahman'.

The four Mutts were also associated with the four Vedas. The Shringeri Mutt in south India with Krishna Yajur Veda, the Mutt at Puri in the east with *Rig Veda*, the Dwaraka mutt of the west with *Sama Veda* and the Joshi Mutt in the north with *Atharva Veda*. He also introduced the Panchayathana worship on all these mutts in which five deities are worshipped namely, Lord Shiva, Lord Vishnu, Adithya, Ambika and Ganapaty. Four traditions are associated with these Mutts. The Sharada Peetam is associated with Bhurivala tradition, the Dwaraka Peetam is associated with Kitavala, the Govardhana Peetam is associated with Bhogavala and the Joshi Mutt is associated with Nandavala tradition. The four Mutts that are established by Shankara in the four directions of India came to be known as the Amnaya Mutts. Their heads have the title' Shankaracharya' after the original founder Adi Shankara or Shankaracharya.

Shankara introduced the tradition or Sampradaya of Dasanami Sanyasins in these Mutts. It is called 'Dasanami' because of the ten titles that suffix their names. They add at the end of their names any of the ten suffixes namely, Saraswati, Bharati, and Puri, used by Sringeri Mutt, Theertha and Ashrama used by the Dwaraka Mutt, Giri, *Parvatha* and *Sagar* used by Joshi Mutt and Vana and

Aranya used by the Govardhana Mutt. He unified all the theistic sects under the Shanmatha system, based on Advaita Vedanta. It centers on the worship of six main deities namely, Shiva, Vishnu, Shakti, Ganesh, Soorya and *Skanda*, who are considered as the manifestation of Supreme Brahman. In this he unified all Gods and Goddesses under six main streams and said that the worship of any of the Deities is as per the choice of the Bhakta because the worship of any one of the forms of God is not in conflict with the worship of any other form of God.

In this manner Shankara revived Hinduism and brought it back to its old glory and fame by reforming several people belonging to different faiths including Pashupata, a variation of Shaivaits, Soura, the followers of Sun God and Kapalikas, a variation of Shaivaites in addition to convincing people belonging to other Vedic doctrines like Mimamsa, Sankhya and so on about Advaita Vedanta and by winning over people belonging to other religions like Jainism and Buddhism. He preached Advaita Vedanta to people. He defeated scholars belonging to other sects and religions and established the superiority of Advaita Vedanta. He stressed the sole reality of Brahman but at the same time he also accepted the phenomenal world and the worship of various Gods. He came, undertook the task of religious harmony and integrated the different sects of Hinduism, established the superiority of the doctrine of Advaita Vedanta over other religions found in India at that time, and brought renaissance to the land and after accomplishing the allotted task of his birth he left. But for Shankara, Hinduism would have got wiped out from the world or at least would have lost all its uniqueness, glory and importance. His impact on Hinduism is profound. Even to day he stands unparallel as the main figure in the tradition of Advaita Vedanta. He is considered as an incarnation of Lord Shiva Himself.

Indian Scenario in Shankara Period

Shankara was born during the 8th century. (There is difference of opinion regarding this) This period witnessed many phases of growth, change and decline of Buddhism. At that time Jainism also had spread through out the country under Mahavira through the teaching of compassion and non -injury and had its influence among the people. Both these religions were different from Hinduism specifically, because, as per common understanding, the concept of God with form was absent in both these religions. Both these religions were opposed to superstitions and cruelty in the name of religion that was found in Hinduism in its corrupted form, practiced at that time. Hinduism itself had disintegrated in to a number of sects, each opposed to and intolerant of the other and trying to prove that one or the other sect was superior to the other. For example there were the followers of *Mimamsa* and *Sankhya* systems who did not believe in the existence of a Universal God, the charvakas who rejected the Vedas and the existence of God and so on. Hindus at that time were in the narrow confines of regionalism, orthodoxy, and excessive and blind ritualism. The excessive emphasis on Vedic rituals together with lack of proper and correct understanding of the Vedic Yagnas, the unwanted, blind and dangerous superstitious beliefs in the guise of religion, and the caste system that threatened to engulf the true spirit of Upanishadic teachings led to fast decline of Hinduism.

In the process the great and eternal principles of Upanishads were almost discarded by the people due to lack of proper knowledge about them. Many temples that were once constructed on the basis of *Agama Sastras* were in the hands of corrupt people who followed corrupt practices in the name of rituals and worship. Hinduism got distorted and was being misinterpreted and precisely at that time Shankara emerged as the champion of Hindu-Sanathana Dharma and re-established its past unique place in the world. He infused the noble principles of Vedic worship. As Vivekananda stated, "Sect after sect arose in India and seemed to shake the religion of Vedas to its very foundations, but like the waters of the seashore in a tremendous earthquake it receded only for a while, only to return in an all absorbing flood, a thousand times more vigorous and when the tumult of the rush was over these sects were all sucked in, absorbed and assimilated in to the immense body of the mother faith".

During such a time of religious chaos Shankara, emerged on the scene and during the brief period of 32 years of life on earth, he firmly established the Advaita vedanta doctrine of Vedanta, and through this he unified the Hindu religion that was at its low ebb at that time. It was he who was responsible for the resurrection of Sanathana Dharma. Due to his efforts Hinduism regained its lost glory and importance, of its philosophy and spiritual principles, and also popularity. He revived the Advaita Vedantic tradition against the growing encroachments of other religions and other Vedanta schools. He unified all the innumerable sects in to a common framework mainly through discourses, discussions and debates. Wherever he went, he won over his opponents through debates. He held discussions with the leading scholars of the various sects particularly those of *Samkhya*, and *Purva Mimamsa* who gave importance to Vedic ritualism and with the religious leaders of Buddhism, Jainism, and also *Charvakas*.

Shankara unified all theistic sects that believed in the existence of God or the Supreme power in to a common framework. He urged the people to give up blind rituals, superstitions and *adharmic* traditions that were widespread due to the wrong understanding of Vedic Dharma. He then imparted the knowledge of the true spirit of Vedanta and tradition and asked the people to know the Vedas in its totality understand their hidden meanings and follow dharmic path shown by the Vedas. His tour called the Dig-Vijaya, through out the country on foot was for spiritual conquest. Disciples came to him in large numbers to obtain spiritual knowledge. Vivekananda stated that when atheists and agnostics had destroyed the nation again, it was found out that Advaita was the only way to save India from materialism. Materialism came to the fore, taking the form of license with the higher classes and superstition with the lower. Then Shankaracharya arose and once more revived the Vedanta philosophy. He made it a ratioanalistic philosophy. Again he says,

> "Shankaracharya had caught the rhythm of the Vedas, the national cadence— His whole life's work is nothing but that, the throbbing of the beauty of the Vedas and Upanishads."

Finally Shankara ascended to the throne of '*Sarvajna Peeta*', as a mark of recognition of his undisputed mastery and scholarship in spiritual knowledge. It is said that during his visit to Nepal, he had a vision of Dattatreya and from there he proceeded to Kedarnath and at the age of 32, after accomplishing his allotted task, he bade good-bye to the world. It is also believed by some that Shankara attained Siddhi in Vrindavanam at the Kamakshi Amman temple at Kancheepuram. Again according to some others he breathed his last at Mahur in Maharashtra, and again to some others it was in Vadakkanathan or Vrashachala temple at Trichur in Kerala.

Religio-philosophical Tradition Opposed to Vedanta Doctrines

Jainism

Jainism that is traditionally known as Jain Dharma is an ancient Indian religion of India. The Jains follow the teachings of the 24 Thirthankaras (a teacher who shows the way) who are called Jinas meaning those who overcome or conquer. The Thirthankaras are pure beings and they show the way to liberation. The 24th Thirthankara is supposed to be Mahavira, meaning 'the great hero', who lived in the 6th B.C. Jainism emphasizes non-violence and self control for attaining Kevala Jnana and later *Moksha*. The first in the line of the 24 Thirthankaras was Sage Rishabhanatha also known as Adi Natha. This religion has no single founder. The truth is said to have been revealed by Theerthankaras at different times. Thirthankaras are considered as teachers only or even as a role model, but not as Gods. The first Jina is traditionally believed to have lived around 8.4 million years ago.

Although many principles of Jainism and Buddhism are similar to Hinduism, as in Buddhism, Jainism also does not believe in the existence of a creator or universal God, who is responsible for all creation, maintenance and destruction. The eternal universe is governed by natural laws only and is inhibited by innumerable souls. According to them, there is no first cause as such for anything in the world and the world is not created by God and has no beginning and end. It is uncreated and indestructible. It is divided in to heaven, hell and earth. There are Arhats, Gods and some higher beings in Heaven who have greater freedom and higher degree of knowledge and intelligence. They have no interest in worldly matters. Worshipping them will result in good *Karma*. The Gods keep watch on the activities of the world. They respond to man's prayers and help man in all good deeds. The *Jeeva* unlike *Atman* of the Upanishads is capable of changing its dimensions depending upon its karmas and circumstances. Before birth it is small like a seed. After birth it grows and at the time of death it contracts and becomes a tiny seed to start the life process again.

There is infinite number of *jeevas* existing in the universe eternally. The souls are uncreated and eternal and exist in all animate and inanimate objects and beings. Their number remains the same but they may move from one plane of existence to another and also can assume different forms in different things depending upon their level of evolution and past *Karmas*. All *jeevas* reap what they sow that forms the basis of *Karma* theory. According to this religion the destiny of each and every being is the consequences of its physical, verbal and mental actions. Through personal efforts *Moksha* becomes possible. But there is no divine intervention. The whole existence is sacred in which some souls are bound while others are liberated. When the jeeva gets freed from all the notions of association with matter and body it becomes *Muktha jeeva* and enjoys unlimited consciousness, knowledge, perception, power, and joy. Ordinary *jeevas* suffer due to ignorance and illusions. They get entangled in matter till they are liberated. Soul exists in inanimate objects as well. So whenever a man does anything that causes pain and suffering to the hidden souls in that, they are forced to find new bodies. So injury to the other beings must be totally avoided.

The central theme of Jainism is compassion to one and all alike. They follow vegetarianism. They cover mouths to prevent the possibility of inhaling insects and small organisms, a principle that has non-violence as the basic idea. *Karma*, a subtle matter, a substance, a flowing energy, enters a living body and forms the Karmic body and envelops the jeeva from all sides. It binds the soul to matter and makes liberation extremely difficult. Lasting bliss is possible only by transcending the cycle of transmigration or birth and death. Rational perception, rational knowledge and rational conduct are means to get detachment that would result in liberation or *Mukti*.

Buddhism

Gautham Buddha was the founder of Buddhism. He was born in Lumbini near Kapilavasthu around 566 B C as a prince in Shakya tribe of Nepal. He was the son of King Suddhodana and Mayadevi. He was named Siddhartha. When he was 29 years old he left the comforts of family and royal life for seeking the cause and remedy for all the sufferings in the world. He reached Uruvilva (Buddha Gaya) and sat in meditation under a Bodhi tree. After six years of rigorous yoga *Sadhana* he became the Buddha or the Bodhisattva, the enlightened one on the full Moon in the month of May. He wandered through out North India preaching his new path. He delivered his first sermon at Sarnath near Varanasi and for full forty years he continued with his preaching. At the age of 80 approximately in 486 B C he passed away on the day of *Vaishakha Poornima*, the day in which he was born and attained enlightenment. His last words are said to be "Impermanent are all created things; strive on with Awareness". The four noble truths as told by Buddha that are His first teachings after attaining enlightenment are; suffering exists, suffering arises from attachments to desires, suffering ceases when attachment to desires also ceases, and freedom from suffering is possible by following the eight fold path that includes, right view or understanding that is free from superstition and delusion, right thought that is worthy of the intelligent, right speech that includes speech that are kind, open and truthful, right action that consists of peaceful, honest and pure actions, right livelihood that does not cause hurt or danger to any living beings, right effort through self training and self control, right mindfulness, that is, the mind that is always active and watchful and right contemplation in deep meditation on the realities of life. According to him, the five aspects of good conduct are, no killing, no stealing, no sexual misconduct, no lying, and no intoxicants. According to Buddha there is no God.

To attain salvation or Nirvana one has to depend on self-effort only. There is no Atman or imperishable self or unchanging eternal soul that is permanent. Buddha rejected all concepts of Atman. The chief objective of all human beings is to attain Nirvana or salvation. According to Buddha nothing perishes in the universe since matter turns in to energy and energy turns in to matter. Secondly all experiences that we experience though our senses are external and are impermanent, unsteady and constantly changing. Life is ever flowing and is also ever changing. So, attachment is futile as it leads to suffering that is lack of peace or a condition of being disturbed. The changes are due to the law of cause and effect. People suffer due to ignorance of the laws of Karma and also due to the greed for wrong kind of pleasures. To end suffering one must cut off greed and ignorance. *Nirvana* is that state where all suffering ends. Death is not the end of life. When one dies one's consciousness leaves and enters one of the six paths of births namely, heavenly beings, humans, *asuras*, hungry ghosts and hell beings. The three poisons namely greed, hatred and stupidity turn the wheel of life and death. By cutting the wheel one can become enlightened and can escape the wheel of life and death. The path towards *Nirvana* or the end of the involuntary cycle of suffering and rebirth can be ended by eradicating its cause and conditions by means of following the eight fold path that is also called as the middle path. According to the Madhyamaka system of Buddhism, the nature of enlightenment is Shoonya or emptiness or void. Buddha rejected relying on Vedas for salvation. He said to attain salvation one need not accept the authority of the scriptures or the existence of God.

From the Buddhist's perspective man created God out of the psychologically deep-rooted idea of self-protection. He asked everyone to see and experience truth through knowledge and wisdom but not believe it through faith. Dr. Radha Krishnan said that Buddha did not look upon himself as an innovator but only a restorer of the way of the Upanishads despite the fact that Buddha did not accept Upanishads. In *Puranas* Buddha is described as an incarnation of Lord Vishnu. In the Bhavishya Purana it is said that 'in the *Kali Yuga*, Lord Vishnu incarnates himself as Gautama Buddha, the Shakyamuni and taught the Buddhist Dharma for ten years. Then Shuddhodana ruled for twenty years and Shakyasimha for another twenty years. At the first stage of Kaliyuga the path of the Vedas would be destroyed and all men would turn towards Buddhism. Those who sought refuge with Vishnu would be deluded.'

Traditional Doctrines Based on the Vedas

With the Vedas as the basis, six traditional systems of Hindu philosophy developed in India. They are known as Darshanas or vision. These are manuals of Indian philosophy. These are the traditional philosophical doctrines based on all Vedas. These are, *Samkhya, Yoga, Nyaya, Vaiseshika, Purva Mimamsa* and Vedanta or *uttara mimamsa*. But the doctrines other than Vedanta are not completely based on the Vedas. For example, *Nyaya* and *Vaiseshika* highlight human reason that functions within certain limitations like time, space and causation. *Mimamsa* rely mainly on Vedic Karmas. But according to Vedanta supreme truth can be known only through self-introspection. Although all these doctrines were in a way complementary to each other, still, they were divergent as far as their views on the concepts of soul and absolute reality are concerned. But the religions of Buddhism and Jainism and all theses six *Darshanas* or the traditional Hindu systems of philosophy agree both in the doctrine of cycle of birth and death and also in the possibility of transcending the phenomenal existence and achieving the supreme state of everlasting *Mukti* or liberation. All the six systems of Hindu philosophy also belive in the law of Karma, rebirth, attainment of Moksha and are concerned with the realization of the self.

Sankhya

Kapila muni was the founder of the Sankhya system of philosophy. It is the oldest philosophical systems of Vedanta and of India. There is rigid dualism in this philosophy. It maintains a rational duality between spirit or consciousness that is termed as *Purusha* and *Prakruti* that is matter. It does not believe in a creator. It is based on the enumeration of the cosmic principles or Tattvas or *Prakruti* that are separate from the consciousness or *Purusha*. It divides the universe in to 25 principles or *Tattvas*. The first 8 *Tattvas* compose material universe and referred to as *Prakruti*. Another *Tattva* is the motive power of the universe. It is the soul or spirit and is referred to as Purusha. The 16 remaining Tattvas are the result of *Purusha* acting on *Prakruti* constituting the universe.

It is pluralistic as it postulates two basic substances, two eternal realities, constituting the Universe, namely, *Purusha*, the pure, unchanging consciousness and *Prakruti*, the natural world, the matter or nature that includes everything else. In these two eternal realities, *Purusha* is the center of consciousness and it is *Prakruti* that is the source of all material existence, the physical and mental phenomenon of the Universe.

The mind, the ego and the intellect are considered to be the manifestation of *Prakruti*. *Purusha* is the seer. The sentient Being is *Purusha* that is limitless and the physical body does not restrict it. Bondage is due to *Purusha* being misled about its own identity and thinks itself as the physical body. In the deluded state, one is not able to distinguish *Prakruti* that is material from the other, the *Purusha* that is pure consciousness. The pure consciousness is identified with its reflection that clings to the phenomena of 'my body' and 'my mind'. *Buddhi* or intelligence and knowledge enable one to realize the difference between the two and with this knowledge the spirit gets liberated. Prakruti is composed of three gunas. When the equilibrium of the three gunas gets disturbed, the world evolves. The Samkhya yoga says that the whole universe evolved out of interaction of *Purusha* and *Prakruti*. There is no place for a creator God in this philosophy. Liberation comes with the realisation of the distinction between Purusha and *Prakruti*. The concept of God however was incorporated in to this system of philosophy after it became associated with the doctrine of Yoga.

Yoga

Yoga is closely associated with *Sankhya* philosophy as it is considered to have developed from *Sankhya*. But it differs from *Sankhya* in that, this system believes in the concept of personal God or *Ishwara* on whom one meditates. It says that *Ishwara* is the only aspect of *Purusha* that is not entangled with *Prakruti*. This system also believes and is in agreement with the concepts Brahman, *Atman* and so on mentioned in Vedanta or Upanishads. *Yoga* emphasizes physical and mental discipline through yogic practices. Patanjali systematised the various yogic practices and traditions of his time through his *Yoga Sutras*. Patanjali's *Yoga Sutra* is the basis of *Ashtanga Yoga* or the eight limbed *Yoga:*

First, *Raja Yoga*, that includes *Yama* or the abstentions, that includes the five truths namely, non-violence, truthfulness, non-stealing, chastity and avoidance of greed.

Secondly, Niyama or the five observances namely, inner and outer cleanliness, modesty and being content with what one has, keeping the body fit, self study of oneself through contemplation or meditation and laying all actions at the feet of God.

Thirdly, *Asana* or posture for doing meditation.

Fourthly, *Pranayama* or the breath control for achieving physical and spiritual health.

Fifthly, *Pratyahara* or abstraction or restraint in which one tries to go beyond senses by ignoring the feelings and perceptions.

Sixthly, *Dharana* or concentration or steadying the mind by concentrating on a single object or aspect.

Seventhly, *Dhyana* or meditation where the mind is totally engulfed by the object or aspect of meditation.

Eighthly and finally Samadhi or deep meditation or liberation in which one's personality gets totally dissolved.

It is the technique of meditation and transcendence to attain *Moksha* or liberation or *Samadhi* that is the union with the eternal self. It gives methods to gain physical and mental control over body, mind and self until one gets the required awareness about one's real self, the soul or the Atman that is different from body, mind and so on.

Nyaya

Aksapada Gauthama wrote *Nyaya Sutras* and he systematized the *Nyaya* Philosophy. *Nyaya Sutras* contain 528 brief aphorisms on metaphysics. There are many commentaries on these *Sutras*. It is a school of logic and epistemology and is based on the science of logic and reasoning as methods of investigation. So it is also known as *Nyaya Vidya* or *Tarka Sastra*. It is also referred to as *Anuviksiki* or the science of critical study. It analyses the nature and source of knowledge and later its validity and non-validity. It says that by getting valid knowledge of the external world and its relationship with the mind and self one can be free from suffering and this is the way to liberation. It emphasizes that logic and clear thinking are the means to bliss. It goes at length to identify the valid sources of knowledge as distinguished from invalid or false knowledge. According to this school there are four sources of knowledge or Pramanas namely, perception, inference, comparison and testimony. The knowledge obtained from each of these four Pramanas can either be valid or invalid and it is necessary to identify valid knowledge. Right knowledge removes wrong notions that are the root of all miseries and ills of the world. Right knowledge will also destroy anger, and ill will leading to detachment or loss of desires that results in freedom or liberation from the cycle of births and deaths. According to this philosophy all sufferings can be got rid of by mastering the logical techniques of reasoning and by applying these in one's daily life. When we are able to get the knowledge of truth, all miseries, births, faults and false knowledge would disappear and finally Moksha would result.

Vaiseshika

This doctrine was founded by *Uluka Kanada.* It postulates an atomic pluralism. It says that all objects in the universe are basically made up of minute, indivisible, formless and immutable particles known as Paramanu or atoms. Atoms have the quality of velocity but by themselves they are incapable of motion. Akasha or Ether is the medium in which atoms move. The indivisible, partless, and eternal particle of matter that cannot be further subdivided is the Paramanu or Atom. The combination of atoms results in creation. Atoms are neither produced nor destroyed and hence they are eternal. The Atoms are of four kinds namely, earth, water, fire and air. These atoms differ from each other quantitatively as well as qualitatively. Originally they exist independent of each other. When creation takes place these atoms join with one another and finally the Universe is formed. Creation is combination of Atoms and destruction of the universe is the dissolution of the atoms. Based on the merits and demerits of past actions the unseen power sets the atoms in to motion and these results in either enjoyment or suffering.

Liberation is the cessation of suffering due to bondage and this liberation happens when true knowledge dawns. Due to ignorance self gets attached to objects and performs actions. The true nature of the self is beyond knowledge. When the self is bound it possesses the qualities of consciousness, bliss, and pain and so on. But when it is liberated the self is pure substance without qualities. This system of philosophy reduces the entire universe in to seven categories or Padarthas. Padarthas are physical and mental objects of knowledge that can be named and also thought of. Brahman causes the consciousness in its creation. All forms originate from the Pimmeval sound 'AUM'. Although the sounds are many, the source of the sound is one namely 'AUM'. According to this philosophy, divinity is the cause and creation is the consequence. The recognition of the atomic nature of the Universe and its difference from the soul paves the way for liberation. Later this doctrine got merged with Nyaya philosophy and became a supplement to Nyaya philosophy. But traditionally Nyaya philosophy accepted four sources of knowledge whereas the Vaiseshika system of philosophy accepted only two sources of knowledge namely, perception and inference.

Purva Mimamsa

Mimamsa means investigation or inquiry. It is an orthodox or Asthika school of Vedic thought. It is called as Purva Mimamsa since it analyses the earlier portions or the Karma Kandas of the Vedas that include the Samhita and Brahmana portions of the Vedas. According to this system, Upasana or worship, jnana or knowledge are important only as the accessories to Vedic rituals. It does not believe in the existence of a universal God. It believes in Vedic rituals, Yagnas or fire sacrifices, and mantras and so on and stresses that only by acting according to the teachings of the Vedas one can attain *Mukti* or liberation. Jaimini in the 3rd century BCE founded it. The Mimamsa Sutra of Jaimini, which is the main text of this doctrine, describes the different Vedic sacrifices, for what they are performed, the sources of knowledge, the validity of the Vedas and elaborates upon the theory of Apurva, the mysterious, transcendental power produced by the proper performance of Vedic sacrifices and yagnas. It says that soul is permanent and it possesses a body to which the results of actions accrue. Atman is one with consciousness. So the self is distinct from the body, senses and intellect. The self is present even when the intellect is in a dormant state as in sleep, and even when the sense organs are destroyed. The body is only a means to an end that is beyond itself.

The soul directs the body to which it is connected until it is liberated. The one soul gets reflected in different bodies having different qualities. The self is the agent, the enjoyer and is omnipresent. The world is eternal and real. It is independent of the mind. The idea of a universal God does not find a place here. This system believed in ritualism, anti- asceticism, and ant mysticism. It investigates the Dharmic path that is described in the Vedas, in the form of Yagnas for achieving the desirable objective. Mimamsa gives great importance to Vedic culture by emphasizing the correct performance of Vedic yagnas and sacrifices. According to this, the knowledge of Dharma can be obtained from Vedas only. It also accepts the notion of *Swarga* or heaven and says that a person, who leads a virtuous life as per the Vedic Dharma or tradition, is bound to go to heaven. Non-performance of the Vedic rituals results in sin. To gain special favours optional karmas are to be performed. However at a later stage, this school changed its views and began to teach the doctrine of God.

Vedanta or Uttara Mimamsa or Later Mimamsa

Of all the schools of ancient Indian thought, Vedanta is the most popular. This deals with the Metaphysical speculation. It deals with the philosophical teachings of the Upanishads, that is, on the mystical aspects of Vedic teachings.

The Vedanta Sutras of Badarayana or sage Vyasa that give the essence of Upanishads or Vedanta are presented in a cryptic, poetic style that are very difficult to understand and therefore have given rise to a variety of interpretation resulting in six different schools of Vedanta namely, Advaita, Visisht Advaita, that is qualified non dualism,

Dwaitha or dualism, Dwaith Advaita or Bhedabheda, Shuddh Advaita and acintya Bheda Abheda. Adi shankara was the champion of Advaita Vedanta. Later the five other vedantic doctrines were founded. The philosophy of *Visisht Advaita* or qualified non dualism or attributive Monism or Advaita with qualification or Shree Vaishnavism was founded by Ramanujacharya, Dwaitha or Dualism or Sat-Vaishnavism was founded by Madhwacharya, Dwaith Advaita or Bhedabheda or differential monism or dualistic dualism was founded by Nimbarkacharya, Suddh Advaita or pure monism was founded by Vallabhacharya and Achintya Bheda Abheda was founded by Chaitanya Mahaprabhu.

The other sects in Hinduism found during the time of Adi Shankaracharya include the Pasupathas, the most ancient sect of Saivism that was dualistic in its approach, Kapalikas, who worshipped Lord Shiva in His most ferocious form, the Bhairava who followed crude religious practices and Tantrikas who misused the spiritual practices invoking *mantra, yantra, kundaliniyoga* and so on.

The Nastika Philosophical System

Charvakas or Lokayata

It is named after its founder Charvaka who authored *Brahaspathiya Sutras*. It is the materialistic and *Nastika* or Atheistic system of philosophy. This system is highly materialistic. It has a down to earth approach. It believed in the reality of this world and the physical existence of man and other beings and intelligence that is a form of matter produced by the combination of the four elements. It does not believe in heaven or hell, in vice or virtue. The Charvakas accepted as reality only those, which they could perceive and interact with. They did not believe in any imaginary world. However they believed in the existence of four elements, namely, earth, water, fire and air only as against the five elements stated in the Vedas that included the element of Space as well. They also did not believe in the existence of God or life after death or in soul. To them, death is the final point and once the body is destroyed, the four elements get dissolved and they return to their respective sources. The main purpose of life, they point out, is to enjoy worldly life with the help of physical body. Anything that one cannot perceive with senses does not exist. Such things are only an illusion. We should believe any teaching only when we can confirm and experience it, not otherwise. The Charvakas did not accept either the Vedas or the Vedic rites, or in Karma. They ask, what is the use of sacrificing anything now with the hope of getting some future benefits about which we do not know or are not sure of?

Shankara's Life and Mission

Shankara based his philosophical arguments on the four Vedas namely, *Rig, Yajur, Sama* and *Atharva Vedas*, which are considered as *Sruti*, the various Upanishads that formed the culmination and gist of all Vedas, and other Hindu scriptures, which are categorized as *Smriti*. He traveled far and wide through out the country, propagated his teachings in the nook and corner of India, and succeeded in establishing the superiority of Advaita Vedanta. His innumerable works both as a devotee and as a philosopher of Advaita vedanta also contributed immensely in the resurrection of Hindu Dharma. Shankara set aside all the misconceptions, misinterpretations, and confusion about ancient Hindu Philosophy and reestablished the Vedic path that formed the foundation or basis of Hinduism that is the Sanadhana Dharma or Universal Dharma or code of conduct and thereby he became responsible in regaining the strength and glory of Vedic Dharma that had lost its appeal and popularity to a large extent, among the people in the country.

Shankara's life reveals to us that he practiced all the three traditional paths of yoga simultaneously. He was a real Bhakta who sought refuge and salvation at the feet of his chosen Deities. The innumerable stotras on Lord Shiva, Lord Vishnu, on Ganesha, Subramanya and Goddess Thripura Sundari who is Goddess Parvati and so on speak volumes about his devotion to God. The verses overflow not only with divinity but also with excellent poetical expressions and the Stotras are ample proof of both these. The Stotras clearly reveal the peak of emotion, the state in which Shankara was while writing the verses that expressed the helplessness of the devotee on the one hand and the mighty power of the Deity on the other in saving and protecting His or Her Bhakta. Shankara also visited many temples, composed hymns on the deities of the temples, installed idols, purified the forms of worship in many places, helped in the reconstruction of dilapilated temples, established Sri and Divine Chakras. He also visited many other temples, which were neglected and revived worship in all those temples. It is said that on one of his visits to Tirupati, he had installed *Dhana Akarshana Chakra* underneath the idol of Lord Venkateshwara (Balaji) and it is a well-known fact that the Tirupati temple is the richest temple in the world today. It is also said that Shankara installed a yantra that is known Akarshana yantra to attract pilgrims to the Srirangam temple during one of his visits there and in the Bharat Mandir at Rishikesh and so on. To Shankara the deity represented Nirguna Brahman, in form and with qualities.

While being a devotee Shankara also proved himself to be a great *Karma Yogi*. The very objective of his life was to reestablish Hinduism in its past glory and to spread Advaita doctrine of Vedanta. To this he was committed and he spent almost his entire short span of life for this purpose. The wide travel that he undertook to cover the length and breadh of the country by teaching, preaching, by giving discourses, by entering in to debates and discussions with the opposing religious, spiritual and academic scholars belonging to other sects in Hinduism and belonging to other religions prove the fact that he was in the true sense of the term a Bhakta as well as a *Karma Yogi* who worked unceasingly and in a selfless manner for common good that is for the welfare of mankind. During his visits he debated with many great scholars including the *Vaisheshikas* of Kanada School, followers of Kapila's Sankhya school of thought, the logicians of Gautama's school, followers of Mimamsa School, Buddhists, followers of Jainism, the tantrics and so on. He won over them and made them his disciples. He also convinced the various Hindu sects about the fact that all Gods are equally important. Lastly his philosophical treatises that explain a method as well as his philosophy of Advaita Vedanta make us realize that he was also, in an equal measure a *jnanayogi* as well who gave the real *jnana* or wisdom to the world.

Thus Shankara was a real *Bhakta*, a real *karma yogi* and a real *jnana yogi* all rolled in one. It was his conviction that *Bhakti* and *Karma* would purify the mind and would pave the way for one to become a Jnani or a man of wisdom who realises Brahman. Knowledge obtained from the teachings of the scriptures by the *Guru* also helps a person to advance in his spiritual path although scriptures become of no use later. One obtains Jnana or wisdom through real *Bhakti*, selfless karmas and knowledge that is obtained through the teachings of the scriptures by the *Guru*. With the help of all the three paths namely *Bhakti*, *Karma* and knowledge or by following any of the paths as desired by the spiritual aspirant, and finally by introspection, Viveka, self study and meditation one attains the necessary Jnana or wisdom about the eternal truth that is Brahman.

Accounts of Shankara's Life

The accounts of Shankara's life could be found in a number of works called 'Shakara Vijayams' or Shankara Digvijaya'. But most of these works were written many centuries after Shankara lived. The Shankara vijayas differ from one another with regard to most of the details regarding Adi Shankara. Actually there is no agreement regarding Shankara's correct date of birth and death and where he breathed his last, where he actually came across his *Guru*, where exactly he wrote his commentaries, where some of the incidents in his life happened, the places he visited, the routes he took, the chronological order of his tour, whether he established only four mutts or even more and also about the authorship of the stotras and philosophical treatises that are attributed to him.

The earliest one is by Chitsukhcharya titled Brihat-Shankara Vijaya. Another is by Ananda giri who belonged to the 13th century titled Pracheena Shankara Vijaya. The authors of these two were the disciples of Adi Shankara. Anandagiri also authored one of the popular Tikas to Shankara Bhashyas or commentaries. This Ananda giriya shankara vijaya is not available now and very little is known about this. Among the Shankara Vijayams, the oldest that is now available and considered as the most authentic and most popular is the Madhaviya Shankara Vijaya or Sankshepa Shankara Vijaya. The author of this is Madhavacharya who is identified with sage Vidyaranya, the 14th century Matathipathy or head of the Sringeri Mutt who had also written one of the best manuals on Advaita metaphysics. Brahmananda Sraswati who belonged to the 17th or 18th century wrote the Brihat Shankara Vijaya. The Sidvilasiya Shankara Vijaya that is also known as Shankara Vijaya Vilasa was probably written between the 15th and 17th centuries by Chidvilasa. It is in the form of a dialogue between Sidvilasa and his disciple Vijnanakanda. This text tells about the tradition of the four mutts that Shankara had established in the four corners of India, at Sringeri, Dwaraka, Puri and at Joshimutt near Badrinath. The Keraliya Shankara Vijaya that is also known as Shankara karyakaritha is attributed to Govindanatha who is also known as Acharyacharita. It states that Shankara's last days were in Vrrashachaleshwara temple in Trichur-Kerala. It dates around 17th century. There are also Shankara Vijayas called 'Shankara Vijaya of Vidya Shankara also known as Shankarananda, also known as Vyasachaliya Shankara Vijaya, Shankara Abhyudaya of Choodamani Dikshitha, Shankara Vijaya of Anantanandanadagiri, also known as *Guru* Vijaya or Acharya Vijaya, Shankara Vijaya of Vallisahayakavi in the name of Acharya Dig Vijaya, and Shankara Digvijaya sara of Sadananda. In addition to these there is a minor work called Krishnanada Shankara Vijaya. There are also works like Shankara Abhyudaya, a short poem, Shankara Vijaya Sara, Shankara Mandara Saurabha, Bhagavad pada Abhyudaya and so on which describe Shankara's life.

●●●

2
Life Sketch of Adi Shankara

There are differing views about the period of Shankara, the incidents in his life, and about his works. There are a few works such as the Shankara Vijayams of Madhavacharya, Anandagiri, Chidvilasa, Swami Sadananda and Govindanatha and works like Madhava Vijayam, Mani Manjari and so on that provide some accounts of this great genius. But in all these we find different accounts of Shankara's date of birth, place of birth, life, works, the date and place of his disappearance and so on. However Shankara's contribution to Advaita Vedanta has been accepted by all without any dispute and this is most important because all other aspects about this great Adi *guru* at best can satisfy academic interest only.

As per the records displayed at the Adi Shankara *Janma bhoomi Kshetram* of the Sringeri Mutt at Kaladi, the birth place of Shankara, the year of birth, important events and the chronological order of Shankara's Digvijaya are:

788	Birth of Adi Shankara
791	Demise of father of Adi Shankara
793	Sacred thread ceremony of Shankara
795	Shankara changing the course of river *Poorna* and installing the idol of Shree Krishna in the temple at Kaladi and Shankara composing the famous *Kanaka Dhara Stotram*

796	Shankara left Kalady, meeting Govindapada near Narmada River and becoming a *Sanyasi*
798	Stay ai Kashi, arrival of Sanandana (Padmapada), writing Bhashyas, meeting Kumaraleela Bhatta, defeat of Mandana Mishra
798-800 A D	Vyasa Darshana, resuming Digvijaya
800-804	Arrival at Sringeri, Installation of Shree Sarada, arrival of Totaka and Hasthamalaka, and writing Granthas
804-816	Demise of mother
819	Resuming Digvijayam, ascending Sarvajna Peeta, Gaudapada Darshan, establishment of four Mutts
820	Attained *Siddhi* at Kedara.

In this chapter this chronological order is followed..

According to another account, Shankara was born in 509 B C and he left his physical body in 476 B C. According to this account Shankara first visited Badrinath as per the command of his master and at Badri he became the disciple of Gaudapada who was 108 years old at that time. According to this, it is after he wrote the Bhashyas that Shankara visited Prayag and the first Mutt that Shankara established was at Dwaraka followed by Jyothir Mutt, then Govardhana Mutt and finally the Sringeri mutt was established. It also says that Shankara established the Kamakoti Peeta at Kanchipuram in Tamil Nadu with Adi Shankara himself as the first Matathipathi.

The Birth of Adi Shankara

The traditional sources of accounts of his life are from Shankara Vijayams, which give the biography of Shankara. The most important and popular of all the Shankara Vijayams is the Madaviya Shankara Vijayam. More than one date is given for the birth and period of Shankara. The traditional date is said to be Kaliyuga 2593 or 509B C. The official date accepted currently is 788-822 CE. This period is based upon the records of the Sringeri Sharada Peetam that has maintained a relatively unbroken record of its Matathipathis or

Acharyas. Based on this, the government of India celebrated the 1200th anniversary of Shankara's birth in 1988. However the correct date is still questionable. Many believe that he lived after Buddha. To some the period of Shankara varies between 509 B C to 788 A D. If Shankara had been the contemporary of Kumarila then according to some his period must have been between 150 B C to 450 A D. As per the astronomical data given in Brihat-Shankara Vijaya, Shankara was born in the year Nandana in the Lunar month of Vaishakha (May- June), on Monday in 805 A D. To some the period of Shankara was between 788-820 C E and 700-750 CE. However they do not claim absolute correctness about this date, as there are no concrete proofs for this date. The Sringeri Mutt, also claim that Shankara was born in the 14th year of the reign of King Vikramadithya. But it is not certain to which King Vikramadithya it refers to. But Scholars accept the Vikramadithya of the Chalukya dynasty of Badami, Vikramadithya-2 (733-746 CE) that is about the middle of the 8th century. The Dwaraka and Puri Mutts and Kanchi Peetam give the period as 509-477 B C. for Shankara that is 5th century. But then, Shankara could not have quoted the Buddhist Logician Dharma Keerthi. Again, Kumarila Bhaṭṭa who was a near contemporary of Shankara is said to have belonged to the 8th century. There are also contradictory versions about the planetary positions at the time of Shankara's birth.

Shankara was born in a poor Nambhooḍari Brahmin family in Kaladi, a village in Kerala. This place Kaladi was known before as Shalaka gramam. It is said that the river Poorna was flowing 3 Kms to the south of this place. But when Shankara marked this place with his feet this place became blessed and it came to be known as Kaladi (In Malayalam the language of Kerala, 'Kal' means leg and 'Adi' means step. Sree Krishna the presiding deity of the temple of this place also came to be known as Thrikkaladiappan. In the Shankara *Janma Bhoomi Kshetra* that is located on the banks of river Poorna one can see the spot where Adi Shankara was born. Shankara's ancestors belonged to the Vedic branch of Krishna Yajur Veda-Taittiriya Sakha. The place Kaladi is located near Thiru Shiva Perur (The present Trichur). It is believed that Shankara was born on an auspicious time in Vaisakha *Sukla Panchami* day (April-May on the 5th day of waxing moon) under the star of Thiruvadira (Arudra) that is supposed to be associated with Lord Shiva. To some he was born on the fifth lunar day of the Sukla or bright fortnight in the month of *Vaisakha*, on Punardam (Punarvasu) *Nakshatra*. His grand father was Vidyadiraja, a Priest in the Shiva temple at Kaladi. He had a son by name Shiva *Guru*. Shiva *guru* was inclined towards asceticism even from his child hood. However as per his father's wishes he got married and entered family life. Shiva guru's wife was Shiva tharaka also known as Aryamba who was the daughter of *Magha* Panditha who belonged to Meppattur that is 40 kms from Ernakulam. For many years they were not blessed with children. So the couple went and worshipped in the Vadakkanathan temple also called as Vrushachala, meaning 'Bull-hill', a hillock that looked like a bull, the vehicle of Lord Shiva, a famous Shiva temple in Thiru-Shiva Perur (Trichur) in Kerala. The hillock was also known as Dakshina Kailasa. According to legends Lord Shiva appeared in the dream of the couple and asked them whether they wished for a mediocre son who would live long or an extraordinary son whose life span would be short. The couple chose to get a son who will be extraordinary. In course of time a son was born to them and he was named Shankara, the bestower (*Kara*) of happiness (*Sam*). It also means giver of prosperity. The child was named Shankara also because he was born out of Lord Shiva's blessings. In Gita it is said that whenever righteousness declines in this world, God the supreme takes an *Avatar* to set it right. Shankara's birth proved this truth.

Shankara's Childhood

Baby Shankara was extraordinary in many respects. It is said that on his first birthday, during the worship of Shiva in the temple it was seen that all the flowers, garlands, and so on that were offered to the God were seen on the child as well. Again at the time of the car festival the parents saw their child in the car seated instead of the Deity. It is said that when Shankara was a small baby, once his mother saw a huge cobra coiled around the neck of Shankara. As she was looking at the snake, it became a garland around the neck of Shankara. It is also said that once there was some argument among the children as to the number of seeds in a melon. Shankara told them that there would be as many seeds inside the melon as there are as many Gods. When the children cut it open, they found only one seed inside. Perhaps even as a child Shankara knew that the ultimate, supreme is only one. He showed extraordinary brilliance even from childhood. He was a prodigy in every respect. It is said that Shankara started talking very clearly even when he was only one year old. By the time he was two years old, he learnt the alphabets of Malayalam, his mother tongue. From the third year he started learning Sanskrit alphabets. Very soon he also started reciting all *Kavyas* and *Puranas* and other scriptures.

Shankara's father Shiva *guru* was a great Bhakta of Mother Parvati. He used to visit the temple daily to offer milk to the Deity. Shankara was later given that milk as Prasad. Shankara thought that the Deity drank the milk and whatever she left was given to Shankara as Prasad. It is said that on one occasion Shivaguru could not go to the temple. So he asked Shankara to take the milk to the temple. Shankara offered the milk to the Deity. But the goddess did not drink the milk. This disappointed Shankara and he began to cry. Taking pity on him the Goddess appeared before him and drank the milk. This made him very happy, but after looking at the vessel Shankara began to cry again as the Goddess did not leave any milk for Shankara to drink. The Goddess took the child in her lap and suckled him. It is said that this made Shankara a great scholar and a poet. It is also said that immediately after this incident, Shankara started composing hymns on the Goddess.

Shankara as the *Brahmachari*

When Shankara was only a child his father Shiva *guru* passed away. His mother brought him up and performed *Upanayana* that is the sacred thread ceremony as per tradition for marking the beginning of his formal education. The *Brahmopadesam*, the *Gayatri Mantra*, the secret of life, that revealed the nature of ultimate reality was taught to him as per tradition, to make him eligible for Brahmacharya or for the life of a student under an enlightened and compassionate master. He wore the sacred thread, the Yajnopavitam that has three threads, representing Goddess Gayatri, the Goddess of mind or thought, Goddess Saraswati, the Goddess of word and Goddess Savitri, the Goddess of deed, with the knot in the middle representing Brahman, the truth that pervades everything. The three threads also represent the trinity of Gods namely, *Brahma* (the creator), *Vishnu*, (The sustainer) and *Maheshwara* (The destroyer).

After his *Upanayanam,* Shankara was sent to *Gurukula.* Shankara had his first education in his village, Kaladi. There he learnt all Vedas and Sastras. He could also recite extensively from *Puranas* and Epics. He also learnt *Nyaya*, *Yoga*, *Sankhya* and *Mimamsa* doctrines. He could master all knowledge even at a tender age including all *Sruti* and *Smriti*, and also the philosophies contained in Bhuddhism, Jainism and so on. While pursuing his education in *Gurukula* Shankara went to seek alms or *Bhiksha.* On one such occasion, he happened to visit the house of a woman for alms and the poor lady of the house had only the dried Amlaka (The Indian Gooseberry) fruit in her possession to offer as *Bhiksha* to Shankara. The pious lady gave that to Shankara as *Bhiksha.* Shankara was highly impressed and moved by her piety. He composed and sang the Kanakadhara Stotram then and there and it is said, that as soon as Shankara completed the stotram, golden Almlaka fruits were dropped from above and showered upon the lady by Goddess Maha Lakshmi- the Goddess of wealth.

Once Shankara's aging mother fell unconscious while returning after taking bath in the Poorna River that was near his house. Immediately through his prayer and will, it is said, that Shankara changed the course of the river and made it flow near his house just to enable his mother to take bath in the river that flowed very close to their house. Thereafter the annual temple festival of this place called Arattu for the presiding deity Lord Krishna began to be celebrated in this place and it came to be known as Arattu Kadavu.

Shankara Embracing *Sanyasa*

Even from childhood Shankara was attracted towards *Sanyasa.* But his mother was opposed to the idea of his embracing *Sanyasa.* She wanted Shankara to get married and lead a normal family life.

But Shankara's eagerness to become a monk was intense. Once when Shankara was bathing in Poorna River near his house, a crocodile caught his leg, and however much he tried he could not get out of its grip. After sometime the crocodile began to draw Shankara in to the water. His mother who was with him at that time could not rescue Shankara from the grip of the crocodile. Shankara told his mother that if she permitted him, Shankara, to become a monk then surely the crocodile would leave its grip over his leg and he will be saved. Finally Shankara's mother had to yield to his wishes just to save him. Immediately the crocodile freed the leg of Shankara, and swam away from him and Shankara was saved without getting hurt by the crocodile. He then told his mother that whenever she thinks of him at any time at any stage he will come to her. He also told her that at the end of her life he would perform all her last rites. The *ghat* where the crocodile caught hold of Shankara's feet came to be known later as the crocodile *ghat* (Mudala Kadavu).

Shankara then went to the temple of Keshava, (Lord Krishna) his family deity. The temple was in a dilapilated condition. He also saw river Poorna eroding the sides of the temple of Lord Krishna. At the request of the priests, Shankara took the idol of the temple to another place and he asked the villagers to construct a temple there. It is said Lord Krishna himself appeared in Shankara's dream and asked him to shift the idol from there. It is said that in 795 AD Shankara reinstalled the idol of Lord Krishna here. On hearing about Shankara the king of Kerala, with a desire to meet him, sent his men to bring Shankara to his palace. But Shankara politely refused to go to the palace of the King. He told the men that a *Brahmachari* is not after any honours or gifts from the king. Thereafter the king himself came to meet Shankara the boy with innumerable gifts. But Shankara asked the king to give away the gifts to the needy people. On request of the king, Shankara blessed the childless king and asked him to perform *Putreshti yoga* for getting a son.

Shankara's Journey Towards His Guru

After obtaining his mother's permission and blessings, Shankara left Kerala, became a wandering monk, at the age of eight and journeyed towards north of India searching for a proper *Guru*. Even while studying in the *Gurukula* earlier, Shankara, while studying the commentary of Patanjali, learnt from his master that Patanjali had stayed in a cave at the bank of river Narmada in deep *Samadhi* since thousand years and he is then known as Govinda and the urge to meet this great soul' came up to Shankara's mind even then. When Shankara reached the Omkarnath temple located near Narmada River, he learnt from the people there, that a great *Yogi* was staying in a cave in trance since a very long time. Shankara immediately went to that place where the cave was located. He saw some monks there near the cave and he enquired about the sage. It is said that the monks were struck by the charm and celestial glow on the face of the young monk who was only a small boy. They told him that they were all waiting there just to meet the sage once he comes out of his trance. They said that they all are waiting for such a meeting since a long time and in that process some of them have even become quite old. Shankara asked them how he could have a look at that great sage. They told him that he could go in to the cave, the entrance of which is quite narrow. He could go inside with a lamp, as the inside of the cave was very dark.

Shankara lighted a lamp and in the presence of all the hermits who were there he went round the cave three times and then after prostrating at the narrow entrance, he went inside the cave. There he saw the great sage sitting in Padmasana posture in Samadhia in a corner. His body was very thin and emaciated. His long hair was spread all over his face. Still, Shankara could see the celestial glow radiating from this great soul. When Shankara saw Govinda, his joy knew no bounds. He forgot himself in total bliss. Automatically even without his own awareness he prostrated before the enlightened sage and with folded hands began to pray to him. The devotion with which Shankara sang the hymn woke up the sage from his super conscious state. He then requested the great soul to make him his disciple and impart the ultimate knowledge. With in a few moments Govinda's rigid body began to relax, and slowly he opened his closed eyes and looked at Shankara. (According to another view Shankara met his *Guru* Govinda at Badri.) Shankara again prostrated before this all knowing soul. Govinda asked the boy who he was. To this Shankara replied in a shloka consisting of ten verses. This Shloka is called Dasa Sloki. Through these ten verses Shankara told Govinda that he was neither earth nor water, nor fire, nor air, nor sky, nor any other properties. He was also not the sense, not even the mind. He was Shiva, the wholesome essence of consciousness. He was the self the pure consciousness, the bliss. Govinda at once knew that –this was the boy for whom he was waiting since long. With great joy, he immediately took Shankara as his disciple. Govinda *Bhagavad pada* was a disciple of Gaudapada. Gaudapada was the author of Mandukya Karika, a treatise in verse of the Mandukya Upanishad, one of the profoundest of all Upanishads. People there considered Govinda as the incarnation of Patanjali. Some also believed that he was born of King Aṇantha or Adishesha and also as the disciple of Shukhadeva, the son of Veda Vyasa.

Shankara the Monk

Govinda Bhagavad *pada* initiated Shankara in to the Paramahansa order of Sanyasa that is considered as the highest order of *Sanyasa.* Shankara underwent *Shravana*, or hearing the spiritual treatises from his master, then Manana, investigating and analyzing and discussing with his master what he had from him and then *Nidhidhyasana* or contemplating on what he had understood from the master. The sage imparted the knowledge of Brahman to Shankara through the four *Mahavakyas* of the Upanishads. He also taught him the Vedanta *Sutras* of Vyasa that contained the essence of Vedic philosophy. Shankara also learnt all *sastras* from his master.

It is said once during the rainy season river Narmada was in spate. The rushing water from the river entered in to the cave where Govinda, Shankara's master was seated in deep meditation. The monks who were present there did not know what to do. They did not have the courage to wake him up from trance. Shankara immediately placed his Kamandal against the using waters and to the surprise of all the monks there, the Kamandal contained the rushing waters. He thus saved his master. When Govinda came out of his Samadhi he came to know everything that took place during the period of his trance, and he blessed his dear disciple and said just like his act then, he would also be able to contain and reconcile all the conflicting doctrines through his commentaries on the Prasthana Traya in to the all inclusive Advaita Vedanta Philosophy. This, Govinda said, would be Shankara's mission on earth. Sage Govinda remembered the prophecy of Vyasa that the best commentary on Brahma Sutras would be written by one who tames the river Narmada. Govinda at once asked Shankara to write Bhashyam on Prasthana Traya- the major Upanishads, the Brahma *Sutra* and *Bhagavad Gita*.

Within a very short time Shankara mastered all *Srutis* and *Smritis* and obtained all knowledge and he got himself firmly established in self-knowledge. It is said even at this very young age, He wrote several hymns on Shiva, a few philosophical treatises and a commentary on Brihad Aranyaka Upanishad. Then Shankara wanted to enter in to Samadhi. But Govinda, his master reminded Shankara of his mission. The *Guru* knew the capacity of Shankara. So after Shankara obtained the required knowledge from him, the master asked him to expound the philosophy of Advaita Vedanta and write Bhashyas on the principal Upanishads, Brahma Sutra and Bhagavad Gita to provide the correct interpretation of the Vedic truths. He further told Shankara that sage Vyasa himself had told Sage Govinda that in course of time a desciple of the highest order of sage Govinda would master all knowledge and that he would reveal himself through his miraculous deeds. The *Guru* then asked Shankara to go to Varanasi and he said that from there Shankara would know his future course of action. He told Shankara that he was not a mere individual, but a whole institution, not a mere star, but the entire solar system. He directed his disciple to spread Vedic truths through his writings. After completing his divine mission of his life in this manner, Govinda left for Badrikarsram. At this point of time Shankara was only eleven Years old.

Shankara in Kashi

To spread Advaita Vedanta, Shankara, reached Kashi, also known as Varanasi situated on the bank of holy Ganga. There he stayed in a secluded and quite spot in Manikarnika Ghat and began his life's mission. He started writing his commentaries on the Prasthana Traya. (According to another view Shankara wrote his commentarie or Bhashyas on Prasthana traya at Badrinath). He met scholars and spiritual leaders of several schools of thought, argued with them and then convinced them. The pride of the opposing scholars was humbled by the convincing arguments of Shankara. Many scholars began to come to him to gain knowledge and to clear their doubts. During this time *Sadananda* became the disciple of Shankara. Later he became the first disciple of Shankara with the name Padmapada. Gradually he began to attract more and more disciples there.

Padmapada-Shankara's Disciple

Shankara's first disciple was sanandana hailing from Chola Kindom in South India. He was very sharp and quick in grasping Shankara's teachings. The other disciples were jealous of him because of this. Shankara, the master noticed this. One day Sanandana went to the other side of the bank through a bridge. In order to make the other disciples know his superiority, Shankara called him aloud and urged him to come at once. Sanandana felt that his master was in some trouble and in danger and that he needed Sanandana's immediate help because his master's voice revealed a distress signal. Without a second thought Sanandana began to walk across the water without going through the bridge so that he could reach his master immediately. He was oblivious of the freezing water or the danger in crossing the wild river. Only his master's call was there in his mind. He was totally immersed in crossing the river as quickly as possible that he did not hear the warning cries of alarm of the other disciples. Sanandana crossed the rushing waters very easily. At every step of Sanandana, lotus flowers appeared and he walked over them and reached his master. The other disciples then understood the superiority of Sanandana. According to some this incident took place in Uttar Kashi. Shankara then composed 'Atma Bhoda' in favour of his disciple and he gave him the name of Padma Pada. He along with another desciple of Shankara by name Sureshwaracharya founded the Vivarana School of commentators.

Shankara and the Untouchable

While Shankara was in Kashi, on his way to Lord Vishvanatha temple, he came across an untouchable with four dogs. Shankara's disciples asked the untouchable to move aside to enable Shankara to walk along that path. At that, the untouchable smilingly asked Shankara's disciples whether they are referring to the everlasting imperishable Atman, the self or the perishable physical body of his. As for the soul, it is pure and omnipresent. He asked "Is there any difference in the reflection of the moon as seen in the Ganges or in a cup of wine? As for the body, it is inert. How can it move away?" On hearing these words of the *chandala*, an outcaste, the disciples were speechless for some time. Shankara was also taken aback. At once Shankara realized that this man who is capable of uttering the greatest truth couldn't be an ordinary person. He realized that the man standing in front of them is none other than Lord Shiva Himself and His four dogs, the four Vedas and it was Lord Shiva who appeared before Shankara in the guise of the outcaste, only to remove his ignorance from him. Shankara immediately prostrated before Him and composed the slokam '*Manisha Panchakam*' that clearly shows that Atman shines equally in both a Brahmana and an untouchable. The Lord then asked Shankara to propagate Vedic Dharma and make it available to all. It is also said that Lord Shiva after blessing Shankara bade him to write a commentary on Brahma *Sutras*. It is said, that He told Shankara that after accomplishing his allotted divine mission, he would be united with Him, Lord Shiva, and it was for the welfare of the humans that Shankara had taken birth in the world as the manifestation of Lord Shiva. After uttering these words Lord Shiva disappeared.

Shankara and the Woman

On another occasion when Shankara was going to Ganges along with his desciples for taking bath, he saw a woman who was in deep sorrow, by the side of the dead body of her husband. She was blocking the narrow path to the ghat and was asking for help from all those who were passing by that side for cremating the dead body of her husband in a traditional manner. Shankara waited there for a long time. Finally he asked the woman to shift the dead body to one side so that he and his disciples could go to the ghat. The woman was so deep in her sorrow. She neither looked at Shankara nor seemed to have heared what Shankara told her. When Shankara repeatedly asked the woman to remove the dead body from the way, she looked at Shankara and told him that he, Shankara himself could ask the dead body to move to one side. To this Shankara asked the woman how a dead body could by itself move. Immediately the woman responded by saying, 'when Brahman is present in each and everything, why can't, he, the Brahman make the corpse move. Shankara was dumbfounded with this reply and he began to ponder over her words. Within seconds he realized that it was all the sport of Mahamaya, the Adi Shakti or the primeval energy. The woman and the corpse receded nowhere and in its place he saw only Para Shakti. Shankara prostrated before that woman and worshipped her as mother Goddess. It is said Shankara composed a Shloka in praise of Goddess Tripura Sundari at that moment. He now understood that Brahman was a mere witness and the whole universe belonged to Adi Para-Shakti, the primordial energy who played her cosmic *leela* on Shankara.

On another occasion, Shankara found a desciple struggling with Sanskrit grammar *Sutras* and he was repeating 'Dukrin Karane' again and again. It is said, that Shankara after seeing him struggling, composed the famous Stotra 'Bhaja Govindam' just to teach the uselessness of such theoretical studies in attaing the supreme knowledge that leads to Liberation.

Shankaras Digvijaya to Badrinath

After some time Shankara proceeded to Badrinath accompanied by Padmapada. He was twelve years old at that time. On his way to Badri he visited many holy places like Prayag, Haridwar, Rishikesh, Srinagar, Rudra Prayag, Nandaprayag, Gomukhi and worshipped the Deities in the temples in those places. At Badrinath he visited the temple of Maha Vishnu. But he could not find any idol, worship or devotees there. Later he came to know that the priests had hidden the idol (It is also stated that it was thrown to the river by the invaders) in the bed of Ganga for fear of attack. But later inspite of all attempts on their part they could not retrieve the idol. Shankara then plunged in to meditation. After coming out of the meditation he asked the priests whether they would restart the worship if the idol could be located. At this all the priests were overjoyed and they requested Shankara to help them in getting back the idol and istalling it in the temple. Shankara then walked for a short distance and he pointed to a particular spot in the Ganges and to every one's surprise the idol was found there. But they could retrieve only a broken idol. Shankara considered that it was God's will to install the broken idol even though broken idols are not usually installed in the temple. Later the idol was installed as per Vedic rites on an auspicious day. He then appointed Namboodari Brahmins from Kerala as priests there.

At Sri Nagar- or Sri Keshetra in Uttarkhand Shankara visited the five *Siddha Peeths* or seats of enlightenment that showed the predominance of Tantric methods. The Tantriks there were performing human sacrifices in the name of religion. Shankara gave discourses about Advaita Vedanta. The Tantriks entered in to debate with Shankara. Through his clarity of thinking and logical analysis and convincing ability, Shankara argued and changed their views about religion and spirituality and they stopped the practice of human sacrifice completely. Wherever he stopped people gathered in large numbers to listen to his discourses. Then Shankara and his disciples reached Joshimutt or Jyotirmutt and then Badrinath. There at Badri, Shankara met several sages of the Himalayan caves and held discussions with them. Shankara visited and worshipped in several temples in the Himalayan region. He stayed there for some time.

Shankara also visited Vyasasrama. There, Shankara entered in to deep meditation for several days. There he wrote his *Bhashya* on *Prasthana Thraya*. It is also said that at this period of time Shankara also wrote several treatises. It was in this place that Shankara had the vision of *Vyasa* in the guise of an old man. (According to another view *Vyasa* appeared before Shankara while Shankara was in Kashi) The old man put several questions to Shankara and Shankara answered all the questions in a very convincing manner. Then the old man entered in to a debate with Shankara and he began to argue. Shankara also argued equally to prove his point. The entire Veda and all other scriptures were analysed during the course of their argument. Then the old man said that he would visit the next day to resume the argument. This went on for seven days. Shankara and his disciple *Padma pada* knew that this old man was none other than *Veda Vyasa* himself. So when the old man arrived on the eight day, Shankara prostrated before him and urged him to reveal his identity. Then the greatest of all sages revealed himself as Vyasa and he blessed Shankara. Instantaneously Shankara composed a hymn in praise of this greatest of all Seers. Shankara then wanted to shed his human form as he felt that he had completed his mission on earth. He was sixteen years old at that time. But *Vyasa* told him that it was not yet time for him to leave the world, as he was to revive Sanatana Dharma and make it available to one and all and after blessing him with 16 more years of life Vyasa disappeared.

Shankara Returning to Banaras

Shankara then returned to Banaras and stayed there for several years. It is said that at this time he wrote commentaries on Sanat Sujathiya, Nrsimhatapani, Vishnu Sahasranama, and Lalita Trishathi. He won over Pashupathas who viewed that Ishwara and jeeva are different and at the time of *Moksha* the qualities of *Ishwara* percolate in to *jeeva*. He also won over the followers of *Nyaya* Philosophy who resided on the banks of the sacred Ganges and many other scholars who belonged to the opposing schools of thought.

According to legend, Shankara wanted to enter in to a debate with Kumarila Bhatta, an elderly Mimamsa philosopher about his philosophy and defeat him. With this aim he came to Prayaga to meet Kumarila Bhatt. Kumarila was born in a Brahmin family in South India. He spent his entire life in upholding Hindu Dharma against Jainism and Buddhist philosophies. It is said that he disguised himself as a Buddhist monk and learnt Buddhism. It is even said, that he was indirectly responsible for the death of his *Guru*, the Buddhist *Sugata*. Shankara found him in slow fire as a penance for his crime against his *guru* from whom he learnt Buddhism in disguise in order to defeat him in a debate. He told Shankara that he had understood Shankara *Bhashyas* and it was his desire to write a Vartika, an explanatory treatise on Shankara Bhashyas, but could not, because of his vow of expiation for his sin in disguising himself and cheating his *Guru*. He told Shankara that he had become sinless as he could see Shankara before he left his body. Shankara then told him that Kumarila was an incarnation of Skanda and no sin can affect him. Kumarila requested Shankara to impart Brahma Vidya to him. Shankara told Kumarila that he could extinguish the fire and save him. But Kumarila politely refused to accept that offer although he had a long cherished desire to write a *Vartika*, an explanatory treatise on *Shankara Bhashya*.

Mandana Mishra Becoming Disciple of Shankara

Kumarila asked Shankara to meet his disciple Mandana Mishra who was also known as Viswaroopa at Mahismathi, the present Maheshwar in Madhya Pradesh and and debate with him so that after defeating Mandana Mishra Shankara could make him his desciple and make him write the Vartika. After imparting Brahma vidya to Kumarila Bhatta Shankara left. Shankara during this time also met Prabhakara and his son Prithividhara. He won over them and they became his disciples. Later he left for Mahishmathi the present-day Bihar where Mandana Mishra was living. When Shankara went to the house of Mandana who was then called Vishwaroopa, he saw Mandana who followed Mimamsa doctrine of the Vedas washing the feet of Vyasa and Jaimini (The founder of Mimamsa school of thought) for conducting a ritual in his house. He could bring them to his house on account of his great Tapas. Mandana was the greatest champion of Mimamsa doctrine that upheld the Vedic ritualism that differed from Advitha Vedanta. It is said that Shankara found that even parrots discussed *Shastra* in the house of Mandana Mishra. Mandana, a householder did not like Sanyasins and he entered in to an argument with Shankara. The scholars present there at that time pacified Mandana. Shankara then invited him for a debate and Mandana accepted the challenge on condition that the loser should become the desciple of the winner of the debate.

Shankara accepted the condition and the debate started. Mandana Mishra's wife, Ubhaya Bharati was the judge. It is said that Ubhaya Bharathi was an avatar of Goddess Saraswati. Once when sage Durvasa was chanting Vedas before Lord Brahma, and his consort Goddess Saraswati before a big assembly, the sage committed a small mistake in chanting for which Goddess Saraswati laughed. The angry sage cursed the Goddess to be born on earth and she took birth as Bharathi. Bharati told Shankara that if Shankara loses the debate then he should become a householder and marry and if Mandana is defeated then he should become a Sanyasi. She threw garlands around the neck of both her husband and Shankara and said, he, whose garland starts to fade first, should accept defeat. While Shankara tried to establish Advaita vedanta that is based on the *Jnana Kanda* or the Upanishads of Vedas, Mandana Mishra tried to establish his doctrine of Vedanta that is based on the *Karma Kanda* that includes the Samhitha and Brahmana portion of the Vedas that emphasized Vedic Karmas or rituals and sacrifices. After fifteen days of continuous debate, Mandana Mishra accepted defeat. Ubhaya Bharathi then wanted Shankara to debate with her because Mandana is only one half and she is the other half. So if Shankara is to be declared as the winner then he should defeat her as well. The debate started and even after 17 days Bharati could not defeat Shankara. Finally she decided to win him over through a debate on *Kamasutra,* the science of sex and love. She asked Shankara about marital life and its obligations and duties. But Adi Shankara had no knowledge about this science, as he was an ascetic even from the age of eight. So for knowing the subject Shankara requested her for some time and by his yogic powers, did *parakaya Pravesham* and entered in to the body of king Amaruka who had just then passed away and was about to be cremated, after asking his disciples to keep vigil over his physical body. The king's body revived. But the king was totally different from his older self and the learned ones began to doubt that a great soul had entered in to the king's body. So they sent people to search for the body of the great one.

Shankara, as the King acquired the knowledge of sex love or Kamasutra. He gradually began to forget his original physical body. His disciples therefore located his whereabouts and revived his memory after singing a few philosophical songs. But by that time the men who went in search of the body of the Mahatma located the body and were about cremate it so that he would remain with them as their king. Shankara on reaching the place saw that his body was set to fire just then. He prayed to Lakshmi Narasimha and composed Lakshmi Narasimha Karavalamba Stotram. By the grace of Narasimha, the rains at that moment extinguished the flames and the soul of Shankara entered in to his original body.

Now Shankara was in a position to argue with Ubhaya Bharati. But by then Ubhaya Bharati declined to debate with Shankara. As agreed upon earlier to the starting of the debate, Mandana Mishra took to Sanyasa. Shankara then cleared all the remaining doubts of Mandana, there upon Mandana prostrated before Shankara and said that Shankara made everything clear by the single statement of '*Tat Tvam Asi*'. He gave all his property to Shankara and Shankara in turn asked him to distribute his wealth to the poor and needy. Mandana Mishra then became Shankara's desciple with the name Sureshwaracharya. He was the first to take charge of the Sringeri Mutt.

Shankara's Visit to Sree Sailam

Adi shankara during the course of his travel visited Srisailam. At Srisailam the Deity was Shiva in the form of Mallikarjuna. He appears as a Linga under a Marutha tree that is also called as Arjuna tree. This is supposed to be the place where Arjuna did Tapas on Lord Shiva and Lord Shiv blessed Arjuna after He humbled Arjuna's pride. It is said that during this time Shankara resumed his work on writing the commentaries. There he composed Shivanandalahari in praise of Lord Shiva – The Mallikarjuna of Sree sailam.

Shankara and the Kapalika

According to another story, Shankara was about to be sacrificed by a Kapalika, the worshippers of the ferocious form of Shiva, the Bhairav when he was meditating in an interior forest at Hatakeshwaram near Srisailam. Their king, Kirakeshan wanted to eliminate Shankara. So he engaged Ugrabhairav the chief of Kapalika for doing away with Shankara. The Kapalika became a disciple of

Shankara and gradually he gained the confidence of all the disciples of Shankara. But Shankara knew his real intention. One day he told Shankara that he should fulfil one of his desires of offering human sacrifice for gaining Lord Shiva's blessings. The Kapalika wanted the head of a king or an all-knowing person as sacrifice to be offered for fulfilling his wish to go to Kailash in human form and he wanted Shankara to be offered as the sacrifice. Shankara readily agreed to this and he asked the Kapalika to cut off his head when he was in meditation. But Padmapada came to know everything and he prayed to Lord Vishnu in the form of Narasimha. Padmapada had performed austerities and Tapas on Lord Narasimha and he had obtained a vision of Lord Narasimha and it is said that Lord Narasimha appeared before Padmapada and blessed him and then he disappeared from his view. Due to his Yogic power, Padmapada in his super conscious state now became Lord Narasimha personified and killed the Kapalika, who was about to kill Shankara. It is said that Shankara composed the Lakshmi-Narasimha Stotra at that moment.

Shankara's Visit to Gokarna

Then Shankara went to Gokarna and worshipped Lord Shiva and Lord Hari- Shankara, the idol that combined both Hari and Hara and composed a hymn on Lord Vishnu and Lord Shiva. After visiting Gokarna Shankara went to Mookambika at Kollur in Karnataka. There, Shankara composed a hymn in praise of the divine Mother. There he stayed for several days. Shankara installed Shree Chakram at Mookambika temple. One can see Shankara Peeta in this temple where Adi Shankara meditated and visualized the form of Devi and realized her. It is also believed that Shankara composed Sondarya Lahari here, at Mookambika temple at Kollur and established Sarvajna Peeta at Kutajadri peak located near Mookambhika temple. Later, he won in debates with the local scholars there. At the requests of the Brahmins there, Shankara visited a village there called Sri Bali that had a temple for Lord Shiva and Goddess Parvati. There, all the Brahmanas were learned in Vedas and performed Yagnas as per Vedic tradition. There, in that village was a Brahmin by name Prabhakara who was a great scholar. He had a handsome son who behaved almost like an idiot. He was also very lazy.

When Shankara visited that village Prabhakara approached Shankara along with his son Prithvidhara. Both father and son prostrated before Shankara, then the father told Shankara about his seven years old son who was behaving like an idiot. Adi Shankara asked the boy who he was. When Shankara asked the boy, "Who are you"? At once the boy started speaking and gave his reply in twelve verses that was known later as Hastamalakiyam that contained the essence of Advaita Philosophy that, "This body is not me, it is *Paramatman* that is my body". Shankara was pleased with this reply. He then named the boy Hasthamalaka that means one with the Amalaka fruit in his hand, since the knowledge of self was so natural to him as the Amalaka fruit in one's hand and he became one of the principle disciples of Shankara.

Establishment of Sringeri Mutt

Then Shankara visited Sringa giri that is known as Shringeri to establish Sharada peetam. It is said that Sage Rishya Shringa had meditated at this place for a long time. There, Shankara preached Advaita vedanta doctrine. He also installed the idol of divine Mother Sharada in a temple there. When Shankara reached Sringagiri, that is Sringeri, he stayed in the old Asrama site of the great Rishis of Vibhandaka and Rshya Shringa. He stayed there for about twelve years, and he established a monastery there. Shankara made his desciple Sureshwaracharya whose original name was Mandana Mishra as the head of this Ashram. This was the Mutt that Shankara established in South India.

At Sringeri a devotee of Saivaite cult told his teacher Neelakhanta about Shankara. Neelakhanta's doctrine was opposed to the Advaita philosophy of Shankara. So he approached Shankara and although Sureshwaracharya, one of the chief disciples of Shankara came forward to argue, Neelakhanta wished that he entered in to debate with Shankara himself. As usual within no time Shankara defeated his opponent in debate and established the superiority of Advaita Vedanta. Neelakantha accepted defeat and became a disciple of

Shankara. According to Madhaviya Shankara Vijayam, Shankara and his disciples reached Sringeri, in the afternoon in hot summer. When they reached river Tunga they witnessed an unusual sight. They saw a frog in intense labour pains. Beside the frog a cobra had spread its hood to protect the frog from the Sun. This sight moved Shankara and the others, as it was unusual for a snake to protect its prey, the frog. Shankara then established a Mutt there.

Totacharya-the Disciple of Shankara

When Adi Shankara was at Sringeri, he met a boy named Ananda Giri'. Shankara took him as his disciple although he was not bright. But he was a very loyal and dutiful servant to Shankara. Once Giri was washing the clothes of his master. So Shankara, his master waited for his disciple Giri to come before commencing his discourse on Advaita Vedanta. Seeing this a desciple of Shankara pointed at a wall indicating that imparting knowledge to Giri or to the wall is the same. At this, Shankara blessed and granted all knowledge to Giri. Giri at once became enlightened and composed Totakashtakam, a Sanskrit poem in Trikuta Meter, which was very difficult, in praise of his *Guru*, Shankara. From that day Anmada Giri came to be known as Totacharya. This incident made all other disciples of Shankara to give up their pride.

Shankara Directing Desciples to Write Sub-commentaries

Shankara later bade Sureshwaracharya (Mandana Mishra), his disciple who was eager to help his master in his writings to write a Vartika that is critical appreciation. But the other disciples felt that this act may bring contrary results as Mandana Mishra, until he embraced Sanyasa and became a disciple of Shankara was a staunch follower of Vedic rituals. They therefore requested Shankara to allot this work to any one of the other three chief disciples of Shankara. So Shankara asked Sureshwaracharya to take up an independent work and Sureshwara wrote Naishkarmya Siddhi, that was an independent work. Shankara also bade him to write commentaries on his Bhashyas on Brihad Aranyaka Upanishad and Taittiriya Upanishad. Shankara told him that he would be born as Vachaspati and would write an extensive critical study of Shankara's commentaries on Brahma Sutras. Later Padmapada (Sanandana) also was directed by Shankara to write a treatise on Shankara Bhashya on Vedanta Sutras. He also permitted Padmapada to go on a pilgrimage as per his wish. Shankara also asked Ananda giri (Totaka) and other disciples to write about Advaita Vedanta.

Shankara Performing the Funeral Rites for His Mother

When Shankara knew through his intuition that his mother was very sick he proceeded to his birthplace Kalady, where his mother was staying. His mother, who was in her deathbed, was very much pleased to see her son. She wanted Shankara to teach her the knowledge of Brahman. Shankara sat by her side and began to instruct her about the self effulgent Brahman. But she could not follow and understand the high philosophy. So Shankara resorted to the path of *Bhakti* and recited a hymn on Lord Shiva. But she could not bear the fearful sight of the *Bhoota ganas* who came to take her. Shankara understood the mental state of his mother and he immediately composed a hymn on Lord Narayana and his mother slowly breathed her last peacefully. Shortly after his mother's demise His *Guru* Govinda also left his mortal body.

His relatives who were against him did not allow him, a *sanyasi*, to perform his mother's funeral rites because it was against the tradition of Sanyasins to take part in any rites. Shankara had to perform all rites alone. They also did not help him in any way. All of them refused to offer any help and even take part in the cremation. They did not help him to carry the dead body to the funeral pyre. Further, they also prevented him from getting firewood for his mother's cremation. So, it is said, that Shankara carried on his shoulders the dead body of his mother. He piled up dry plantain stems from the backyard of his house on his mother's corpse for the last rites. From that time onwards due to Shankara's curse Vedic study did not flourish in that village. In the Adi Shankara Janmabhoomi Kshetra one can see the Samadhi of Aryamba, Shankara's mother, in the place where she was cremated. A big lamp on a lamppost made of Blackstone is kept lit there always. The Poorna River is located towards its south.

Shankara Resuming His Digvijaya to Tamil Nadu, Karnataka and Andhra Pradesh

After performing the funeral rites for his mother Shankara resumed his Digvijaya towards the south. With King Sudhanva, a malayalee King Shankara passed through the present Tamil Nadu, Andhra Pradesh and Karnataka and Vidharbha. It is said that when Shankara was touring the present Tamil Nadu, he visited Thiruvidaimarudur in Tanjore dist of Tamilnadu. Lord Shiva was the Deity in the temple there. The scholars of that place did not have faith in Advaita Vedanta. They stated that when Lord Shiva was the creator, how can both the creator and created be the same. Then Shankara entered the temple along with them, and it is said that when they reached the sanctum Sanctorium a hand came out of the *Lingam* and at the same time there was a thunderous voice stating three times, "Satyam is Advaita". The scholars who were there then accepted the doctrine of Advaita Vedanta and Shankara became their *Guru*. On his way to Rameshwaram Shankara met a few who belonged to a sect similar to Sakthas who drank liquor during their worship. Shankara changed their views and they then started following the code of worship as per Shankara's advice. From there Shankara went to Pandya and chola kingdoms.

Shankara visited Tiruvanaikkavu in Tiruchirappalli and worshipped Jambukeshwarar and Akhilandeshwari. It is also said, that Shankara found Goddess Akhilandeshwari, the presiding deity of the temple at Thiruvanikkavu to be fierce looking and he made the fierceness disappear from her face. He then presented two sets of earrings called Thathangam to the deity in the temple there. Shankara also visited Chidambaram, Sree Rangam, Tiruchendur, and Vaitheeswaran Koil and so on. At Kancheepuram Shankara built a temple for Goddess Kamakshi. There, Shankara defeated the Sakthas in debate. From there Shankara proceeded towards north of India. Then he traveled towards northern India.

Shankara visited Lord Venkateshwara at Tirupati. There he recited a *shloka* in praise of the Lord and established a *Yantra* underneath the idol. It is believed that from that day onwards devotees began to throng to this temple. It is also said that Shankara installed Shree

Chakras in many temples like Kamakshi temple at Kanchi, Bharat temple at Rishikesh, Nara Narayan temple at Badri, Guhyeshwari temple in Nepal and so on. Shankara then went to Karnataka along with his disciples. On his way, Krakacha the leader of the Kapalika cult opposed Shankara. But Shankara's disciples drove him away. Later Krakacha approached Shankara in great anger and it is believed that at that moment Kapali appeared from nowhere and cut off the Kapalika's head.

Shankara's Visit to the Western India

Shankara also toured Vidarbha and Ujjain and put down the atrocities of Bhairavas in the name of religion. Through his discourses he converted them to the Vedic dharma path. But after some time Shankara had some trouble with a few of the Bhairavas there. But with the help of the King Shankara could come out of it. Then Shankara went to Saurashtra and visited Dwaraka and established a Mutt there. Padmapada, who was one of the four chief disciples of Shankara, was made the head there. In Shourashtra Shankara visited several shrines including the shrine of Somnath and Prabhasa and arrived at Dwaraka. In Dwaraka, Shankara defeated Vaishnavas in debate. He debated with Bhatta Bhaskara of Ujjain who was a great proponent of Bhedabheda Philosophy, and defeated him. All the scholars of Ujjain accepted the philosophy of Shankara. At Bahlika and Kamboja Shankara defeated the jains in debate. All the scholars of Ujjain (Avanthi) accepted Shankara's philosophy. At Ujjain he worshipped Maha Kaleshwara. Shankara defeated many Jains and great scholars like Khandanakara and several others.

Shankara's Visit to Eastern Part of India

Shankara then went to the eastern part of India to preach his philosophy of Advaita Vedanta. He established the Govardhana Mutt at Puri. His desciple Hastamalaka whose original name was Sanandana was made the head of the Mutt there. During his travel Shankara defeated several scholars in debate, including Jains, Madhyamikas, Lingayats, and followers of Bhatta Bhaskara and so on. At Kamarupa, the present Gauhati in Assam, he humbled Abhinav Gupta, the Shaktha commentator. He was a leading scholar of Shaktha School of thought. Abhinav Gupta accepted defeat and pretended to have become a desciple of Shankara. But he wanted to take revenge upon Shankara. So through his black magic, he made Shankara suffer from a severe form of piles namely rectile fistula. But Shankara's desciple Padmapada removed all the evil effects of the Black magic through his mantras and he transferred the evil back to Abhinav Gupta and Shankara was saved by the divine grace. But Abhinav Gupta died of the same disease. From Kamarupa Shankara went to places like Kosala, Anga and so on. On his way he won over many scholars like Murari Mishra, Udayana, Dharma Gupta and others. Many followers of other sects like Sakthas, Pasupathas, and Kapalikas and so on became Shankara's followers.

Shankara Ascending Sarvajna Peetam

After a few days of his stay in the eastern parts of India, Shankara resumed his journey. Now his destination was Kashmir. Shankara then visited the Sarvajnapeeta; the throne of Omniscience in Kashmir that is now located in the Pakistan occupied Kashmir. Only that great one who has mastered all branches of learning can ascend this throne. This throne of knowledge is in the temple dedicated to Goddess Sharada or Saraswati, the Goddess of knowledge. Philosophers engage themselves in debate here to establish their superiority and to win over their opponents and to ascend this throne or *Peeta*. This peetam had four doors for scholars from all the four directions of India. The southern door was never opened because no scholar from the south India had entered the Sarvajna Peeta. Shankara had to answer the questions put to him by the followers of other religions like Buddhism, Jainism, other non-Vedic doctrines as well as the other vedanta doctrines. Shankara after defeating all the scholars assembled there ascended the throne of Sarvajna Peeta or the throne of transcendental wisdom.

Last Days of Shankara

Shankara then proceeded to Badrinath. On his way, He established a Mutt at Joshimutt. One of Shankara's chief desciples by name Totakacharya whose original name was Anandagiri was made the Matathipathi or chief of the Mutt there. From there he went to

Badrinath. It is believed that at Bhadrinath, Shankara had a vision of his Guru's *Guru*, sage Govindapada who is regarded as an incarnation of Adi sesha. Shankara showed him his commentary on Mandukya Upanishad and Gaudapada's Karika on that Upanishad. It is said that Sage Gaudapada became highly pleased with Shankara and after blessing him he disappeared. It is also believed that Shankara visited Nepal.

Shankara finally went to Kedarnath and visited several holy places there including Goumukh, Gangotri and so on. He was 32 years of age at that time. There are several views regarding where Shankara spent his last days and where he left his mortal remains. Some say that Shankara went to Kailash from here and there he merged with Lord Shiva. According to some he attained final liberation at Kedarnath. Behind the Kedarnath temple one can see the Samadhi Mandir of Shankara. But according to some Shankara went to Kailash and brought the Sphatika Lingas and a portion of Soundarya Lahari verses from there and attained Videha Mukti at Kancheepuram. Still others believe that his end came in the Vadakkanathan temple at Trichur-Kerala after establishing a Mutt there that is known as Naduvil Madam. In the Vadakkunathan temple there one can see a raised platform with emblems of conch and discuss in stone that mark the Samadhi of Adi Shankara. Again according to still others he breathed his last and merged with Dattatreya at Mahuripuri (Mahur) or Mohuragad in Marathwada. To some others Shankara spent his last day Dattatreya Guha in Badrinath. It is also said that Shankara in the end left to a place that was dear to him and what was that place no one actually knows. According to Madhaviya Shankara Vijayams Shankara shed his human form in 820 A D. It is also believed that he attained *Maha-Samadhi* either in *Vaishakha* (April-May) or *Margazi* (Dec- Jan) in 837 A.D.

●●●

3

Adishankara's Works

Adishankara was supposed to have written many works numbering around 300 but there are doubts regarding the authorship of the books that are ascribed to him. According to another view 153 works are attributed to Shankara that includes 23 *Bhashyas*, 54 *Prakarana Granthas* and 76 *stotras*. The doubtful authorship may be, because, his successors in all the four Mutts that Shankara established in the four corners of India also are called as Shankaracharyas and the possibility that some of the works attributed to Adi Shankara might have been probably written by them. The controversy may also be due to the fact that it is felt that Shankara could not have written so many *Granthas* and commentaries with in a short span of life of only 32 years and also because according to some, the language and style is not uniform in all the works attributed to Shankara. But for a genius like Shankara writing so many *granthas* and commentaries might have been only a child's play.

The difference in style might also be due to the fact that Shankara wanted his works to be suitable and approachable to all people irrespective of their level of knowledge. But these controversies have no importance because the purpose behind all these writings is spreading of Vedic Dharma. However, as far as his life and teachings are concerned there is no controversy. All his works are in Sanskrit and in his works he had quoted extensively from the Vedas, Upanishads, and other ancient Hindu scriptures. His philosophical works are also mainly Polemical in nature and are against the other Indian Philosophical systems both in Hinduism and in the other religions that were non-Vedic and that had spread their influence in the country during the time of Shankara. His works are mainly divided in to three categories.

Shankara's Commentaries

Shankara *Bhashyas* or commentaries on *Prasthana Traya* that is known as the triple canon rank among the greatest works of Shankara. *Prasthana* means system or course and *Traya* means threefold. The Upanishads, *Brahma Sutras* and *Bhagavad Gita* form the *Prasthana Traya*. Shankara has been acclaimed as the commentator par excellence of *Prasthana Traya*. The commentaries on Prasthana Traya provide logical interpretation of principal Upanishads, Brahma Sutras and Bhagavadgita from the point of view of Advaita Vedanta. In his commentaries Shankara had mentioned the earlier commentaries of Dravida, Bhartraprapancha and others. It is said that Shankara's presentation of his commentaries on *Prasthana Traya* is both *Prasanna* and *Gambhir*, meaning that they are easy to read and understand but at the same time are profound and with enormous depth. It is said that to learn logic and metaphysics one has to read Shankara's commentaries.

In fact Shankatra's *bhashyas* stand at the pinnacle of Indian philosophical writings and also have given rise to a long tradition of sub-commentaries that are known as *Vritti* or *Deepikas* that explain the aphorisms in a more elaborate way, Tikas that is a gloss on a particular work giving only a brief explanation of the verses, and Tippanis explaining the difficult words or phrases of the original and *Varthikas* that is a critical study and the ways of making the *Bhashya* perfect by supplying the omissions. One of the chief disciples of Shankara wrote a sub commentary on Shankara *Bhashya* called 'Pancha Padika'. Vivaran Acharya wrote a further commentary on this sub commentary. Vachaspati Mishra wrote another sub commentary on Shankara Bhasya that is called 'Bhamati'.

Amalananda wrote a further commentary on this. Ramananda's sub commentary on Shankara *Bhashya* is known as '*Ratna Prabha*'. Again, Anandagiri, a disciple of Shankara wrote a commentary called '*Anandagiriya*'. Trayambaka Bhattacharya wrote a sub commentary on Shankara *Bhashya* about one hundred and fifty years ago with the title '*Bhasya bhanuprabha*'. Raghunatha Suri wrote a sub commentary for one pada or section of the Shankara Bhasya. It is called '*Shankara-Pada-Bhushana*'.

(A) Upanishads

The Upanishads form the last section, after Samhita, Brahmana and Aranyaka section of the Vedas and form the end or culmination of the Vedas that are known as Sruti. (Sruti means what is heard or revealed. Vedas are called as Sruti because the sages of yore heard this knowledge from nowhere. The knowledge of the ultimate reality was revealed to them as vibrations of Space). It is also called as Vedanta or *Uttara Mimamsa* that means latter enquiry. The Upanishads are known as *Upadesa Prasthana* or injunctive texts. This section of the Vedas is also known as *Jnana Kanda*. There are 180 well known Upanishads. Shankara wrote his commentaries on ten of them. (There is no unanimity of opinion regarding this number. According to some Shankara wrote commentaries for 11 of the Upanishads and for still others it is 12 and so on.) The Upanishads are referred to as the *Gnana Kanda* of the Vedas as they discuss philosophy, meditation, the individual soul or *Jeevatma* and the Universal soul namely Paramatma and their relationships. These are composed over several centuries by several sages of the past. They are affiliated to different Vedas. Arthur Schopenhauer said that in the whole world there is no study so beneficial and so elevating as that of Upanishads. According to Vivekananda "The Upanishads are the great mine of strength. There in lies strength enough to invigorate the whole world; the whole world can be vivified, made strong, energized through them".

Shankara commented upon ten of the earlier Upanishads, which are considered as the principal or *Mukhya Upanishads* and brought out the Advaita Vedanthic principles found in them. In his commentary of the Upanishads Shankara explains the meaning of the Upanishads and how they supported his Advaita doctrine. In his commentary on *Chandogya Upanishad* Shankara wrote that his commentary is a brief book for those who want to know the summary of the Upanishad. The Upanishads for which he wrote commentaries are:

(1) *Aitareya Upanishad Belonging to Rigveda*

This Upanishad is associated with *Sage Aitareya.* It is a short prose text with three chapters containing 33 verses. It is found in the 4th, 5th and 6th chapters of the second book of the *Aitareya Aranyaka* of *Rig Veda.* This Upanishad is written in symbolic language. It many tells about creation, the cosmic power in the human body, the embodiment of self in the human body, the three births of the self, and the three classes of people who aspire for liberation. This Upanishad gives the deeper inner meaning of Vedic sacrifices for elevating the mind of men from the outer ceremonial worship to inner sacrifice. In this Upanishad Atman or the inner self is described as the divine creator. This Upanishad says that only when man realizes the Atman he gets release from repeated births and deaths. The realized being then becomes immortal. This Upanishad also answers the question as to who is this self. The self is Brahman and everything is based and governed by Brahman. All beings are the creation of Brahman. This Upanishad contains the *Maha Vakya*-'prajnanam Brahman' that means Brahman is knowledge or Gnana.

(2) *Brihadaranyaka Upanishad Belonging to Shukla Yajurveda*

It means the great forest book. It is in the Shatapatha Brahmana of the *Shukla Yajur Veda.* It is ascribed to sage Yajnavalkyavalkya and is known for its philosophical statements. This Upanishad has six chapters in three sections namely, *Madhu Kanda, Muni Kanda* or *Yajnavalkya Kanda* and *Khila Kanda. Madhu Kanda* explains the basic identity of the individual self or Jeevatman and the Universal Soul or Paramatman or Brahman. In *Yajnavalkya Kanda*, the conversations between sage *Yagnavalkya* and his wife Maitreyi are found. The saint says that everything in this world is loved not for its sake but only for the sake of the one who loves them. The *Khila*

Kanda explains the various methods of worship and meditation and the three stages of religious life namely, Shravana or hearing the instructions of the teacher, Manana or reflection and Nidhidhyasana or contemplative meditation. This Upanishad says that one should meditate with the awareness that one's soul is with all the things in the world. Whosoever is aware of this becomes Brahman itself. While soul is real *Prana* is covered by name and form. As the soul cannot be seen it is very difficult to comprehend it. It is nothing but consciousness. When the senses and desires are controlled, then one would attain God- the Brahman-that is Liberation. This Upanishad mentions three cardinal values namely, Damana or Self restraint, *Dana* or giving alms and *Daya* or compassion. This Upanishad says that Brahman is realized through mind alone. The famous doctrine 'NETHI NETHI' or negation of all concepts while knowing Brahman is found in this Upanishad.

(3) *Isa Upanishad Belonging to Shukla Yajurveda*

Isa Upanishad is also known as *Isavasya Upanishad* or *Isopanishad.* It derives its name from the first word of the first verse of this Upanishad. 'ISA' means 'Lord of the Universe'. The name is derived from the verse '*Isa Vasyam Idam Sarvam*'- that means 'This Universe is enveloped by the Lord'. It is a small Upanishad and contains only eighteen verses in total but it is a well known Upanishad. This Upanishad is found in the final *Adyaya* of *Shukla Yajurveda Samhita.* The verses cover ritualism, religion, philosophy and metaphysics in a very deep manner. It belongs to a later period, approximately, the Maurian Era. Mahatma Gandhi once remarked that even if all the Hindu scriptures disappear, and if this one alone remained, Hinduism will still survive. This Upanishad begins with the statement that God pervades the entire Universe and it belongs to Him. The last three verses deal with death and departure of the soul from the body. Usually these verses are chanted during the cremation ceremonies.

This Upanishad explains why we should live in this world and perform duties without attachment, since everything belongs to God- the dynamic force. Nothing belongs to man as his own. It is only delusion or ignorance that makes us assume the doership of action performed. It is like coveting what does not belong to us. So while living in the world one should perform his duties without claiming any rights of ownership of actions or things of the world. This Upanishad also teaches the unity of God and the world. It further says that a man's material and spiritual goals need not be contradictory to each other. One while living in this world should see the glory of God in everything. One should understand that everything belongs to God, and he is only an instrument of God. Man should cultivate absence of possessiveness and renunciation of doership of actions. This Upanishad says that Brahman is both moving and non moving, near and also far and is within and without every being. The senses and mind cannot perceive Him. It remains static but it overtakes those who run. He moves and moves not. It is far yet near, it is within all, and it is without all. He is the source of everything. He is pure. He does not possess a body. He is all pervading and transcendental. He is eternal. He is independent of the Universe but the entire Universe is dependent on Him. He is above, below and everywhere. He is all pervading, radiant, bodiless, soreless, pure, untainted by sin, all-seer, Lord of mind, transcendent and self-existent. The one who perceives oneness in all beings will have no delusion or grief. Such a one does not entertain or perceive any hatred. He who knows both the unmanifested and the destructible world together transcends death by the worship of destructible or *Saguna Brahman* and attain immortality by worship of the unmanifested.

This Upanishad ends with a prayer to Surya, Agni and the Creator for helping the Atman to realize and follow proper paths of knowledge and action. It describes the supreme person, God as the controller of the Universe. The later prayers are for the effulgence or supreme light for understanding the true nature of the Supreme Lord and to free one from the sins of past misdeeds. It also discusses karma or action, advocates a simple living, knowledge over ignorance, seeing all living things in connection with the Supreme power and the negative reactions of those who kill another human being. The worship of the Supreme Lord is advocated against worship of Devas or Demi Gods for bringing about eternal life, knowledge and Bliss. Its essence is that everything in the Universe is that of God. One may enjoy whatever He has given. But one should not covet the wealth of the other. It gives several descriptions of the supreme and also a series of prayers for seeing that supreme effulgence in order to understand the true nature of the Supreme Lord. Worship of the supreme is given importance here.

(4) *Taittiriya Upanishad Belonging to Krishna Yajurveda*

This Upanishad is associated with *Krishna Yajur Veda* that is also called as *Taittiriya Samhita*. The eighth and the nineth chapters of *Taittiriya Aranyaka* form this Upanishad. It is divided in to three sections called Vallis namely, the *Siksha Valli*, the *Brahmananda Valli* and the Bhrigu Valli. Each valli is divided in to smaller verses called Anuvak. *Sikshavalli* is concerned with the phonetics or pronunciation of *Mantras*. It highlights the importance of phonetics and right pronunciation along with the meaning of *Mantras*. It also explains the intimate connection between the syllables. It tells about the *Mantras* and rituals performed by those who seek divine knowledge or *Medha Kama* and wealth or *Shree Kama*. It says that in the space inside the heart, resides the immortal golden being *Hiranya Purusha*. Through the subtle route in the middle of the head, a self realized *Yogi* travels when he leaves the body and joins the Brahman. This Upanishad explains about meditation in which Brahman is meditated upon as a set of five called '*Panktha*', the greatness of the holy syllable 'Aum', and tells about the pious way of life for realizing Brahman. It also gives a *mantra* for meditation that is supposed to have been given by Sage Trishanku who had realized Brahman and gives a prescription for an ideal life.

The Brahmananda Valli is noted for its philosophical contents. It states that the one who knows Brahman becomes one with Brahman. It defines Brahman as truth, divine knowledge, and infinite. In the space of the heart, resides Brahman who is known through knowledge and who is immortal and effulgent. The five sheaths of subtle bodies or the five Atmans that reside in the human body namely, the *Annamaya Kosha* or body formed of food, *Pranamaya Kosha* or body formed of vital life force, *Manonmaya Kosha* that is formed of the mind, the *Vijnanamaya Kosha* that is formed by knowledge and the most subtle *Ananda Maya Kosha* that is formed by Bliss are explained here.. It says that to the knower of Brahman there is no good or bad since for such a person only Brahman remains and nothing else.

The Bhriguvalli describes how Bhrigu, the son of Varuna, who is supposed to be the God of Oceans, realized Brahman through his repeated Tapas under his father's guidance. When Bhrugu approached his father Varuna to teach him the knowledge of Brahman, he asked his son to crave for that knowledge, from which all beings take birth, live after being born, towards which they move and in to which they merge, that is Brahman. Bhrigu meditated and realized that food is Brahman, later vital force as Brahman, still later mind as Brahman, then knowledge as Brahman and finally Bliss as Brahman. He realized that from Bliss all beings emerged. All beings that are born are sustained by Bliss, move towards Bliss and merge with Bliss that is established in the cavity of the heart. This section also tells about the greatness of feeding the hungry and also the greatness of food. The knower of Brahman attains the highest, says this Upanishad and that Brahman is truth, knowledge, and infinite. He who knows that Brahman as existing in the intellect, lodged in the supreme space in the heart enjoys identity with Brahman and all desirable things simultaneously. If any one thinks Brahman is non-existing, and then he himself is non-existent says this Upanishad. If any one knows that Brahman does exist, then he exists by virtue of that knowledge of Brahman. About creation, this Upanishad says that in the beginning everything was unmanifest- the Brahman. From the unmanifest emerged the manifest. Brahman was called the Truth. One becomes blissful by coming in to contact with that Brahman and realization of Brahman is the highest goal of all. Whenever a spiritual aspirant gets fearlessly established in this unperceivable, bodiless, inexpressible, and non- supporting Brahman, he reaches the state of fearlessness. On the other hand whenever the aspirant creates the slightest difference in it, he is caught with fear. This very Brahman is a terror to the so-called learned men who has no intuitive outlook. One becomes blissful by coming in to contact with that.

(5) *Katha Upanishad Belonging to Krishna Yajurveda*

This Upanishad has two chapters and each chapter contains three Vallis or sections. Some of its passages are found in *Bhagavad Gita*. This Upanishad tells the story of a pious Brahmin, Vajasravasa, and Nachiketa, his son. This Upanishad begins as a story but later expounds great philosophical truths. This story is given in *Rig Veda*. It says that all feelings are of the body and mind but do not belong to the self and when one tries to view them objectively then he will come to know this truth. One remains as the immortal self with the realization of this truth. Such a person is free from the cycle of birth and death and he becomes a *jeevan mukta* because he lives in this world without any body consciousness.

Vajasrava performs a sacrifice and gives a few old and feeble cows as Dakshina to the priests who performed the sacrifice. Nachiketa, his son felt disturbed at this act of his father and he asked his father a few questions. This perturbed his father. In anger the father told his son, "I give you to Yama", and Nachiketa goes to the abode of Yama, the Lord of death. He waits there for three days and nights to meet *yama*. Finally after three days *Yama* comes and he offers three boons to Nachiketa to compensate for his long waiting. As the first boon the boy, Nachiketa asks Yama to enable him to return to earth alive, to relieve his father from all anxieties and tensions of life and become free from anger towards him, recognize him and talk to him. *Yama* grants this boon to Nachiketa. Secondly, he asks yama how his good deeds may become in exhaustible through Vedic sacrifices that enable him to go to heaven and attain immortality. *Yama* enlightens him about Vedic sacrifices and Nachiketa repeats all that *yama* told him. This pleases *Yama* and he tells Nachiketa that the sacrificial fire would be known after him as Nachiketa in future. Thirdly he askes *yama* the means by which death can be defeated, and what happens to man after death. *Yama* tells Nachiketha that the answer for this question is very complicated and very difficult to understand. Even great sages had put this question. Yama tries to dissuade the boy and tells Nachiketa to ask for any other boon. He also tells the boy that he would instead, offer any material pleasures like wealth, gold, horses, cattle and so on. But Nachiketa is persistent in getting the answer to this question and did not yield to any other alternative. He craved only for the knowledge of immortality. Yama became highly impressed by the maturity shown by the young boy. He then began to unfold that knowledge and this forms the central theme of this Upanishad.

World appears as real only due to ignorance. Such a person has to go through repeated births and deaths, as he cannot be free from it. The knowledge of self that makes one immortal without undergoing the repeated births and deaths should be obtained from the knower of self-only. It can never be obtained through arguments. The wise through concentration of mind has understood that the self is hard to perceive. The self has neither birth nor death. It is unborn, eternal, imperishable, everlasting, ancient, is not slain when the body is slain, all pervading, and so on. Everything shines after him that shines. By this light everything shines. It is the subtlest of all and greatest and resides in the heart. The one who has no desires know the self and becomes free from all pains and sorrows of life. The self is near, far, everywhere, joyful, greater than the greatest, smaller than the smallest. The self cannot be attained by studying Vedas, or by intelligence or by hearing. One has to seek the self to know it. One who has not abstained from bad conduct, who has no restraint of senses, whose mind is not controlled and who does not possess a tranquil mind cannot attain self even through knowledge.

The soul is the lord, the body the chariot, the intellect or intuition the charioteer, the mind the reigns, the senses the horses, and the objects of the senses the paths. Those who are not disciplined and have no control over their senses are like wild horses of the chariot, that go astray not reaching the destination. These people cannot become free from the cycle of birth and death. But the one who has discrimination and possess a controlled mind, his senses are controllable like the good horses. He attains the goal and he is not born again. The self cannot be known by studying Vedas or by hearing or by intelligence. It can be known only if one restrains from bad conduct with control over senses and mind. Senses are to be controlled by mind and mind is to be controlled by the self. The senses can be held back by Yogas. The self is present in all beings. Only seers who are endowed with subtle and pointed intellect and capable of perceiving subtle objects see it. This Purusha that is, the self is of the size of a thumb and dwells in the body. It is the lord of the past, and future.

This Upanishad says that one should approach the excellent enlightened one because the path of knowing it is as sharp as razor's edge and hard to perceive. The one who knows this self gets liberated from birth and death. When the Prana goes out of the body, the self alone remains. It is by its light that everything in this universe shines. The highest state is when all the five senses and mind are at rest and the intellect is inactive. This truth is very difficult to comprehend. But it can be understood if one enters in to the hidden secret place in the depth of the heart. Nachiketha, after obtaining this knowledge from Yama attained immortality.

(6) *Chandogya Upanishad Belonging to Samaveda*

This Upanishad is associated with *Sama Veda*. The last eight chapters of the *Chandogya Brahmana* form this Upanishad. Each chapter here is sub divided in to Khandas. This Upanishad is one of the important sources of Vedanta philosophy. *Brahma Sutra* of Vyasa has references of this Upanishad in a number of places. This Upanishad explains several important spiritual practices.

The first chapter contains 13 Khandas. It tells the glory of 'Udgitha' or the holy syllable 'Aum'. In the second chapter, it is said that Udgitha should be meditated as vital force or *Prana*. A story to explain the sanctity of *Prana* that is untouched by evil unlike the five senses that get tainted by evil is told here. The method of meditating on 'Aum' as the eternal and ultimate refuge for achieving prosperity is explained in the fourth *Khanda* with the assertion that the one, who meditates in this manner, himself becomes the eternal and ultimate refuge. The nineth and tenth *Khanda* describe another method of *Udgitha* that is supposed to result in superior divine essence. The first chapter also explains the *Upasana* of different parts of the body separately.

The second chapter contains 24 *Khandas* and deals with the *Upasana* of the whole body. The third chapter has 19 *Khandas* and deals with the Upasana of Sun, teaching of Brahman through Gayatri, the meditation of *Sandilya Vidya*, *Kosha Vidya*, *Purusha Vidya* and finally the meditation on Brahman is taught. In the fourth chapter the story of King Janushruthi Pautrayana and the seer Raikva and meditation called *Samvarga Vidya* are explained. In the fifth chapter the *Panchagni Vidya* or the knowledge of five fires is given. The sixth chapter gives the most important message about the oneness of Atman with all beings and non-Beings. The story of Uddalaka and his son Shvetaketu also is told. This chapter has the Mahavakya 'Thou art that' or 'TAT TVAM ASI'. The seventh chapter describes the dialogue of sage Sanat Kumara and Narada that establishes the fact that realization of the ultimate principle of Universe is the only way to tide over sorrows. The last and final chapter is about *Dahara Vidya*, the technique of meditation of concentrating on Brahman located in the cave of the heart.

This Upanishad says that this entire Universe is Brahman. From Him all things originate and unto Him all dissolve and he sustains all. On him one should meditate in tranquility, for, 'As is one's faith, such indeed one is, and as is one's faith in this world, such one becomes on departing'. So, one should cultivate faith. This *Atman* residing in the heart is smaller than a grain of paddy, than a barleycorn, than a mustard seed, than a grain of millet or than the kernal of a grain of millet and it is also greater than the earth, sky, heaven, and all the worlds.

This Upanishad says that those who have purified their mind through withdrawal of senses and other means and who know Brahman see Brahman, the seed of the Universe, everywhere. When one reflects then alone one understands. That which is infinite alone is happiness. Finite cannot give happiness. To understand the infinite or immortal one should see, hear and understand everything as Brahman- nothing else other than that. This infinite is not worldly possessions. It is above, below, behind, in front, to the south, to the north- only Brahman is everywhere. That person who sees and understands and derives pleasure and delight in *Atman*, union in

Atman, joy in *Atman*, he becomes self-sovereign. He who sees this does not see death or illness or any sorrow. Whatever is there in this world and whatever is not, are contained in the inner core of the heart and that is Brahman.

The one who is not conscious of his body is not affected by desire or anger. Several stories are given here to emphasis the ultimate truth. The Vedic rituals are explained in the initial chapters. The later chapters are mainly concerned with the meditation of 'Aum'. A well-known passage in this Upanishad is the dialogue between *Satya Kama Jabala* and his mother. It asserts that it is only through character one can become Brahman and is not by birth in a particular caste.

(7) *Kena Upanishad Belonging to Samaveda*

This Upanishad derives its name from its first word 'Kena', meaning by whom? It belongs to the *Thalavakara Brahmana* of *Sama Veda*, so it is also called as *Talavakara Upanishad*. This Upanishad is divided in to four sections. The first two sections are in verse and the remaining two sections are in prose. The verses deal with the supreme unqualified Brahman and the prose section deals with the supreme as Ishwara or God. It is said that Adi Shankara wrote two commentaries on this Upanishad. One is called *Kenopanishad Pada Bhashya* and the other is known as *Kenopanishad Vakya Bhashya*.

This Upanishad says that the power that illumines everything and every being is whole and indivisible. It is this power that makes the senses perform their functions and makes the mind to think. This Upanishad says, that which is not uttered by speech, but by which the word is expressed, that which does not think with mind but by which the mind is thought, that which is not seen with the eye, but by which man sees, that does not hear but by which man hears, that which does not smell but makes the nose smell, that alone is Brahman. Those who think they know it know not, and those who know it do not think that they know it. It is known only when man knows the innermost witness of all cognitions. Then one attains immortality. The wise realize Brahman in all beings and thus become immortal. This realization of Brahman is similar to that which is like a flash of light or like the twinkling of the eyelids. The mind attains it by continuously remembering it by the mind. For this, knowledge, austerity, self-restraint and actions are the feet, the Vedas are the limbs and truth is the abode.

According to this Upanishad once the *Devas* won over the Asuras and they became very proud and thought that their victory was because of their strength and power. Then, Brahman appeared before them in a visible form of *yaksha* but the *Devas* could not recognize Him. Each one of the *Devas* tried to prove his strength but it was seen that fire or *Agni* could not burn even a straw, *Vayu* or air could not blow it away and so on. Finally Indra the Lord of all *Devas* came nearest to find out, who that *Yaksha* was. But the *Yaksha* disappeared by the time Indra could approach Him. Before him was a woman standing who was in the name and form of Uma- the Gnanambika- the Godess of Gnana or Supreme knowledge. She revealed the identity of the Yaksha who was only Brahman and imparted to Indra the knowledge of Brahman. She said that all power originated from Him alone. The wise one knows it and he attains eternal freedom from all sorrows of life. Since it is beyond the reach of all no one is able to impart instructions about Brahman as this or that precisely. It is known yet unknown. It cannot be described in words. It is the one about which the mind thinks but is unable to grasp. It cannot be seen, heard or felt or smelt. But it is that by which the being sees, hears, feels and smells. It is both known as well as unknown and also beyond the unknown. It is that spirit or energy that makes everything work. When Brahman is known as the inner self in all states of consciousness then only it is known. One attains *Mukti* by giving up all material pleasures of life.

This Upanishad points out that the knowledge of Ishwara or Saguna Brahma is *Apara Vidya* and it helps in knowing the path that leads to self-realization or *Mukti* from actions that are performed. Gradually the soul would acquire higher wisdom, the knowledge of the Absolute or *Nirguna Brahman* that is *Para Vidya* that results in identifying oneself with the supreme Brahman and this leads to Mukti or Liberation. For the one who understands this truth all sins would be eradicated and he becomes peaceful and blissful by identifying himself with Brahman.

(8) *Mandukya Upanishad Belonging to Atharva Veda*

This Upanishad is one of the shortest of all Upanishads. It explains the spiritual- mystic syllable 'Aum' and attainment of reality through introspection but not through senses. This Upanishad is considered to be the most profound and subtle of all Upanishads leading to enlightenment. This Upanishad is in prose and contains twelve sentences. Mandukya Upanishad means the scripture of toads. It is believed that Varuna, the Lord of oceans took the form of a toad to preach this Upanishad. Mandukya also means a particular kind of abstract meditation in which an ascetic sits motionless like a frog. *Mandukyasana* is also one of the 32 *asanas* of *Yoga.* Some also associate this Upanishad to sage Mandukya. The Mukthikopanishad says that if a person is unable to study all the 108 Upanishads, it is enough if he reads the *Mandukya Upanishad* alone. Even before Shankara, Gaudapada, Shankara's *parama guru*, wrote a commentary on this Upanishad that is known as Mandukya Karika. It is the earliest known systematic analysis of Advaita Vedanta system of Vedanta. Shankara merged the Karika with this Upanishad and wrote his commentary.

This Upanishad teaches the oneness of the individual Self and the Brahman through the four *Padas* of *Pranava*, *'Aum'*. It states that in the *Pranava Mantra*' Aum', 'A' stands for the wakeful state, 'U' stands for the dream state, 'M' the dreamless deep sleep state. The self in the waking state is called *Vaisvanara* and enjoys gross objects and has the consciousness of the external world. In dream state the self is called Taijasa and it enjoys the subtle objects. It has the consciousness of the interior. In the dreamless deep sleep state the self is called *Prajna* and everything is unified in this stage and it is full of consciousness-and enjoys Bliss. The one who sleeps does not desire anything of enjoyment and does not see any dream. It is the door to knowledge-which is the Lord of all- omniscient, the indwelling controller of all. It is the source, origin and dissolution of all beings. After the third state there is no consciousness of the internal or external world or both. It is not filled with consciousness, neither simple consciousness nor unconsciousness. It is actionless, incomprehensible, unthinkable, and indescribable. Its only proof is its identity of the self in all states. All phenomena come to nothing. This point cannot be explained but it has to be experienced. This point is beyond thought, duality and knowing. He who knows this enters the self by the self.

In the wakeful state, we experience the gross body and experience this world through sensory organs. In the dream state of sleep, only mind is awake. The experiences belong to the mind only. In the dreamless sleep state, there is no consciousness of any experience. The mind is absent but the awareness of deep sleep remains even after one wakes up. This Upanishad says that in this state Atman alone is the witness. One becomes aware that one has slept deeply and the objective consciousness is present in the unmanifested seed form only in deep sleep. When one practices and chants 'Aum' steadily and constantly, then he experiences the Turiya. At this stage only Atman' remains and the Self is realized. The *Ardh Mantra* after the syllable 'm' in 'Aum' corresponds to this state of Turiya. At this point only silence remains. This is however the basis of all the earlier stages. At this stage one merges with *Atman*- the consciousness. Even the objective consciousness that is present in an unmanifested form in the third state of deep sleep is transcended in this final moment of *Turiya*. This cannot be called as any stage because it is consciousness itself.

(9) *Mundaka Upanishad Belonging to Atharva Veda*

It is in the form of *Mantras* written in verses for teaching the highest knowledge of Brahman that cannot be obtained by sacrifices or worship. This Upanishad is considered to be the most poetic of all the Upanishads. It is said, that if the teaching of this Upanishad about the knowledge of Brahman is properly understood, then one will be able to get rid of all illusions of the material world- as they will be cut like hairs in the process of shaving or one will be, with such a knowledge become a sanyasi or monk who is with shaven head. *Mundaka* means shaven head. It is also possible that it was particularly meant for the monks with shaven head. It is also said that the term '*Mundaka*' also means the son of *Manduki* and '*Mandukyas*' are his disciples. It is said in this Upanishad, that Lord Brahma first uttered this Upanishad to His son *Atharva.* From him it was passed on to Satyavaha and from him to Angiras and from him to Shaunaka. This Upanishad is in the form of dialogue between Angiras and Shaunaka. It contains three chapters and each chapter has two sections.

This Upanishad mentions six disciplines of Vedanga. There are three chapters in this Upanishad and each chapter is further divided in to *Khandas.* There are 64 *Mantras* in this Upanishad. This Upanishad divides knowledge *Para Vidya* or great divine knowledge that leads to Self-realization and *Apara Vidya* or worldly knowledge and points out the greatness of *Para Vidya.* It also says about renouncement of all actions for realizing the Self. This Upanishad stresses the importance of '*Sarva Karma Sanyasa*' or renouncement of all actions. It says that to attain *Moksha* the knowledge of the ultimate should be attained through Sanyasa because the desires are the root cause of birth and death and for the one who has renounced desires there is no birth or death. It also describes the *yoga* for self-realization with a simily of bow and arrow.

The Mantra 'Aum' or 'Pranava' as told in this Upanishad is said to be the bow; the *Upasana* of the seeker on Atman is the arrow that is sharpened with meditation and the target, the supreme Reality-Brahman. With mind totally absorbed in the thought of Brahman, one should become one with it like a released arrow that hits the target. Brahman that is self-effulgent cannot be comprehended by the senses or speech or austerity or *Karma* or through any other means. One can realize it only through meditation through *gnana* or wisdom. It also says that the self is not attained by study, through intellect or by hearing. It is attainable only through seeking. It is also not attained by one devoid of strength, nor through delusion or worldly knowledge. This self is to be perceived by that, by which the mind and the motor and sensory organs of all beings are pervaded. Having attained this knowledge the seers became established in self, freed from all attachment. They, by seeing its all pervasiveness get merged with this. The story of two birds sitting on the *Pippana* tree that is the body and one of the birds representing the individual self or *jeevatma* and eating the fruits of the tree while the other bird representing *Paramatman* or the universal soul that merely witnesses everything is given here. When the bird representing *Jeevatman* or the individual soul sees the universal soul or *paramatman* it becomes liberated. This Upanishad asks the spiritual aspirant to give up all talks.

The distinction between lower level of knowledge and higher level of knowledge is explained here. The lower knowledge consists of knowledge of *Vedas*, science and pronunciation and so on, code of rituals, grammar, meter and so on. But the imperishable could be obtained only through higher knowledge. Through higher knowledge the wise realize that which cannot be perceived or grasped, which is without source, features, or sense organs, hands or feet, which is eternal, multi formed, all pervasive, extremely subtle, undiminishing and is the source of all, that is located in the heart. This *Purusha* is transcendental. He is formless. He is birth less, without a vital force and without mind. He is pure and supreme. It is one without a second. It binds heaven, the earth, the interspace, mind, and vital organs together with all other organs. One should meditate with the *Mantra* '*Aum*' on this self that shines as blissfulness and immortality, that is supreme, the bright sheath that is free from taints, that is without parts, is pure, is the light of lights, that becomes multiformed like spokes on the hub of a wheel, to go to the other shore beyond darkness. Those who penetrate and know this self, this supreme immortal, immutable Brahman that is everything, and that exists in the heart destroy the knot of ignorance. To them all doubts vanish, and all actions get dissipated.

Men engaged in *karma* with desire of its fruits do not understand the truth due to attachment. So they get afflicted with sorrow once the results of karma get exhausted. The hermits on the other hand, who resort to their duties as per the stages of their life and meditation and have their senses under control, attain *Purusha* that is immortal and un-decaying and from whom everything in this Universe originates.

It also points out that out of the imperishable universe, the phenomenal creation emerged. The different kinds of beings originate and finally merge in to the imperishable. This Upanishad explains the way for the knowledge of the self or Brahman and the state thereafter. Just as the space inside the pot gets merged with the space out side when it is broken, similarly, the individual identity as different from *Para Bhrahman* also vanishes with knowledge and the self becomes one with the supreme self. Another Simile is that of a river merging with the ocean and losing its individual identity as river finally. The individual illumined soul becomes free from name and form and reaches the self effulgent Purusha that is supreme. The one who knows the supreme Brahman becomes Brahman itself. It goes on to say, that once Brahman is realized all doubts vanish and the knower of Brahman no longer engages himself in Karma because he then goes beyond all good and evil and sees only oneness in all beings. From the imperishable several things are born and finally all of them merge in to it again. The one, who knows the Supreme self as residing in the heart, destroys all ignorance. To obtain this knowledge and to become one with it one should constantly meditate with mind absorbed in the thought of Brahman. It is said that the national motto of India, the phrase 'Satyameva Jayathe' has this Upanishad as the source.

(10) *Prasna Upanishad Belonging to Atharvaveda*

Prasna means question. This Upanishad is supposed to belong to a period after Buddha. This Upanishad contains six questions and the answers for them. Six pupils who were interested in knowing Brahman come to sage *Pippalada* and request him to clarify their spiritual doubts. The sage asks them to take up penance and *Brahmacharya* for one year and after one year the sage clears their doubts. The first question was that of *Kabandi* the son of *Katya.* He wanted to know the root cause of the universe. The second question was put by Bhargava, belonging to *Bhrigu gotra* about the supremacy of the vital force of life or *Prana* over the sense organs of man. Kausalya the son of Ashwala put the third question concerning the origin and functioning of the vital force of life. The fourth question asked by Sauryayanee, the decedent Garga was about the dream state. The fifth question put by Satyakama the son of Shibi was related to the fruitfulness of meditating the syllable 'Aum'. The sixth and the last question asked by Suhesha, son of Bharadwaja was about that which is the cause and about the creator of the Universe, who is called as *Shodasha Kala Purusha* or the one who has sixteen vital things, that is Brahman.

The root cause of the world, the sage said was Prajapati who created a couple first and creation proceeded from there. As to the relation between senses, vital force and *Prana* in the body, it is to be understood that *Prana* is the main sustainer of the body because it is the master from whom the other divine elements derive their strength. This Prana originates from the soul or *Atman* like a shadow of a person. By the will of *Atman, Prana* enters the body due to the actions of mind. Prana itself divides in to five forms of Prana, and performs different functions of the body. As the answer for the fourth question, the sage says that just as the sunrays merge with the sun at the time of sunset all the senses go back to mind in sleep. But even at that time, the five *Pranas* are awake. It is the mind that witnesses the dream in this state. In deep sleep the mind merges with the supreme reality – the *Akshara* or non- perishable Brahman. At this stage there is bliss. Then the sage gives the answer for the fifth question. '*Aum*' indicates supreme reality and the Para Brahman and the one who meditates upon '*Aum*' merges and becomes one with it. For the last question about the being that created this universe, the sage says, that the ultimate Supreme source for all existence is nothing but Brahman. It is also said that in addition to his commentaries on the Principal Upanishads Shankara wrote *Bhashyas* on *Svetasvatara Upanishad, Kaushitaki Upanishad, Narsimha Tapani* and so on, the authorship of which are doubtful.

(B) Brahma Sutras

Veda Vyasa is believed to be the author of *Brahma Sutras* that contain the essence of Upanishads. The *Brahma Sutras* contain sutras that are very cryptic and intricate. It consists of 555 Aphorisms or Sutras in four chapters or Adyayas. Each chapter is divided in to four padas or quarters. Each quarter has several groups of *Sutras* called *Adhikaras* or topical sections. There are 192 *Adhikaras*. There are several or one *Sutra* in each *Adhikara.* For example, the first four *Adhikaras* of the first chapter contains only one *Sutra* each and are referred to as Chathur Sruthi. Each *Adhikara* deals with separate question to discuss. The Sutras systematize the *Gnanakanda* of the *Vedas* that form the Upanishads. They discuss the role of *Karma* and God and refute the arguments found in other religions like Buddhism, Jainism, and other Vedanthic doctrines like Nyaya, Shaiva, Shakala, Yoga, Sankhya and Atheism. It is believed that before the final composition of Brahma Sutras there were differences among the various sages namely, Audulomi, Karshnagni, Kasakrtsna, Jaimini, and Vyasa.

In *Brahma Sutras* Vyasa reconciles the seemingly contradictory statements found in Upanishads. The seemingly contradictory statements are made in to unified, consistent and logical arguments here. Brahma Sutras are known as *Vedanta Sutras* because it is the Aphoristic text on Vedanta. It is called as *Uttara Mimamsa* because it is an enquiry in to the final mystical section of the Vedas. It is known as *Sareerika Sutras* or *Sareerika Mimamsa Sutras* because it covers the nature and destiny of the soul and *Bikshu Sutras* because Sanyasins are competent to study it. It is known as *Nyaya Prasthana* or *Yukthi Prasthana* that is the logical analysis of Advaita Vedanta. It is also termed as, Badarayana sutra, and Vedanta Darshana. In the Brahma Sutras, Vyasa systematized the ideas of the *jnanakanda* of the Vedas in the form of one coheret treatise. The sutras tell us about the teachings of the Upanishads and also establish in an argumentative manner the specific interpretation of the Upanishads through the sutras. Further these sutras also critically discuss the role of Karma and God, the doctrines associated with Buddhism, Jainism, Sankhya, Yoga, Nyaya, Vaiseshika, Shaiva, Shaktha philosophies and Atheism and so on.

Shankara Bhashya on Brahma sutra is known as Sareerika Bhashya. It is titled as Vedanta Suhirdashya. The earliest known and the most popular of all commentaries on *Brahma Sutras* is by Adi Shankara. It is considered to be "very profound with subtle reasoning and power of illumination". It was later commented upon by many, the most important being Vachaspati and Padmapada. Later many derivative texts from these commentaries followed. *Brahma Sutras* are so terse that they are very difficult for comprehension and so unintelligible. Further they are also capable of multiple interpretations. These factors led to many commentaries, and sub commentaries and further derivative texts by Vedantins following different schools of Vedanta philosophy.

Shankara in his commentary categorically states that one can become enlightened and know Brahman only through direct knowledge of Brahman. The philosophy of Advaita Vedanta is logically presented and discussed by Shankara in his commentary on the Brahma Sutras. It is seen that Shankara in his Bhashya or commentary quoted extensively not only from the principal Upanishads but also from other Upanishads. Paul Denessen, the German Indologist points out that Shankara quoted the Upanishadic texts in His commentary on *Brahma Sutras* as many as 2000 times. He says that Shankara had quoted 810 times from Chandogya, 567 times from *Brihad Aranyaka*, 142 times from *Taittiriya Upanishad*, 129 times from *Mandukya*, 103 times from *Katha*, 88 times from *Kaushitaki* and 53 times from *Swetasvatara Upanishad*. It is also stated that he quoted 39 times from *Prasna Upanishad*, 22 times from *Aitareya*, 13 times from *Jabala*, 8 times from *Isa* and 5 times from *Kena Upanishads*. In addition it is also understood that Shankara had made references of the Samhitha, Brahmana and Aranyaka portions of the Vedas and from the *Dharma Sastras*.

Through his commentary, Shankara established the non- dualistic or the Advaita Vedanta interpretation of Vedanta. Shankara's commentary of *Brahma Sutras* stands pre eminent in the explanation of Advaita Vedanta. Shankara's introduction to his Bhashya on *Brahma Sutra* is called as the 'Adhyasa Bhashyam'. It is a short text. In this he quotes from other Shastras in support of his arguments. It summarises all the major points of his commentary on *Brahma Sutra*. He says that his commentary explains how *Brahma sutra* identifies the fundamental obstacles to knowledge and how the methods advocated in Sruti remove such obstacles for acquiring the supreme knowledge. Shankara clarifies that the obstacle to enlightenment is due to misconception on our part on account of superimposition of the non- real on real that leads to duality. Shankara defines Adhyasa and says that Adhyasa is a mental notion. It is superimposing the qualities of a thing on another or their attributes that are of opposite nature. It is just as one moon appears as many in its reflection. It is due to the confusion to discriminate. Once this Avidya or Adhyasa is removed, Vidya or knowledge, that is the knowledge and experience of Brahman, the ultimate reality alone will remain and shine. Shankara then says that the cause of Avidya need not be analysed since when once it is recognized and removed it will be known that it never existed at all. In this Shankara the opponent who is the Vedantin argues and Shankara, the Advaitin answers and clears the doubts through arguments. Shankara the opponent puts the question as to how the Atman that is claimed to be the subject is confused with something else that is not Atman. In reply Shankara the Advaitin answers that such superimposition is not unusual since in empirical life the Atman is referred as the object of the notion of 'Me'.

Further he says that there is no rule that such confusion should not arise. So it is only natural that the imperceptible Atman is confused with objective factors. In his own style, Shankara begins the Bhashyam with an objection. He asks; when it is crystal clear as to what reality is, as it is totally different from the unreal, where is the need to write an entire book about reality, and how to perceive reality. Then Shankara himself gives the answer. It is due to lack of discrimination or Aviveka that the superimposition arises. Though there is no duality, we mistake one for the other and there comes duality. This ignorance is a mental notion that leads to confusion of seeing one for the other. The imperishable Atman that is eternal is confused with the objective phenomenon of the world. The confused understanding of the non-real as real is *Adhyasa* and this results in duality of subjects, objects and means of knowledge. Then Shankara explains about *Avidya* and *Vidya*. *Avidya* according to Sastras is the confusion of real and non-real that results in duality of subject, object and means of knowledge. This is *Avidya* or ignorance.

On the other hand ascertaining the true nature of things through proper discrimination is called *Vidya*. However *Avidya* that results in superimposition does not affect or taint Atman that is the substratum of everything. One knows the true nature of things through discrimination that is called *Vidya*. However, the effects of *Avidya* or ignorance can never taint the self or *Atman*. As long as one falsely identifies the self as an agent or doer, then he is in *Avidya*. Due to *Avidya Atman* is confused with non- *Atman* and until this basic confusion remains enlightenment becomes an impossibility. The purpose of all Vedanta texts is to remove this ignorance and establish *Atman* as the true reality. Shankara also says that all discussions of injunctions, Vedic rituals, worship, meditation and even the talk of liberation are due to ignorance because only for a man who identifies himself with his body, he becomes a knower. It is due to the notion of duality.

Actually there is no duality between the knower and known. Then Shankara the opponent asks as to how can all Shastras along with the means of knowledge be called ignorance? For this the reply of Shankara the Advaita Vedantin is, the means of knowledge cannot function for a man without identifying himself with body, mind and senses and perception and other activities are possible only by accepting the senses, mind and so on as belonging to one. But self is unattached. It becomes a knower because of the notions of body, mind and senses. All means of knowledge told in the sastras are due to avidya as they are all based on the notion that one is a knower and the notion of a doer is because of the superimposition on the unattached Atman. When one thinks and identifies the self as the agent or doer then it is only Avidya resulting in the notion of duality of knower and known that is nothing but illusion.

In the next section he says, that this Avidya is a matter of common experience. However, it is due to misconception arising due to non- discrimination between Atrnan and non- Atman. Before the dawn of knowledge all shastras are within the area of Avidya. For example when it is said that a Brahmin should perform sacrifice, the notion of caste, agent, a certain stage in life are all implied and are superimposed on the eternal Brahman. But the activities themselves are not Avidya. It is the sense of doership that makes the sastras as ignorance. When such acts of worship and sacrifices are performed without the notion of doership then it is not Avidya. Such superimpositions are beginningless and endless and are quite natural. The purpose of all Vedas is to eradicate this Avidya that is an obstacle to knowledge and establish the unity of *Atman* and Brahman, the knower and the known that transcends all plurality that is the only reality that shines in its own glory. It is also said in the *Bhashya* that repeated meditation on the Lord as taught in the scriptures should be continued until the realization of the reality.

The first chapter is *samanvaya* or harmony. It explains all the texts of Vedanta about Brahman that is the ultimate reality and goal of life. In this Shankara establishes the harmony. He says that the basic purpose all Upanishads is to reveal Brahman- the ultimate goal in life although terms other than Brahman is used in some Upanishads that may lead to some misunderstanding and misinterpretation of the terms. Shankara then makes it clear that all such terms refer to Brahman only. To Shankara Brahman is the one and the only reality. Brahman is the being, consciousness, bliss, infinite, formless, all pervading, indivisible, all powerful, all knowing, without beginning and end, the source of all beings and so on. It cannot be described as it transcends all names, classification, and character and so on. It cannot be known through reason but it can be known through intuition. The absolute unity of the self that is jeevatma with Brahman that is the *Paramatman* transcends all pluralities. To know self is to know Brahman. *Atman* is the spirit of the self in the individual being. The individual soul is an appearance of *Atman*. The reality of *Atman* is that, that it is the same as Brahman. This *Atman* is the self of all beings. It is not created and it is eternal. It resides in the body but does not depend upon the body. The false perception that is because of *Avidya* or ignorance, leads to the notion that the self belongs to the body. But even after the body perishes the self continues to exist. Even mind also is an appearance of the self like body. By removing *Avidya* that is ignorance or nescience and also wrong or illusory knowledge plurality arises with the tendency to superimpose non-self on self. In Brahman there is no duality. With the realization of the ultimate truth, that is Brahman, the subject, object, the knower and the known all merge in to that one single Brahman. The knowledge of the empirical world is not the ultimate knowledge. It is like objects of dream. A man who wakes up from ignorance is like a man who wakes up from dream realizing the fallacy of superimposition and duality.

The second chapter is Avirodha that is non-conflict. It discusses and refutes all possible objections against Vedanta philosophy. After discussing the objections that may be raised against the metaphysics of Vedanta by other schools of thought, Shankara after proving the fallacy in them establishes the superiority of the tenets of Vedanta. In this process Shankara refutes the arguements of 'Sankhya', 'Yoga', Vaiseshika, Buddhism, Jainism, Pasupata system, Saktha system and so on.

The third chapter is *Sadhana* or the means. It describes the process of liberation. In this chapter the means or Sadhanas that include *Upasana, Tattva Gnana*, and rituals that are presented in the Upanishads are discussed. Shankara says that in some Upanishads Brahman is mentioned with attributes because it is needed for performing *Upasana* or meditation. Many a time one term is used in two different Upanishads for two different *Upasanas*. In some other case for the same Upasana, or meditation, different names are given. Shankara also stresses that a Sanyasi should give up all rituals. Only with negation of everything, 'Nethi, Nethi', direct knowledge of liberation is possible.

The fourth chapter is about *Phala* or fruit of *Sadhana*. It tells about the state attained in Liberation. *Saguna Upasana* in which idols are worshipped and *Tattva gyana*, knowledge of the essence, are both discussed here although the man of real knowledge realizes his real nature as Brahman in this very life.

(C) Bhagavadgita (the Song of God)

The Bhagavad Gita or the 'Song of God' is a part of the great epic *Mahabharatha*. It is known as the *Sadana Prasthana* or practical text. It is a Universal Gospel. Shankara hails *Gita* as the essence of

Vedas. *Bhagavad Gita* or The song of God is found in the Bheeshma Parva of the epic *Maha Bharatha*, the authorship of which is attributed to Vyasa. It consists of 700 verses in 18 chapters. It is also called as *Gitopanishad* and also *Yogopanishad-* giving it the status of *Upanishad-Sruti* as well as *Smrithi- Prasthana* as it is a part of the epic *Maha Bharata.* It is one of the most sacred and popular scriptures in Hinduism. This book is considered as a practical guide to Hindu philosophy and life. Shankara himself stated that from a clear knowledge of the *Gita* all goals of human existence become fulfilled and *Bhagavad Gita* is the manifest quintessence of all Vedic teachings. Shankara's main objective of *Gita Bhashya* is to probe in to Dharma and to explain the divine incarnation. He also says that the path of *jnana* takes one directly to liberation while the man whose mind is purified by work is competent to tread the path of knowledge and to him alone jnana or wisdomwill come.

As the verses of *Bhagavadgita* are very difficult to understand and are also confusing, many commentators tried to comment upon this sacred scripture. Shankara's commentary is supposed to be the earliest one that is available to mankind. Shankara says that he wrote a brief commentary on *Gita* just to show what this scripture signifies. The ultimate objective of this scripture is the attainment of the highest knowledge obtained through *Bhakti marga* that paves the way for self-knowledge attained through renunciation of actions or *Karma* that is Vedic sacrifices. yagnas and so on. Renunciation here refers to performance of karmas with no notion of doership and with no expectation of the fruit of action. Karma marga or the path of action is to be followed with a spirit of self-surrender to the Lord and also without the desire of its results. Such actions are bound to lead to purification of mind. A man with a purified mind becomes fit for obtaining the ultimate wisdom.

Just before the epic battle of *Mahabharata* at Kurukshtra, Lord Krishna preached *Bhagavad Gita* to Arjuna about ethical matters, the nature of God and the methods of realizing Him. The scripture teaches one how to do one's duty in the world like a lotus leaf on water. The content of this scripture is a dialogue between Lord Krishna and Arjuna that took place on the battlefield of Kurukshetra, just before the commencement of the war. Arjuna becomes nervous after seeing his teachers, kith and kin on the opposite side in the battlefield. He becomes depressed and dejected and he refuses to fight. At that moment Lord Krishna instructs Arjuna about his duties as a *kshatriya* and as a prince. He teaches the path of right action, right knowledge and right devotion. He elaborates on the different yogic and vedanthic principles through examples and analysis. He gives the essence of the Upanishadic teachings to Arjuna. He then reveals his universal cosmic form and blesses Arjuna.

The first chapter has 46 verses. It is titled 'Vishada Yoga'- The dissolution or dejection of Arjuna. Arjuna, the third among the Pandava brothers becomes disillusioned after seeing his relatives, teachers on the opposite side in the battlefield at Kurukshetra. Arjuna becomes intensely dejected and laments over the anticipated loss of his kith and kin in the war. He then laments over his despondency and lack of self-confidence in fighting the war and overwhelmed with grief and despondency he sank on the seat of his chariot.

The second chapter has 72 verses. It is about *Samkhya Yoga* or the path of knowledge. In this, Lord Krishna encourages Arjuna the warrior in him to fight and to uphold the path of Dharma as a warrior. Lord Krishna says that the duty of a Kshatriya, especially of a prince is to fight and instructs that only the body is killed while the eternal self is immortal. So Krishna asks Arjuna to do his duty of fighting by developing a balanced mind in which pleasure and pain, gain and loss victory or defeat are the same. Such evenness of mind, the Lord says is Yoga. Lord Krishna says, a *jeevan mukta* is one who is free from all desires longings, ego sense, and attachment and also fear. He is totally indifferent to all sensual pleasures. He has perfect control over his senses and mind. His mind is ever poised and even under all circumstances. He is always fixed in Brahman He also tells Arjuna that one has only the right to work but not with its fruits. So, one has to act without any motive or desire in a selfless manner. In this chapter the immortality of the soul is explained. He asks Arjuna to wake up from ignorance and dejection. While the gross body is unreal, perishable, inferior and subject to birth, death, pain, and so on the self is real, non- perishable, and not subject to birth and death. Lord Krishna says that one actually does not kill any one nor get killed by another since that which is birthless, eternal, undecaying, and ancient is not killed when the body is killed. If that is the case, then, who is the killer? Who is the one who gets killed? Various types of Yogas namely, Karma, jnana, Sankhya and so on and Atma, the soul are explained here. Body is referred here as the field and Atman the indwelling self is referred as the knower of the field. But the body has no reality in the absolute sense. Brahman alone is real. Due to superimposition, or Adhyasa or absence of discrimination or viveka body appears as Atman or Brahman just a rope appears as snake in darkness. Once the distinction is known as a result of awareness, knowledge dawns. And the false knowledge gets eradicated. The verses from 39 to 53 explain Karma yoga. And finally the Lord explains the marks of a man of stable mind and his glories.

The third chapter with 43 verses explains *Karma Yoga* or the Yoga of action- the duties of a human being. Arjuna asks Krishna when knowledge is stated to be superior to action, why Krishna is asking him to perform his karma of fighting. Krishna starts by telling the importance of *Karma marga*, the necessity of performing Vedic sacrifices and so on. He says that every one is obliged to perform his duties as per his or her stage in life and in accordance with the rules and regulations of society in which one lives. It is not possible for any one to be inactive. Each one will pursue actions according to his nature. The Lord says that there is need for action even on the part of the wise and even of God for the welfare of the universe. But a man should perform actions without the sense of doership and with detachment to the results of his actions. The egoistic man thinks that he is the doer. But actually Prakruti is doing everything. A wise one is free from all bondages of action. Mentally, he renounces all actions. The Lord further points out why the duties are to be performed, the benefits of performing them, the harm caused by not performing them, what actions lead to bondage and which actions lead to salvation. Actions are to be performed as non-action. Lord Krishna says that to action alone one has a right but never for its fruits. He says, 'let not the fruits of action be thy motive; neither should there be any attachment to inaction'. So one should do one's duty abandoning all attachment, with an even mind in success and failure for, evenness of mind is called Yoga. Finally the Lord explains how to overcome desire. One should do one's duties and control desire and anger which are the two enemies of wisdom. After mastering the senses one should kill the enemy that is desire by restraining the self by the self and there by knowing the superior self that is superior to intellect.

The fourth Chapter contains 42 verses and this chapter is on Jnana - Vibhaga Yoga or the Yoga of wisdom and the disciplines of knowledge and action. In this the Lord explains both the path of action as well as the path of knowledge and the wisdom or supreme knowledge that results from both the paths. The Lord here explains how it is possible for one to ascend on the spiritual path and how there is also the possibility for one to descend fast in to the material world. He starts by telling the glory of god with attributes or Saguna Brahman and he also describes the path of Karma that is the path of selfless action. The Lord says that he who sees inaction in action and action in inaction is wise and a Yogi even when he performs actions. The sage is one whose actions are burnt by the fire of knowledge. Though he acts yet he is not bound. He is one whose mind is controlled, and without any attachment to the fruits of actions and is free from all opposites like pleasure and pain, success and failure, always contented and happy and balanced. The one who sees Brahman in all actions attains Brahman. The different types of sages and sacrifices with their results are also described here. But wisdom is superior to sacrifices that are actions made with material objects, because all actions end with wisdom. Wisdom will enable one to cross all sins because the fire of wisdom will reduce all actions to ashes and the one who obtains this wisdom by controlling the senses attain peace. On the other hand the ignorant and the doubting mind pave the way for destruction. So Lord Krishna asks Arjuna to cut and annihilate doubt of the self that is born out of ignorance.

The fifth chapter has 29 verses. It explains *Karma sanyasa yoga* or the *Yoga* of renunciation and action. Arjuna asks the Lord to tell him whether renunciation of action or *Yoga* is better. For rihis the Lord said that both renunciation of actions as well as Yoga lead to the highest bliss. However of these two, he says, *yoga* of action is superior to renunciation of action. However both *yoga* of renunciation and *yoga* of action are not different from each other because the one who is firmly established in one reaps the results of both the *Yogas*. For sages everything is the same. They look everything with an equal eye. With the self always engaged in meditation on Brahman the yogi attains infinite bliss. He does not rejoice in the pleasures of senses that always bring misery ultimately. Such a wise man is ever happy. For such a person there is everlasting peace and happiness. The Lord differentiates between the concept of action with attachment and action without attachment and says that *Karma* performed with detachment and renunciation of actions both lead to the same goal of liberation. The verses from 1 –12 describe *Sankhya Yoga* and the *Yoga* of disinterested action, the features and the glory of *Sankhya Yogi* and *Nishkama karma Yogi*. The remaining verses explain *jnana Yoga* or the *Yoga* of wisdom as well as *Dhyana Yoga* or meditation along with devotion.

The sixth chapter with 47 verses is about *Adyatma Yoga* or the *Yoga* of meditation. It is the science of self-control and realization. He who performs his duties without the sense of doership and without any expectation of the fruits of his actions is the real *Sanyasin* and *Yogi*. Action is the means for the sage who wants to attain *Yoga*. But once *Yoga* is attained inaction is the means. The self is both a friend as well as enemy. It is a friend for the one who has conquered the self by the self. But it is an enemy for the one who has not conquered the self. Again, *Yoga* that destroys pain is possible only for one who is moderate in everything, in eating, actions, sleeping, and wakefulness and so on. He should gradually bring his mind under the control of the self. Gradually he sees the self-abiding in all beings and all beings in the self. No doubt it is very difficult to control the wandering mind. But by constant practise and dispassion, mind can be easily controlled. Though one has faith, still, if he is unable to control his mind he will not be in a position to attain perfection in Yoga. He cannot be freed from the cycle of birth and death. But the knowledge that he obtained in his earlier birth will help him and he may be born in the family of pure, wealthy, or even yogins and he strives for perfection even more than before. The Yogi is supreme. He is superior to ascetics, knowledgeable men who have mastered the sastras, and also men of action. *Astanga Yoga* or the eight-limbed Yoga and the process of practicing it are explained in this chapter. This chapter discusses Dhyana Yoga in great detail and also about control of mind. It tells about this path, how it is practiced, how to mastermind through Yoga and it is said here that Yoga reveals the spiritual nature of man. Only a man who has control over the mind and transcends the mind is fit to seek liberation. Usually the mind is restless, unstable and is attached to sense objects. Through self-discipline and intense desire for God the supreme, and also by developing detachment for worldly objects, one can achieve tranquility of mind that will lead to the end of all sorrows and miseries of life. Then one will be able to fix his mind on the supreme and attain liberation. So, all mental desires and tendencies to enjoy the pleasures of life must be curbed. Lord Krishna says that when a man dwells in his mind on the object of senses then attachment to them is created. From attachment comes desire and from desire anger results. From anger arises bewilderment and loss of memory. Loss of memory results in destruction of intelligence and he perishes due to destruction of intelligence. After explaining the difficulty in controlling the mind, the Lord explains in detail the procedures of gaining mastery over mind through yoga. The fate of one who falls from this Yoga and the glory of Dhyana Yoga are also dealt with in detail.

There are 30 verses in the seventh chapter. It is about *Paramahansa Vijnana Yoga*- the knowledge of ultimate truth or the Yoga of wisdom that when known, then, there is nothing remaining to be known. The Lord says that His *Prakruti* is of two kinds. The inferior *Prakruti* that is eightfold, namely earth, water, fire, air, ether, mind, intellect and egoism and the other higher Prakruti, that is the very life element or the energy or the essence of everything in this Universe and by which the world is upheld. He says that he is the sapidity in water, light in the moon, the syllable *AUM* in all the Vedas, sound in space and the virility in men. The four kinds of men, who worship the Lord, Krishna says, are those who are distressed, those who seek knowledge, those who seek wealth and finally the wise ones. Of all these, the Lord says that He is dear to the wise because the wise one is the very self of the Lord. He is ever established in the Lord, the self and that is his supreme goal. Finally the wise man reaches the abode of God, Vasudeva that is nothing but the innermost self. But such a person is very difficult to be found because all beings are subject to illusion and delusion of the pairs of opposites. This chapter tells about the *Yoga* of *jnana* that is the knowledge of *Nirguna Brahman* and *Vijnana* the knowledge of *Saguna Brahman. The* illusory energy, the *Maya* that is found in the material existence and the difficulty in overpowering *Maya* or ignorance is explained here. It also shows the greatness of divinity, the presence of God in all objects as their cause and the four types of people who are attracted and opposed to divinity. Men who are ignorant of the glory and the true nature of God are condemned. The Lord says that it is very difficult to overcome Maya or illusion or the ignorance born out of it and concludes saying that, a spiritual aspirant takes refuge in God without any reservation to reach God that is the goal or ultimate truth.

The eighth chapter with 28 verses is about *Akshara Para Brahma Yoga* that emphasizes the science of Yoga and the attainment of salvation, that is, the Yoga of the indestructible Brahman. Lord Krishna tells Arjuna that Brahman is the supreme and imperishable and is knowledge. Action is performance of Vedic sacrifices. The last thought that arises in the mind at the moment of death is very important because one attains whatever one thinks and remembers at that moment. One who remembers the Lord at the time of death is sure to attain Him, the Lord. The ever stead fast Yogi who constantly remembers the Lord as the imperishable and the unmanifest, that is Brahman, reach Brahman that is the highest abode of Lord. That stage one can reach only by unwavering devotion to Lord, the Brahman in whom all beings dwell and by whom everything in this universe is pervaded. Again, the creation of the material world and the distinction between the material and spiritual world is explained here. This chapter also explains the different paths for leaving the material existence and the destination to which both the paths namely, the path of Devayana or the path of light that lead Yogis to Brahman and the path of Pitriyana or the path of darkness by which the Yogi attain the lunar light and returns.

The ultimate secret of *Raja Vidya-* the *Guhya Vidya-* The Yoga of sovereign science and the sovereign secret- the confidential knowledge of the ultimate truth that is realizable by direct intuitional knowledge is revealed in the nineth chapter that has 34 verses. The verses 1-6 explain *jnana* or wisdom. It also says about *bhakti*, description of God as the soul of everything and his glory, worship with and without motive, and the glory of practicing true devotion. How the entire world is created, maintained, and annihilated by that energy that pervades everything is explained. One should do everything as an offering to him. Even the unrighteous become righteous if he worships him with devotion and attains everlasting peace and happiness and that those devotees are never destroyed.

The *Vibhuthi Yoga-* or the Yoga of infinite glory of the ultimate truth that is the Yoga of divine glories forms the tenth chapter with 42 verses. God's glories, *bhakti yoga*, its reward and glory, the glory and powers of *yoga* are all explained here. The Lord reveals himself as the cause of all causes and also His manifestations with infinite glories.

The eleventh chapter is known as the *Vishvaroopa Darshana yoga* or the Yoga of the vision of the Universal or cosmic form and it contains 55 verses. As per Arjuna's request Lord Krishna reveals His universal form exhibiting the entire universe and existence. He also describes His Universal form and blesses Arjuna with divine eyes to behold His supreme cosmic form. Arjuna witnesses the Universal form of Krishna with all that are moving and stationary. He then askes Arjuna to stand up and fight as they, the opponents in the war have already been slain by Him and Arjuna happens to be only an instrument for their death. Then overtaken by fright Arjuna pleads Keshava for a sight of Lord's four-armed gentle form.

The glory of *Bhakti yoga* or the Yoga of devotion for attaining the supreme truth is elaborated in the twelfth chapter- *Bhakti* Yoga-that has 20 verses. Arjuna asks the Lord to tell him who of the two categories of People, the devotees who worship God with form that is the manifested form of Brahman or the enlightened who worship the unmanifest Brahman are better versed in Yoga. For this question, the Lord says that those who worship him with faith and with one pointed mind are the best in Yoga. It is because fixing the mind on the unmanifested Brahman is very difficult for the beings. So he asks Arjuna to fix his mind and intellect on the Lord. But if he is unable to fix his mind then he asks Arjuna to do constant and continuous practice, Abhyasa Yoga to reach the Lord. If that also is difficult then the Lord asks Arjuna to perform actions for God's sake. If that also is difficult then, take refuge in God with a controlled self, renouncing the fruits of all actions. Knowledge is better than practice, meditation is better than knowledge, and renunciation of the fruits of actions is still better than meditation because peace results with renunciation. Then the Lord tells Arjuna about those people who are dear to Him. He says, the one who has no hatred, who is friendly, kind and compassionate to one and all, who is not attached or egoistic, who is equanimous and balanced in all opposites like pleasure and pain and so on, who is forgiving, who is always contented with mind and intellect fixed on the Lord, who is free from envy, anxiety, wants, who is pure, untroubled, who has renounced all selfish actions, who is always balanced and renounced all good and evil, who is full of devotion, who has no foe, honour or dishonour, who is the same in cold and heat, pleasure and pain, who is free from attachments, who is silent, contented, has a steady mind and full of devotion are dear to him. Those who follow these Dharma or immortal qualities with faith and regard Lord as the supreme goal, such devotees are very dear to Him. The merits of the worshippers of God with form and without form, the means of God realization, and the mark of a God realized soul are all explained here. This chapter also explains the different forms of spiritual disciplines that are required for achieving this end.

The *Kshetra-kshetrajna Vibhaga Yoga*— the individual and ultimate or universal consciousness with 35 verses is the thirteenth chapter. This chapter deals with yoga of discrimination between the field and the knower of the field. As per Arjuna's request the Lord also explaines about Prakruti or matter, Purusha or spirit, the field that is the *Kshetra*, the knower of the field, that is Kshetrajna, and knowledge. Lord Krishna says the body is the field or *Kshetra*. The one who knows it is called as the Kshetrajna or the knower of the field that is the Lord. The knowledge of both the field and the knower of the field is considered as knowledge. The *Kshetra* is described as consisting of the elements, egoism, intellect, the unmanifest, the ten senses, and one mind, five objects of senses, desire, hatred, pleasure and pain, intelligence and courage. Knowledge includes all good qualities like humility, non injury, forbearance, service to the *Guru*, purity, steadfastness, non attachment to objects of senses, self control, absence of egoism, non attachment even towards kith and kin, balance of mind at all times of opposites, unflinching devotion to the Lord, aloofness, and applying spiritual knowledge of truth. Knowledge is that awareness about that, which pervades everything in this universe, who is within and without all beings, who is movable and immovable at the same time, who is incomprehensible, who is near yet far, that supreme light that goes beyond all darkness, the knowledge, the knowable, and the goal of all knowledge that resides in the core of the heart of all beings. Only he that sees that all actions are performed by Prakruti while the self is actionless and they who see with the eye of wisdom the difference between Kshetra, the field and the Kshetrajna who is the knower of the field and the liberation of all beings from matter, such wise ones only attain the supreme. The difference between the gross physical body that is perishable and transitory and the immortal soul that is immutable and eternal is explained here. He also discloses the precise knowledge about the individual soul and the universal or cosmic soul.

The fourteenth chapter of *Guna-traya- Vibhaga Yoga* contains 27 verses and deals with yoga of classification of the three *Gunas* that includes the glory of knowledge, the evolution of the world from *Prakruti* and *Purusha*, the three qualities of *Sattva, Rajas* and *Tamas*, the means of God realization and the features of one who has transcended the three gunas. The three qualities, Sattva, Rajas and Tamas bind the body of all beings. Of these three qualities the quality of *Sattva*, is stainless, is healthy and luminous and binds the body to happiness and knowledge. The quality of *Rajas* is passion, which is the source of desire for life, objects and it binds one to attachment of action. Tamas that is born of ignorance deludes all beings. It binds one to heedlessness, indolence and sloth. When the light of wisdom shines in one then it is an indication that Sattva is increasing in him. The increase of *Rajas* is seen in greed, activity, actions and restlessness. When Tamas is increasing, darkness, inertia, delusion and so on are found in a being. When a being breathes his last when the quality of *Sattva* is predominating in him then he reaches the highest spotless worlds. When the quality of Rajas is dominant in him when his end comes, then, he will be born among beings that are attached to action. If Tamas is predominant at the time of death then such a one is born in the family of the senseless. The fruit of all good actions is pure and *Satvic*, the fruit of all rajas is pain and the fruit of *Tamas* is ignorance and sorrow. Those who are *satvic* rise upwards, the *rajasic* stay at the middle level, and the *Tamasic* go downwards. The one who can cross over and goes beyond all the three gunas or qualities gets freed from birth, death, old age and pain and reaches the immortal. Then Arjuna requests the Lord to explain to him about the features of one who has crossed over all the three qualities, his conduct and how he goes beyond all the three qualities. The Lord in answer states that the one who does not hate radiance or activity or delusion, when they are present and does not long for them when they are absent, thus who always remains neutral, who views all opposites as the same, who always remains in the self, and who views every one and everything alike, who is same in honour and dishonour and one who abandones all actions such a one is said to have crossed all the three qualities.

The fifteenth chapter of 20 verses is about *Purushottama Yoga* –the *Yoga* of the supreme *purusha*- the realization of the ultimate truth, that describes the virtues, glories, and transcendental features of God who is omnipotent, omniscient, and omnipresent and the purpose and value of knowing God and the ways by which God can be realized. The means of God realization, the *Jeevatma*, God and His glory, the perishable body, the imperishable Atman and the supreme are all explained here. Those wise ones who are free from pride, delusion, from opposites like pleasure and pain and attachment reach the eternal, the supreme abode of the Lord and there is no return to this world for such beings as they abide in the self constantly with no desires. He further says that an eternal portion of him become the living soul in the world, with five senses and mind and abides in *Prakruti*. He abides in the body of living beings as the fire – Vaisvanara that is united with *Prana* and *Apana*, digesting the food. From the Lord who is seated in the hearts of all arise the presence or absence of memory and knowledge. All beings are perishable. The immutable and unchanging one is imperishable. The highest self who is indescribable and imperishable, creates, sustains and pervades all the worlds. He is *purushottama* or the highest *Purusha*. The one who knows this worships Him with all his being and becomes illumined.

In the sixteenth chapter of *Daivasura-Sampad-Vibhaga Yoga*—The *yoga* of discrimination between the divine and demonical properties, with 24 verses, Lord Krishna explains in detail the divine properties, conduct and actions that are conducive to divinity, and also the evil or demonical nature and the conduct that are opposed to divinity. The features of a man with demonical properties and his destruction, conduct that are opposed to scriptures and the need to follow the path laid down by scriptures are also told here. The Lord lists out the characteristic features of those with divine properties and also of those with demonical properties. He says the one who possesses divine qualities exhibit fearlessness, purity of heart, constancy in the yoga of wisdom, charity, self restraint, performs sacrifices, studies scriptures, possess austerity, straight forwardness, non-injury, calmness without anger, renunciation, peacefulness, absence of crookedness, compassion and kindness, uncovettousness, gentleness, modesty, firmness, vigour, forgiveness, fortitude, purity, friendliness to all, without hating any one, and absence of pride and so on. These qualities pave the way for liberation. At the same time, hypocracy, arrogance, self-conceit, anger, harshness, ignorance, and attachment and so on are the properties of one with demonical nature. These people are always confused as to what to do and what not to do. They have no purity, no good conduct, or truth in them. They have no belief in the creator. They possess uncontrollable worldly desires, are full of hypocracy, pride and arrogance. They hold firmly the evil notions due to ignorance. They are overpowered by lust and anger. They seek wealth even by immoral means just to satisfy the sensual pleasures of life. They are full of pride. They are born again and again only to suffer. One must abandon lust, anger and greed, as these are the triple gates to hell. These features pave the way for bondage and lack of freedom from the cycle of birth and death. So the one who acts under the impulse of desires cannot attain perfection nor does he reach the supreme goal. So he asks one and all to perform and live in this world as told in the scriptures.

The seventeenth chapter with 28 verses is about *Shraddha-traya-Vibhaga yoga* or the *yoga* of the three-fold faith. It tells about the three-fold faith and also how they determine the features of living beings. The different kinds of food, sacrifices, penance and charity are also discussed here. Arjuna asks the Lord about the sacrifices performed with faith that is not as per the ordinances of the scriptures. What type of faith is that, whether it belongs to the category of Sattva, Rajas or Tamas. For this the Lord says, the faith of each one of the beings is in accordance with his nature. That is whether he is *Satvic, Rajasic* or *Tamasic*. A man is as per his faith. Those people who perform terrible austerities by torturing their body in which the Lord, the Self resides, are demonic, because these austerities are not prescribed in the Vedas, they perform these because of hypocracy, egoism, impelled by desire and passion. These people are senseless. The satvic people enjoy food that increases vitality, energy, strength, health, joy and cheerfulness, food that are agreeable to the body. On the other hand, the *Rajasic* people like foods that are bitter, sour, saline, excessively hot, pungent, dry, burning, that cause pain, grief and diseases. The *Tamasic* ones cherish food that is stale, tasteless, putrid, rotten, and impure. The sacrifices that are performed without the sense of doership and in a selfless manner and are done as a duty are pure. But the sacrifices that are done with a view to obtain its fruits and with a sense of doership are *Rajasic* in nature. If the sacrifices are performed contrary to the scriptures, where no food is distributed, and are without the utterances of *Mantras*, gifts and faith are indeed *Tamasic* in nature. The Lord then explains about the austerity of body, speech and mental austerities. He says, worship of the gods, *Gurus* and men of wisdom with purity, straight forwardness, and non-injury is known as austerity of the body. Speaking that which is pleasant, beneficial, that is told in the scriptures and is truth that does not hurt others, is the austerity of speech. Mental austerity consists of serenity of mind, equanimity, silence, self-control and purity of nature. All these three fold austerities practiced with utmost faith without any expectation of reward is pure or *satvic*. The austerities performed with the expectation of honour, fame and name is said to be *Rajasic* and those actions, which are performed in a foolish manner by self-torture, or with bad intention of destroying others are called as *Tamasic*. The alms given as duty to one who does not serve in return, in a fit place and time to a worthy person, such alms is *Satvic*. Those alms that are given with a view to get some results are *Rajasic*. Those gifts that are given in a wrong place and at a wrong time to unworthy persons, in an insulting manner are *Tamasic*.

The final, the eighteenth chapter that has 78 verses tells about the *Yoga* of liberation by renunciation. It is called *Moksha Sanyasa Yoga*. Arjuna requests the Lord to tell him about the essence of *Sanyasa* and *Tyaga* and the Lord says, *Sanyāsa* is renouncing actions impelled by desires. This is what the sages understand by *Sanyasa*. *Tyāga* according to the wise is abandonment of all fruits of actions. Therefore one should not stop activity. The activity of sacrifice, giving gifts, and austerity should always are to be performed because these purify the wise. Further the Lord says that the one who is free from egoism and whose intellect is not affected by good and evil although he kills people, he does not kill because he is not bound by his actions. An action is Satvic if it is done for its own sake without love or hatred and without the least expectation of its results. But the action that is done with a view of its results and with a sense of ego and with great effort is *Rajasic*. Finally those actions that are done out of delusion without concern for its consequences, or that results in loss of wealth or injury to others or to oneself is *Tamasic*. That intellect is Satvic that knows and differentiates action and renunciation, what should be done and what should not be done that is beyond fear and fearlessness, bondage and liberation. That intellect by which one knows Dharma or the right conduct and *Adharma* or wrong conduct, that is, what to be done and what ought not to be done is *Rajasic*. That intellect that is covered by darkness and perceives everything in a perverted manner wrongly regards *Adharma* or wrong as Dharma or the right is *Tamasic*. The happiness that is like poison in the beginning but becomes nector like in the end is born out of the self and is therefore *Satvic*. That pleasure which is the result of sense contact with objects, and that is like nector like in the beginning but turns to be like poison in the end is *Rajasic*. That intellect that is covered with the delusion of the self and arising from sleep, indolence and heedlessness is *Tamasic*. After thus telling Arjuna about the three types of qualities Lord Krishna finally tells Arjuna that the one who dwells in solitude, eating moderately and has a controlled body and mind, is always engaged in meditation and concentration, taking solace in dispassion, and has abandoned egoism, violence, arrogance, desire, anger, covetousness, and who is free from the notion of me and mine is fit to become Brahman itself. He is indifferent to everything and attains supreme devotion to the Lord. Through devotion he realizes who and what is the Lord and finally he comes to know the Lord and enters the supreme reality. Then Krishna concludes His sermon by stating that the Lord dwells in the heart of all beings, and His Maya, causes all beings to revolve. Lord Krishna asks Arjuna to take refuge in Him with all his heart so that by his grace Arjuna will be fit to attain the eternal abode with supreme peace. He asks Arjuna to abandon all actions born out of desire and attachment and take refuge at the feet of the Lord alone so that the

Lord will take care of him and liberate him from all sins and then he asks Arjuna whether his delusion caused by his ignorance had vanished. Arjuna in greatfulness tells the Lord that all his doubts got destroyed because of the Lord's teachings and His grace and with a clear mind he becomes ready to fight.

The *Bhashya* of Shankara on *Bhagavad Gita* is considered to be one of his masterpieces. Shankara's main objective of Gita Bhashya is to probe in to Dharma and explain the divine incarnation. In his commentary Shankara deals with the different aspects of Advaita Vedanta as found in this great text. Trivor Leggett in his book on 'Realization of the supreme self- the Yogas of the *Bhagavad Gita*' says "Shankara explains the revelatory flashes of the Gita by putting them side by side with Upanishadic texts and with each other. He presents a system which is internally consistent, and which resolves the apparent contradictions of some of the texts".

In his introduction to the commentary Shankara states that the famous *Gita Shastra* is an epitome of the essentials of the whole Vedic teaching. He also states that it is very difficult to understand, as it appears to teach diverse and quite contradictory doctrines and he intented to write a brief commentary on *Gita* in order to state precisely what it signifies as many of he commentaries on *Gita* convey different contradictory meanings. He also says that *Gita* explains the two paths of works and knowledge, the two Vedic paths which are mutually exclusive at the same time stressing that salvation is possible not through works but through wisdom. He says that the path of *Gnana* takes one directly to liberation. While the man whose mind is purified by work is competent to tread the path of knowledge and to him alone wisdom comes. The ultimate aim of *Gita*, according to Shankara is attainment of the highest good that is denoted by complete cessation of all relative existence. This is realized through self-knowledge attained by means of renunciation of all actions. Lord Krishna himself states in the *Gita* that knowledge is characterised by renunciation. Dharma through activity no doubt is a means to secure worldly welfare to attain heaven but when it is practiced with a spirit of self-surrender to the Lord and without desire for the result, then it leads to purity of mind. A man with a pure mind acquires the required knowledge. Thus through unselfish *Karma* one realizes the ultimate. The scriptures however help us in the eradication of superimposition on the self. They cannot reveal the self directly. He further says that the object of *Gita* is to remove the cause of *samsara* or transmigration such as grief and illusion and not to enjoin action for its own sake. Actions are to be performed as a means for attaining self-knowledge by purifying the mind. The self is also imagined to be the knower of objects. But the objects are perceived by the intellect and sense organs. Thus due to ignorance the self is identified with mental state. Similarly self is said to become enlightened. This notion is due to *Avidya* or ignorance that identifies self with intellect. However neither ignorance nor enlightenment pertains to self. They relate to intellect and mind but are wrongly attributed to self. Self is ever free from *Avidya.* Similarly *Atman* also cannot be known through any means of knowledge or *aumana* or inference, as it has no form or mark that can form the basis of any inference. *Atman* has no sound, form, taste, smell or touch. *Atman* cannot be known by analogy as it has no parts or by implication or by scriptures because *Atman* has no features and is not manifest and it is ever existent and is the witness. The intellect, mind and senses, the entire body are insentient matter. But they appear to be sentient because of the self that is pure consciousness. Liberation consists in removing *Avidya* and identifying oneself with Brahman while living in the physical body.

Other Bhashyas of Shankara

It is said, that Shankara, in addition to his commentaries on the Prasthana Traya wrote commentaries on Gaudapada's Karika that became very popular, on Vishnu Sahasranama, Gayatri Mantra, Adyatma Patala of the Apasthamba Dharma Sutras, Patanjali's Yoga Sutras, Sanat Sujatheeya, and Sahasranama Adhyaya and also wrote Yogasutra Bhashya Vivarana.

SHANKARA'S STOTRAS

The Stotras of Shankara are the devotional hymns in praise of Gods. These are rich in poetry and devotion. It elaborates the relationship between the devotee and his Deity through devotion. The verses are the emotional outpourings of the helplessness of the *Bhakta* while seeking refuge at the feet of his dear God who is everything to him and who is compassion personified. Shankara's devotional hymns highlight *Bhakti Marga*. Swami Vivekananda said,' the modern civilized world marvels at the writings of this sixteen year old boy'. Some of the devotional hymns associated with his name are: *Ananda Lahari, Annapurna Stotram, Bhaja Govindam or Moha Mudgara, Bhavani Ashtakam, Bhavani Bhujangam, Ganesha Ashtakam, Ganesha Pancha Ratnam, Ganga Ashtakam, Gauri Dasakam, Govindashtakam, Guru Ashtakam, Guru Paduka Panchakam, Guru Paduka Stotram, Hanumath Pancharatnam, Jyothir Linga Stotram, Kala Bhairava, Ashtakam Kalpa Shakthistavam, Kanaka Dhara Stotram, Kashi Panchakam, Krishnashtakam, Lakshmi Narsimha Karavalamba Stotram, Lalitha Pancharatnam, Mantra Matruka Pushpa Malatsavam, Meenakshi Pancha ratna Stotram, Panduranga Shatakam, Rama Bhujangam, Ranganathashtakam, Shanmuga Stotram, Shat- Padi, Shiva Aparadha Kshamapana Stotram, Shiva Bhujangam, Shiva Manasa Pooja, Shivananda Lahari, Shiva Panchakshara stotram, Shivashtakam, Soundarya Lahari, Subramanya Bhujangam, Tripura Sundari Ashtakam, Uma Maheshwara Stotra, Vishnu Bhujanga Prayata Stotram, and Vishwanathashtakam and so on*

Shankara's *Prakarana Granthas*

The philosophical treatises of Shankara are known as *Prakarana Granthas*. In addition to these some of the stotras also provide methodologies for understanding the doctrine of Advaita Vedanta. It is said that for gaining practical knowledge, one has to read Shankara's philosophical treatises like Viveka Choodamani, Atma Bodha and so on. Some of his philosophical treatises and philosophical hymns include, *Aparokshanubhoothi, Atma Bodha, Atma Panchakam, Brahmha Gnanaval Mala, Dakshina murthy Ashtakam* (devotional hymn explaing philosophy of Shankara), *Dhanyashtakam* (Devotional hymn explaining philosophy of Shankara), *Kaupeena Panchakam* (Devotional hymn explaining the philosophy of Shankara), *Maneesha Panchakam, Maya Panchakam Nirguna Manasa Pooja, Nirvana Dasakam* or *Dasa Sloki, Nirvana Manjari, Nirvana Shatakam, Panchi Karanam, Pratha Smaranya Stotram, Sadana Panchakam, Sata Sloki, Siddhantha Tattva Vindu, Tattva Bodha, Vakya Sudha, Vakya Vritthi, Viveka Choodamani,* and *Upadesa Sahasri* and so on. Some people attribute the authorship of works like *Jaya Mangalya* that is a *Sankhya* philosophy work and *Sthira Siddhi* that is a *Nyaya* Philosophy work to Shankara.

●●●

4

Shankara as the Poet and Devotee

Shankara who was also a great devotee composed several hymns on Lord Shiva, Mother Parvati, Goddess Bhavani, Goddess Thripura Sundari, Goddess Lakshmi, Lord Vishnu, Lord Ganesha, Lord Karthikeya, and Lord Hanuman, and so on. In all these stotras he explains the greatness of *Bhakti* or devotion that would pave the way for reaching the supreme goal of liberation or *Mukti* or freedom from all sorrows of life that lead to the endless cycle of births and deaths. Though Shankara taught that Brahman is the sole reality and that reality could be known only by Jnana or wisdom, he was not against *Bhakti*, *karma, Yoga*, rituals, worship, *Thantras* and *Mantras*, idol worship and so on. He was as much a *Bhakta* as a *Jnana Yogi* and a *Karma Yogi*.

In composing hymns in praise of Gods and Goddesses he revealed himself as a *Bhakta*. Further, his intention in composing hymns was also to help the common man who cannot understand Shankara's complex philosophical teachings. He helped such people to reach the ultimate through *Bhakti* that automatically lead one to Jnana or wisdom. He also did not categories scriptural study as unimportant in spirituality. In fact he emphasised that *Sruti* is the greatest of all *Pramanas* or means of knowledge. To him each *Pramana* has its own importance and its own field of operation and it is totally valid in that sphere. As long as the senses of duality exist as long as one sees the world as real he needs idol worship, and has to perform Karmas. For example, in the Shloka 'Aparokhanubhuthi' Shankara says that the means to attain Vairagya or detachment is got by praying to Hari and by performing duties as per one's social order and stage of life. He also stressed that *Bhakti* and Karma would pave the way for Jnana and that the same Brahman that is the highest reality manifested itself as Ishwara or personal God.

In *Shivanandalahari,* Shankara says that the one who allots some time for worshipping the lotus like feet of the mother Goddess for doing meditation upon Her and to interact with Her, for doing Pranams to Her, for listening to Her holy stories, for being in Her presence, for singing Her glories and being happy to offer his mind to Her would become *Jeevan Mukta*, that is, would attain liberation even while he is alive. In the same hymn Shankara also refers the *Bhakta* or devotee as Muktha or the liberated one. Again, he says *Bhakti* as described in the hymn 'Lalitha Sahasranama' is the outcome of pure devotion and inner knowledge. In his 'Sadana Panchakam' Shankara explains what a spiritual aspirant who leads a normal life should do while preparing himself for the spiritual path. Shankara says that such a one should study scriptures, perform *Karmas* as told in the scriptures, worship God through Vedic Karmas, have unflinching devotion to God and so on until the notion that' I am the body' leaves him and gets the firm conviction that 'I am Brahman'.

Some people view that Hindu religious hymns that are in praise of Hindu Goddesses show an element of vulgarity, because such hymns describe in detail the beauty of the body parts of the Goddesses. Shankara's Stotras in praise of Goddesses are not an exception to this. But it must be understood that the Goddess represents the feminine form of the formless Brahman, the cosmic energy in dynamic form. All her body parts are worshipped with reverence as symbols of the source of all life and cosmic energy. She is worshipped as the primordial creative principle that forms the basis of cosmos and the energizing force behind all divinity as well as beings. Further, one must understand that for a true devotee who is on a higher plane or dimension, all parts of the body are the same. The description or analogy of any of the body part of the mother Goddess is the same for him. Further, a Bhakta as the child of the mother Goddess sees only these divinity in his mother Goddess. To him the sex aspect of any of the body parts is irrelevant and has no significance. The Bhakta is overwhelmed with both the creator and His or Her creation, which are one and the same for him. He only marvels at the beauty of creation through his poetry. To him truth is beauty and beauty is truth.

In the hymn '*Soundarya Lahari*', Shankara says that the learned poets describe Mother Goddess as manifestation of beauty in human form. In another sense, the *Bhakta*, like a scientist describes, without any passion involved in it, the biology and the physiology of the human body. To him his chosen Deity looks very beautiful and he expresses the beauty through poetical expressions and analogies. In another sense it can be said that any form of energy whether it is love, passion or anger or compassion or any other emotion, only when that energy in its totality is focused in one direction and is in its peak, the results would be quick and high. So the *Bhakta*, perhaps channelises all his passion and love towards his chosen Deity, and becomes one with his chosen Deity whom he considers as his lover, partner, Lord or master or child, through his intensity of passion that is translated in the form of poetic expressions as passion is not considered a taboo in Hindu religion. Further, for a poet even if he happens to be a *Bhakta*, a thing of beauty is a joy forever. It is natural for a poet to describe the feminine beauty of the Goddess in the same manner as he describes the masculine strength and valour of Gods. More than anything else, the poetical expressions and analogies of body parts of the Goddesses convey some inner, spiritual and mystic meanings, as in the case of Soundarya Lahari of Adi Shankara that can be interpreted only by the enlightened beings. In some of the hymns on Goddesses Shankara states that Her form can be known only through Upanishads.

Ananda Lahari (The Wave of Happiness)

This is a prayer to Goddess Bhavani, who is Parvati the consort of Lord Shiva, for Her blessings. It contains twenty stanzas and is very devotional and also poetic. Shankara says,

"Oh, Goddess Bhavani, Gods like Lord Brahma even with His four heads, Lord Shiva who is your consort and who destroyed the three cities or Tripura even with His five faces, Lord Subramanya, your son even with His six faces, and Lord Vishnu, your brother even with His thousand faces are unable to sing your praise, if that is so, how can the others sing your glory?"

"One cannot explain in words the pleasant taste of *ghee*, milk, resins, and honey unless one tastes them with tongue. Similarly ordinary beings cannot describe your beauty because your beauty is known only to Lord Shiva".

"Hey, Goddess Gauri, I always sing and salute you. Your mouth is red with Thambhoola, your eyes are always black with Khajal, your forehead shines always due to the Kumkum of Kashmir, your neck is adorned with sparkling chains, and you are decorated with shining silk from Kancheepuram that is tied as saree by the golden belt of your waist".

"Hail *Sathi*, who is the consort of Lord Shiva, your eyes are like the lotus flowers, you shine with the garland of Kalpaka tree flowers over your bosom, your earrings shine because of the melodious music from the *veena*, you are very beautiful and your majestic walk is like that of the she elephant".

"Oh, Goddess, Your body is covered by the golden ornaments that are made of precious gems, you shine like the morning sun, your pretty looks of your eyes conquered the love of Lord Shiva, and your anklets are covered by the yellow silk dress that you wear. May you with your several faces appear before me with your kind and beautiful face."

"Your two hands are as soft as buds of the Himalayan Mountains, you wear flowers and gems, you have soft hair, you embrace Lord Shiva, who is your consort, and you who appear like a tender creeper, destroy all my sorrows and bring me eternal happiness".

"Several people with varying qualities depend on the creepers that are full of leaves but in my mind I feel that, you, who is without leaves is the only creeper that is to be served because by winding around you who is the everlasting, ancient creeper that is without leaves we can obtain *Mukti*".

"Oh, Goddess, who is the consort of Lord Shiva, you are the creator and Goddess of Dharma and the Vedas, you are the source of all prosperity, who is being worshipped by Kubera the God of wealth, you are the mother of the very first desire, you have won over the God of love, and you are the seed of devotion".

"I am fickle minded so I do not possess unflinching devotion to you. You are full of all riches and so you should show mercy on me. Just as the clouds pour rain water to the throat of the Chataka bird, similarly my brain also is being powered by you only".

"Oh, the ever shining goddess, kindly show me mercy, because it is not proper on your part to be indifferent towards me, who has taken refuge in you for solace. It is also not becoming of you, who is the wish fulfilling plant not to fulfill my wishes because in that case, what difference is there between you who is that wish fulfilling plant and the other plants?"

"I have come in search of your feet with great faith and hope because I have taken refuge in you alone but not in any other God. If, inspite of that if you do not bother to be merciful towards me, then, I will become the most helpless with no support at all, oh, mother of Lord Ganesha".

"Just as iron turns in to gold by the touch of the holy who are the lucky ones, just as the impure sewerage water becomes pure when it gets mixed with the sacred Ganga waters, although my mind is filthy and is full of sins, it is sure to be purified because my devotion to you has merged my mind with you".

"It is told by the ancient seers that by serving Gods other than you, one can fulfill one's desires, but you are more capable because you bless one with more than what he desires. My heart is throbbing for you day in and day out, Oh, Goddess, it is upto you to do whatever you think I am worthy of".

"Oh, Goddess, who is the consort of Lord Shiva, who is the emperor of all the three worlds, your form is reflected by the walls of your beautiful home that is full of precious gems and crystal. Its dome reflects the moving moon of the sky in which Gods like Brahma, Vishnu and other Gods reside".

"Oh, the daughter of the great Himavan, your abode is Kailasa, your fame is sung by Lord Brahma and Indra, all the three worlds are your family, you have all the occult powers within you and you are the consort of Lord Shiva, and you are uncomparable in your luck".

"Hey Goddess, all people view Lord Shiva as the one who rides over an old bull, who drinks the poison *halahala*, who wears the directions, who dances in the grave yard and wears snakes as His ornaments. But they do not know that he is gifted with all the wealth of the world due to your luck".

"Lord Shiva, who is the Lord of all beings, has the natural desire to destroy and recreate this universe by staying in the cremation ground and by smearing ashes over His body, by swallowing the poison *Halahala* to show His mercy in saving this universe. Oh, Goddess, He does all these good things because of His association with you".

"You are the most pretty in the entire universe, Oh, daughter of the mountains, Due to mercy, Lord Shiva the Lord of the mountains placed *Ganga* who is in the form of water with a disappointed face, on His head permanently".

" The saffron that is mixed with sandal and musk that you apply all over your body for taking your oil bath with water, along with the dust of your feet while you walk, oh, Goddess, the creator took for creating the most beautiful maidens of heaven".

"He who always thinks of you as the one who plays along with your friends in the pond that is full of fully blossomed lotus flowers of the happy spring season, that are intertwined, that shine because of the swans that are in the moving water due to wind, and that has the sandal wood powder of your body, would never suffer from fever that causes all ailments."

Annapurna Stotram

This is a twelve verses prayer on Goddess Annapurna, the Goddess who grants food.

"Oh, mother Annapurna, who is the personification of compassion, the bestower of everlasting happiness, who is the giver of all blessings, who protects, who is the ocean of beauty, who is the destroyer of all sins, who is the purifier, the supreme Goddess, who purifies the family of Himavan in to which she was born. and the great Deity of Varanasi or Kashi, kindly, grant us food".

"Oh, mother Annapurna, who is the personification of compassion, whose ornaments are made of different valuable gems, who wears silk, golden threaded garments, whose chest shines with the pendent of garland of pearls, who is very pretty looking, and who is the presiding deity of Kashi, kindly grant us food".

"Oh, mother Annapurna, who is the personification of compassion, who blesses happiness that is obtained through yoga, who is the destroyer of enemies, who is the cause of righteousness in beings, who shines in all the three worlds, who grants all riches, who bestows the fruits of all penance, and who is the presiding deity of Kashi, Kindly grant us food".

"Oh, mother Annapurna, who is the embodiment of all compassion, who lives in the caves of mount Kailash, who is shining like gold, Oh, Uma, who is the consort of Lord Shiva and who is always youthful, who makes His beings understand the content of the great Vedas, whose basic syllable is the Pranava *mantra* 'AUM', who opens up the door for *Mukti*, and who is the presiding deity of Kashi, please grant us food".

"Oh, mother Annapurna, who is the embodiment of all compassion, who bestows both material and spiritual wealth, who contained the primordial universe, who directs Maya of the world, who is the flame of the lamp of true knowledge, who is the source of mental happiness of Lord Vishwanatha, who is the presiding Deity of Kashi, kindly grant us food".

"Oh, mother Annapurna, who is the embodiment of all compassion, who is the maker of all the alphabets from the beginning till the end, who is the cause of all the three causes of creation, preservation and destruction by Lord Shiva, who wears saffron colour dress, who is the consort of the destroyer of Tripura or the three cities, Lord Shiva, who governs this universe, and who is the form of Goddess of night, who opens up the gate to heaven and who is the presiding Deity of Kashi, kindly grant us food".

"Oh, mother Annapurna, who is the embodiment of all compassion, who is the cause of earth, who governs all beings, who is the mother of compassion, who possesses dark hair that resembles the colour of the flower of the indigo plant, who grants food daily and grants *Mukti* and eternal bliss, and who is the presiding deity of Kashi, kindly grant us food".

"Oh, mother Annapurna, who is the embodiment of all compassion, Oh, Goddess, who is decorated with various kinds of costly gems, who is the daughter of Daksha Prajapati, and who is the most beautiful, who bears benign breasts, who does good to all, who is prosperous, who fulfills the desire of all Her devotees, who performs auspicious acts and who is the presiding deity of Kashi, Kindly grant us food".

"Oh, mother Annapurna, who is the personification of all compassion, whose lustre is like that of innumerable suns, moons, and fire, whose red lips resemble the red pearl, and the bimba fruit, who wears shining earring that resembles moon, sun and fire, who has a goad, and who is the presiding deity of Kashi, kindly grant us food".

"Oh, mother Annapurna, who is the personification of all compassion, who protects the universe, who is the remover of all fears, who is the ocean of compassion, who is the cause of happiness of all beings, who does good always, who is the consort of Lord Vishwanatha, who is the form of Lakshmi, who is the consort of the destroyer of the sacrifice performed by Daksha Prajapati, who deliverse all beings from all ills and who is the presiding Deity of Kashi, kindly grant us food".

Oh, mother Parvati, Annapurna, who is partless, who is the dear consort of Lord Shankara; kindly give us food, knowledge and detachment".

"Goddess Parvati is my mother, Lord Maheshwara is my father, all my relatives are the devotees of Lord Shiva and my country encompasses all the three worlds".

Bhavani Ashtakam

This stotra contains eight stanzas. This stotra reveals the intense devotion of Shankara in seeking refuge at the divine feet of the divine Mother. Shankara, the Bhakta who is tossed hither and thither by all problems that are physical, psychological and who is overcome with grief prays and seeks protection from mother Bhavani whom he calls as his ultimate and only refuge. It is the heart felt prayer of a helpless devotee who is represented by Shankara, who is entangled in the mire of *Maya* to Mother Bhavani who is his only refuge. He starts this Shloka by saying "none of those who are considered as mine or my *karmas* are my refuge except you, mother Bhavani who is my sole refuge".

"Oh, mother, I am tied in the ocean of samsara, birth, and death. I am a coward who has no guts to face the sorrows. I am filled with lust and sin, greed and desire. I am entangled in this useless life. Be my refuge, Oh, mother Bhavani".

"I do not know how to meditate, or perform austerities. Nor do I know any Tantra, prayer, how to worship and also the art of Yoga. Oh, Bhavani, you are my only refuge".

"I do not know to be righteous, the methods of salvation, or the sacred places or the merging of mind with God. I have no knowledge of Tantra, or prayers, or the art of devotion or Yoga. Oh, mother, you are my only refuge".

"All that I do is to do bad things, keep company with bad people, have bad and sinful thoughts, and serve bad masters. I belong to a bad family immersed in sinful deeds. I have bad intentions, utter bad words and am a coward with no guts to face sorrows; I am filled with lust, greed, and desire, attached to the world all the time. So, Mother Bhavani, you are my only refuge".

"I do not know anything about the creator, the maintainer or the destroyer of the universe, who is the Lord of all the worlds, or the Lord of Goddess Lakshmi, the Lord of all day and night or the Lord of the Devas or the almighty God. All that I know is only to bow to you, Mother Goddess, you who is my only refuge".

"Whenever I am in the midst of dangers, engaged in severe arguments, am in sorrow or suffering from an accident or traveling in distant places in the midst of water or fire, on top of a mountain surrounded by enemies, or in deep forest, I always think of you and seek protection from you. Oh mother you are my only refuge".

"I am an orphan who is extremely poor, and affected by diseases and old age, terribly tired, in a pitiable state, and overcome by problems of life, sorrows and sufferings, and when I am in the midst of danger I always think of you and bow before you who is my only refuge".

Ganesha Pancharatnam

This Stotra is a garland of prayer with five stanzas. The sixth stanza tells about the result of singing this prayer. It is a prayer to Lord Ganesha who is described by Shankara as the one who removes all obstacles, who is the God of wealth, Vedas and elephants, destroyer of Asuras and evil, the protector of the world, who grants salvation, who shines like sun, who is the bestower of peace to all the worlds, the annihilator of Gaja Mukheshwara, who has a big belly, and the face that of an elephant, who is kind, bestower of blessings and fame to his devotees, the remover of poverty, the eldest son of Sadashiva, who kills the pride of enemies of Gods who wear serpents and Dananjaya as ornaments, who is fierce with a single pretty tusk, the one who has a form beyond all imaginations, who is endless, who removes all obstacles, and who dwells permanently in the heart of Yogis. This Stotra tells about the result of charity. Shankara says the one who remembers Him with respect every morning these five gems of garlands of this great Lord, Ganapaty and the one who meditates on Him in His heart is sure to be blessed with a healthy life, with the absence of all problems of life and he will be blessed with great peace, great sons, longevity, physical and spiritual health.

"I prostrate before Lord Ganesha, who holds the big Modaka in His hand with great joy, who bestows salvation, who wears the moon as a crown on His head, who is the leader for those who have no leaders, who destroyed the elephant demon Gajasura and who destroys the sins of those who bow down to Him".

"I bow to that Lord who is a terror to those who are not His devotees, who shines like the rising sun, to whom all Gods and demons are alike, who removes the distress of devotees and who is also the best among the best."

"I bow to that luminous Ganapaty, who brings happiness to all the worlds, who killed Gajasura, the demon, whose belly is big, has a beautiful face of an elephant, who is immortal, who gives mercy, forgiveness and happiness to those who bow to Him and who bestows fame and a well disposed mind".

"I worship that ancient elephant God, who destroys the pains of the poor, who is the abode of 'AUM', who is the first son of Lord Shiva, who destroys the pride of the enemies of Gods, who has a frightening look during the time of deluge, and who is fierce like an elephant in rut and who wears Dananjaya and other serpents as His ornaments".

"I reflect upon that single tusked God alone, who has a lustrous tusk that is very beautiful, who is the son of Lord Shiva, the destroyer who removes all obstacles and who dwells in the hearts of Yogis for ever".

"He who recites this shloka of five gems on Lord Ganesha every morning with devotion and remembers this great Lord Ganesha will be blessed with a healthy life devoid of all blemishes, will obtain learning, good sons, long life, material and spiritual prosperity".

Gangaashtakam

This is a prayer to Mother Ganga with eight verses. The nineth verse tells about the result of singing this prayer. Shankara describes Goddess Ganga that is full of waves, as the remover of all dirt and as the ladder to heaven. She who is the garland on the head of Shiva is meant for His happiness. Shankara says that those who are lucky to taste a drop of Her water will get relieved of all sins and will also be loved by heavenly maidens. He further says that let the pure waters of mother Ganga protect and save all of us. She also makes those who bathe in Her waters to cross the ocean of life and those who take a sip of the water would get permanent residence in Vaikunta. For the one who merely touches her waters, even becoming a monarch in the kingdom of heaven becomes worth less. Finally Shankara says, "Let my devotion to Lord Vishnu and Shiva be permanent" and the holy devotee who reads this Ashtakam on mother Ganga is bound to get rid of all sins and reach Vaikunta.

"Oh Goddess Ganga I came to your shores and sat there praying on Krishna and taking nothing else except water, Oh, Ganga, who removes all dirt, who is the ladder to heaven, who is full of waves that are spreading. Oh, Ma kindly be pleased with me".

"Oh, Goddess, who adorns the head of Shiva as a garland meant for His happiness. Those who are lucky will touch a drop of your water and will get relieved of all their black sins and would enjoy the love in the laps of the heavenly maidens who hold fans in their hands".

"Let your pure waters of heaven, originating by the breaking of the Universe into two, water the curly hair of Shiva from heaven above. The water that rush through the sandal wood trees of the caves of Meru and falling continuously on the earth with force, wash away the sins of one and all who use these waters. Kindly take care of us all".

"The waters of Ganga that is full of bees crowding to drink the water coming out of the bathing elephants, that is fully red because of the saffron colour, and that is full of grass and flowers, that flow from the head through the bust of holy women, that is full of waves created by the playing elephants and their calves by beating the water with their trunks is being saluted by sages both in the morning and evening".

"This Goddess is brought down to earth by king Bhageerath. It was originally seen as water of worship from the pot of Brahma. Later it became the purest of all waters, washing the feet of Lord Vishnu and then became an ornamental gem on the head of Lord Shiva and later it was born as the daughter of sage Jahnu".

"Hail to that pretty Ganga who took birth from the king of mountains, who also makes people dip in Her waters to cross the ocean of life, who finally reaches and merges in the ocean. She annihilates all sorrows of life, and like Adisesha bends and flows, appears like leaves on the hair of Lord Shiva and flows near the city of Varanashi or Kashi".

"Oh mother Ganga there are no sufferings for the one whose eyes see even one of your waves. You give permanent residence in Vaikunta for the one who takes a dip in your water. For one whose body touches your water, even the post of Indra becomes worthless".

"Oh, mother Ganga, you who are the most important in all the three worlds who is so wide and big that all heavenly women dip and bathe in you. You are the full form of eternal truth; you flow carrying the dust of the feet of Lord Vishnu. You flow in the path of heaven and even a single drop of yours is the cure for all sins including the killing of a Brahmana. Oh, mother Ganga, no one is capable of adequately praying you who is the only one capable to wash away all sins in the three worlds. Kindly be pleased with me".

"Oh, mother Jhanavi, finally at the end of my wandering of searching for the company of Lord Shiva, my soul came to your bank, meditating, holding both my hands on my head with happiness and in salutations to the lotus feet of Lord Vishnu. Oh my Goddess. Let my devotion to Lord Vishnu and mother be always permanent".

"That holy devotee who reads this holy octet on Ganga would become free of all sins and reach Vaikunta, the abode of Lord Vishnu".

Guru Ashtakam

This Stotra of eight verses stresses the importance of bowing to a teacher and acquire knowledge from him. The nineth verse tells about the effects of singing these verses of prayer. It says whether you have beautiful and passionate wife, great name, wealth, children, grand children, relatives, or belong to a great family, is an expert in all the six Vedangas and Vedas, a good writer and a poet, great in the world, rich, virtuous, or even a great monarch who is served by several kings, charitable, famous, possess priceless collection of jewels, whether your mind is in forest or house while performing your duties, or in great thoughts, - What is the use of all these if your mind does not bow at the feet of the teacher? Whether one is a saint, king, bachelor, or householder, if he has reverence to the words of the teacher, then he would be blessed with the great gift of knowledge of Brahman".

"Even if you have pleasing and beautiful life, great fame, highly prosperous, if your mind does not bow at the teacher's feet what is the use of all these?"

"Even if you have wife, wealth, children, and grand children, house, relations, born in a great family, If your mind does not bow to the teacher then what is the use of all these?"

"Even if you are an expert in all six limbs of Vedas and the four Vedas, and also a great writer of prose and poetry, if your mind does not bow at the teacher's feet then what is the use of all these?"

"Even if you are well known through out the world, and a wealthy person in your own native place, well respected in life, if you do not bow at the teacher's feet what is the use of all these?"

"Even if you are a king of great region, who is served by all great kings, if your mind does not bow at the teacher's feet then what is the use of all these?"

"Even if your fame is well spread, and the entire world praises you because of your charity and fame, if your mind does not bow at the teacher's feet then what is the use of all these?"

"Even if your mind is indifferent towards passion, yoga, fire sacrifice or in family pleasure or in the affairs of wealth, if your mind does not bow at the teacher's feet what is the use of all these?"

"Even if you have priceless collection of jewels, a passionate wife, if you do not bow at the teacher's feet what is the use of all these?"

"That blessed one who reads these eight verses, whether he is a saint, king, bachelor or householder, if his mind concentrates on the words of the teacher, he would get the gift of attaining the everlasting Brahman".

Guru Paduka Panchakam

These five verses are believed to have sung by Shankara when he first met his master Govinda Bhagavapada. The sixth stanza gives the effects of singing these verses. These verses praise the sandals of the *Guru*. In these verses Shankara salutes the sandals of the *Guru* who is the cause of creation, maintenance and destruction of all the worlds. The sandals of the *Guru* are the sun that removes all darkness of dangers. His sandals are like water in the lake that washes and cleans the imperfect knowledge attained by false arguments. His sandal provides cool shade to those who are burnt by sufferings. This sandal also makes all knowledge bow down in shame. Shankara finally says that Goddess Lakshmi would bless those who read this 'Paduka Panchakam' daily morning with devotion.

"Salutations and salutations to the sandals of the *Guru*, that is the cause of creation, upkeep and destruction of all the worlds; the cause that can be attained only through unlimited amount of good deeds and that is explained in Vedanta."

"Salutations and salutations of *Guru* that is the sun dispelling the darkness of dangers and that increases the invaluable wealth of knowledge and that bless the people to attain everything they desire".

"Salutations and salutations to the sandals of *Guru*, which is like water in the lake that washes and clears the wrong knowledge attained by false arguments and gives the knowledge of Brahman that is not dependant on any other thing but everything else depends upon it".

"Salutations and salutations to the sandals of *Guru* that provides cool shade, considering it as the most important duty, for those who are burnt by sufferings and protection to those affected by dangers".

"Salutations and Salutations to the sandals of *Guru* that puts all knowledge to shame and that is praised by Brahma, Vishnu and Shiva".

"The king of teachers will live in the houses and the mother of wealth will bless them through Her glance of those who read these five verses on Sandals with devotion every morning."

Guru Paduka Stotram

This is a shloka of eight stanzas in prayer to the sandals of *Guru* who removes all darkness arising out of ignorance by shedding the light of knowledge. The nineth verse tells about the good effects of singing this prayer.

"Salutations and salutations of the sandals of my *Guru*, that is like a boat that helps me to cross the endless ocean of *Samsara*, that helps me to be devoted to my *Guru* and by worshipping of which I attain the domain of renunciation".

"Salutations and salutations to the sandals of my *Guru*- the one who prostrates before it would be blessed with great wealth even if they had been poor before, and also would make even the dumb people great orators".

"Salutations and salutations to the sandals of my *Guru*, who is the ocean of knowledge resembling the full moon that puts out the fire of misfortunes like water and that helps in removing all miseries of those who bow to it".

"Salutations and salutations to the sandals of my *Guru*, that attracts one to the lotus feet of the *Guru*, that eliminates the unwanted desires and at the same time helps those who bow before it to fulfill their desires".

"Salutations and salutations to the sandals of my *Guru* that shines like gems on the crown of a king and also like a maid in the stream full of crocodiles and that make devotees attain the status of a king".

"Salutations and salutations to the sandals of my *Guru*, that is like a collection of several suns that drive away all dark sins, that is like the king of eagles that drives away the cobra like miseries and that is like a terrific fire that dries up the ocean of ignorance".

"Salutations and salutations to the sandals of my *Guru* that gives us the six glorious qualities of *Samadhi*, that gives the students the ability to go into eternal trance and that helps to get the eternal devotion to the feet of Vishnu".

"Salutations and salutations to the sandals of my *Guru* that bestws all desires of the disciples who are serving, who perform service that helps spiritual aspirants to the state of realization".

"Salutations and salutations to the sandals of my *Guru* who is like Garuda that drives away the serpent of passion, that provides treasure of wisdom and renunciation, blesses one with enlightenment, knowledge and quick salvation".

Hanumath Pancharatnam

These are five gems of verses on Bhakta Anjaneya. The sixth verse tells about the greatness of singing this prayer. Shankara says, "My mind thinks of the son of *Vayu*, who is devoid of all desires of enjoyment, who sheds tears of joy, who is a great devotee of Shree Rama, and the great emissary of Sita Devi".

"I yearn to see such a Hanuman who is the son and good fortune of Anjana Devi, whose face is red like the rising sun, who has glances that are full of mercy, who brought back the dead in the Rama- Ravana war, and whose fame is great".

"He is the only refuge for me. He has reddish lips like the Bimba fruit. He is the enemy of the arrows of Manmada who is the God of Love, and has broad eyes like that of Lotus leaves. His neck looks like a conch"

"His very sight drove away Sita's sorrows. Let Him, who praised Rama's greatness and destroyed the arrogance of the ten headed Ravana shine."

"I see Him, who is the result of penance of Vayu Deva. He is the leader of all monkeys, demons and water lily. He is similar to sun God. He is the protector of all the suffering humans"

"Who ever read these five verses that are in praise of the son of Vayu Deva would become the devotee of Shree Rama and would enjoy his life for long."

Jyotirlinga Stotram

This stotra is also known as Dwadasa Jyotir Linga stotra. There are twelve verses in this prayer. The thirteenth verse is about the effects of this prayer. There are twelve places where Lord Shiva is worshipped in the form of Jyothi or flame. It is said, that the one who is at a higher level of spiritual attainment sees these Lingas as columns of fire, that pierces through the earth. In this stotra the location of all the twelve Jyotir Linga keshtras are given. These are, Somanatha in Sourashtra, Mallikarjuna in Sri Sailm, Maha Kala in Ujjain, Omkareshwar in Amaleshwara, Vaidyanath in Pareli, Bheema Shankara in the south, Rameshwar near the bridge in Setu, Nageshwar in Daruka forest, Visveswara in Varanasi, Trayambhakeshwar in the shores of Godavari, Kedareshwara in Himalayas and Grushmesha in Sivalaya. Through these twelve verses of prayer Shankara the devotee salutes and seeks refuge in each of the twelve Jyotir Linga Shrines. The thirteenth stanza describes the greatness of singing this prayer of twelve verses.

"I seek refuge of Somanada who resides in the holy and beautiful Saurashtra, who is ever shining, wears the crescent moon, and who gives the gift of devotion and mercy".

"I salute the one who resides in Shree Saila, who is the bridge to cross the ocean of life, who has the company of all Gods and who resides on the peak of Thula and is called Mallikarjuna".

"I salute that Mahakala, who is the God of all Devas, who resides in the city of Avanthi for granting salvation to all and to save people from untimely death".

"I meditate on Lord Shiva who is 'AUM', who resides in the city of Mandathipura that is located at the holy confluence of Kavery and Narmada rivers for helping good people to cross the ocean of life that is full of miseries."

"I salute Vaidyanatha, whose Lotus like feet are worshipped by all Asuras and Devas alike and who resides along with his consort Goddess Parvati in the place that shines always in the north east of India".

"I seek refuge of Lord Naganada who resides in the beautiful town of Sadanga in the southern part, who is well decorated who grants all pleasures of life and who is the only God who grants devotion and salvation".

"I meditate on that Shiva who is the Lord of Kedar, who enjoys the valley of the great mountain, who is worshipped by sages, Devas, Asuras, Yakshas and Nagas always."

"I meditate on that Lord Trayambaka who resides on the peak of western Ghats, in the holy bank of river Godavari and who destroys all sins of His devotees who come and worship Him".

"I meditate on Lord Rameshwara with devotion, the Lord who resides in the confluence of the river Tamaravarunee with the sea, where a bridge has been built with the help of innumerable arrows by Lord Shree Ramachandra".

"I salute that Lord Shankara who is the darling of His devotees, who is worshipped even by the demons, who is in the company of demons like Dakini and Sakini and who is also known well as Bheema".

"I seek the protection of the Lord of the Universe- who resides happily in the forest of joy and who is also the basis of all joy, who destroys all accumulated sins, and who is the Lord of the city of Varanasi and who is the Lord of all those who have none".

"I seek refuge of Ghushreneshwar who stays and plays in the beautiful place of Illapura, who is also the greatest in the Universe and who is extremely kind".

"Those who read this prayer with devotion that tells about the twelve Jyotir Lingas would be worshipped by others".

Kalabhairavashtakam

This is a prayer to Kalabhairava in eight verses. The nineth verse tells about the results of singing this prayer. Kalabhairava is the fearful aspect of Lord Shiva. He is supposed to be protecting the city of Kashi. Kalabhairava was created by Lord Shiva to cut the fifth head of Lord Brahma who was later pardoned by Lord Shiva. But the sin of beheading Lord Brahma's head followed Kala Bhairava wherever he went, in the form of a lady. The head that was cut got stuck to Kala Bhairava. So Kala Bhairava entered the city of Banaras but the sin could not enter the city. So Kala Bhairava was made the protector of the city. He is supposed to be black and riding on a dog. Kalabhairava is also identified with Veerabhadra who cut the head of Daksha, the father of Sathi Devi, consort of Lord Shiva. Out side every Shakti peets where the dead body of Sathi that was carried by Lord Shiva fell, there is a temple of Kala Bhairava. He is also said to be that form of Lord Shiva that controls 'Kala' or time. Again He is also considered as the guardian of Shiva temples. In this Shloka of eight verses Shankara salutes Kalabhairava and offers prayers to him. The nineth verse says about the good results of singing this prayer. In this Kalabhairava is identified with Lord Shiva who is the Lord of Kashi- Kashi Vishwanath. He is the one who helps in crossing the miserable ocean of life. He is imperishable, primeval cause, deathless; the one who fulfills all desires and grants salvation. He is a form of Shiva, God of the world, but assumes different forms. He maintains Dharma, destroys all bad paths, saves one from the ties of Karma, bestows everything, takes away the fear of death, grants salvation, destroys all sins, grants occult powers, as chief of all the Bhootha Ganas grants fame, judges good and bad and is the Lord of the Universe. Shankara through these verses bows to such a Lord.

"I salute that Kalabhairava, who is merciful, who is served by Indra, the Lord of Devas, who wears on His forehead the moon, who wears snake as His sacred thread, who has different directions as His attire and who is worshipped by Narada and other sages".

"I salute that Kalabhairava, who shines like billions of suns, helping us to cross the miserable ocean of life, who is the supreme Lord with blue neck who has three eyes and who grants the desires of His Bhaktas, who is the God of Yama, the God of death, who has Lotus like eyes and is imperishable, and who has the Trident that is undefeatable."

"I salute that Kala bhairava, who has the weapons of spear, a chord and a stick, who is black and the primeval cause, who is deathless and is the first God who has no decay or ill health, who is the Lord and great hero, and who likes the vigorous steps of '*Thandava Nritya*".

"I salute that Kalabhairava, who fulfills desires and grants salvation, who is known for His pretty looks, who is a form of Lord Shiva who is static and loves His devotees, who is the God of the entire world assuming various forms and who has a golden waist thread on which jingling bells are tied".

"I salute that Kala Bhairava, who maintains the Dharmic path and destroys the unrighteous path, who saves us from the bondage of Karma, who is the Lord who makes us feel ashamed whenever we commit wrong things and who has a shining body with a golden rope that has jingling bells".

"I salute that Kalabhairava, whose feet are adorned with gem studded sandals, who is eternal and one without a second, who is our favourite God and who grants everything to us, including liberation that removes the fear of death".

"I salute that Kala Bhairava, whose loud roar destroys all creation of Brahma, whose looks destroy all sins, who can also grant the eight occult powers and wears the garland of skulls".

"I salute that Kala bhairava, who is the Lord of Bhootha Ganas, who grants lasting fame, who judges good and bad deeds of the residents of Varanasi, who is righteousness, who is ancient and Lord of the Universe".

"Those who read this source of eternal knowledge of eight verses of prayer to Kala Bhairava would find increase in the effects of good deeds, destruction of grief, passion, poverty, want and anger and finally would reach Kala Bhairava".

Kalpashakthistavam

This is a prayer in fifteen verses to Goddess Ambika who is Thripura Sundari. The sixteenth verse is about the good effects of singing this prayer. Thripura Sundri means the beauty of the three cities. She is so called because she existed even prior to the trinity of Gods, she has the form of three deeds namely, duty, worship and wisdom. She recreates the world after the great deluge or Pralaya. She can be easily attained by practicing Yoga of devotion. She has immense power that gives protection to all beings that are in danger. She is the searchlight during Vedic discussions. She is the ultimate limit of Lord Shiva's blessings. She has the capacity to reduce all types of sins. She is ever present. Shankara says that those who sing these verses in the mornings with happiness will become wealthier than Kubera, the Lord of wealth. They will have a happy life while living and after death they would reach the perinnial state of Bliss.

"I pray to Her who sits on the throne of gems of thought, located on the pretty mountain Meru, that is full of bees in ecstacy due to plenty of honey that they drank from the innumerable flowers of the forest that is full of the wish fulfilling trees, that is on account of Her Maya, and that can be got by Yoga of devotion".

"I yearn for Her protection, who has the colour of early morning, with a body that is dazzling remarkably, resembling crores of Suns, that are rising in the morning. Her power is indescribable. She gives protection to all beings who are in danger and she is the search light in the discussion of the Vedas".

"I always seek Her protection who has thick hair, that is made more pretty by the crescent moon that is made even prettier by the stars that look like the just opened flowers of the wishfulfilling tree, the Kalpa Vriksha, whose hair is bluish black in colour, whose two long eyes are ornaments to Her forehead and who is the ultimate limit of Lord Shiva's blessings"

"I meditate upon that Tripura Sundari, in my mind, whose lotus like face is capable of defeating millions of moons, who has great eyelashes that can be compared to the bows of God of Love, who is capable of reducing all types of sins, who is the result of meditating upon Lord Shiva, and who is always present in full."

"I seek protection of that Tripura Sundari, who is the consort of Lord Shiva, whose eyes are always shut due to Bashfulness of youth, that shows a mixture of passion, curiosity and mercy that again is a mixture of white, red and black colours that are crystal clear, tired looking and long, who has pretty gem like lips that shines while smiling and that look like the brightest moon light".

"I always seek protection of that Tripura Sundari, whose cheeks are very pretty and shine like mirror made of gems polished by hands, whose lotus face is made more beautiful by a pair of ear studs that hang from Her ears like pretty bunch of flowers, whose nose is like the lotus bud, who is the sister of Lord Krishna, the friend of Arjuna, the enemy of Karna, and who was born to Yasoda while Krishna was born to Devaki"

"We always meditate upon that Tripura Sundari who has clear nector like ponds, described by words as resembling the sweet taste of honey from the flowers, who is surrounded by playful bees that are attracted by the natural scent around Her face, who is Ambika, who is always good to Her devotees"

"I pray to that Tripura Sundari, whose neck is decorated by chain of gold beads and the gem studded Mangala Sutra, the lutre of which defeats the stars in the sky, and steals the dazzle of the white coloured conch, whose pretty ear drops touch Her low level shoulders and who is the bountiful treasure of Lord Shiva, the enemy of the God of Love".

"I make that Tripura Sundari, reside in my heart, who shines because she holds sugar cane bow, rod, rope and flower arrows, who wears golden bangles, rings and armlet and who has beautiful breasts".

"I always see Tripura Sundari in my mind whose middle is small because of the heavy breasts and attractive ornaments that she wears and who is the darling of Lord Shiva".

"I carry in my mind that Tripura Sundari who is worshipped even by the Devas, who wears a golden belt, who wears pretty silk dress, who has a broad lucky and heavy middle that is capable of carrying Her beauty".

"I meditate on that Tripura Sundari in my mind whose thighs and knees are very pretty, who is capable of granting salvation".

"I always see my mother Tripura Sundari, reflected in my mind with shining legs, that defeats the beauty of the long tender neck of peacocks and the softness of which is similar to the inside of the Lotus flowers".

"I meditate upon that Tripura Sundari whose lotus like feet are worshipped by great, wise and blessed men, and whose pretty and holy form gets showered by the golden buds from the wish fulfilling tree and who is like the holy bee playing in the lotus lake of wisdom".

"I meditate upon that Tripura Sundari whose form is defined by 'Hreem', who is the daughter of the mountains, the daughter of the ocean and the wife of Brahma who sits on the Lotus, who is the wish fulfilling cow of Her devotees, whose fame is told in all the scriptures, who contains the entire Universe within Herself".

"The wise men who sing this prayer with a clean mind, in the morning with happiness would defeat even the Lord of wealth by his properly earned wealth. He would be liked by all men and women alike, would be blessed with wealth, wife, and children, and after the end of his life he would reach the ever lasting state".

Kanakadhara Stotram

This is a Stotra with twenty-one hymns on Goddess Lakshmi. The last verse tells about the result of singing this prayer. Goddess Lakshmi is praised for Her glance that would bring prosperity. She is prayed for removing poverty, for driving away sins that are committed. She is also the one who creates, maintains and destroys this Universe. She is worshipped in all the three worlds. She is the Vedas, She is Rathi who gives the most beautiful qualities, She is Shakti who resides in the thousand petalled Lotus, and She is the Goddess of wealth and the consort of Purushotthama. She is the leader of the universe, showers mercy on the Devas, She is the light, and she is earth as well as the mother of earth. She is worshipped by Devas. She gives wealth, pleasure to senses and makes one rule kingdoms. Shankara composed these verses when he received a gooseberry as alms from a poor woman when once he went, as per tradition of Brahmacharis, to seek alms or Bhiksha. It is said that Shankara was very much touched by the act of the poor woman and these verses flowed out from his heart. It is also said that Goddess Lakshmi showered golden gooseberries as rain on the poor woman's house. Shankara says that those who sing these verses of prayer daily will be blessed with all graceful qualities with all great fortune, and would live in recognition even from the learned.

Through this stotra Shankara says, "Let Goddess Lakshmi who is born of the oceans and is the Goddess of all good things, attracted to Lord Hari, who wears supreme happiness as ornament, shower her glance of prosperity on me like bees getting attracted to the unopened buds of forest tree called Tamala and like honey bees that shower on a blue Lotus".

"Oh mother, who is born of the ocean of milk, give those glances that is filled with love and that looks again and again at your Lord Murari, who gives immortal bliss. Like the honey bees to the beautiful blue lotus flower, let those glances of yours shower wealth on me".

"She who looks at the blissful face of Her Lord, Mukunda with her half closed eyes that are filled with happiness, shyness and signs of Love, let she who is the consort of that Lord who lies on the snake shower wealth on me".

"Let the glances of Her whose Lord has vanquished the demon Madhu, and who wears Kausthuba as His ornament and blue Indraneela as garland and who grants all the wishes of his consort goddess Lakshmi who lives in the Lotus, fall on me and grant me all that is good".

"Let the glance of Goddess Lakshmi, the Universal mother, who shines like a streak of lightning on a dark cloud on the dark and broad chest of her Lord who killed the Asura Kaidaba, and who is the daughter of sage Bhargava who did penance to have the Goddess as his daughter, fall on me and bring me prosperity."

"Let the power of Her kind side-glance that is auspicious and loaded with love and blessing, that made Her Lord Hari, kill the demon, the *Asura* Madhu fall on me".

"Her single side glance of a moment, that has the capacity to make one as the king of the Devas, made Indra the Lord of the Devas to regain his kingdom of heaven, and made her Lord the killer of Madhu extremely happy. Let the glance of her Lotus eyes fall on me a little."

"To Her devotees and great souls she grants a place in heaven that is very difficult to attain. Let Her compassioanate looks with sparkling eyes that are like the fully opened Lotus fall on me for granting me all my wishes".

"Oh, mother, kindly send your mercy like rain to this dried up land and quench the thirst of the little Charaka bird, the mystical bird that is always thirsty. In a similar manner, drive away all my sins, Oh, mother who is the beloved of Lord Vishnu, by the glance of your cloud like dark eyes."

"You are the Goddess of knowledge, the beloved of Lord Narayana whose flag is Garuda. You are the power at the time of deluge. You are the wife of the Lord who does creation, maintenance and destruction at the appointed time. My humble salutations, to you oh, mother, who is worshipped by all the three worlds".

"I salute you as Vedas that teach all good actions. I salute you as Rathi, the consort of Kama, the God of Love for giving the most beautiful qualities. I salute you as Shakti, as Goddess Parvati, who resideds in the hundred petalled lotus. My humble Salutations to you oh, mother, who is the Goddess of wealth, and who is the consort of Lord Purushotthama, the best among men".

"My salutations to Her who is most beautiful like the full blossomed lotus, who is born of the ocean of milk, who is the sister of nectar and moon, and is the consort of Lord Narayana".

"Salutations to you, who has the golden lotus as Her seat, who is the leader of the universe, who showers mercy on the Devas, and who is the consort of the Lord with the Saranga bow".

"Salutations to you, oh, mother, who is the daughter of sage Bhargava, who resides in the holy chest of Lord Narayana, who resides in the Lotus and who is the consort of Damodara".

"Salutations to you, who gives light to the Lotus flower by living in it, who is earth as well as the mother of earth, who is worshipped by the Devas, and who is the consort of the son of Nanda (the foster father of Shree Krishna)".

"You are the giver of all wealth, pleasures, and the right to rule over kingdoms. You have lotus like eyes that would remove all miseries quickly. You are my mother, my salutations to you".

"The one who worships your glances are bound to be blessed with all prosperity. My salutations, to you, by word, thought and deed to that queen, who resides in the heart of Lord Vishnu, who killed Murari".

"You, the goddess sitting in the lotus, who has lotus in her hands, dressed in dazzling white, who shines with garlands and sandal paste, who is the Goddess and consort of Hari, who gladdens the mind, and showers prosperity on all the three worlds, kindly show compassion on me".

"Eight elephants that come from different directions bring and pour Ganga water that flows in heaven, for your sacred bath. My salutations this morning to you, oh mother of all the three worlds, who is also the consort of the Lord of the worlds, and who is the daughter of the ocean that gave Amrit or nectar."

"Oh mother, who resides in the lotus, and who is the consort of the Lord with lotus like eyes, whose glances are filled with mercy, kindly turn your glances at me, who am the poorest among the poor. But before that make me the vessel that is fit to receive your kindness and compassion".

"He who recites these prayers daily on Her who is the personification of Vedas, who is the mother of all the three worlds, who is Goddess Rama, will undoubtedly be blessed with all good qualities, fortunes and would lead a life with great recognition. Even learned people will hail such people".

Krishnashtakam

These eight verses are in praise of Lord Krishna. The nineth verse tells about the good effects of singing this prayer. Krishna is the one who removes all sins. He pleases the mind of devotees. He grants supreme Bliss. He helps one to cross over the miserable ocean of life. He is the treasure house of good qualities, pleasure and mercy. He shines in all directions. The one who reads these verses would be born as a great Bhakta of Lord Krishna in all his births.

"I pray to Him who cuts off all sins, who pleases the mind of His devotees, who is the divine son of Nandagopa. Salutations to the sea like Lord Krishna who wears the peacock feather on His head, and who, with His flute in His hand is music of the ocean of Love".

"Salutations to Him who has the eyes like lotus, who only can win over the pride of the God of love, and who has broad eyes that shines always, who consoled the Gopas when He had to leave, Salutations to that elephant like Krishna who lifted the Govardhana mountain by His soft, lotus hands, who has a very pretty smile and gaze, and who alone could kill the pride of Indra".

"My Salutations to Lord Krishna who is not easily reachable, who wears the earrings of Kadamba flowers, who has beautiful cheeks, and who is the Lord of the women of Vrija. Salutations to that chief of all Gopas, who gives supreme bliss to His parents and all others".

"Salutations to the son of Nanda whose lotus like eyes is ever in my mind, whose curly hair falling on His forehead, Salutations to Him, who makes Nanda His father happy, who reduces the effects of all sins, who protects the entire Universe and who is the mind of every cowherd."

"I bow to Him who steals the hearts of all, who was incarnated to reduce the burden of mother earth, who helps to cross the miserable ocean called life, and who is always a child to Yashoda, His mother. I bow to that son of King Nanda whose eyes are very pretty, who is always followed by bees everywhere, who is always new to understand for His devotees".

"I salute that Gopa lad who is the treasure house of good qualities, happiness and mercy, who Himself is above the need for mercy, who removes all problems of the Devas. I salute that dark, handsome one who has the colour of the cloud, who wears yellow coloured silk dress and who appears new and is interested in new things everytime."

"I salute that Krishna, the lad, who is always happy and shines like the sun, who is the darling of all gopas, who is the Bliss of all the hearts. I salute that Krishna who is the leader of all gopa lads, who plays divine music with His flute, who grants happiness and whose glances are like defenceless arrows that has no match".

"I salute Him who swallowed the fire in the garden of forest of Vraja land, and who was in the mind of all gopis. I salute Him who is with the Goddess of wealth and who gave salvation to Gajendra and who is surrounded by divine glow and shines in all directions".

"Wherever I live and exist I should be immersed in your stotras continuously so that I am blessed with your grace. That great man who sings these verses of prayer would be born with devotion to Lord Krishna in all His births".

Lalita Pancharatnam

This is a shloka on Goddess Lalita with five verses. The sixth stanza is about the good effects of singing this prayer with devotion. Goddess Lalita is like a boat that helps one to cross the ocean of life. She is the power behind Lord Shiva. She is the Goddess who slays arrogance. She is known through Vedas and Upanishads. She is the auspicious form of mercy. She is the cause of creation, maintanance and dissolution. She is the Goddess of the Universe. She is beyond the comprehension of mind and words. She is the mother of the world, Goddess of words and languages. Shankara says that those who read this Shloka would be blessed with knowledge, riches, and endless fame by the blessings and grace of Goddess Lalita.

"I meditate this morning on the lotus face of Lalita, Whose lips are deep red in colour, whose nose shines like pearl, who has long eyes extending to her ears, has ear drops made of very precious gems, who has a very pleasant smile and has a very pretty shining forehead".

"I pray that hand that is like a wishfulfilling creeper and that wears shining gem studded rings, golden bangles with precious stones, and who holds flowers and Goad in Her hands".

"I worship that Lotus feet of Lalita that blesses Her devotees. Her feet are like a boat to cross the ocean of life. Indra, the leader of the Devas, worships her. She sits in the Lotus posture, holds a lotus, goad and a flag and wheel in Her hands".

"I pray in the morning that Lalita, who is the power behind Lord Shiva, who is the Goddess and also slayer of arrogance, who is known by Vedas and Upanishads, who is pure and auspicious form of mercy, who is the cause of creation, upkeep and destruction, who is the Goddess of the Universe, and who is beyond the reach of words and mind".

"I repeat this morning the holy name of Lalita, who is the Goddess of passion and love, who sits on the Lotus, who is the greatest of all Goddesses, who is the consort of Lord Shiva, and who is the mother of the world, the Goddess of all languages and the Goddess of all the three cities".

"He who reads these five verses of prayer in the morning praising Mother Lalita would obtain luck, knowledge, riches, and, everlasting fame by the grace of Goddess Lalita".

Mantra Matruka Pushpa Malastavam

It is a prayer of garland of seventeen verses of *Mantra* to the divine mother. The first sixteen stanzas in this shloka explain the sixteen types of offerings worship and services, the Shodasa Upacharas that a devotee performs to his God. The last stanza describes the benefits, which a devotee would get by reciting these verses. She, the mother Goddess is worshipped as the protector of the entire world and its beings. She is the giver of all boons. Her form can be understood only from Upanishads says Shankara the devotee, the poet. Shankara says, that the one who offers this garland of verses and worship the Goddess daily during dawn, noon and dusk and bow before Her wholeheartedly would soon find the mother dancing in his mind. On His face Goddess Saraswati and Goddess Lakshmi would dance in his house always.

"I pray to your throne, mother, that is made of jewels of thought and is placed on the altar made of one thousand pillard precious stones, which is the garden of the precious Kadamba trees surrounded by Kalpaka trees, that is in the island of gems, that is in the middle of great tide of the ocean of nector that shines with its ever beating waves".

"I meditate on you who has a beautiful smile, who is located at the centre of the Chakra, which is the shining dress of Sun, Moon and fire God and who shines like the rising sun, who holds bow and arrow, goad and noose in Her hand, who has a pleasing smiling face, who wears red silk and who wears crescent decorated crown".

"You are the ocean of nector of mercy. With all my devotion I offer you a throne of jewels the legs of which are Lord Vishnu, Brahma, Rudra and Ishwara, the seating plank is Lord Shiva. I also offer pots of holy water for you to drink; holy rice mixed with saffron, sandal and rare gems and pure water for your inner purification and let all these contribute to your happiness".

"Oh my Devi, whom the sages meditate, and who protects the entire world with its beings and who has long broad eyes, holy water mixed with saffron, camphor, cow's milk, tender coconut water, and rose water, are kept ready for you with holy chants. So kindly take your holy bath".

"Oh, my Devi, whose form is the aim of the chants 'Hreem', I offer you with devotion in my mind, beautiful upper cloth with golden borders and with precious stones embedded in it and also red silk cloth with gems hanging from it and a triple holy thread of sacrifice woven with golden threads. Let all these contribute to your happiness".

"Oh my Devi, even swans are jealous of your beautiful gait. Kindly accept the beautiful shining chain of garlands, diamond armlets that resemble the ray of the Moon, bangles, anklets with jingling bells, hair crest that resembles the crescent moon, crown, noose, stud made of gems, rings and golden belt".

"The perfumed paste of camphor, and saffron sandal wood I offer you with great devotion, for you to apply on your body. I offer musk to apply Tilaka on your forehead, Gorochana to apply on your cheeks, holy black *kajal* to apply to your eyes, mixtures of musk to apply to your conch like neck and let all these contribute to your happiness".

"Oh Goddess, who is giver of boons, I have offered many pretty garlands made of lilies, jasmine, sweet smelling herbs, golden coloured lotus flowers, champaka flowers, sweet smelling pandanus flowers and so on with all my devotion in my heart. Let all these contribute to your happiness".

"Oh my mother, let me offer to you the perfumed *Dasanga* smoke, Gulgulu and ghee to add fragrance to your holy body, by which you arose the passion of Lord Shiva who burnt the God of Love and to add to the fragrance of your long black hair that appears as a string of bees that tied the heart of Lord Shiva and which became the play house of perfumes".

"Oh Goddess, who is the daughter of the mountain, I imagine your house the interior of which is decorated by gems, where the pillars are gem studded in which hang garlands with lights in the hands of various types of golden statues and where the lamps are lit with cow's ghee that increase the sparkle of the room. I seek your happiness".

"Oh, Goddess, who is pleased with the sound of 'Hreem', shining golden vessels cleaned by fire filled with *ghee*, and *Dal*, dishes made of leafy vegetables mixed with holy rice, mixed rice made of honey, sugar and curds, and milk rice are all kept. Thousands of Vada made of black gram *Dal* and several types of such are offered to you, Oh, Mother, please accept them".

"Oh, mother, Uma, Tamboola is kept in the gem studded plate full of betel nut of superior quality that shine with camphor light and also with betel leaves that are as thin as the Pandanus flower petals, lime prepared from the pearl oyster that adds fragrance to your face is kept on the eastern side to contribute to your happiness"

"Several beautiful damsels who are dancing to the pleasant music with their Lotus like feet according to the beats of the drum and melodious singing, accompanied by chanting of Mantras carry camphour lamps that are decorated with gems in clean plates. They are arranged very beautifully in a pictorial design to offer worship of lights to you. Please accept them oh, Mother".

"Goddess Lakshmi Herself is holding a white umbrella made of pearls for you, Indrani, the wife of Indra and Rathi, the wife of God of Love, fan you from both sides with white fans, Goddess Saraswati is playing on *veena* to give you melodious music and the pretty Devathas are dancing with elegant movements of their body and mind for producing nine different emotions. Oh mother, please enjoy them all".

"Oh Goddess Ambika, who should me meditated with the three *Mantras* starting from 'Hreem' and whose form can only be understood from the Upanishads, and by the one who is an expert in composing songs praising you, let all my conversations be prayers to you, let all my walks and travel be perambulators around you and all my lying down be salutations to you"

"The one who offers these items of worship to the daughter of the mountains, using this prayer of garland of Mantras, daily during morning, noon and dusk and salute Her with his entire mind would soon find that in his mind Goddess Parvati would dance and on his face Goddess Saraswati would dance and in his house Goddess Lakshmi, the daughter of the ocean and who brings all good would dance".

"Let these words which are like ornaments to the lotus feet of mother that drips with honey woven by me as a garland of mantras to the mother make the bee like poets full of joy".

Meenaksi Pancha Ratna Stotram

This is a hymn of five verses on Goddess Meenakshi, who is Parvati, the consort of Lord Shiva.

"I always salute Meenakshi, who is the embodiment of mercy, who shines like innumerable rising suns, whose crown is shining, whose lips are red like that of the Bimba fruit, who has sparkling teeth, who dresses in reddish silk, whose feet is worshipped by Lord Vishnu, Lord Brahma and Indra, the king of the devas, who is the better half of Lord Shiva and who is the personification of the sacred eternal truth".

"I always salute Meenakshi, who is the embodiment of mercy, whose crown is made of rows of shining pearls, whose face is like that of the shining full moon, whose tinkling anklets are made of precious gems, who, like a fully blossomed lotus shines, who blesses and grants the wishes of all Her devotees, who is the daughter of Himavan and who is being assisted by Goddess Lakshmi and Saraswathi".

"I always salute Meenakshi, who is the embodiment of all mercy, who is Vidya, the sacred knowledge, who occupies the left half of Lord Shiva, who shines with 'HREEM', the sacred sound, who occupies the central place in the holy Sri Chakra, who presides over the court of Lord Shiva, who is the mother of Lord Ganesha and Lord Subramanya and who enchant the whole universe".

"I always salute Meenakshi, who is the embodiment of all mercy, who is the consort of Lord Sundaresha, who is the remover of all fears, who is the bestower of all knowledge, who is the purest, who is dark, whose feet is being worshipped with lotus flowers, who is Lord Narayana's sister, who is fond of the music from veena, drum and flute and who is the Goddess of all the varied aspects of the universe".

"I always salute Meenakshi, who is the embodiment of all mercy, who resides in the hearts of yogis and saints, who grants different types of wealth and occult powers, whose feet are being worshipped with different kinds of flowers, who is worshipped by Lord Vishnu, who is the sound of the holy spirit that is all pervading, who is the greatest and who is the source and meaning of the varied philosophies".

Pandurangashtakam

These eight verses praise the virtues of the deity of Pandaripur in Maharashtra. The nineth verse tells about the good effects of reciting this prayer. It is believed that there was a merchant by name Pundarika here. He never looked after his old parents. Instead he drove them away as he thought that they were a stumbling block to him. The old couple set out to Varanasi on foot along with a group of pilgrims. Afterwards Pundarika also proceeded to Varanasi on a horse drawn carriage. On the way although he saw his parents, he ignored them. On his way he met Rohit Das, who was very poor. He was a dutiful son who was taking care of his parents extremely well. That night Pundarika saw three ugly women-taking baths in the pond near the place where Rohit Das was staying. When they rose up from the pond they looked divine and beautiful. Pundarika learnt from them that they were the holy rivers Ganga, Yamuna, and Godavari who had to bear loads of sins committed by people who bathed in them. They got cleansed up by coming to the place near the hermitage of Rohit Das. This knowledge changed Pundarika completely. He repented for all his wrong doings towards his parents. Thereafter as a penance he spent the rest of his life in looking after his parents. Once, Lord Vishnu visited his place in the guise of a cowhered. But Pundarika was so busy in caring his parents that he asked the Cowhered to wait until he completed his work. He gave a brick to Lord Vishnu who was in the guise of a cowhered to stand until he completed his work. This act pleased Lord Vishnu and He decided to stay there at Pandaripur as Vittala that is brick. These verses are worship to Lord Vishnu, Panduranga, who is the absolute Brahman, the source of immense happiness, who stays as Yogi in the banks of river Bheema along with the great seers and who stood on bricks to fulfill the boon to Pundarika. By keeping His two hands on His waist, he teaches that this worldly life is only kneedeep. He is the protector of the world, self-born, supreme light, God of Gods and removes problems of those who take refuge in Him. Shankara says, he who reads this Shloka daily with devotion would cross the ocean of life easily, and would attain Vaikunta, the abode of Lord Vishnu in the end.

> "I worship that Panduranga who is the supreme Brahman, who is the source of unlimited happiness, who resides on the bank of Bheema River along with great rishis in yogic posture for fulfilling the boon to Pundarika".
>
> "I worship that Panduranga who is the supreme Brahman whose feet are placed on bricks, dressed as lightning, having the colour of blackish blue of clouds, in whom resides Lakshmi and who is handsome and is the shining at the core of the beings".
>
> "I pray to that Panduranga who is the supreme Brahman, He, by keeping His two hands on His waist explains to us that all worldly pleasures are only knee deep. He created the lotus on His navel for the creator Brahma to live"
>
> "I pray to that Panduranga who is the supreme Brahman who has the Kausthuba gem around His neck, who wears the most beautiful armlets, who is the source of all prosperity, who is calm, peaceful and who safeguards the universe".
>
> "I pray to that Panduranga who is the Supreme Brahman, who is bright like the autumn moon, who has a charming smile, whose cheeks are covered by His shining ear drops, whose red lips resemble the hibiscus flower and the bimba fruit and who has lotus like eyes".

"I pray to that Panduranga, who is the supreme Brahman, whose crown illuminates all directions, whom the Devas worship with very valuable gems, whose form has three bend postures and who wears garland and peacock feathers".

"I pray to that Panduranga who is the supreme Brahman, who is all pervading and plays flute, who is the destroyer of all bad ones, who wears the dress of a cowhered just for play and who with His lotus like smile brings bliss to the herd of cows".

"I pray to that Panduranga, who is the supreme Brahman, who has no origin, who is everything to the soul of Rukmini His consort, who is supreme splenldour, who is the only refuge for salvation, who is always in the fourth state of transcendence, who is always contented, who is the supreme God and who solves the problems of miseries of His devotees".

"He who reads this prayer to Panduranga daily with devotion and concentration, would cross the ocean of life with the least effort and finally would attain Vaikuntha, the abode of Vishnu".

Rama Bhujangam

This is a prayer of twenty-eight verses to Shree Rama for His grace. The twenty-nineth verse tells about the blessings of reciting these verses. These verses are composed in the Bhujanga meter. Shree Rama is described in this shloka as pure, the eternal truth, personification of ultimate happiness, the greatest above all characters, whole and within Himself, the ultimate pleasure, the way to salvation, the way to cross the ocean of life, who is formless, complete Bliss, the greatest and supreme God who removes fears, who is God of the Vedas, the primeval man, father of the Universe as well as the eye of the Universe, and destroyer of sorrows of life. In the end Shankara says, those who worship Him would get what they desire at the end and will not face death. He is the eternal Bliss, the greatest of the Devas, eternal happiness beyond mind and words, the object of salvation, and the sign of eternal truth.

"I worship that Rama, who is pure, eternal, truth, personification of ultimate Bliss, who is the greatest of all characters, who is whole, who is the ultimate, and also the ultimate wealth and pleasure and the way for Himself".

"I worship that Rama who is the king of this earth, always peaceful and alone who is the path to cross the ocean of life to attain *Mukti* or liberation, who is the personification of pleasure, who is formless, who is revered, who is the supreme goal, and God of all knowledge, Lord of Devas, Lord of the ultimate, God of all beings and who has no Lord superior to Him".

"Salutations to you many a time, to that eternal, great form of Taraka Brahma *Mantra* that Lord Shiva uttered in the ear at Kashi at the time of death –Rama, Rama, Rama".

"I always bow again and again that Rama who occupies the throne embedded with jewels that is placed below the wish fulfilling tree, seated there in a pleasant style, the face radiating the lutre of innumerable Suns and who is always served by His consort Sita and brother Lakshmana".

"I worship that Ramachandra whose lotus like feet is adorned by the jingling anklets, who dresses in red silk that is tied by a golden belt, who wears flower garland that attracts bees and also garlands that are made of valuable gems and Kausthubha".

"I worship that Ramachandra whose lips are reddish and reminds the beautiful moon, who has the splendour of innumerable suns and moons, whose feet is worshipped by the light of billion studded gems of crowns of Brahma and Rudra because they bend and worship His feet".

"I always worship that Ramachandra who is in the midst of Hanuman and others who are worshipping Him, who teaches the eternal knowledge through His hand *Mudras* or symbols. I cannot and do not think of any other God except you".

"When Lord Yama, the Lord of death comes before me and frightens me with his soldiers, then please appear before me with your Kodanda bow that would destroy all fears and dangers from me".

"Kindly be pleased, oh, Ramachandra, come and reside in the temple of my mind along with Bharata, Lakshmana and Sita and protect this devotee with your power".

"Kindly be pleased with me, oh, Ramachandra, who is in the midst of great devotees, great monkey kings and other kings and chieftains. I bow to you, Oh, Lord, kindly be pleased with me and bless me again and again with your light".

"You are the only God to me, the eternal fact; I acknowledge only your power because all the five elements or the *pancha Bhhoothas* have got originated from you only".

"I bow to Him, who is eternal happiness, God Rama, the consort of Janaki who is bearing Lotus on His belly."

"I bow to Him, who loves His devotees and who can be seen only by good Karmas. I bow to that God of the Vedas and the primeval man, salutations to you, who is the handsome consort of Sita".

"Salutations to You, who creates, maintains, uses and destroys, rules over and is the eye and who wins over all and is the father and mother of the Universe".

"Salutations to You, who is an expert in maintaining and controlling the entire Universe, Oh, my Lord, my mind is engaged in serving Your feet with the aim of knowing the eternal, real truth".

"Even the stone that was Ahalya got her life because of the mere touch of the dust of your feet, when that is the case then; it is not at all strange that by serving and worshipping you, the humans get permanent salvation".

"Those beings who remember your strange, holy story and those who chant your name that destroys the sorrows of life, would achieve what they desire and in the end go beyond death".

"That person who understands that you are the greatest of all Devas with a form, that is eternal happiness, that is beyond mind and words, and who is Rama, the object of *Mukti* and those who have surrendered themselves to you alone are the blessed".

"My Lord Ramachandra, the greatest, very famous everywhere, the killer of His enemies, has indescribable powers because even as a young boy you broke the Holy bow of Lord Shiva".

"Who else other than you could kill Ravana, the ten headed demon King and his sons and his friends in his own place of Lanka that is surrounded by sea"?

"Always praying Rama, Rama, drinking the necter of His name that is always beautiful and is an ocean of real bliss, and saluting you is Hanuman with a smiling face- To Him I pray always".

"I who always chant Rama, drinking the necter of His name am never afraid of death because of Rama, Your continuous grace".

"Only you Rama, who is with His consort Sita, who has the Kodanda as His ornament, who is always served by Lakshmana, and who is known for His heroism, who is Yama, the God of death to Ravana, the demon king of Lanka and who at the same time is the friend of Sugreeva, the king of monkeys, only you are needed for us".

"Only you are needed for us, Oh, Rama, who sits on the hero's throne, who is the eternal truth, exhibiting eternal principles to His devotee Hanuman and other devotees, and who sits on the roots of Mandhara tree wearing the garland of Mandhara flowers"

"Only you are required, Oh, Rama, who got wild with the ocean, who is respected and saluted by all, who traveled with friends, who is always with a smile, who lived in the Dandakarunya forest and who taught the supreme knowledge".

"Oh, God, you are the kith and kin of the whole world. I spend all my time chanting the name of Lord Hari, who is the consort of Sita, and who is the enemy of Ravana, and who killed Khara and Mura and Asuras and who is the eternal truth. Kindly give me your graceful looks".

"My saltations to Him, who has been worshipped by Lakshmana, the great son of Sumitra, by Bharatha, the son of Kaikeyi, and the friend, Sugreeva the King of monkeys, Oh, Ramachandra".

"Shower your grace, Oh, my Lord, Ramachandra, who is very famous, who is death to His enemies and who is kind to His devotees".

"He who reads or always thinks in his mind daily, this Bhujanga prayer, that is the summary of Vedas on Lord Ramachandra, would attain Ramachandra and would be blessed".

Ranganathashtakam

These nine verses of prayer are in praise of Lord Ranganatha who resides in Shree Rangam in Tamil Nadu. The tenth verse is about the good effects of reciting this prayer. According to one belief, the first stanza of the poem was not composed by Shankara but by the great Vaishnavite saint Parasa Bhatta. It is said that Brahma first worshiped this idol of Shree Ranganatha. Later it was given to king Raghu who belonged to the Ikshvaku dynasty, to be worshipped in his capital Ayodhya. After wards Shree Rama who was a descendent of the Ikshvaku dynasty worshiped this. At the request of Vibheeshana, Rama gave this idol to Vibheeshana, the brother of King Ravana whom Shree Rama killed in the war, on condition that he should not place the idol anywhere during his journey to Sri Lanka. But it so happened, that Vibheeshana had to place this idol in Shree Rangam on his way to Lanka and he could not take out the idol later. It is believed that this Deity that faces the south towards Sri Lanka to bless Vibheeshana and that Vibheeshana visits once in every twelve years to worship Shree Ranganatha in this place. Shankara prays to Ranganatha, who is considered as the epitome of happiness, who is true knowledge and who is the abode of the Universe. Shankara also says that the wishes of those who read these verses every morning would be fulfilled and finally he would attain Liberation.

> "I salute that Lord Ranganada who resides in yogic pose, on the bed of king of snake *Adisesha*, below the *Vimana* or dome in the sanctum, that resembles the lotus bud, who is in the midst of seven ramparts and the Kaveri river, with His right hand near the crown and His lotus like merciful left hand pointing at His feet taking care of all of us".
>
> "Let my mind always think about Ranganada, whose form is an epitome of happiness, and who is true knowledge as described in the Vedas and is like that of the pleasant moon".
>
> "Let my mind be always fixed on that Ranganada, who resides on the bank of river Kaveri, who is merciful, who sits below the Mandhara tree, who plays in a pretty and speedy manner and who destroys all demons by His worldly sport".
>
> Let my mind always think of Ranganada, who resides in Shree Ranga, who is the abode of Goddess Lakshmi and the universe, who is the Lotus in the heart, who is the abode of mercy and resides where good conduct is present".

"Let my mind think of Him who is saluted in Shree Rangam and worshipped by the Lord of the Devas and Gods like Brahma and also by the entire universe and sages like Vyasa, Sanaka, and others as Mukunda".

"Let my mind always think of Him, who is the Lord of Shree Ranga, who is the King of the Gods like Brahma, the holy bird Garuda of *Vaikunta*, of Devas, and the entire universe".

"Let my mind think of Him who protects the city of Shree Rangam, whose power is never failing, who is in perfect yoga state and reclines on the ocean, who protects Goddess Lakshmi and in whom the whole world resides".

"Let my mind think of Him who sleeps in the city of Shree Rangam like a pretty picture, on the king of serpents, on the lap of Nanda, on the lap of Lakshmi, on the ocean of milk and on the *banyan* leaf"

"He who dies in this city of Shree Rangam never has birth again, as Ranganada has the Chakra in His hand, the Garuda as his vehicle, the serpent as His bed, and His feet drenched by the waters of the sacred Ganga".

"Any one who reads these verses of prayer on Lord Ranganada in the early morning would get all his wishes fulfilled and finally attain salvation".

Shanmuga Stotram

These eight verses are in praise of the six-faced Shanmuga who is residing in Tiruchendur in Tamil Nadu. It is said that the evil chants of Abhinav Gupta affected Adi Shankara. It is said that Shankara composed these verses at that time to get rid of all the evil effects of the chant. It describes the glory of Lord Subramanya, who is the son of Lord Shiva, who destroys all diseases, sorrows and sins, who killed the demon Tarakasura, who is as cool as the moon, and who is worshipped by all the Devas, Yakshas, Siddhas, Kinnaras and so on.

"I bow down to that six faced one who resides on the seashore, and in the hearts of sages like Narada, who rides a peacock, who is the son of Lord Shiva, who destroys diseases, sorrow and sins of His devotees".

"I bow down before that six faced one who is the killer of Taraka and worshipped by Indra and the other Devas, who decorates Himself with sandal paste and is as cool as the moon, who is our source and who is worshipped by Indra, Yakshas, Siddhas and Kinnaras".

" I bow down before that six faced one who is decorated with garlands of flowers like Champaka and Jasmine, whose heads are adorned by six holy crowns and six garlands and rare ear drops, who is anointed by a mixture of saffron and sandal paste".

"I bow down to that six faced one who has eight elephants that protect the world, whose weapon is spear, who is praised by Lord Vishnu, Indra, and Lord Brahma and who helps devotees to fulfill their wants and wishes".

"I bow down to that six faced one who joined Veerabahu with innumerable soldiers and gave salvation to Soorapadma who fought with His countless soldiers and provided permanent solace to Indra and the other Devas."

"I bow down to that six faced one who fulfilled the wishes of Indra who was the enemy of the demon Jamba, who gave the essence of all Dharmas to sage Agasthya who was born from a pot, and who protected me everyday, from all miseries of the ocean of life".

"I bow down to that six faced one who has lotus like face that is like innumerable moons, who grants all that they desire to those who explain this holy story, who is the one who has a strong body with a golden colour and who punishes all cruel people".

"I bow down to that six faced one who destroys the countless sins of many previous births, who makes available the blessings of good deeds and charity done in previous births, who destroys all the enemies and who is the son-in-law of Indra".

Shiva Manasa Pooja

It is a mental worship to Lord Shiva in seven verses. Lord Shiva is requested here to accept all the offerings and worship that are at the portals of mind and shower His blessings. Shankara says "My soul is your temple, my activities your attendants, my body your home, my acts your worship, my act of sleep the meditation, and the words the prayers. In short everything that I say and do is your form of worship". Finally Shankara asks the Lord to pardon him for all those acts committed by hands, by action, by body, by hearing, by sight, by mind, whether they are proper or improper.

"I worship that Linga that stays in me as my soul, residing in the lotus of my heart, bathed in the water of my devotion and duly worshipped by the lotus of my meditation to avoid another birth".

"I offer you my imaginary throne made of precious jewels, Abhishekam with water from the melted snow of the Himalayas, silk cloth to wear, I adorn you with many precious jewels, musk and sandal paste, Bilwa leaves and Champaka flowers, and the holy light. But all these I offer mentally, oh, my God, who is merciful, the Lord of all beings. Kindly accept my offerings and bless me".

"I offer you sweet rice in golden bowl that is inscribed with nine jewels, five kinds of food that is made out of milk and curd, bananas, vegetables, sweet water scented with camphor, and betel leaves, All these I have prepared mentally with devotion. Oh, God, please accept them".

"I offer you a beautiful dias, decorated fans, shining mirror, instruments like Veena, Drums, Mrudanga, big drum, along with song and dance. I offer my full prostration and several prayers. All these I offer to you mentally oh, my Lord, Kindly accept all these mental offerings".

"My soul is your temple, my activities are your attendants, my body is your abode, my acts that please my senses are a form of worship to you, my sleep is meditation upon you, my walks are your perambulations, and whatever I utter are prayers to you, whatever I say and do are the different forms of worship to you".

"Oh, God, kindly pardon all my acts committed by me by hands, by action, by body, by hearing, by sight, or by mind which may be proper or improper. Oh, ocean of mercy, hail to you, you are the most benevolent and the greatest of all Gods".

"My mother is Goddess Parvathy, my father is Lord Shiva, my friends are Shiva's devotees and my native place is all the three worlds".

Shiva Panchakshari Stotra

This stotra of five verses is about the Panchakshari Mantra of Lord Shiva-'NAMASHIVAYA'. Each verse starts with the letter NA, MA, SHI, VA, YA. The sixth verse tells about the good effects of uttering this *mantra*.

"My salutations to Lord Shiva, who wears the garland of snakes, who has three eyes, who smears His body with ashes, who is the great Lord, who is eternal and pure, who has as His garment the directions, and whose *mantra* starts with the letter 'NA'.

"My salutation to Lord Shiva, who is worshipped by giving Him Abhishekam or bath with the sacred waters from the Mandakini River that is, Ganga, and with sandal paste. He is the Lord of Nandi, the bull that is His vehicle, He is the Lord of all ugly looking evil spirits and ghosts, He is the great Lord, who is worshipped with the chanting of *Mantras* and with flowers and whose *Mantra* has the second letter 'MA'.

"My salutations to Lord Shiva, who is the embodiment of all auspiciousness, who is like a sun to His consort Gauri who is like a Lotus, who destroyed the Yaga performed by Daksha Prajapati, and who is Neelakhanta or whose throat is blue, whose flag has the emblem of the bull, Nandi, that is His vehicle, and whose Mantra has the third letter 'SI'.

"My salutations to Lord Shiva whose form as Shiva Linga is being worshipped by great sages like Vasishta, Agasthya, Gautama, and so on and Indra, the Lord of the devas, and whose eyes are the sun, moon, and fire and whose Mantra has the fourth letter 'VA'".

"My salutations to Lord Shiva, whose form is also that of a Yaksha, whose hair is matted, who holds the Pinaka bow in His hand, who is the primeval God and brilliant, who is naked or Digambara and whose *Mantra* has the last letter 'YA'."

"The one who chants this sacred five syllabled Mantra namely, 'NAMASHIVAYA', in front of Shiv Lingh finally would reach Shiva and would attain bliss."

Shivashtakam

It is a prayer on Shiva in eight verses. The nineth verse tells about the good results of reciting this prayer on Lord Shiva. Lord

Shiva here is addressed as the real cause of all causes and His appearance is described in these verses in a beautiful manner.

"I salute that Shiva who is the source of all causes, who has eyes that are reddish brown and shine like light, whose garlands and ear drops are made of the king of snakes, and who alone is capable of granting boons to Lord Brahma and Lord Vishnu".

"I salute that Shiva, whose head shines with the ornaments like the clear moon and snake, whose eyes are kissed by His consort, whose residence is the peak of Kailash and Mahendra Mountains and who destroys all the sorrows of all the beings of all the three worlds".

"I salute that Shiva whose neck is blue like that of the colour of the Lotus, whose earrings are made of Padmaraga gem, who rides on a bull, whose body has the fragrance of Aloe and Sandal paste that are applied, who smears Himself with ash all over His body, and wears fully blossomed Lotus flowers as garland".

"I salute that Shiva who is worshipped by the Gods of all the three worlds, whose hair is matted and is reddish brown, whose appearance is fierce and fearful because of His pointed teeth and who looks handsome by wearing the skin of the tiger".

"I salute that Shiva who is the personification of *Yoga* and is worshipped by Yogis, and who destroyed the sacrifice performed by Daksha Prajapati, who killed the great demon Tripurasura and who also cut off the fifth head of Lord Brahma because he was proud".

"I salute that Shiva who wears the tiger's skin, whose function is destroying and recreating the world, who takes care of the demons as well as the yogis, and who is worshipped by sages, serpents, planets and Bhootha Ganas".

"I salute that Shiva who is as white as the cow's milk, who applies ash all over His body but is strikingly handsome, who is the refuge of all pious beings who are hermits in the forests, and who sees the side glance of His consort Gauri with His half closed eyes".

"I salute that Shiva who protects the bull that worships Him, to whom the sun, moon, the God of rain and the God of fire bow down, who lives in the place filled with smoke of the fire of sacrifices and who is praised by sages who are well versed in *Rig* and *Sama Veda*".

"He who reads these eight verses on Lord Shiva, in front of Lord Shiva's temple would reach Kailash that is the abode of Lord Shiva and would be happy along with Lord Shiva".

Subramanya Bhujangam

This is a shloka of 32 verses on Lord Subramanya who resides in Tiruchendur. Shankara composed this hymn in *Bhujanga* meter. The 33rd verse is about the good effects of reciting this prayer. It is said, that when Adi Shankara meditated upon Lord Subramanya of Tiruchendur, he saw a light shining within the core of his heart and he composed this song. The first stanza is a prayer to Lord Ganesha, the elder brother of Lord Subramanya.

"Though He appears like a child, He can crush the mountains of obstacles. Though He has the face of an elephant, even His own father, Lord Shiva, honours him. Lord Brahma, Indra and other Devas approach Him to fulfill their wishes. He is Ganesha, who possesses vast glory. May He bless me with all types of prosperity".

"I know nothing, the words or its meanings, prose or verse, but in my heart I can see the effulgence of the six faced one and because of this I am able to compose shlokas and words flow from me instantaneously".

"I pray to that protector of the Universe who is seated on the peacock, who is the essence of the *Mahavakyas* of the Upanishads, who possess an attractive body, who resides in the heart of great sages, who is the God of all Gods, who is the essence of the four Vedas and who is the son of Lord Shiva".

"Oh, Lord Subramanya who is the son of the pure Para Shakti who is the mother of the cosmos, who resides in Tiruchendur near the seashore as though telling His devotees who take refuge in Him that they can easily cross the ocean of life, the eternal cycle of birth and death and safely reach the other end of the shore, the very source".

"Just as the waves of the sea that hit the sea shore become weakened and disappear finally, likewise, the waves of miseries of your devotees get destroyed like dust when they take refuge in you, Oh, Lord Guha, that is, the one who always resides in the cave of the heart of beings".

"You, who live on the Sandal mountain look as though you are telling that 'he who climbes my mountain abode climb the greatest mountain'- Let that one protect me always".

"That Lord who resides in the cave of the heart, who destroys all sins on the bank of the ocean, who resides on the sandal mountain for protecting the sages who are His devotees and who is self illuminating, and who destroys all miseries of beings, He is the refuge".

"I continuously worship that Lord of the Devas who was brought up by the Karthika maidens, who fulfills all desires of people, who is engulfed by flowers while sitting on His throne made of gems and rubies in His residence made out of gold and who shines like innumerable suns".

"My mind is like a bee and it is full of sorrows of life that come around your lotus feet that are pretty and red in colour, adorned by anklets that are very beautiful and steal my imagination".

"Oh, Skanda, I meditate upon that waist of yours that is adorned by the sacred golden cloth, with belt of tingling bells that is shining".

"I bow to you, oh, slayer of Tharaka, whose chest get the saffron colour by the embrace of the hunter's daughter, Valli. For your devotees this marks your love to them".

"Oh, Lord Subramanya, I meditate upon your knee long arms that are longer than the trunk of the elephant that punished Lord Brahma and that carried the universe in a playful manner, that gave a shudder of death to your enemies, that killed many demons, that are shining and capable of protecting this entire world".

"Your six faces are comparable to the six full moons that are without blemish and shine simultaneously always".

"Oh, son of Lord Shiva, your six lotus like face are shining like a group of swans with captivating smiles and side glances and nector flow from your lips".

"Oh, Lord, you will not lose anything by showering small little side glances on me with your twelve broad eyes that are long and extend up to your ears and that also shower the nector of mercy".

"You are the Lord of the universe. I salute all the six shining heads with crowns that are kissed by Lord Shiva uttering repeatedly for six times that His child should be immortal".

"Oh, Lord, who is the son of God who destroyed Tripura, whose garlands are studded with rubies and gems, who has beautiful cheeks that are touched by the ear studs, whose waist is wrapped by yellow silk and who holds the spear in His hand. Oh, Lord, kindly appear before me".

"My salutations to child Subramanya, who jumps from the lap of Uma, His mother, to the extended arm of His father, Lord Shiva who took His son in His hands".

"Oh, Kumara, you are the son of the Lord of the Universe, you dweli in the core of my heart, you are the chief of the army of devas, you hold the holy spear, you ride on the peacock, you are the beloved of the daughter of the hunter, and you destroy the sins of His devotees. You, who are the enemy of Tharakasura, kindly, protect me always".

"When I calm down all my senses, intelligence and cannot move, when my throat is filled with phlegm, when my body shiver with fear, when my soul is on the verge of leaving my body, without any one to give me a helping hand, Oh, my Lord, please come to me running, Oh, Lord, who is in the cave of my heart, I want your presence at that moment".

"When the terrifying messengers of Yama, the God of death come to take me, kindly come to me fast with your spear, riding on your peacock chariot, to console me and to be my support".

"I prostrate before you and salute you and pray to you again and again, because at that moment of death, I may not have the strength to utter any prayer, Oh, ocean of mercy, do not be indifferent to me at that moment of my death".

"You vanquished Soora Padma, who was the monarch of all the worlds, you killed the demon Taraka and the lion faced *asura*, but you are indifferent about the one, that is, the misery in my mind. Oh, Lord. What should I do and where shall I go for refuge, protection and help?"

"I am always in the midst of sorrows, but I know you are the friend of all those who have none for them. I do not wish to approach any other God, Oh, son of Goddess Uma, destroy all my sorrows that bother me and interfere in my meditation to you".

"Serious sicknesses like epilepsy, leprosy, tuberculosis, consumption, diabetes, fever, madness, veneral diseases and the troubles from all evil spirits all vanish in no time when they see your holy ash on the leaf, Oh, destroyer of Taraka".

"Let me be blessed with the sight of the holy form of Skanda, let my heart fill with His holy stories, let my mouth tell His great heroic stories, let my hands be engaged in His service, let my body be His servant and let all my actions be devoted to my God Skanda".

"For great sages and devotees there are Gods ready to fulfill their wishes. But to me who am downtrodden, there is only Lord Subramanya, who fulfills my wishes".

"Let all my kith and kin and my pets all bow, worship and sing your praise and meditate on you always, Oh my God, Kumara".

"Oh, God who crushed the Krouncha Mountain, kindly crush and kill all those animals, birds, insects and diseases that harm my body".

"Oh God, who is the Lord of the army of devas- as a father pardons the mistakes of his son, you, as father, pardon all my mistakes of your child, that is myself".

"Salutations to everything that are yours, the peacock, holy spear, animals like sheep, rooster, ocean, and the temple by the seashore at Tiruchendur. Oh, Skanda, I offer my Salutations to you, again and again".

"Victory to you, oh, the one, who is the source of bliss, who is the ever shining light, lasting fame, personification of happiness, ocean of bliss, and friend of all beings. Hail to you, who is the son of Lord Shiva who grants *Mukti*".

"He who worships daily that, that resides in the core of the heart, with intense devotion, and with this prayer composed in *Bhujanga* meter, would be blessed with good children, wife, prosperity, longevity, and would also attain the everlasting bliss that is Skanda".

Tripura Sundari Ashtakam

This is a shloka of eight verses on the beauty of the three world's Tripura Sundari, the prettiest woman in all the three worlds that is one of the names of Goddess Parvati. It also means the consort of Lord Shiva, the Tripura that is Lord Brahma, Lord Vishnu and Lord Shiva all in one who dwells in the Kadamba forest.

> "I bow to Her who is the charm of Tripura, who roams in the Kadamba forest, who looks like a collection of dark clouds who satisfies the spiritual hunger of sages, who has a mountain like hip, who is served by heavenly maidens, whose eyes are like the lotus flower, who is like rich black cloud and who belongs to the family of Lord Shiva, the three eyed one".
>
> "I bow to Her, who is the charm of Tripura, who lives in the Kadamba forest, who holds in Her hands the holy golden *veena*, who wears a garment embedded with collection of rare gems, whose nector like face shines, whose mercy grants prosperity, who wanders every where and who belongs to the family of Lord Shiva, who is the three eyed one".
>
> "I bow to Her, who is the beauty of Tripura, who lives in the Kadamba forest, whose garland beautifies the mountain like bosom, who showers never ending mercy, whose cheeks are red like wine, who can sing divine music, and who belongs to the family of Lord Shiva who is the three eyed one".
>
> "I bow to Her, who is the charm of Tripura, who resides in the middle of Kadamba forest, who is seated near the golden planet, who resides in the six lotus flowers, who enlightens the sages like lightening, who is more beautiful than the just opened flower of Hibiscus, who has crest jewel of moon and who belongs to the family of Lord Shiva who is the three eyed one".
>
> "I bow to Her, who is the charm of Tripura, who keeps *veena* over Her bosom, whose residence is a lotus flower, who punishes the evil minded ones, who has eyes that are intoxicated and hence red, who attracts Lord Shiva, and who is the daughter of Matanga rishi, and has a sweet voice".
>
> "I bow to Her, who is the charm of Tripura, who holds the first flower of Manmada, the God of love, who wears blue dress with red dots on it, who holds in Her hand a bowl containing wine, whose eyes are unsteady due to intoxication, whose breasts elevate Her chest, whose hair is partitioned, who is black beauty and who belongs to the family of Lord Shiva, who is the three eyed one".

"I pray to that Goddess Ambika, who applies saffron all over Her body, and Musk on Her hair, whose smile is quite charming, who captures all beings with Her bows and arrows, who wears red garland and valuable ornaments, and whose colour is that of red Hibiscus flower".

"I pray to that Goddess Ambika who is the celestial mother, whose servants are heavenly maidens, who rules over Sri Pura, whose hair is tied by the celestial maidens, whose body is anointed by sandal paste by Goddess Saraswati the consort of Lord Brahma, and who is decorated with gems by Goddess Lakshmi who is the consort of Lord Vishnu".

Uma Maheshwara Stotra

This is a shloka of twelve verses on Lord Shiva and His consort Goddess Parvati, the Lord and the lady of the entire Universe and who create, maintain and destroy the Universe. The thirteenth verse tells about the good effects of this prayer.

"My salutations to you, Lord Shiva and His consort Goddess Parvati again and again, who always look very youthful, who are always together, and one of whom is the daughter of the mountain, and the other one's symbol is the bull".

"My salutations to Lord Shiva and His consort Goddess Parvati, again and again, whose love making is a festival, who grants boons to devotees, whose feet is worshipped by Lord Vishnu".

"My salutations again and again to Lord Shiva and His consort Goddess Parvati, who ride on the divine bull, who are worshipped by Gods like Lord Vishnu, Brahma and Indra, whose bodies are smeared with ash and anointed by sandal paste".

"My salutations to Lord Shiva and His consort Goddess Parvati, again and again, who are the God and Goddess of the universe, who always are victorious, who are worshipped by devas and their chief Indra".

"My salutations to Lord Shiva and His consort Goddess Parvati again and again, who are the very medicines that cure all ills, who revel on hearing the Panchakshari Mantra, 'Om Namashivaya' being repeated, who are the three Gods in one, the creator, maintainer and the destroyer, all in one".

"My salutations to Lord Shiva and His consort Goddess Parvati again and again, who are very beautiful, and who are always interested in the devotion of their devotees and the welfare of the world".

"My salutations to Lord Shiva and His consort Goddess Parvati again and again, who destroy the evil effects of Kaliyuga, who is Ardha Nareeshwara, where one side is famished and the other is very pretty, and whose residence is mount Kailasa".

"My salutations to Lord Shiva and His consort Goddess Parvati again and again, who destroy all that ends in bad and who are the only ones with sharp intelligence in the entire world and whose memory is very remarkable".

"My salutations to Lord Shiva and His consort Goddess Parvati, again and again, who are the refuge of those who surrender themselves to Them, whose eyes are the sun, moon, and fire, and who have face like that of the full moon on the sky".

"My salutations to Lord Shiva and His consort Goddess Parvati, again and again, who attract all beings, who are devoid of old age, death, and other imperfections and worshipped by Lord Vishnu and Lord Brahma".

"My salutations to Lord Shiva and His consort Goddess Parvati, again and again, who are the only solace during difficult moments, whose garlands are made out of Bilwa leaves and Jasmine flowers, and who are the embodiments of peace".

"My salutations to Lord Shiva and His consort Goddess Parvati, again and again, who protect one and all on earth, and whose objective is protecting the universe and who are worshipped by all asuras and devas".

"The devotees who recite these twelve stanzas of prayer to Lord Shiva and Goddess Parvati, in the morning, noon, and at twilight time, would be blessed with a life of hundred years with all luck and attain Kailash, the abode of Lord Shiva".

Vishnu Bhujanga Prayata Stotram

This is a prayer to Lord Vishnu in *Bhujanga* meter. It means moving like a snake. It has sixteen verses and the seventeeth verse is the *Phala stuthi* that tells about the effects of this stotra. Shankara wrote several slokas using this meter. It is said, that Shankara composed Shiva *Bhujanga Prayata Stotra* in praise of Lord Shiva when his mother was in deathbed for helping her attain salvation. But when Lord Shiva's attendants came to take her to heaven, she became terrified to see them. So Shankara composed another poem on Lord Vishnu to pacify her and the attendants of Lord Vishnu who did not have the fearful look as those of Lord Shiva's attendants could come and take her to heaven.

> "My salutations to that God who is beyond Brahman mentioned in the Vedas, who is the principle of life itself, who is clarity personified, who is eternal, who does not possess desire, form and is known through the Mantra 'AUM', who is beyond the three qualities, who cannot be understood easily, who is without parts and is therefore whole, and who is always in transcendental state or in Turiya".
>
> "My salutations to Him, who is told in the Vedas as the Trinity of Gods, namely, Brahma, Vishnu and Maheshwara, who is an embofdiment of purity, peace, and is patient, who has no beginning or end, whose limits cannot be measured by the concept of time".
>
> "He is the light of innumerable rising moons and suns that simultaneously appear on the sky, that the naked eye cannot see, who is beyond heat and cold, pretty looking as gold, and who is always blissful".
>
> "His nose and eyelids are very pretty, His forehead very broad, and beautiful, His hair curly with a crown on it, His eyes beautiful like the petals of the lotus flower, and His ornaments include the Hibiscus flowers".
>
> "His shining ear drops touch His beautiful shoulders. His lips while smiling are like that of the red Hibiscus flower that opens up beautifully and the bees get attracted to Him because of the Hibiscus garland that he wears, and His chest shines because of the garland of Kauthubha gem".

"The armlets that He wears is made of pretty gems, His four arms are decorated by golden bangles. His stomach is tied by yellow silken cloth and His two feet are prettier than the pretty Lotus".

"He appears to His devotees in this manner. The one who meditates upon this form of Him, with control of the five sense organs, which dispel darkness or ignorance easily, crosses the miserable ocean of life. I salute that form that removes all darkness".

"I salute that Lord Vishnu who is found in every household in all the three worlds, whose life is happy with His two wives, one of whom is Goddess Lakshmi who is beautiful and shines like gold with a slender waist and the other is Bhoomi Devi, who is black like the Dhoorva grass".

"After leaving all my kith and kin and friends, all possessions like land, wealth and servants, I have been traveling for long in search of you in my sorrow."

"Old age is having its toll upon me like a devil. It is destroying my blood, bones, flesh, and strength, Oh God, who is merciful to the downtrodden, how is that, you seem to be not bothered about me at all?"

"I am terribly afraid of death. When I struggle with phlegm, heavy breathing, pains in all joints of my body, kindly tell me what should I do?"

"Oh, the unlimited one, I am crying aloud, Hey, Govinda, He, Lord Vishnu, the destroyer of the asura Mura, Hey, Hari, Hey Ram, Hey Narayana, and I think about you alone in my heart with deep devotion. Kindly be pleased with me, oh, the merciful one".

"Hey the embodiment of mercy, Hey Hari, Hey, Keshava, who is the cause and source of everything, Hey Lord, of the universe, Hey Narayana, Hey, Vishnu, Hey the blissful one, I am calling you loudly and saluting you. Kindly make me a devotee at your Lotus feet".

"My Salutations to Lord Vishnu, who is Vasudeva, My salutations to you Lord, who took the form of Lord Narasimha with a body, that was half lion and half man, who destroys all fear, and who also took the foam of a boar".

"My Salutations again and again to Lord Vishnu who is the Lord of the universe, who has a mace and wheel, who destroys all miseries of His devotees, Oh, Lord of everything, kindly pardon all my mistakes and deficiencies".

"I salute that Lord who is with a lotus on His belly, whose face is ever smiling, and whose nails shine like the moon, who holds pretty *Sudarshana Chakra* in one of His hands, who is worshipped even by the Devas, and who sleeps on *Adisesha*, the king of serpents. Again and again, I say that there is no other God except you, Oh, Hari".

"Oh, the killer of demon *Mura*, that devotee of yours who reads these verses of this prayer to you, may, he get rid of all worldly attachments and attain yogic state and after death become imperishable".

5

Shankara: The Devotee and Philosopher

In some of the shlokas of Shankara that are Stotras in praise of the Gods and Goddesses one can see the undercurrents of great philosophical truths of Advaita Vedanta. However, the philosophical content found in the shlokas are very difficult to understand and can be interpreted in their full meaning only by the great ones. A few of such Shlokas are presented here and an attempt is made to give a glimpse of their philosophical contents. In Soundarya lahari Shankara brings forth the great Tantric principles in a very subtle manner. These hymns clearly show that Shankara was both a Bhakta and a philosopher at the same time.

Bhaja Govindam or Moha Mudgara

This Stotra is one of the most popular works of Adi Shankara. It is one of the masterpieces of Shankara. It has 31 verses. This shloka is a prayer to Govinda- Lord Vishnu and through this Stotra Shankara brings out the futility of worldly desires. In this stotra Shankara deals with the imperishable and illusionary nature of the phenomenal world as well as life and stresses the need for *Bhakti* towards God that is devoid of dogma and unnecessary ritualism and that results in the wisdom of the ultimate truth. When the mind turns towards Lord totally, then one becomes detached from the phenomenal world and becomes fit to gain the eternal truth that leads to *Mukti* or liberation. This Stotra reveals *Jnana* through *Bhakti*. This Stotra is also called as Moha Mudgara as it destroys delusion. This stotra stresses the need to cultivate an attitude of detachment to all worldly pleasures and have intense devotion to God as a means of spiritual progress because at the moment of death nothing will come to the aid of a person. It is only detachment that will lead to liberation or *Mukti* from the cycle of birth and death.

The first stanza in this hymn is a chorus and it is repeated at the end of each verse. It is said that after the first stanza that is a chorus Shankara composed twelve verses that was titled as Dwadasa Manjarika Stotram, that is, a hymn containing twelve verse blossoms or pearls of wisdom and the fourteen disciples of Shankara who were following him at that time composed fourteen other verses that came to be known as Chjathurdasa Manjarika Stotram that is, a hymn with a bunch of fourteen verse blossoms. Shankara is supposed to have added five verses finally. The set of 31 verses is called *Bhaja Govindam* or *Moha Mudgara*. This Stotra has a story associated with it. When once Adishankara was walking along the streets of Varanasi with his disciples, he heard one old Pandit, a scholar repeating blindly, the grammar rules of Panini to his students. Adi shankara went to him and asked him not to waste his time on grammar, instead turn his mind inward towards God in worship and total devotion. Adi Shankara is believed to have composed this stotra at that point of time.

In this *shloka* Shankara addresses the common ignorant man and says, "You fool, Pray to Govinda because when the time of your departure from this world comes near, no one including your relatives you will find with you".

> "Give up the thirst to amass wealth. Devote your mind to the thought of the real. Be content with what you have as a result of your past actions".
>
> "Do not become passionate and lustful when you see a woman's navel and chest. Bodies are only flesh, fat and blood. Remember this always".

"Life is uncertain like a raindrop on a lotus leaf. Always remember that disease, ego, and grief prey upon you".

"Your kith and kin will love you as long as you possess wealth and you support the family. But when once you become old and helpless no one will care for you".

"Only when a person is alive all his kith and kin enquire about his welfare. But, once, the soul departs from the body, all his kith and kin become afraid of the dead body".

"Childhood is totally engaged in play, Youth goes away in passion and the thoughts of the beloved. Old age passes away by thinking about all the past things and is full of worries. Alas, hardly there is any who is lost in Para Brahman".

"This worldly life is strange. Who is your son? Who is your wife? Who are you? From where did you come from? Ponder over all these things".

"Non attachment comes from Satsang or the company of the good and wise people. From non- attachment freedom comes; freedom from illusion and delusion results in self-settledness. *Jeevan Mukti* finally results from self settledness".

"Lust is seen only in youth but not in old age. What is the use of a dried up lake? Similarly, when there is no wealth there are no relatives. Where is worldly life when once the truth is realized"?

"Do not be proud of wealth, friends and youth. All these are momentary and they are all destroyed in no time. Try to be free from the worldly illusions and attain the eternal truth".

"All seasons, day and night all come and go in a repeated manner. Time plays its toll and life sneaks away gradually even without your own knowing. But alas, the desire never leaves man".

"Oh, mad man, why are you so much after the thoughts of wealth? Is there no one to teach you? Only one thing in all the three worlds can save you from the ocean of samsara. Get in to the boat of Satsaung quickly and save yourself".

"There are many who are with matted locks, shaven heads, are clothed in saffron and also in various other colours. All these outward show is for one's livelihood and to fill one's belly. Even if the truth is revealed to one still the fools do not see the truth".

"In old age, body becomes weak, head becomes bald, gums are without teeth and one leans on stick while walking. Even at this time attachment and desire are very strong and they never leave man".

"There is the man who sits up warming up his body in the sun or in front of the fire to keep him warm. In the night he curls up his body and sits with folded knees to keep away from cold. He eats food by begging and sleeps under the tree. Still in his heart of hearts he is entangled by passions".

"One may take a dip in the holy Ganga, observe penance, and give away wealth in charity to the poor and needy. That is what all scriptures teach you. But if you do not realize the truth behind all these even in hundred lives, you will never attain the Lord, the supreme goal. So, one needs *jnana* ultimately to attain *Mukti*. Without *jnana* nothing can give *Mukti* or liberation even after hundred births".

"Live in a temple or under a tree, wear deerskin as clothes, sleep on the floor, Give up all attachments and renounce all comforts. When one has such *vairagya* or detachment to all pleasures of life, then such a man is the happiest and the greatest in this world."

"One may be delighted in Yoga or Bhoga or attachment or detachment but only the one whose gaze is steadily fixed on the supreme- the Brahman enjoys bliss".

"If a man reads even a little from Gita, drinks just a drop of the Ganga water, worships Lord Vishnu event once, then he will have no fear of death".

"Birth and death come repeatedly. It is very difficult to cross the ocean of life. Oh, Lord Murari, save me from by your mercy".

"Like collecting rags one accumulates all good and bad deeds. Monks wear rags that are discarded by the people. They wander free of all virtues and sins. The one who lives in communion with God enjoys bliss that is pure and he is uncontaminated like a child and is like one who is intoxicated or mad".

"Who am I? From where did I come from? Who are my father and mother? Ponder over all these and see that everything is senseless and give up the illusory phenomenon, senseless world as a dream".

"Lord Vishnu dwells in all of us. Give up your anger and impatience. Have equanimity or Samabhava towards all always, see the self in all things, and remove ignorance that causes the notion of duality, if you want the quality of Lord Vishnu".

"Do not waste your effort in winning over love or in fighting with a friend or foe, your children or relatives if you want to attain Godhood. See yourself in every one and become one with all, giving up the notion of duality".

"Give up lust, anger, infatuation, and greed. Ponder over your real nature and ask, "Who am I"? Fools are those who do not think of the self and have no self-knowledge. Such people are imprisoned in the hell and suffer endlessly."

"Recite the verses from the Githa and the thousand names and glories of Lord Vishnu regularly. Take delight in *Satsang*. Distribute your wealth to the poor and needy."

"He whose body yields to passion becomes a prey to all diseases. Although death puts a full stop to all these, yet man is not giving up the sinful ways".

"Joy lies not in wealth but in welfare. Remember this always, The way of wealth is such that a rich man fears even his own son".

"Do *Pranayama*, remain unaffected by external influences, withdraw from the senses and discriminate between the permanent and the impermanent. Silence your restless wavering mind by chanting the holy name of God with great devotion".

"The devotee who is at the Lotus feet of his *guru* would get freedom from repeated births and deaths quickly. The indwelling Lord can be experienced through disciplined and controlled senses and mind". Worship Govinda always, Oh, fool, Other than this there is no way to cross the ocean of *Samsara*".

Through these verses Shankara says, "The wealth that one earns cannot and does not give lasting happiness. Man is repeatedly born and dead and again enters in to the womb of mother to be born again. Once you attain the real knowledge you will have no desire for this life that is full of miseries and problems. Thoughts about the shapely body of a woman, is nothing but foolishness. The joys and pleasures of flesh and fat is the entrance of deceit and misery. Understand and remember this truth always day in and day out. This world is strange. You may have plenty of wealth, many people around you and you may be strong in youth. Leave all your passions, give up your anger and love for money, yearning for life and ponder over who and what you are. Realise that this world is only like a mirage. So leave this dream world and sing Githa and the thousand names of that Lord. Meditate on Lord Narayana, the Lord of Lakshmi. Spend time in *Satsang* or with wise and good souls. Lord Govinda is staying in you and me and in all. So have no different attitudes to different people. See all in one and one in all. Control wants, desires and understand what is permanent. Always meditate upon the Lord. That only will lead you to the supreme. Life is like a tiny drop of water floating on a lotus leaf. The world is full of sorrows. Then why think of this world? Think about the Lord only. With loss of desires you would lose passion for life and with that you will realize the truth. Cross the sea of life with the help of a *Guru*. Once you cross the sea of life you will see Govinda in your heart. You have to identify yourself with *Para Brahman* that only is permanent joy"

Bhavani Bhujangam

In this Stotra of seventeen stanzas, Adi Shankara sings the glory of Bhavani, who is represented as the Kundalini Shakti, or the cosmic energy that is the everlasting immortal bliss or power that flows in Sushumna, the subtle body in a being. It is a salutation to the Almighty Mother. This Stotra also describes Her beauty and the ornaments and other decorations of the Mother Goddess. Her form, Shankara says is much above the Universe in its micro aspect. She, the consort of Shiva, is addressed as Blissful knowledge. She is also the great essence beyond sun, moon and the five elements. The devotee Shankara pleads to Mother Bhavani, who is a form of blissful knowledge and is everything, to reside in his heart and protect him from all sorrows of life. Shankara finally says that who soever repeats the holy name of Bhavani thrice a day with devotion is bound to get rid of sorrows, passions, sins and fear for all the time and for ever and would attain wealth, occult powers, and Salvation. Shankara says:

"I bow before that which is the personification of nectar, which is the everlasting immortal bliss, which is the luster in the Sushumna that lies in the midst of the six subtle charkas of the body, and that melts the moon and drinks its light".

"I sing about that Bhavani who sits in the triangle and also in the great Lotus, with the luter of crores of rising suns, who is immensely beautiful, and who attracts the entire universe with Her charm".

"Oh, great Goddess, keep your feet that is adorned with jingling bells made of gems, that shines- the feet that is worshipped even by Lord Vishnu, Lord Brahma and others, on my head".

"I worship the streak of hair on your belly, your shining navel, bent towards the left slightly, your hips dressed in red clothes, and your waist adorned with belt of gold studded with costly jewels".

"I worship your breasts full of milk, that are round like the gem studded pot, shining with milk, and who has lotus like eyes".

"I worship that mother, Bhavani, whose arms are delicate as Sirisa flowers, that carry arrow, bow, noose and goad and that shine with bangles and bracelets".

"I worship that Bhavani who is very pleasant looking; who shines like the full moon in the autumn season, whose lotus like face is full of peace, and who shines with gem studded necklace and earstuds".

"With these verses I am praising you, who apply musk on your forehead and cheeks, you who have pretty nostrils, and forehead, well formed beautiful lips and who blesses Her devotees with Her side glance".

"I sing in praise of your head that is radiant and decorated with gems forming the crescent moon and who has a thick hair that is decorated with jasmine flowers where bees enter and play".

"This form of yours, Oh, Bhavani, is much above this Universe in its micro form. Oh, mother, kindly shine in the lotus of my heart and bless me in your lustrous form so that I have the mastery and wealth of words".

"Oh, mother, I meditate upon you, who is the wife of Lord Shiva and who sits on His lap and is Tripura and Rajarajeshwari, surrounded by and led by Lord Ganesha".

"I sing about you as a form of blissful knowledge, which is superior most, as you are the sun, moon and all the elements and the great essence of everything".

"I know nothing about your greatness but still I have the desire to praise you, Oh, Bhavani. Please pardon me for my guts in doing so. You are the knower of Vedas and Agamas and who is not reachable even by the study of scriptures".

"You are my teacher, my Lord Shiva, Goddess Shakti, my mother, father, knowledge, relations- in short, you are everything to me. You are my ultimate refuge, the only thought that I can think of".

"Oh, mother Bhavani, my Salutations to you again and again. You are my refuge and my boon. You are the embodiment of all mercy, the greatest among the Devas, Oh, holy mother; please protect me from this forest snare of life".

"Who ever can read these verses correctly and with devotion, these verses which form a prayer praising the entire form of Bhavani, who is the essence of Vedas would attain salvation, wealth and all the eight occult powers".

"Repeat the holy name of Bhavani with devotion three times and always. You would get rid of all sorrows, passions, sin and fear, for ever and always"

Gauri Dasakam

These are ten verses of prayer on Mother Gauri, the consort of Lord Shiva. The eleventh verse is about the good effects of singing this prayer. Shankara extols the virtues and beauty of Mother Gauri-Goddess Parvati through these verses.

"I adore you Oh mother Gauri, who has beautiful lotus like eyes, who playfully creates and destroys the world, and who is sought after by great yogis. You are beyond the phenomenal world of existence. You are bright as the collection of several suns at dawn".

"I adore my mother Gauri who has lotus like eyes, who can be visualized by the sages in their deep state of meditation and trance. You reside in the minds of all of us giving pure bliss. You are the source of all living and non-living things in this world. You, who is endowed with a slender waist are full of pure bliss of wisdom".

"I adore my mother Gauri who has lotus like eyes, whose face is always smiling because of the happiness that is created by Her Lord, Shiva, who wears the crescent moon. She wears long thick blue dress that shines by the moon that she wears. Her Lotus like feet is worshipped even by Indra and Upendra".

"I adore my mother Gauri, who has lotus like eyes who shines as the indestructible primary being from whom all living and non-living beings originate and who is the primeval sound that shines like lightening and flame".

"I adore my mother Gauri who has lotus like eyes who, the Kundalini Shakti or the cosmic energy that arises from the Mooladhara Chakra attains the effulgent form that is similar to Sun, Moon and shines like a flame. She is pleasure personified and is subtler than the subtlest."

"I salute my mother Gauri who has lotus like eyes, who is the one eternal, pure, stainless Goddess of the universe who also witnesses creation, upkeep and destruction of the Universe and who is the consort of Lord Shiva".

"I adore my mother Gauri, who has lotus like eyes in whose womb exist the entire Universe like an egg and also the innumerable visible and invisible forms. She is half the body of Her Lord Maheshwara and wanders in the silver peaks of Himalayas".

"I adore my mother Gauri who has lotus like eyes, who is like a garland in which all the movable and immovable beings are woven together on a thread that are similar to beads and flowers and who can be obtained only through the path of spiritual knowledge".

"I adore my mother Gauri, who has lotus like eyes, who, in different forms represent the collection of powers, who pervades the entire Universe and plays with it as per Her liking, who is auspicious and is the wish fulfilling plant for those who bow and worship Her".

"I adore my mother Gauri who has Lotus like eyes, who destroys the miseries arising due to desire and attachment and bondage of those who meditate on Her Lotus like feet, and who occupy half the body of Lord Shiva who is ever pleasing".

" Even if one murmers these ten verses on mother Gauri in the mornings with a pure mind, right conduct and pure devotion, for such a person, whatever he utters would become true and such a person would have great devotion to Lord Shiva and the daughter of the mountain would act as per the desire of such a devotee".

Govindashtakam

This is a shloka on Govinda in eight verses. The nineth verse is about the good effects of singing these verses. It is praise about the form and glories of Govinda- Lord Vishnu. Govinda is described in these verses as the limit of extreme happiness, truth, wisdom, that is eternal, stable, not bound by space, is with the cows, is the end of all miseries and problems, appears with and without forms due to illusion, is the Universe, is the lord of all lords, is ultimate bliss of all the three worlds, is both visible and non-visible, is lord of earth and its goal, cures all miseries of life, is ever detached, eats earth and mud, shines only when the mind is pure, is peaceful and peace itself. He is beyond the reach of ignorant men, appears in different forms but is actually without any difference. He is realized by meditation and devotion in thought although. He is beyond thought. He is the one who destroys sorrow and passions. He is wise, is the limit of wisdom, and has a body undisturbed by senses. He is pretty, the cause of all causes, primeval, without beginning, time and qualities.

"I salute that Govinda who is the limit of happiness, who is truth, wisdom, eternal, stable, not bound by space, who is happy with cows, who is beyond and is the end of all miseries and problems of life, who appears with and without forms due to illusion, who is the Universe, is the Lord of Goddess Lakshmi and has no Lord above Him".

"I salute that Govinda who is the boundary of all happiness, who showed in his mouth all visible and invisible parts of all the fourteen worlds to Yashoda, His mother, and who as a child was punished by His mother Yashoda for eating mud, who is the basis of all the three visible and invisible worlds and who is the Lord of earth and the eternal goal of all".

"I salute that Govinda who is the extreme limit of happiness, who reduced the burden of earth by killing all the enemies of devas, who cures all sorrows of daily life, who is always unattached, who likes and eats butter, who eats mud as His food, who shines and reveals Himself in the mind when it is tranquil, but not known by anything else and who is peace personified".

"I salute that Govinda who is the extreme limit of happiness, who looks after one and all in His playful form of a cowherd, who protects those who look after cows, who playfully lifted the Govardhana Mountain where the Gopis and Gopa lads play happily. His name is Govinda. He is known by many other names as well. His plays or leelas are beyond the reach of the ignorant minds".

"I salute that Govinda who is the extreme limit of happiness, who is seen with each one of the Gopis, who also appears in different forms but actually is one and the same. The dust raised by the hooves of cows cover his pretty form. He can be realized by concentration and devotion in thought. He is also beyond thought. His greatness can be realized only with the gem of thought of a person."

"I salute that Govinda who is the extreme boundary of happiness, who took away the clothes (the false ego) of women taking bath and climbed the tree, Who wanted the women to get their clothes by coming near Him in nude (that is by leaving all passions, attachments and egoism), and who destroyed all sorrows, passion, who is wise, who is the limit of wisdom and whose body is unaffected by senses".

"I salute that Govinda who is the extreme limit of happiness, who is pretty, the cause of all causes, primeval, without beginning and end, who danced standing on the head of Kaliya in river Yamuna, who is black in colour, who lives ever in the present, and destroys the evil effects of Kali and who is the cause for the movement of present to the future".

"I salute that Govinda who is the extreme boundary of all happiness, who is in Brindavan, is worshipped by all Devas, whose nector like smile is as pretty as the jasmine flower and who gives happiness to all His friends, whose feet are worshipped with reverence by sages and who is the ocean of all good qualities and who is worshipped by one and all."

"He who dedicates his mind by chanting the holy names Govinda, Achutha, Madhava, Vishnu, Lord of Gokula and Krishna and reads these eight verses on Govinda is sure to get drenched by the nector of meditation. Their sins get washed away. They reach the blissful world of Govinda and attain the nector like supreme bliss."

Kashi Panchakam

These five verses of prayer are about the glory of Holy Kashi. This is the place where the ultimate real knowledge of the souls shines. It is the form of eternal joy. There is no need for other sacred waters when the body becomes the temple of Kashi, when devotion becomes the sacred Ganga who is the Universal mother who is spread everywhere and is the personification of all knowledge. Devoted attention is Ganga; realization got through the teacher is Prayaga, the inner soul, the God of the Universe who is the witness in the minds of all beings.

"I am that Kashika, that is the form of real knowledge of the soul, that pacifies the mind, Manikarnika among the holy waters and Ganga, the clear flow of knowledge"

"I shine in this place, in this world, with its moving and stable things, considered as real and eternal joy. I am the eternal knowledge and ultimate soul"

"Kashi exists in Kashi and makes everything shine. He who knows this reaches Kashi"

"I am that Kashika, that is knowledge and realization that shine in the home called body as Bhavani, the wisdom of the five Chakras of the body that is Lord Shiva, the king of the inner soul who is witness"

"I have no need of the other sacred waters as my body is the temple of Kashi, my devotion is Ganga, the universal mother who flows everywhere and who is the personification of all knowledge. My devoted attention is Gaya; the knowledge I get through my devotion to the teacher is Prayaga. My inner soul is the God of the Universe who stands as witness of all beings"

Lakshmi Narasimha Karavalamba Stotra

This is a prayer to Lord Vishnu as Lakshmi Narasimha. It is also known as Lakshmi Narasimha Karunarasa stotram. It has sixteen verses and the seventeenth verse tells about the result of singing this prayer with devotion. Lord Lakshmi Narasimha, the permanent protection of the sages is the boat that helps us to cross the ocean of misery that is called life. The devotee in these verses pleads for protections from desire, passion, and attachment to the pleasures of senses like taste, touch and so on and from worldly illusions, from senses that steal the sense of discrimination from worldly attachments. Those who are blessed with devotion to Hari are bound to attain the Lotus feet of Brahman. It is said that Shankara composed this stotra when his disciple Padmapada who appeared in the form of Narasimha saved Shankara from the Kapalika who was about to sacrifice Shankara's head as his offering. It is also said that Shankara composed this hymn after returning from the body of the king in to whose body he entered to learn the art of family life to win over Mandana Mishra. When Shankara was about to reenter in to his own body he saw his body being lit and in flames. It is said that the grace of Lakshmi Narayana extinguished the fire when Shankara sang this hymn.

"Oh great Lord of Lakshmi Narasimha who resides in the ocean of milk, who wears the gems of *Adisesha* on His head as ornaments, who is good and holy, who protects the sages, and who is the boat that helps one to cross the miserable ocean of life, kindly give me the protection of your hands".

"Oh, great Narasimha, your feet has been touched by the crowns of Brahma, Indra, Shiva and sun, you, who are the Lord of Goddess Lakshmi, please give me the protection of your hands".

"Oh, great Lord Narasimha, who killed the *Asura*, *Mura*, I am traveling everyday in the dark forest and am terrified by the lion of desire, I am scorched by the heat of competition, please give me the protection of your hands".

"Oh great God, I have touched the dangerous bottom of my life and am troubled by innumerable serpent like miseries. I am really miserable and reached the state of wretchedness. So please give me the protection of your hands".

"Oh great God, I am caught by the black, deadly crocodiles called time in the ocean of miserable life, that are killing me. I am afflicted by waves of passion, and attachments to desires of senses. So please give me protection of your hands"

"Oh great God, I have climbed the tree of life that grew from sin, that has innumerable branches of past Karmas, and leaves that are parts of my body, flowers that are the results of Vasanas or tendencies, or sorrow. I am falling down rapidly. Please give me the protection of your hands".

"Oh great God, who rides on the enemy of snakes, who resides in the ocean of nector, the serpent of family life has opened its fearful mouth with dangerous fangs filled with terrible poison that has destroyed me. So, kindly give me the protection of your hands".

"Oh great God, I have been scarred very badly by the fire called life, and every single hair of my body got affected by it. So I have taken refuge at your lotus feet. Pleas give me the protection of your hands."

"Oh great God, I am caught in the net of life and all my organs too are caught in that web, the five senses make my head reel. So, kindly give me protection of your hands".

"Oh great God, I am struck by the fearful elephants of worldly illusion and my vital parts have been totally crushed and I suffer from the thoughts of life and death. So kindly give me protection of your hands".

"Oh great God, I have become blind because the sense of discrimination or Viveka has been stolen from me by the thieves called senses. I am blind and have fallen in the deep well of passion. So please give me the protection of your hands."

"Oh great God, I am being tied by the soldiers of the Lord of death, by innumerable ropes of worldly attachments, that are dragging me along by the noose around my neck and I am alone tired and afraid. So, merciful one, please give me the protection of your hands".

"Oh Lord of Devas, the Lord of Lakshmi who has lotus on His belly, who is Vishnu, Lord of all heavenly beings, who is in Vaikuntha, who is Krishna, who slayed the demon Madhu, who has lotus like eyes, who is the knower of Brahman, and who is Keshava, Janardhana, Vasudeva, Please give me the protection of your hands".

"Oh great Lord, who holds *Sudarsana Chakra*, the holy wheel in one hand and conch in the other, who embraces His consort, the daughter of the oceans in another hand and the fourth hand that gives protection and boons, please give me the protection of your hands".

"Oh great God, I am completely drowned in the ocean of life, please protect me, Lord of compassion. Just as you took a form to remove Prahalada's sorrow, Please give me the protection of your hands".

"Oh great God, who dwells in the hearts of sages like Prahlada, Narada, Parashara, Pundarika and Vyasa, and who loves His devotees and is the wish fulfilling tree, that protects, kindly give me the protection of your hands".

"This prayer that blesses the earth with all good things is composed by Shankara who is a bee, drinking deeply the honey from the lotus feet of Lakshmi Narayana, and those humans who are blessed with devotion to Hari will attain the Lotus feet of Brahman".

Shat Padi

It is a poem of six verses or the six-legged bees that is a prayer to Lord Vishnu. The seventh verse is a request to Lord Narayana to bless the poet and devotee Shankara to retain the stotra in his mouth always. Through these verses Shankara pleads Lord Vishnu to remove all delusions and fear of life and make his mind peaceful.

"Oh, Lord Vishnu, lead me away from arrogance, give me peace to my mind, and destroy the desires and grant me liberation and take me across the cycle of birth and death".

"I sing and pray to the lotus feet of the Lord of Goddess Lakshmi who is like river Ganga fragrant and full of eternal pleasures that breaks the shackles of the cycle of birth and death".

"Oh, Lord, I am not different from you as I am part of you, just as waves are part of the ocean and vice versa".

"Oh, Lord Krishna, you lifted the Govardhana hill, you are the enemy of the demons, you have sun and moon as your two eyes, your very appearance destroys the attachment to this world".

"Oh, supreme Lord, you protect this earth through different incarnations including that of Matasya or fish. I am being torn by the cycle of birth and death, so, I am worthy of being protected by you"

"Oh, Damodara, Govinda, you are the source of all qualities, who has lotus like body, you are like the Mandara mountain for rebirth that is like ocean Ksheerasagar, kindly drive away the fear from my life"

"Oh, Lord Narayana, you are full of compassion. I am taking refuge at your lotus feet. May these verses of prayer be retained in my mouth always".

Shiva Aparadha Kshamapana Stotram

This prayer has ten beautiful verses. In the eleventh verse Shankara hastens Lord Shiva to protect His devotees always inspite of all mistakes committed by them.

"Due to effects of past *Karmas* in this world and placed in my mother's womb with all filth, I had to suffer a lot due to the heat and bad smell of that. No one can describe the sufferings that I had to go through in the womb of my mother. Therefore Oh, Mahadeva, kindly pardon all my sins".

"Because of sorrows I had to roll in dirt during my childhood with a dirty body, Then, I was only interested in drinking my mother's milk. Insects that are like flies and many ills at those times also hit me and I was not able to prevent any of these. Because of all these I never thought of you, Oh, Parameshwara and so Oh, Shambhu, kindly pardon me for all my sins, Oh, Mahadeva".

"During my youth, I was bitten by the snake like five senses in all parts of my body, and I lost all my wisdom and began to get attached to worldly pleasures of progeny, wealth and women and therefore I did not remember you, Oh, Parameshwara, and so, Shambho, kindly pardon me for all my sins, Oh, Mahadeva".

"When I became very old, all my senses became very weak, I lost all my memory, my body became very weak due to the sins, sickness and pain that never left me and my mind now rewinds all my past, the useless passions and desires that I had and my act of not remembering you Oh, Parameshwara, Shambhu, kindly pardon all my sins Oh, Mahadeva".

"I am unable to observe the complex rules of Dharma daily, am unable to follow the teachings of the Vedas as told by the wise, I am unable to know Dharma even by listening to Vedas and also by meditating, so, what is the use of learning all these daily, and so, Shambho, kindly pardon my sins, Oh, Mahadeva".

"I never gave anything in charity to the devotees even by thinking of you, Oh, Lord Shiva. Neither did I perform any Vedic sacrifices by chanting many mantras, nor did I meditate sitting on the holy banks of the sacred Ganga, or performed any penance as prescribed in the Vedas or chant the name of my Lord Rudra, and so, Shambhu, kindly pardon my sins, Oh, Mahadeva".

"I did not sit in a lonely place in Padmasana posture, and awaken the Kundalini Shakti or the cosmic energy in me and send the breath in the form of *Prana* that is 'AUM', through the subtle path of the two main Nadis to reach the ever shining Sahasrara, that is pure Para Brahman, I did not calm my mind and meditate on Parameshwara who is beyond the physical body and who is the essence of the Vedas. So Shambho, kindly pardon my sins, Oh, Mahadeva".

"I have not concentrated on the tip of my nose and try to imagine you in my heart that is naked truth, that is alone, that is always pure, that is beyond all the three qualities of Sattva, Rajas and Tamas and that is capable of removing all ignorance and so Shambho, kindly pardon my mistakes, Oh, Mahadeva".

"Hey my Lord, who wears the moon as a decorated crown, who has burnt Manmadha, the God of love, who carries Ganga on His head, who gives eteral peace to His devotees, who wears snakes on His neck and ears, who has fire in His third eye, who wears the hide of the elephant, and who is the Lord of all the three worlds, please show me the path of Liberation that is the only useful path".

"Oh, my mind, what is the use of charity or riches, or horses, or getting kingdom or son or wife or friends or cows or houses or the physical body because all these are perishable in no time? So be away from all these and for the upliftment of the soul, meditate on the consort of Goddess Parvati, as per the teachings of your *Guru*".

"Please listen, the life span is closing down, so also youth is disappearing fast, the days that are gone will never come back, time swallows everything on earth, life and wealth like tide and lightning last for only a split second, So, my Lord Parameshwara, protect your devotees for ever".

Shiva Bhujanga Prayatha Stotram

It is a prayer to Lord Shiva in the meter of *Bhujanga.* It contains fifteen stanzas. It is said that when Shankara sang this hymn to his mother who was in her last moments, she became so terrified when Shankara described the form of Shiva. So he sang another shloka describing Lord Vishnu to pacify his mother. It starts with a prayer to Vigneshwara. From the second stanza onwards it is a prayer to Lord Shiva who has no beginning or end, who is always in Turiya or the transcendental state of consciousness, who is the ultimate truth. In the final verses Shankara makes a few requests to Lord Shiva. He says, " be pleased with me, remember me, take care of me, see me with your three eyes, save me, look after me, pardon all my mistakes and appear before me, be kind to me, give me a stable devotion towards you, give me recognition always and by all means that you that you think is fit enough".

"I pray to Lord Ganesha, the one tusked God who is the darling of Lord Shiva, whose cheeks are drenched by the water of exuberance, who is surrounded by the bees that are flying, who has a trunk that waves slowly, who protects the entire universe, who has a thick, long, shining tusk and who is capable of saving us from all dangers".

"I meditate the great flame that is Shiva, that has no beginning or end, which is the essence of philosophy, the only one form of the holy knowledge, who is the Turiya, the fourth blessed state, the unknown, who was searched by both Lord Brahma and Vishnu and who is the supreme Truth".

"I salute that God who has five faces, who sits along with Adi Shakti, who wears shining ornaments made of jewels, who has matted locks of hair, has snake, moon, and river Ganga on His head. His eyes are the sun and moon, he is the eternal God with Goddess Adi Shakti with Him eternally".

"No one can know you, my Lord by any means, who is with Brahman like Shiva, Ishana, Tatpurusha, Aghora and Vama, who has Hrudaya, who is beyond all the thirty six principles".

"I meditate on that Shiva who is the source of all pleasures and pains, whose half body is red as coral and the other half blue as

Topaz, who is the mixture of all qualities, who is the cause for the rise and fall of God of love".

"I salute your lotus like feet that is decorated by garland of flowers by the Devas and Indra who come to worship you. You who are fondled by Goddess Parvati are the boat that helps us to cross the ocean of life."

"Oh, Lord of the universe who is my Lord, the Lord of Goddess Gauri, who has mercy towards His devotees and destroys sorrows, and who has a body that is a column of fire, salutations to you again and again".

"Oh, great God, who is the God of all Gods, I always pray to you with great devotion. You are the one who is beyond thought and the one who destroyed the cities, who killed the God of death as the destroyer. Oh, great Lord of mercy, kindly be pleased with me".

"Oh my God, who has a different eye, who is the Lord of the universe, the God of knowledge, the cause of the three Vedas, Lord Trayambhaka, kindly be pleased with me, remember me, take care of me, see me with your three eyes, look after me, save me, pardon all the mistakes committed by me and come before me".

"To devotees you are the most kind. So be kind to me. I am seeking your blessings, God of mercy, be kind to me without any hesitation".

"This is the proper time for giving and I am the receiving vessel, Kindly, Oh, Lord, be the giver, I do not ask for anything else from you, grant me a stable devotion towards you, you who are merciful by nature, kindly show me your kindness".

"If you consider me as a bull, ride over me, If you consider me as blemished, wear me on your head as moon, if you consider me as a two tongued liar, wear me on your neck as the two tongued serpent, and in whatever way you give me recognition, I would ever be satisfied".

"I do not know how to trouble others or how to please you, Oh, Lord of the mountain, How was it possible for you, you the Lord of Kashi to become pleased with the one who troubled his wife and son and another who troubled his father"?

"I do not know how to sing your praise or meditate upon you, or the ways of worship. I only salute you with intense devotion your

Lotus like feet that killed the God of death for the sake of your devotee Markandeya who was terribly scared to see the God of death before him".

"I will not pray any other God, who does not possess a blue neck, who does not wear a serpent around His neck, who does not hold a skull in His hand, who does not have an eye on His forehead and who does not have His wife on His left side".

Shivanandalahari

This is one of the greatest poetic prayers that Shankara had composed. It literally means 'Waves of auspicious bliss'. It consists of 100 stanzas in various chandas or meters. The verses contain several figures of speech or *Alankaras*. It was composed when Shankara visited Shree Shailam that is one of the twelve Jyotir Linga shrines in India. This stotra is in praise of Lord Mallikarjun, - Lord Shiva, residing at Shree Sailam. This shloka starts with a salutation and prayer to Lord Shiva and then goes on with a request to enlighten the Bhakta. The Bhakta also seeks protection from the Lord. In this hymn Shankara praises Mallikarjuna who is Lord Shiva, and Brahmaramba, who is Goddess Parvati, the presiding deities of the temple at Shree Shailam. Through these verses Shankara asks people not to waste time in going after sensuous pleasures that are like quickly fading fruits, like a monkey or an elephant in rut and also engage the mind in unnecessary debates, instead, worship Lord Shiva to attain supreme happiness. Once the Bhakta starts worshipping the Lord wholeheartedly, and sincerely with pure devotion, and once real knowledge dawns, the scriptures become of no use. Instead of searching for material offerings, it is enough if one offers that single Lotus from the lake of one's own mind to God, to get everlasting bliss. In ignorance people search for different kinds of flowers all around them to worship the Lord without knowing that the actual flower of worship is there already in the mind of man. Whatever body one possesses, what is important is to have a mind that is engaged totally on meditation. In whatever stage of life one may be, if the Lotus in his heart is in the custody of Shambhu, then the Lord will belong totally to that person and help him to get out of all miseries of life. Wherever he lives whether in a cave or in a forest or home it does not matter as long as his inner mind rests at the feet of Lord Shiva and that is Yoga and he is the greatest Yogi. This phenomenal world is not fit for real meditation. So only God can protect and save any one from all sins. This Shloka ends by pointing out the importance of obtaining Lord's grace for everything including controlling of one's mind.

"My destiny makes me incapable of meditation. Kindly change my destiny so that my mind gets immersed in meditation always. Shankara asks the Lord, "Lord, if you say that you cannot change my destiny then how did you crush the head of the creator Brahma using your nails. You are the one who protects the poor- poor in all respects. I am unable to see your Lotus feet oh, Lord. I am caught up in the whirlpool of maya, filled with desires that are evil. Kindly give me solace from the mire of sorrow. Please take care of my mind that is like a monkey that wanders in all directions without any control on itself. Oh, Lord, kindly tie that mind with your grace and blessings. May the Lord be seated in my heart along with mother Shakti. Oh Lord, take control of my mind that acts like a thief and wanders at its will. Kindly show me mercy. Where can I see you? When can I see the holy feet? and be able to hold it, carry it on my head, keep on my eyes and chest, embrace and smell the scent of the Lotus feet to attain Bliss? You have everything under the Sun. What can I offer you except my mind? In worshipping you, by singing your praise, by uttering the names of my lord Shiva, by sweet conversation with the devotees, and by thinking of you constantly, I get *Mukti* in this birth itself. I am ever grateful to you for that. My mind wanders in evil desires. So Oh Lord kindly take me to your fold and tie me up with the rope of your affection and change my destiny. Kindly come and occupy my mind. My mind wanders in all evil ways. Kindly show me mercy and take me under your control. I can give only my mind as an offering. By worshipping you I am sure that I shall attain *Mukti* and become you. I offer my devotion to your Lotus feet. Bless me with merciful divine sight and a lesson for a happy living. It is sufficient to perform service to Lord, to salute Him, to sing about Him, worship

Him, meditate upon Him, listening to the stories about Him, and seeing Him atleast once for attaining Liberation. I, who am a devotee perform the ceremony of purification by devotion, happiness, clear mind, real knowledge, chant the five letter *Mantra*, purify my body that carries my soul, and search good things that are pleasant to the mind. The devotee churns the ocean of Vedas with dedication, by using the rope of stable devotion. The churning stick is the attentive mind to attain the Lord who is with His consort Uma. He can be seen with and through the mind. When Lord Shiva rests in the mind then, Dharma will be observed properly, sins would vanish, so also passion, anger and arrogance. By using wisdom, words brought through poems the devotee makes devotion to grow in his heart that gives the infinite yield. To get out of sin, to obtain immortal wealth, the only way is to pray and meditate upon Lord Shiva. Lord, kindly stay in my mind forever. Kindly live in me. Kindly hunt all evil tendencies in me and kill them. When the Lord lives in the cave of my mind fear will never come near me. May my mind stop wandering and instead start meditating for peace. With meditation on Lord Shiva all good would result in the form of removal of all sins, glowing of devotion, performance of good deeds, gaining good character, and also the joy of knowledge. Let me meditate upon Lord Shiva constantly, instead of going towards the worldly life full of sorrows. Devotion would result in firm character and mind that has sinless actions and deeds of devotion, and give salvation. I meditate upon that Shiva who is Mallikarjuna, residing on top of Sri Giri (Shree Sailam in Andhra Pradesh). May He come and be in my mind. I pray and my *pranams* to that Sadashiva who is everything. I prostrate before Him, who is all pervading. Remove all darkness from me and become visible to me. Oh Lord who has the luture of billions of Suns my mind longs for you like the Chataka bird that longs for the blue-black clouds, like the Chakravaka bird that longs for the sun and like the Chakora bird that longs for the moon everyday. My mind longs for your Lotus like feet that can be searched only by the path of knowledge and which bestws the bliss of emancipation. My mind intensely craves for the Lotus feet of Shambhu that removes fears and phobias and gives bliss. When the spirit of my mind reaches the Lotus feet of Lord Shiva, then, that is the state of devotion. For the one who sings about you there is no death and he attains liberation. I am devoted to you, I meditate upon you, I seek refuge in you, and I beg you to bless me with your divine and kind look. Your swallowing the Halahalam itself is ample proof of your mercy in protecting the entire universe and all its beings. It is sufficient to serve you, sing about you, worship you, meditate upon you, and hear stories about you to obtain liberation. When all the Devas lose their balance, when all the sages tremble with fear, when the whole world is destroyed at the end of the great *Pralaya* or deluge, you appear in intense rapture and in great joy. The creation of the world is your play and all beings are your toys. The cow of my devotion yields the Ambrosa of happiness. With the bowstring of devotion and bow of meditation, the memory of Lord Shiva as a collection of arrows, the intelligent one becomes victorious after winning over the enemies of sins and attains the stable kingdom of heaven. The Lord removes desire, bondage, suffering, and bad conduct of men. Upon such a person, let my mind meditate. Kindly teach me the method of serving great men, with devotion with a clean mind and attachment to the good and exhault my intellect. The one who worships Lord Shiva meditates upon Him to become one with Him to salute Him, hear His stories, be in His presence, sing His fame and be happy and offer his mind to Him who is Lord Shiva. Such a person attains salvation even when he is alive. Worship of this birthless and deathless Lord leads to supreme bliss. Oh Shiva, my Lord, pull my mind that is like a wandering bird that is like wild elephant that wanders uncontrollably by tying it with the chain of devotion granting devotion and intellect. For the one who meditates, sins fall off, devotion will grow, good character and good actions would result, and the joy of knowledge and the fruit of knowledge would appear. I meditate and worship on your Lotus feet that bestws auspiciousness. You are the repository of Liberation". These verses show the devotion of Shankara.

Shankara starts this hymn by dedicating the first stanza to the one who wears the moon on His head, who is the personification of penance, who teaches devotees about the results of penance, who grants good to all the three worlds, whose memory becomes newer and newer always, who is always in ecstacy due to His superior knowledge and Bliss that is the result of the mystic union of Shiva and Shakti. Then Shankara goes on to say, 'oh, Shambho, you who grant happiness, let the waves of bliss from Lord Shiva that is the result of wisdom and that annihilates the sins that fall on the whirlpool of life quench the fire of sorrow that lives in my heart as senses, let that be victorious".

"I pray with all my heart to Him who is known by the Vedas, who is pleasant to the mind, who destroyed the three cities, who is the first and foremost in everything, who has the all seeing three eyes, who has the matted lock of hair, who is the most eminent, who wears snake as the necklace around His neck, who holds the jumping deer in His hands, who is the greatest among the Devas, who is the self luminous, who showers mercy upon me, who is the Lord of the universe with its beings, who is the sole support and holy wisdom, who is always with mother Goddess and who is the great entertainer".

"I would never worship those other Gods who offer small gifts to those who pray to them. But I would beg only for the Lotus feet of Lord Shiva who is close but at the same time very difficult to be reached even by Lord Vishnu, Brahma and the other Gods".

"Oh God, I am ignorant in the science of law, life, medicine, in interpreting events, in composing poems and songs as per grammar which is very difficult, in the knowledge of the ancient holy books, in the teachings of the Vedas, in praising your great deeds, and in the arts of dance and comedy. When that is the case, how can I get any favour from the Kings? Oh Lord of all beings who is the knower of all, who is the most eminent, who is all pervading, kindly tell me who am I? Be pleased to protect me by showering your sea of mercy upon me."

"All debates such as "This is the pot, no, it is only mud. This is earth, no, it is only atoms, this is smoke, no, it is only fire, this is cloth, no, it is only the thread", can all these stop the cruel God of death? It is only futile that you exert your energy unnecessarily in all such debate. Instead the intelligent seek the Lotus feet of Shambhu only and attain supreme happiness".

"Oh supreme God, let my mind dwell upon your two lotus like feet, my words on your praise, my hands on your worship, my ears in hearing your holy stories, my mind meditating upon you, my two eyes on your beauty. I am sure then there will not be any need for me for other great books."

"Like the intellect that considers the shell as silver, the glass stones as precious gems, water mixed with flour as milk, the mirage as water, similarly, Oh, God of all beings, the ignorant people worship Gods other than you without thinking of you who is the supreme God".

"The ignorant people go on searching and hunting in the deep dark lake, in the lonely dangerous forest, on the broad high mountains for a flower for worshipping you. Alas, Oh God, who is the Lord of Uma, these people do not understand that they can remain where they are instead of searching everywhere and become blissful by merely offering you that single lotus from the lake of one's own inner chamber of the heart".

"In whichever form it may be, no matter whether it is in a human form or in the form of Gods, or in the form of an animal that wanders in the forests and hills, or in the form of a small mosquito, or that of a domestic animal, or even in the form of a worm, or flying birds; it matters nothing if the mind is always engaged in meditating the lotus like feet of the Lord that are the waves of supreme Bliss".

"Whether one is a famous seeker of truth, or a Grahastha or a householder, or a monk or a Vanaprasthin or the forest dweller, or none of these, if his lotus heart is engaged in your meditation, oh, Lord of all beings, Shambhu, then you would belong to Him and help him lift the heavy burden of life."

"It does not matter whether one resides in a cave or in a house or in the open or in a forest or on top of a mountain, or in water or fire, if his inner mind always rests at the feet of Shambhu then that is Yoga, he is a yogi and he will be happy always."

"This useless worldly life is unfit for real meditation. I who am blind and foolish am always on the move. You have to protect me, Oh, Lord, of all beings. Who is poorer than me in this whole world for you to show your mercy? Which protector is there for me in all the three worlds except you, who alone is the protector of the poor?"

"Oh Lord of all beings, you are the only close relation to the poor. What other proof should there be to explain my relationship with you when I am the poorest among the poor? You have to pardon all sins that I had committed and then you have to protect me with your effort because that is the only way between close relations."

"Oh Lord, you are indifferent towards me because you are not putting in any effort to erase my fate that makes me incapable of meditating upon you. Oh Lord, if you cannot change my fate, I who am filled with evil desires to the brim, then how did you crush the head of Brahma the creator by merely using the tip of your nails?"

"May Lord Brahma with His four remaining heads under your protective care live for ever. But He is the one who wrote 'poverty' on my head. Oh God, who is crystal clear and good, let your act of protecting the poor tenderly protect me as well".

"Oh Lord who is omnipresent, due to my past good deeds or due to your mercy you have appeared before me. But I am unable to see your pure, and holy feet because the ruby studded crowns of Devas who bow down and worship your feet cover your feet from my vision".

"You alone grant great blessings and holy status to ordinary people of the world. Lord Vishnu and others who carry the holy positions that is given by your kindness pray to you for getting more and more of such great positions. Just as your grace is immeasurable, my desire also is immeasurable. So, when are you going to protect me by your merciful glance?"

"Oh Lord, I am being caught in the whirlpool of Maya of life that is filled with evil desires, that takes one to evil masters, and that ends in evil and that is a store house for all sins leading only to sorrows. Oh Lord, when are you going to give me solace from this mire of sorrow written on my forehead by Brahma, the creator? If that is your grace and affection then I am more than satisfied."

"Oh Lord Shiva, who is omnipresent, my mind wanders in the forest of evil desires and my mind always thinks of charming young maidens and it wanders in uncontrollable manner at its will on all the four directions, from one branch of desire to the other. Oh, Lord, who holds the skull for begging alms, kindly take my mind that is like a monkey to your control and tie it up with the rope of your affection."

"Oh killer of Manmada, the God of love, let the pretty, lotus shaped crystal clear white tent house of my mind that is built daily anew in the good, spotless path that has courage as the central pillar, tied by the ropes of determination be occupied by you along with Shakti. Oh the Omnipresent, who has around Him the Bhootha Ganas to serve, Oh, Lord, may you be victorious".

"My mind is wandering in many paths. It is filled with desires, jealousy, is intent on stealing other's wealth and tries to enter rich men's house. Oh Lord of all thieves, I am not able to tolerate such a mind that is a thief. So Oh, Lord Shankara, the omnipresent, take my mind under your control and shower mercy upon me who is an innocent one".

"I am worshipping you. Appear before me soon and grant me all pleasures, Oh, Lord who is omnipresent. But if you grant me the position of Brahma, the creator, or of that of Lord Vishnu for that matter as a reward for my worship, then I have to become a swan like Brahma to search for your top and fly in the sky or become a boar, an animal and dig down the earth to find your beginning. In that case how can I bear the sorrow of not seeing you Oh, Shankara, the Omnipresent?"

"When can I live in your stone studded golden mansion on Mount Kailash along with your attendants in servitude and devotion, hands raised and clasped, chanting with joy, "Oh God save me" and spend all time and the Kalpa (432 million years) flies like a second? Oh, God, who is the giver of all happiness, present everywhere, who is always with Goddess Uma, who is the master, who is above all and is good".

"When will I be able to see Him, who is praised by Brahma and the other Gods, who has the ascetics chanting 'hail, hail' all around Him, who is crowded by His Bhootha Ganas, who sits on His vehicle Nandi the bull, who has a blue neck and three eyes, who is embraced by His consort Goddess Uma and who has the deer and axe in His hand?"

"When will I see your holy pair of feet, Oh, Lord of the holy mountain of Himalayas and be able to hold your feet, carry them on my head, eyes and chest, embrace it, smell the scent of lotus flowers from it and attain the Bliss that even Brahma and the others could not enjoy?"

"You have with you the golden mountain, near you is Kubera, the Lord of riches, in your house is Kalpa Vriksha, the wish fulfilling tree, the cow Kamadhenu that grants everything, the precious stone that fulfills any wish that enters your mind and so on. On your head You have worn the moon with cool rays, and all the good in the world are at your feet. When that is the case, what can a slave like me offer to you my Lord, except my mind that can be given as an offering to you?"

"The *Mukti* of my becoming is in worshipping you, the *Mukti* of my coming near you is in singing about you and your glory, and calling you 'Oh, my Shiva, Oh, Madhava'; The *Mukti* of living with you is in conversing with your devotees who live with you in their mind, and the *Mukti* of mixing with you always is in thinking of you and your stable form that is the universe. Since I got all these in this very birth, Oh, God, the Lord of Bhavani, I am grateful to you for all these".

"I offer my devotion to your lotus like feet, I meditate upon you, who is the greatest, I seek your refuge, Oh, my Lord, I beg you by my words, Oh, Vibhu, bless me with the merciful divine sight, that is sought after even by the Gods. Oh, Lord and teacher of the universe, teach me the lesson of happy living."

"Like the Sun God, I do not possess a number of hands to dress your holy idol, like Lord Vishnu I do not have the ability to worship you who is omnipresent, like Vayu Deva, the God of wind, I do not have the ability to spread incense of sandal and other fragrance, like Indra who presides over fire I do not have the ability to cook and offer you food, like Hiranyagarbha, I cannot offer you gold vessels. Oh, God who wears the crescent moon on the head, the God of all beings, and who is the teacher of all the three worlds, if only I had the capacity for all these then I would have served you in a better manner".

"Oh Lord of all beings, your help alone is what is needed. To give protection to all those movable and immovable things that you hold inside your belly and also to those who are placed outside, the fearful herbal poison that emitted intense fire that made all the Devas to flee in great fright, was stopped by you in your neck by neither swallowing it nor by spitting it out".

"Oh Lord, how did you see the fierce flame of poison that frightened even the Devas? Did the fire that your hand held look like fully ripe plum fruit? Did it appear as pills from the *Siddha* doctor when you put it on your tongue and when you wore it around your neck? Did it look loke a blue gem studded ornament? Oh Lord, kindly tell me".

"Oh God of Gods, is it not sufficient to do either service to you, or salutations to you, or singing about you or worship you, or meditate upon you, or hear your stories, or seeing you once to attain liberation for people like me? Indeed what other liberation can one think of apart from these? If I can attain liberation by these acts then what else is there for me to attain more than that by worshipping other Gods?"

"Oh, Pasupathe, who else can ever estimate your courage Oh, Shambhu? How can one attain your state of mind? At the time of delusion or *Pralaya*, when the entire world gets destroyed, and when all the Devas lose their stability and the crowd of sages tremble with fear, you in solitude carry out your play of destruction and recreation of the universe in intense rapture and joy".

"You are engaged in gathering and preserving and then giving all the good things of life, you the great teacher of the known and unknown, you who have spread within and without, you who are the knower of all that is to be known, you who shower all possible mercies, what else is there for me to tell you? You are residing within me all day and night and as such you are very close to me. You only protect me Oh, Shambhu".

"Oh Lord, who is always with his concert Goddess Uma, I, your devotee am tied with the thread of devotion, and is filled with the water of happiness in the pot of my mind that is spotless. I keep the mango leaves of your feet, the coconut of real knowledge and chant the holy and peaceful *Panchàkshara Mantra* and with all these I am purifying my body that carries my soul. I am also searching for more good things that are pleasant to the mind for performing the ceremony of purification".

"A large number of good minded people with lots of dedication are churning the ocean of Vedas with dedication with the rope of stable devotion and with the churing stick of the attentive mind. They are able to get from it the Lord with His consort Uma who is like the Kalpaka Vriksha, the wish-fulfilling tree that is like the wish giving Kamadenu and the wish-yielding gem Chintamani. For the knowledgeable it is like nector of happiness and permanent granter of all luck bestowed by Goddess Uma who is Rema".

"Oh Lord, you, who are the personification of happiness and the nector of divinity, you are the doer of all good and you hold dear in your hand. You are the whole and you remove the darkness of ignorance. You who is always with your beloved Uma is seen clearly by the mind through the path of mountain like good deeds and if such a sea of happiness rises within ourselves then good people like us will know how to lead our lives".

"When the only Lord that is Shiva who is respected and royal sits in the city of the Lotus of the pure mind, then, the four legged Dharma namely, penance, cleanliness, mercy and truth is fallowed properly, the sins committed get wiped out, passion, anger and arrogance disappear for ever; then the seasons come properly and the curative crop of happiness of knowledge give one good returns".

"When irrigated with the machinery of wisdom, by using the pot of words, that flow through as canals and sub canals of poems, the nector like water of the story of Sadashiva is brought forth, then the crop of devotion growing in the field of heart bloom and yield beyond expectations. When that is the case, Oh, Maheshwara, and Vishveshwara, the God of Gods and God of the universe, how can this servant of yours ever fear any famine?"

"To wipe out the sins, to taste the immortal wealth, Oh, God, who is the Lord of death, each of the karmendriyas or the organs of senses, *jnanendriyas* or the organs of perception and the mind request me to praise you, to meditate upon you, to prostrate before you, to circumambulate you, to see you soulfully and clearly and to hear your glories and stories. Therefore, Oh, Lord, kindly order me to perform all these, and remind me about these time and again. Above all kindly do not snare at me for any reason".

"Oh God, who resides in the unapproachable fort of the inner cave of the heart, that has deep trench around it, with strong determined courage as its walls, excellent qualities as its army, with senses as its gates, with unlimited knowledge as its wealth- these describe the fort of the core of my being that is blessed with all that is needed, May you reside there for ever".

"Oh, God of the mountains, do not go anywhere else. Kindly reside in me. Oh, the primeval hunter, wild, wicked animals like envy, delusion and others similar to them live within the jurisdiction of the dense forest of my mind. Therefore kindly enjoy your sport of hunting by killing all these and enjoy yourself there".

"Oh, Lord, when you, the one who holds the deer in his hand, who killed the demon Gajasura, who cut the cruel demon Vyagrasura in to pieces, who makes all beings merge within Him, who is the Lord of the mountains, who has a white body with the ashes smeared all over, and who has five faces lives in the core of my heart, then how can fear approach me?"

"Hey, my mind, that is the greatest bird sitting on the tree that has parts of Vedas as its branches, Upanishads as its crown, served by learned Brahmanas as birds that are indestructible, that gives pleasure and joy, that destroys sorrows, whose fruit gives nector as its juice that shines always, that greatest bird lives in the cage of the two lotus feet of Shankara. Oh, my mind, enough of your wanderings. Stop wandering and stay in that cage for ever".

"Oh my mind, the king of swans lives in the house of the lotus like feet of the Lord of the daughter of the mountains along with the damsels of devotion to God. Live as you like with peace in that house of the Lord that glitters with nector, pretty red rubies and that is surrounded by ascetics who are like swans."

"During the spring season of devotion to Lord Shambhu, in the garden of the heart, the dried leaves of sins fall off and then the creepers of devotion and the leaf buds of good actions appear, the birds of good character, the flowers of prayer, the fragrance of good deeds, the flow of honey like fragrance of the joy of knowledge and the fruit of knowledgeable experience glitter."

"May you reach and stay permanently by your mind, that is the best of swans of discrimination, in the lake of meditation, on Lord

Shiva that is filled with the water of everlasting happiness, that is the seat of the Lotus like heart of the sages and Devas alike, that is approached by good people, that destroys all sins and that emit the fragrance of goodness. Instead of that why go in to the mire of aimless worldly life of the mean minded and suffer its strains?"

"The creeper of devotion that is nourished by the water of nector like joy and sprouted out of devotion to the lotus like feet of Lord Shiva, climbs the branches of firm character and spreads over the mind that has got branches and sub branches and grow extensively with actions that are sinless and deeds full of devotion. Oh Lord give me the fruit of salvation that is sweet to the mind everyday and always".

"I worship and serve Him who is the Lord who enjoys dancing in the twilight, who resides in all the Upanishads or Vedanta, who is quite rugged and handsome, who is deeply in love with His consort Uma or Brahmarambika, who always contains the fragrance of devotion of the sages, who wears the king of serpants as His ornament, who is worshipped by all those with good mind, who is well known for all the good qualities, who is embraced by Goddess Parvati, His consort, and who lives as Mallikarjuna on top of Shree Giri".

"May the Lord who likes to dance as per the request of sage Bringi, may He who tamed Gajasura, may He who got attached to Lord Vishnu in His Mohini Avatara, may He who is the holy 'OMKARA' sound, may He whose body is crystal white due to the smearing of ashes, may He who was caught by the arrow of Manmada the God of love, may He who is interested in protecting all the good ones, may He who resides on top of the Shree Shaila mountains, may He who is omnipresent, and may He who is the Lord of Goddess Brahmarambika give darshan to me and dance in the lotus of my heart".

"Oh Lord Shambhu, my mind that is like the Chataka bird craves for you, who is the God with a blue neck, who showers the nector like mercy, who cures the miseries of the mind that are like the trouble caused by the scorching heat of summer, who is worshipped by good people who aspire for the good harvest of the plant of knowledge, who can take any form as He likes, whose devotees dance like peacocks, who resides on the mountains and who has curly tuft of hair".

"I pray and worship that Lord whose plume is the vast blue sky, who has innumerable eyes like *Adisesha*, the king of serpants, who imparts the knowledge of *Pranava Mantra*, who blesses and wishes those who bow to Him and seek that knowledge, who is sung "Ke-Ki' like the peacock that dances with joy on seeing the cloud coloured Goddess Parvati, who likes to play in the garden of Vedanta and who has got a blue neck like that of a peacock".

"I pray to that blue necked God who is like a peacock excelling in glittering dance performed in front of Goddess Parvati, at twilight at the end of summer, along with the drum beats that are like thunder from the clouds of Lord Vishnu, and with the Devas shifting their sights that look like bright changing lightening, and with tears of devotion from the devotees like the rain from the sky".

"My prostrations to that one who is the Primordial cause, who is lustrous, who is known by the Vedas, who can be known, whose form is knowledge and happiness, who is interested in the protection of all the three worlds, who is being meditated upon by all sages, who is being praised and worshipped by the Devas, who keeps the illusions or Maya with Him, who is interested in vigorous dance, who has a matted lock of hair and who is the personification of all that is good".

"My prostrations to that one who is ever lasting, who is the soul of the trinity of Gods, who won over the three cities, who is the fame of Karitiyayini or Parvati, His consort, and who is the personification of truth, the first householder of the universe, who appears before the minds of the sages, who created the three worlds by His Maya, who is the end of all Vedas, who enjoys dancing in the twilight time, who has the matted lock of hair and who is Lord Shambhu."

"I approached many for filling my stomach and also for wealth, wandered aimlessly. But then I was not aware of the service to you, who is all pervading. Oh, Lord of all beings, Oh, Lord, who destroys the sins of His devotees, due to my previous birth's good *Karmas*, I know that you reside within all beings. Therefor I am fit to be saved by you".

"The Sun that is the friend of the Lotus flower becomes visible to the eye once it rises and removes the darkness that pervades the sky and earth. But you, who has the luster of billions of suns, is not making yourself visible to me. I know it is because of the thickness of the darkness of ignorance that surrounds me. Oh, Lord of all beings, kindly remove all that darkness and become visible to me".

"Oh, God of all beings, and the Lord of Goddess Gauri, and who is all pervading, just as the swan desires the cluster of lotus flowers, just like the Chataka bird that drinks rain water directly, intensely longs for the dark clouds that would bring rain, just like the Chakravaka bird that is the heavenly bird longs for the Sun, who is the Lord of the lotus flowers and just like the Chakora bird that craves for the moon light, every day my mind also longs for your lotus like feet that can be reached only by the path of *Jnana* that ultimately leads to the Bliss of liberation".

"Oh, my mind, your longing for the lotus feet of Shambhu that eradicates all fears and gives pleasure is like that of a man who is dragged by flood, craves to reach the shore, like the tired traveler who longs for the cool shade of the tree, like one who is afraid of rain longs for the soothing home, like the tired traveler longs for the sight of a hospitable householder, like the poor longs for the benevolent rich man, like the one who is frightened by darkness longs for light and like the one who is shivering from the biting cold longs for the warmth of the fire".

"Just as the seed of Ankola tree reaches for its mother the Ankola tree, just as the iron needle reaches for the iron ore, just as the chaste woman reaches for her husband, just as the delicate creeper reaches out to the nearby trees, just as the river reaches for the sea, if my spirit craves for the lotus feet of Pasupati and stays there for ever, then such a state is termed as devotion."

"Oh, my Lord, the mother called devotion takes care of her child the devotee, bathes the child with tears of joy and feels most happy, dresses the child using the clean and pure mind, feeds and fills the stomach of the child with the nector of stories about you, protects the body of the child with Rudraksha beads and ash as amulets and places her in the cradle of your memory".

"The sandals are the *Kusa* grass of crown for Pasupati, the gargled mouth full of water is the holy water for *Abhishekam*, the just tasted pieces of the remaining meat are the holy offering to the Lord who destroyed the three cities and the wonder of wonders is that, the hunter Kannappa who lived in the forest became the king of all devotees. Oh, Lord, what is there in this world that devotion to you cannot achieve?"

"Hey, the lord of Goddess Gauri, your tiny tender feet is always engaged in kicking the God of death, in trampling upon the heard hearted Apasmara, in wandering over the mountains, bearing the crowns of the Devas who prostrate before you, Oh, Lord Shambhu, kindly be pleased to see and wear the gem studded sandals of my mind".

"There is nothing that is impossible to attain for the one who sings the glory of your holy feet, Oh, Lord, who is the Lord of Bhavani. The Lord of death runs away from you fearing the kicks of your feet. The glitters of the crowns of Devas who worship you show the camphor lights. The pretty bride called liberation or *Mukti* embraces you as soon as she sees you".

"Oh Lord of all beings, you have to necessarily protect me because, you who is the bestower of all happiness created the world for your sport only and all the beings are your mere toys. So, all that I do is for your pleasure only and that all my actions are good instruments to bring pleasure to your devotees".

"I seek refuge in meditating upon that eternal Sadashiva, that is the prettiest land where various types of tears of joy, the real inner thrills of life that also indicate the eternal stable state sought by people who search for the results grow".

"Oh, Lord, you are the store house of mercy, the Lord of all beings, be kind enough to take care the cow of my devotion towards you that always yields the fragrance of happiness that resides at your feet and which is the result of all great deeds done by me".

"Oh Lord, I do not possess the qualities of those who wear the egoism of a tiger, irrationality of the deer, blemishes of the moon and the crooked mentality of the snake. But suppose I had all these,

I would have been a suitable ornament to you, Oh, Lord, who wears the moon on the crown".

"Oh, Lord, you can be worshipped in public as well as secretly, with independent intellect. Oh Lord, who is the pinnacle of graciousness, and who grants unlimited blessings, you who hold the moon on your head always is in my heart more than the impermanent world".

"With the bow string of utmost devotion, with the bow of meditation, with the constant thought of Shiva as the collection of arrows that never get less in numbers, the best of all the intellects, win over the enemies like sins and become victorious and they attain the stable kingdom of heaven".

"If any one can understand your lotus feet with the serpentine ornaments that is worshipped by the great Devas through great sacrifices or repetition of your great story or by means of constant meditation that throws light and destroys darkness and that uses the name of the Lord- they alone understand the meaning of life".

"Oh my good mind, chant the names of the lotus like feet of the Lord of the universe, in search of which Lord Vishnu who has Sree Devi and Bhudevi as His consorts took the form of a boar, and which is the fertile land from where the cure for salvation from the cycle of birth and death grows. What more is there for you to attain in this world?"

"The lotus feet of Him who wears ether or space as garment ceaselessly with a divine smell is engaged in removing the desires, bondage and suffering and bad conduct from us. So let the box of my mind get filled with the divine fragrance".

"Oh, Lord, you who are the enemy of Manmada, the God of love, you, who are the leader of the universe, who travels on a bull, kindly mount on my mind that is like a horse that is sacred, that exhibits different charming features, that moves with speed, that understands the gestures of others, and that does not possess blemishes but has only auspicious looks".

"The devotion to the great God stays in the sky of the lotus like feet of the Lord, and clusters of clouds pour sweet rain. Those whose lake of mind is filled by this rain, the crop that is their whole life becomes highly profitable. In what other way can it be?"

"Like the sweet heart who is separated always craves, remembers, gets sweet dreams, recollects the early meetings and sings about those meetings, my mind in a similar manner, utters the names of Lord Shiva in a trance and becomes anxious to get fixed on the lotus feet of the Lord".

"Like the noble groom who leads his bride, you teach me the method of serving the great ones with devotion, with a clean mind and attachment to the good and in this way, enlighten my intellect, Oh my Lord".

"Oh, Lord, who is the bestower of happiness, you move daily in the soft petalled mind of the Yogis, but my mind is worried about your pair of lotus like feet that are tender and soft that got hurt when you kicked the hard doors of the chest of God of death. Oh, God, kindly make your feet visible to my eyes so that I can gently massage them with both my hands".

"Thinking that this one will be born with a hard mind and I have to dance on it to save him, in the past, you walked on the rugged mountains with your tender soft feet and there by practiced and learnt to walk on the hard surface. Is this the meaning of your dance on the rocky mountains instead of walking in divine homes, on bed of flowers and on the properly laid out paths?"

"Oh Lord who is always with His consort Uma, the one who allots some time for worshipping your lotus like feet for doing meditation upon you and to interact with you, for doing *pranams* to you, for listening to your holy stories, for being in your presence, for singing your glories and being happy to offer his mind to you, would become *Jeevan Muktha*, that is, would attain salvation even when he is alive".

"Oh, Lord of Goddess Parvati, Lord Vishnu became your arrow to destroy the three cities. Half of your body transformed itself into your consort Parvati. Lord Vishnu became your lady love to serve Amrita, the nector and occupied the other half of your body as Hari hara. Nandi the bull on which you ride became the player of drum while you danced and the hunter Kannappa offered his eye at your foot in worship. He became your most glorified Bhakta or devotee. Who else is there who is greater than Lord Shiva?"

"Worship of mortal Gods without any doubt would yield happiness but in a limited manner; whereas the worship of birthless and immortal Lord who is with His consort Amba would lead to supreme bliss and those who worship Him are the blessed souls".

"Oh, my lord Shiva who is the ruler of the universe and who is the friend of all the world, who is the ocean of bliss, you are the store house of mercy; To serve you and worship you who is by the side of your consort Goddess Gauri, I am offering you the maid of my intellect that possesses all good qualities along with the request that you may reside in the inner core of my heart always".

"I do not know how to churn the ocean or dig and go to the underworld; I am also not capable as a hunter of wild animals. When that is so, how can I perform worship, Oh, my Lord, who wears the moon on the head with food that is *Halahala*, with ornament that you like namely, snakes and clothes that are the hides of elephant and tiger".

"Oh Lord of Goddess Uma, who is omnipresent, heaps of offerings are ready for your worship. But how will I be able to worship you? Because I can neither become a swan nor fly above to search for your top, the crown, nor become a boar to go under the world to search for your beginning that is your tender feet, especially when even the creator Lord Brahma and the maintainer Lord Vishnu could not be successful in knowing about these".

"Oh, Shambhu, Your food is Halahala, the poison from the ocean, your ornaments are the snakes, your clothes are thick hides of elephant and tiger and your vehicle is the big and majestic bull. Which one of these will you offer me? Apart from these what else have you got? It is more than enough if you kindly give me devotion to your lotus like feet".

"Oh, God, how will I worship you, Oh, my Lord, as I did not build a bridge across the sea like Sree Rama, I did not subdue the king of mountains like Agasthya by the palm of my hands, and I am not born out of the lotus like Brahma who is born from the navel or *Nabhi* of Lord Vishnu. If and when I am able to attain these, then I would be able to offer you flowers, sing your praise and meditate upon you".

"Oh Lord who rules over the universe, it seems to me that you become more pleased with arrows and pestle as was thrown at you by Arjuna or with the throwing of stones at you as was worshipped by Sankhya or Chekkiya Nayanar who was a Buddhist monk but became a devotee of Lord Shiva, rather than by worshipping you, by prostrating before you, and singing hymns about you or by meditating upon you or by reaching the state of *Samadhi*. Oh, Lord, kindly tell me which of these you like most, so that I also will do the same to please you".

"Oh Lord Shambhu, I will sing in words your story, because I am not suitable for the hard yogic practices. I would also worship you with my mind, Oh, Ishwara and I would bow my head before you, Oh, Sadasiva".

"Oh Lord who shines with the moon on His crown, by your grace, the ignorance of my heart that I had from my birth onwards got wiped out by your blessings and in that place resides knowledge that solves all problems. Hence I meditate on your lotus like feet that gives only good and that bestows salvation".

"Oh, Lord, all that is bad, namely, illluck, bad fate, sorrow, egoism, bad words all have disappeared from me now. Kindly uplift me, who is constantly hearing the tasty stories about you, with your divine and graceful looks, Oh, Lord of Goddess Gauri".

"Oh, Lord, who wears the crescent moon on the head, who has a dark blue coloured neck, that is the colour of the dark cloud, who is the brightest of all lights, who possesses everything, who is the Lord of Girija; let my heart be blissful always".

"The tongue is that which speaks of Lord Shiva, the eyes are that which see the Lord, the hands are that worship Him and the one who ever remembers Him is the fulfilled one".

"Oh, Lord of Goddess Bhavani, give up doubts such as 'My feet are tender and your heart is hard', because if that is the case, then how could you enter and stay on the hard mountains?"

"Oh, Lord who destroyed Tripura the three cities, kindly control the uncontrollable elephant of my mind with your goad of courage, pull it strongly with the chair of devotion towards you and tie it with the chain of intellect to the post of your holy feet".

"My mind that is like a big rutted elephant that wanders everywhere in an uncontrollable manner, Oh, Lord, kindly tie it tactfully with the rope of devotion and hold it and lead it to the ultimate state of bliss".

"Oh, Lord, who is the darling of Goddess Gauri, be kind enough to accept my poem by marrying my poem that is like a girl who is beautiful and decorated with ornaments, who has pretty and lovable appearance, who has a very good character, who has pretty and attractive complexion, who is praised by all good people, who has a very sweet and pleasant behaviour, who is the role model for all the girls, who has all ideals, who wears shining ornaments, whose behaviour is very descent, whose palm shows the line of prosperity and who is the store house of all good qualities".

"Oh, Lord, who is the ocean of mercy, is it proper on your part that you appeared and made me know about you easily when Lord Brahma and Lord Vishnu after taking the forms of swan and boar could not locate your end and beginning even after searching in vain the sky and earth".

"Oh Shambhu, I think all these praise is enough for you. However I did not state here anything that is not the truth. When Lord Brahma and other Gods list out all the great Gods, you always top the list and when your devotees search for the greatest Gods, all the other Gods disappear like chaff from the grain and you are recognised as the best among the best of grains".

Soundarya Lahari

Soundarya Lahari means waves of beauty. It has hundred verses. It is one of the best stotras and it is full of *Bhakti*, vedanta and *Sringara rasa*. There are different views about the authorship of Soundarya Lahari. It is said that sage Pushpadanta carved the hymn on Mount Meru and Goudapada memorized it and transferred it to his desciple Govinda who in turn passed it on to Shankara. It is also believed that when Shankara visited Kailash Lord Shiva gave him five Sphatika (crystal) Shiv Lingas and Goddess Para Shakti gave Shankara palm leaves that contained the hymn containing 100 verses that praised Her. It is said that Shankara installed these five Sphatika lingas one each at Sringeri (*Bhoga Linga*), Kanchi, (*Yoga Linga*),

Kedara (*Mukti Linga*), Nepal (*Vara Linga*), and Chidambaram (*Moksha Linga*). It is said that Nandi, the bull, the vehicle of Lord Shiva stopped Shankara while he was taking the Lingas and the verses and in the scuffle Shankara could take only the first 41 verses and the remaining 59 verses he added to it. It is stated in Linga Purana that Lord Ganesha Himself had inscribed the verses on the walls of Kailash. It is said that Shankara was asked to read these verses and while he was reading, Lord Ganesha erased the shlokas from the 100th verse in a reverse order and when Shankara found that the shlokas from 42nd were erased, he added the rest of the 59 verses up to 100th verse. Many also refer the entire 100 verses as Soundarya Lahari.

These hundred verses are supposed to be the best among all the Mantra literature. It tells about many *yantras* and describes the Tantric ways of performing worship and its effects. The dictim that truth is beauty and beauty is truth is expounded in this hymn. These verses equate Para Brahman with Parashakthi. It is a devotional hymn to the mother Goddess that contains secret *Mantras* and *Yantras* of the Sree Vidya Upasana. A form of Hindu worship that unites all aspects to attain both material as well as spiritual well being and ultimate liberation is the *Tantra* practice of Sri Vidya, that is, the supreme wisdom. This hymn contains the essence of Sri Vidya practice. In Sri Vidya knowledge, Devi is worshipped as Tripura Sundari, that is, the beauty of all the three worlds and she is considered as the power and knowledge that is supreme.

This hymn is full of figurative expressions and hence extremely difficult to understand. *Bhakti* is explained in these verses as attraction and love towards Mother Parvati. Bhakta is Mukṭha or the one liberated says Shankara. The Bhakta need to offer only his mind to the Lord, but not anything else. It explains the greatness of the Grace of Mother Parvathy, the consort of Lord Shiva. The verses contain explanations about Sree Chakra, Kundalani Yoga and so on that are extremely difficult to understand. Shankara himself in these hymns says that his attempt of describing the Goddess is like showing a lamp to sun, like offering the Chandrakantha stone to the moon or offering the seawater as Abhisheka to the sea. He says that he used the words of mother Goddess herself to praise Her.

The first part that consists of 41 stanzas is also called as *Ananda Lahari*, which means waves of Bliss. This part though are mostly devotional also contain extremely subtle ideas relating to *Mantras, Kundalini Yoga* and the esoteric worship of Shakti that contain great Mantric potency. These verses have hidden inner meaning and are highly philosophical and mystical and therefore are extremely difficult to grasp. In these verses Goddess Parvati is described as the creator of Dharma and the mother of all the Vedas, the mother of primeval desire, and the seed of devotion. The verses from 1 to 41 describe the mystical experience of the union of Shiva- Shakti. This part deals with *mantra, tantra* and *Yantra* practices. These verses are on the metaphysical level. They describe the philosophical and spiritual aspects of worship of Mother Goddess. These verses are highly philosophical and mystical and very difficult to understand. Each *mantra* given here is for fulfilling a certain wish. The first 41 verses give a detailed account of internal worship of Mother Goddess that included the concept of Kundalini, Sree Chakra, mantras and so on. The supreme reality is depicted as nondual but a distinction is made between Shiva, the holder of power, and Shakti, the power itself. The verses here state that without Shakti, Shiva is incapable of even movement. There are also verses that speak of equality of Shiva and Shakti that is Purusha and Prakruti. It is believed that by making suitable *Yantras* and by reciting particular stanzas and worshipping the *Yantras* everything could be obtained. The verses are full about attracting all the worlds, attainment of knowledge, removal of fears and curing of all diseases, attraction of opposite sex, getting sons and progeny, winning over enemies, avoidance of birth and death, for the safe return of people who have gone on a journey, for getting wealth, for getting a strong body, to get a meaning of life, to attain Lord Shiva and to make a dumb one speak, victory in the matters of love, avoidance of famine, about dacoity and epidemics, for getting ability to become scholar and a poet, for mastery over Vedas, for mastery over words and knowledge and science, victory in love, curing of poisons and fevers, attracting everyone and making them happy, for getting all powers, getting all riches, getting higher posts and powers, destroying enemies, realization of self and ultimate truth, getting rid of fear of poison and untimely death, avoiding abortions, taming bad persons, *parakaya Pravesa* or entering in to the body of another for powers, long life, getting power for attracting all, to obtain all benefits, for developing mutual liking, curing of tuberculosis, curing of all diseases, removing *bhootha, pretha, pisacha* and *Brahma rakshas*, curing childhood sickness, the capacity to see in a dream what we think about, to obtain blessings from Goddess Lakshmi, seeing good but not bad dreams, seeing the Goddess in person and curing of sexual diseases and so on.

The second part with stanzas from 42 to 100 (59 verses) is called as Soundarya Lahari that is believed to have been composed by Adi Shankara. Like the first part this latter part of the hymn known precisely as Soundarya Lahari is also very difficult to interpret and understand. Outwardly it describes the physical beauty of the Goddess as a vision experienced by Adi Shankara. In deeper sense, the verses in this part are supposed to describe Goddess Shakti from head to foot for the fulfillment of all wishes like attracting everything, curing of all diseases including that from water, victory over all, to get wealth, for obtaining a son, to get victory in all efforts, overcoming problems due to position of plants, to locate treasurers, for farsightedness, curing of small pox, victory in love, curing diseases of ears and eyes, attracting all worlds, seeing the Goddess in person, destruction of sins, power to protect, cure of kidney diseases, to get freedom from imprisonment, for all round luck, giving power of speech to the dumb, making correct predictions that come true, victory over mind, for wealth, good sleep, attracting all, getting all knowledge, control over speech, sweet words, mastery in music, attracting king, compensation for the mistake done towards Lord Shiva, conquering fear of darkness and getting grace from the Goddess, for good fame, renunciation, attracting all micro and macro aspects of the Universe, getting magical capability, remarkable beauty, getting expertise in magic, stopping fire, flood and so on, getting power like Indra, stopping the army, getting redemption from sins, parakaya pravesam, removing fear of ghosts, victory over enemies, attracting serpants, making wild beasts obey, getting rid of all diseases, coming out of bad spells that are cast, getting of land and riches, getting power to rule, fulfillment of desires, getting all desires, attainment of knowledge and wealth, redemption of soul, and attainment of ultimate bliss and occult powers. Some of the terms used in this hymn convey hidden meanings as well. For example, it is said that the noose described in this hymn represents the power of love, the sugar cane stands for mind, the five arrows represent the *Tanmatras* or the subtle elements and so on. However only great scholars and spiritual masters can interpret hymns like this in its deeper and hidden meanings. This difficulty of interpreting this poem both in its outward as well as in its inner meanings has given rise to many commentaries. It is said that there are more than 36 Sanskrit commentaries on this Shloka.

Soundarya Lahari of Adi Shankara

Shankara says, "Oh, mother, to those who sing about you and for you, a rainbow becomes visible in the moon worn by you in your crown because what is impossible to see, know and fulfill for others becomes possible for one by meditating upon you".

"Oh, Mother, nothing in this world except your hair is as dense and dark as the darkness of ignorance. But by thinking of your hair all darkness gets removed from us. An infinitesimally small part of the fragrance of your hair makes the Kalpa flowers of the garden of Indra quite famous for its fragrance".

"Oh, Mother, our lives become illumined and bright by meditating upon the brilliance of that *Sindoor* on the parting of your hair".

"Oh, Mother, let me meditate upon the beauty of your face on seeing which Lord Shiva who destroyed even Kamadeva forgot Himself".

Oh, Mother, already you have half of the moon on your crown. May I meditate upon your shining forehead that looks like the other half of the moon".

"OH, mother, may I meditate upon your eyes and eye brows that look to me like the bow of Kamadeva".

"Oh, Mother, may I meditate upon your eyes that are the sun and moon and that create the day and night, dusk and dawns".

"Oh, Mother, may I meditate upon the qualities of your eyes that are denoted by the names of the places like Vishala, Kalyanee, Ayodhya, Dhara, Mathura, Boga- Vathika, Avantee and Vijaya".

"Oh, Mother, let me meditate upon your red third eye that has the power to desire the entire universe".

"Oh, Mother, kindly shower on me your benovolence that is in the form of reflections in your eyes".

"Oh, Mother, with your eyes alone you are capable of winning over Lord Shiva who is pure, unstained and who destroyed the three worlds and also Kamadeva, the God of love".

"Oh, Mother, you recreate from yourself, in a playful manner as if in a game, Lord Brahma, Vishnu and Maheshwara who are the creator, maintainer and destroyer of the universe at the end of each Kalpa. Such a creation by you from yourself is seen as the Satva- Raja- and Tamo gunas in your eyes as the red, white and black colours. Hence there is nothing that is not you and beyond you. You alone are both the creator and the created".

"Oh Mother, why should any one take a holy dip in Triveni Sangama when a merciful glance from your eye can remove all sins?"

"Oh, Mother, without closing your eyes, you watch over day and night tirelessly, and protect the entire universe created by you from being destroyed".

"Oh, Mother, I wonder whether the fishes that resemble the shape of your eyes hide themselves in water fearing the envy of your eyes. It is certain that Mahalakshmi whom you hold in your eyes enters the water lilies during nights to bloom to give the beauty of your eyes".

"Oh, Mother, like the moon that showers its rays equally on the forests and palace and still lose nothing, similarly, you also shower your benevolent gaze upon me. Even when I am far away from you and do not think of you, even while I am sick and need your presence, shower the glance of your long eyes upon me".

"Oh, Mother, the beauty of your face is unparalleled. To me the beautiful curve of the side of your face resembles the bow of cupid and your side glance is like the arrow that is fixed in perfect union with the bow to fly across both your ears".

"Oh, Mother, your ear rings are reflected clearly on your mirror like face. This sight makes me feel as if they are the four wheels of a chariot that is your face in which Kamadeva is seated to the distress of Lord Shiva".

"Oh Mother, even Goddess Saraswati, who is the mother of all the worlds with the sound of Her earring can only echo the sweetness of your words that can belittle even the sweetness of nector like life that saves one from death and old age".

"Oh, Mother, your nose looks like a beautiful golden chip of bamboo that is filled with pearls and when the moonlight passes through it, there comes a pearl on top of it that is your nosestud. May I meditate upon your nose and the nosestud".

"Oh, Mother, I can compare the beauty of your lips only with a fruit yielded by a plant made of coral".

"Oh, Mother, how can I explain the sweetness of the smile that you shower upon your devotees ? It is no wonder that the poets describe the Chakora birds sipping on moon light alone every night to have lost their sense of taste for ever after having tasted the sweetness of your smile".

"Oh, Mother, Goddess Saraswati, who is the mother of all worlds, music and art stays always at the tip of your tongue that utters only the glory of Lord Shiva, who is the ultimate Bliss and the everlasting truth. But when seated at the tip of your tongue, Goddess Saraswati has to lose Her crystal clear colour and take on the red colour of your tongue that prevails over Her own words".

"Oh, Mother, your special devotees like Lord Subramanya, Indra and Lord Vishnu after winning over come to see you even before removing their armours. Then their evil ones chew the betel leaves of your mouth instead of partaking the *Naivedya* of Lord Shiva that anyway belongs to *Chanda*. It is like after every *Pooja*, you give your Prasad to all your devotees".

"The only comfort of your devotees who are immersed in the abyss of solitude and sorrows is the sweetness of your voice. On hearing your sweet voice, Goddess Saraswati silences Her *veena* and hides it in shame".

"Oh mother, let me meditate upon your chin that is touched like the rest of your body only by pure truth, the beauty of which is known only to Lord Shiva who is the ultimate truth and inner knowledge and as far as your source is concerned it is unknown and unexplored as the mighty Himalayas".

"Oh, Mother, *Bhakti* described in Lalita Sahasranam, that is swept off your feet is the outcome of pure devotion and inner knowledge. The garland of white beads that adorns your neck and that is stained by the smearing of black paste has the beauty stem of lotus in muddy waters".

"Oh, Mother, you are the origin of the entire music in the world, you gave everything to your devotees who binds you with them in devotion. The three beautiful lines on your neck look like the lines drawn to limit the scale of music".

"Oh, Mother, kindly protect your devotee from death and the sorrows of the world. Lord Brahma who is more powerful than the Lord of death approached you for protection from being destroyed by Lord Shiva".

"Oh, Mother, who is the most beautiful, even the beauty of the most beautiful lotus is only a gift from you, but only if you will it that way".

"Oh, Mother, may I meditate upon the beauty of your bosom on which the devotees rest, which the poets describe as the beauty of the royal elephant's head".

"Oh, Mother, one need not pass through all the stages of life and then in to old age and death after having enjoyed the nector of life granted by you. When one knows you and what you have to offer, how can he engage himself in small pleasures of life?"

"Oh, Mother, may I meditate upon that garland of pure pearls on your bosom that indicate the knowledge of the inner self that can be attained by devotees after destroying the Gajasura, that is, the intense darkness engulfing the world".

"Oh, Mother, by mere taste of what you offer, one is able to achieve the impossible".

"Oh, Mother, people are carried away by the pleasures of the world. But the world can offer only a fraction of what you offer to your devotees. Finally when the worldly pleasures burn one, then one seeks refuge in you who is an ocean, the depth of which is impossible to measure".

"Oh, Mother, the one who dwells in you sees with your very fine light, that destroys the darkness of the whole world, but he is not seen by the others".

"Oh, Mother, a holy dip in the sacred Ganga purifies one of all sins. You yourself are the everlasting flow of Ganga that removes all sins forever. You are the source of ultimate beauty in which *Rathi*, the consort of *Kama* dissolves herself. Those who seek such a state get a small fraction of that. One has to open his inner eye to experience you like your Lord Shiva".

"Oh, Mother, the learned poets describe you as a manifestation of beauty in human form. May I also fix you in my mind as a woman with the most beautiful qualities so that I need not seek any other form".

"Oh, Mother, may you alone like the most beautiful woman fill all thoughts of my mind".

"Oh, Mother, your greatness, vastness and unlimited self make the entire universe infinitely small".

"Oh, Mother, I meditate upon the beauty of your legs that defeat the shape of the trunks of elephants and the smoothness of the banana plants and that are uncomparable and on which you kneel before your Lord Shiva, the Lord of all the worlds to show us how to respect what is to be respected".

"Oh, Mother, before you even Indra and the other forms of Gods bow with their crowns touching and rubbing the nails of your toes. The Lord of love Kamadeva won over the whole world through your unimaginable and incomparable beauty".

"Oh, Mother, the Upanishads place your feet on top of them and Shiva bows before those feet by washing them with the sacred water of Ganga that is placed on His matted locks and Lord Vishnu falls before those feet that shows reflections of the glow of His crown. Kindly bless me with those feet of yours, Oh, Mother".

"Oh, Mother, we bow before those feet of yours that even Lord Shiva who is the Lord of the worlds wished to touch but could not".

"Oh, Mother, let me meditate upon your anklets that jingled loudly in victory because you could capture Lord Shiva with your feet with the help of Kamadeva who lodged in his mind anger against Lord Shiva for destroying him in to ashes with the flowers of anger".

"Oh, Mother, poets refer your feet which are bent day in and day out for granting the wishes of the devotees as 'Pada Padma', or 'Pada Pankaja' and thus compare your feet to the lotus that becomes worthy due to Mahalakshmi who is seated on it".

"Oh, Mother, when I am at your feet, that is the source of all fame, name and greatness, then there is no fear from dangers. When that is the case, why is such a feet of yours are compared to the hard shell of the Tortoise in Lalita Sahasranama".

"Oh, Mother, when the heavenly nymphs become aware of the greatness of your feet that grant blessings, they close their palms in shame like the lotus that sees the moon after the sun sets because they know only about the Kalpa trees that grants wishes to the Devas of heavens".

"Oh, Mother, let me dissolve in you who is the inner knowledge and ultimate Bliss, like a bee that is inside a flower enjoying the honey and getting maddened by the taste of honey that is flowing out of the flower".

"Oh, Mother, let me meditate upon your gait. It looks as though the swans whose graceful gait have been praised by poets, learnt the art of walking from you".

"Oh, Mother, let me meditate upon that Shiva who is the innermost Bliss and ultimate knowledge, who is your Lord and who is the reflection of your own beauty that is irresistibly fascinating".

"Oh, Mother, to save the world, that is immersed in sorrows, death and loss, you manifested yourself as the perfect beauty of red glow to take refuge by those who are in misery and sorrows".

"Oh, Mother, to me it looks as though the moon wanes because you take away its light for your pleasure and when the moon becomes empty of its light Lord Brahma fills it up as per your command for you to make use of it again".

"Oh, Mother, for the wandering and unstable mind that is not able to concentrate on you, you seem to be far beyond reach. So such people have to be satisfied with only the small little pleasures and attractions that you grant. But even then, they seem to be far away from you".

"Oh, Mother, the one who meditates upon Goddess Saraswati becomes a poet, the one who meditates upon Goddess Lakshmi becomes prosperous but you manifest yourself only in the minds of people who possess purity of heart but not even in the Dharbha plants that are used in worship. You manifest in such people as the inner knowledge and ultimate bliss".

"Oh, Mother, you are far beyond the four Vedas and the knowledge that they give".

"Oh, Mother, I seek knowledge that takes me to your feet. The knowledge that is obtained at your feet grants everything. It could make even the dumb, a poet like Kalidasa your devotee".

"Oh, Mother, you grant the gifts of words of a poet, like Goddess Saraswathi, prosperuity like Goddess Lakshmi and physical beauty beyond that of God of love-Kamadeva, and beyond everything enlightenment to your devotees even while they are still alive".

"Oh Mother, who is mine, Kindly accept this hymn in praise of you that makes use of your own words. It is like offering water to the ocean and offering light to the sun".

Vishvanathashtakam

This is a shloka of eight verses in praise of Lord Vishvanatha of Kashi or Banaras. The nineth verse is the Phala Sruti. It tells about the good results of reciting this prayer of eight verses to Lord Shiva. Through these verses Shankara asks the devotee to sing and praise Lord Vishvanatha, who is like a lion to the ego called elephant, who is like Garuda, the king of birds to the snake like *Asuras*, who is like the forest fire that swallows sorrow, death and old age, who is the reason for all happiness in this world, who is beyond reasoning and so on. Such a one is in the centre of the heart of all beings, when the heart is bereft of all desires, is not of fault finding nature, not attached to sinful acts, and when it rests in the deep state of Samadhi. Such a one is without any passion; he is the source of detachment and peace, and has a pleasing form.

"Sing and praise Lord Vishwanata, the Lord of the universe, who is Kashinatha or the Lord of Kashi, who has a tufted wet hair due to the waves of river Ganga, on whose left side stands Goddess Gauri, His consort, and who is also the friend of Lord Narayana and who crushed the pride of Manmada, the God of Love".

"Sing and praise Vishwanatha, the Lord of the universe, who is Kashinatha or the Lord of Kashi, who is beyond all words, who is the treasure house of all good qualities, who has lotus like feet, that are worshipped by Gods like Brahma, and Vishnu and by Devas and who keeps His consort Parvati on His left side".

"Sing and praise Vishwnatha, the Lord of the universe, who is Kashinatha or the Lord of Kashi, who is the Lord of all beings, who has snake as His ornament, who has the skin of tiger as His garment, whose hair is matted, who has three eyes, who holds Trident, rope, and goad and who is the giver of all boons".

"Sing and praise Vishwanatha, the Lord of the universe, who is Kashinatha, or the Lord of Kashi, whose crown glitters with the moon on it, who burnt Manmada the God of love with the fire from His third eye and whose earring is the king of snakes".

"Sing and praise Vishwanatha, the Lord of the universe, who is Kashinatha, the Lord of Kashi, who is like the king of animals to pride that is like an elephant, who is like Garuda that is the king of birds to asuras who are like snakes, who is like the forest fire that can swallow all sorrows, old age and death".

"Sing and praise Vishwanatha, the Lord of the universe, who is Kashinatha, the Lord of Kashi, whose bearing is shining, who is first among all the forms and the formless, who is the source of all happiness, who can never be won over, who is beyond the comprehension of all reasoning, who is the soul of all serpents and whose soul is both pure and mixed".

"Sing and praise Vishwanatha, the Lord of the universe, who is Kashinatha, the Lord of Kashi, Sing about Him, who resides in the core of your lotus like heart when it is beyond desire, beyond any differentiation, attachment and when it remains in Samadhi, or deep state of meditation".

"Sing and praise Vishwanatha, the Lord of the universe, who is Kashinatha, the Lord of Kashi, who is beyond all passion, who loves all good beings, who is the source of all detachment and peace, who is assisted by Parvati, His consort, who is the daughter of the mountains, and who has a pleasing appearance that is full of sweetness and courage and who wears the strongest poison *Halahala*".

"That one who reads these eight verses of prayer with its meaning that sings the glory of Lord Shiva who is the Lord of Kashi or Varanasi, would obtain knowledge, wealth, happiness and great fame and in the end would attain *Mukti* or liberation"

6
Shankara: The Philosopher and Mystic

The *Prakarana Granthas* or the philosophical treatises and some of the hymns that Shankara composed reveal his philosophy of Advaita Vedanta. The summary of some of these is presented here.

Aparokashanubhoothi or Self-realisation

This poem contains 144 shlokas or stanzas. In this Shankara explains the means to attain self-realization for liberation. The means to attain *Vairagya* or detachment is got by praying to Hari through austerities and performance of duties as per one's social order and stage of life. Pure Vairagya means indifference and detachment to all objects of enjoyment. Discrimination is the conviction that *Atman* the seer alone is permanent. *Shama* means abandonment of all desires and *Dama* means restraint of external functions of the sense organs. Uparati is turning away from all objects and Titikhsa is the endurance of all sorrows and miseries of life. Shradha is deep faith in the Vedas and also the implicit faith on the teacher who teaches the Vedic knowledge. *Samadhana* is concentration of mind on 'SAT' that is Brahman. Mumukshuta is the burning desire for detaching oneself from all bonds of the world. Only such a one who has this knowledge should try to attain the supreme knowledge. *Vichara* or self-enquiry is the only means to obtain *Jnana*. The way to *Vichara* is to enquire, "Who am I? How is the world created? Who is the creator? Of what material is the world made of?" Once the knowledge that "I am neither the body, that is a combination of the five elements nor the combination of the sense organs, I am different from these. Every misconception in this world is due to ignorance" dawns every misunderstanding will disappear and they get dissolved. Brahman is the cause for all the modifications of the Anthakarana or the various thoughts. It is the one without a second, is subtle, unchanging existence, just as the earth is the material cause of the pot. One should know that "I am that one, subtle, the knower, the witness, the imperishable and unchanging Brahman". Unlike the body, *Atman* has no parts. Still people mistake *Atman* for the body due to ignorance. *Atman* is internal, while body is external. *Atman* is the ruler and the body is being ruled. *Atman* is all consciousness while body is made up of blood, flesh, and is impure. *Atman* is the supreme illumination and it purifies itself. Body's nature is darkness. *Atman* is existence itself, and therefore eternal. Body is transient and in essence it is non-existent. Due to the light of *Atman* all objects get manifested. The body is not the 'I' but due to ignorance people identify themselves with the body. Body is with parts and *Atman* is without parts. They cannot be one and the same. Atman is the ruler and the body is the ruled. *Atman* is internal while body is external. *Atman* is all consciousness but body is made up of fresh and blood and is impure. *Atman* is eternal while body is transient. Knowledge is the awareness that "I am not the body but Brahman, that is nothing but absolute existence and Bliss, changeless, pure, imperishable, not subjected to diseases, beyond all understanding, that is all pervading, without attributes, or activities, ever free, immovable, unlimited, holy, immortal and so on. The ignorant should know himself as the *Purusha* with the help of Sruti or Vedas or intuitive knowledge or reasoning, that he is different from the body. And that he is ever existent, residing in one that is *Purusha* and the only one. The supreme *Purusha* is only one. The gross bodies are many. If that is so, how can *Purusha* and the gross bodies be one and the same? The gross body cannot be *Purusha* because when we refer to our body, we say, 'It is my body".

The *Purusha Suktha* in the *Vedas* declares that everything is verily the *Purusha*. The *Brihad Aranyaka Upanishad* also says, that "*Purusha* is totally unattached". Body has innumerable impurities and it cannot be *Purusha* that is the purest and self-luminous. The Vedas also state that *Atman* is different from the body and is permanent because it remains even after one's death and it reaps the fruits of good and bad *Karmas* of a person during his lifetime. Even the subtle body, unlike *Purusha* has many parts, is unstable, and is an object of perception, limited, and in essence non-existent. So, even the subtle body is not *Purusha. Atman* is different both from the gross and subtle body. It is the substratum of ego, Ishwara, the Lord, and the self of all. It is present in every form but transcends all forms. In this way logic establishes the difference between Atman and body. Consciousness is one and the same. The individuality of *jiva* also is false. It is like the delusion of snake in a rope. Just as a rope appears as snake in darkness, for the ignorant, pure consciousness appears as innumerable worlds. The cause of this universe is Brahman. This whole universe is Brahman. The Sruti says, 'all this is *Atman*'. All beings are born from Brahman. Only when there is duality there is another; with identity all become one. *Atman*, the self of all is Brahman. Everything is illusory. When once the supreme truth is realized then one understands that there is no distinction between the cause and effect. Since Brahman is all pervading the phenomenal world also is included in that. The one who is engulfed by *Maya* or ignorance sees multiplicity in Brahman and goes through repeated births and deaths. All beings are born of Brahman that is the supreme *Atman*. So everything is Brahman. Sruti states that Brahman is the basis of all names, forms and actions. A thing that is made of gold is bound to have the qualities of gold. Similarly everything that is born of Brahman has always the nature of Brahman. Fear is there for one who differentiates between *Jeevatma* or the individual soul and *Paramatma* or the universal soul. Duality appears due to ignorance only. When knowledge dawns, duality disappears and everything becomes Brahman. Once this knowledge dawns, there is no illusion or delusion or sorrow.

In the *Brihad Aranyaka Upanishad* it is said that the *Atman* that is the self of all is nothing but Brahman. The world serves all practical purposes but essentially it is a dream world. It is really non-existent. Just as a dream appears to be real in dream state, world appears to be real due to ignorance. But in the waking state one realizes that the objects of the dream are not real and they were illusory. Similarly, when once the knowledge dawns the world that appeared as real hither to would be known as essentially unreal. But the waking experience is absent in dream state. In dream less, deep sleep state the experience both in the waking as well as in dream state is seen as non-existent. The witness behind all the three states is the reality that is beyond all gunas, eternal, and consciousness itself. When once the illusion vanishes, the earth with which the pot is made will be known as the same that is outside it. Similarly *Jeeva* also will be seen as the same as *Atman*. Brahman is seen differently as *Jeeva* just as earth and gold are seen different from the objects that are made out of it and so on. Just as a pot is all earth, similarly, body is all consciousness. The distinction in to self and non-self is due to ignorance. Just as for a person, who is going in a boat everything seems to move, or just as for a person who suffers from jaundice everything appears yellow, just as when clouds move moon appears to be moving, as the moon seen in its reflection in water look unsteady, in the same manner, for a person who is ignorant, *Atman* would appear as body. But when the realization comes and knowledge dawns then this ignorance would also disappear once for all. There is nothing in this universe that can exist apart from *Atman*. So, one should contemplate on *Atman* always while experiencing the results of all past *karmas*. However Prarabda, that is the effects of past *Karmas* or actions cease to exist for one who attains the supreme knowledge that everything is Brahman because then the body becomes non-existent. For the one who has attained the real, *Prarabda* also ceases to exist. When one realizes that what he has considered hitherto due to ignorance was only a rope but not a snake, the snake disappears and in its place rope only will be seen. Similarly when Brahman or *Atman* that is the substratum is known, then the phenomenal world would disappear completely. The body also belongs to the phenomenal world and therefore it is also unreal. So body and *Prarabda* exist only for the ignorant but not for the realized one. *Prarabda* is only for the ignorant but not for the wise. For attaining real knowledge there are fifteen steps through which one can practice meditation always. Only through constant practice *Atman* or the Absolute existence that is knowledge can be realized. So to attain the desired goal one should practice meditation constantly.

The steps of meditation are; control of senses, or *Yama*, control of mind or *Niyama*, renunciation, maintaining silence, space, time, posture, restraining *Moolabhanda*, equipoise of the body, firmness of vision, control of vital forces, withdrawl of mind, concentration, self contemplation and complete absorbtion. Restraint of senses with the knowledge 'That all is Brahman' is *Yama* (The first of the eight steps in Yoga) that should be practiced always. *Niyama* that is the second step in Patanjali's Yoga is the continuous flow of a single thought by eliminating all the other thoughts to be practiced regularly. The real renunciation is abandonement of illusory universe with the knowledge that everything is Atman only. This knowledge results in immediate liberation. Silence is where words and mind are turned back. No one can describe Brahman. It is beyond words. So silence becomes inevitable. The solitude of this type is known as 'space' where the universe becomes non-existent but is always pervaded. Time denotes the non-dual, indivisible Bliss that is Brahman. Brahman is the source and support of everything. It is immutable and the wise merge in to it completely. Restraining *Moolabhanda* or the root is the restraint of the mind on Brahman that is the source and root of all existence. This is fit for those who practice Rajayoga. Equipoise of the limbs or Dehasamya is the merger in to that Brahman when everything is viewed as Brahman and where the distinction between the seer and the seen disappears totally. Practicing Pranayama is restraining the mind and concentrating on Brahman alone. Rechaka or breathing out is the negation of the phenomenal world. Breathing in or *Puraka* is the thought "I am Brahman". Kumbhaka is the steadiness of that thought. This is the real course of *Pranayama*. *Pratyahara* or withdrawal of mind is the absorption of mind in the supreme consciousness by seeing *Atman* in all objects. *Dharana* is concentration or steadiness of mind through the realization of Brahman. *Dhyana* or meditation is remaining aloof from everything as a result of the understanding that 'I am Brahman'. It results in supreme bliss. Samadhi is complete forgetfulness of all thoughts by making it steady and then identifying it with Brahman. The spiritual aspirant should practice this meditation until the knowledge, the Bliss arises. Then the yogi who thus has attained perfection becomes free from all practices. While practicing Samadhi many obstacles may arise like idleness, desire for sense pleasures, sleep, dullness, distraction, a sense of blankness and so on. A yogi should overcome such obstacles. When the mind thinks of an object it identifies with the object, when the mind identifies itself with void, it becomes blank, with the thought of Brahman, it becomes Brahman and attains perfection. Life without thinking Brahman is in vain. Shankara says blessed are those who are conscious of Brahman in the beginning, and then develops this consciousness. All people always respect them. Those who are conscious of Brahman attain the state of Brahman. Merely talking about Brahman is of no use. These people who merely talk about Brahman are the ones who are highly attached to the world and therefore undergo repeated births and deaths. Like the great *Rishis* of yore one should always think about Brahman. Usually the cause is inherent in the effect. One should see the cause in the effect and then dismiss the effect altogether. Intense meditation with conviction makes one to become that on which he meditates upon. Through this alone the state of awareness of Brahman and finally merging oneself with Brahman can happen. This is the path of *Raja Yoga* to attain perfection.

Atma Bodha

It is a treatise on self and consists of 68 stanzas, for those wise ones who have purified themselves with austerities and possess a calm, peaceful mind that is free from desires. The basis for liberation is knowledge of the self that destroys the darkness of all ignorance. Action or *Karma* cannot lead to liberation. Due to ignorance soul appears to be finite. But with knowledge the self reveals itself by itself. It is like the sun that becomes visible when the dark clouds pass away. Constant practice of meditation leads to purification of the self or the *jeevatma* that is stained by ignorance. The soul is infinite and body is finite. So soul cannot be body. The world is like a dream. It appears as real as long as one is ignorant. But when the true wisdom dawns, one understands that the world is only unreal. Brahman is the basis or substratum of everything. As long as this is not understood, world appears to be real. It is like the illusion of silver in the pearl. Like a bubble that bursts in water, the world exists and then dissolves in the supreme self. Akasha or sky appears to be different due to its association with various things. When these limiting factors are destroyed, space becomes one. Similarly the truth or Brahman appears to be manifold due to its association with various Upadhis or conditionings like caste, colour, or position that are superimposed on Brahman and once these are destroyed Brahman becomes one. The gross body that experiences pleasure and pain is the result of past actions and it is constituted by the five elements and its five fold self division and combination. The subtle body is formed with the rudimentary elements or Tanmatras namely, the five pranas, the ten organs, the mind, the intellect and the five elements before their five fold self division and combination with one another. The causal body is *Avidya* or ignorance. But *Atman* is different from all these three conditioning bodies or Upadhis such as gross, subtle and causal bodies. Because of its association with these bodies it appears to get their qualities. It is like the crystal acquiring the colour of that object that is kept near it. Just as rice is separated from the husk, similarly, the pure self is to be separated from the bodies through discrimination and self-analysis. Further *Atman* appears to be active when it is seen through sense organs just as moon appears to be moving when the clouds move on the sky. The ignorant superimpose the varied functions of the body and senses on the *Atman* just as blue colour is attributed to the sky. The ignorant think that limitations which belong to the mind, as the nature of self or *Atman*. Only as long as the intellect and mind function, there will be attachment, desire, pleasure, pain and so on.

In deep sleep when the mind is absent, they also cease to exist. Therefore they belong to the mind but not to the Atman. The nature of Atman is eternity, purity, reality, consciousness and bliss. It is like the nature of heat is of the fire, and so on. The notion 'I know' is because of the thought wave of the intellect. Actually, intellect by itself has no capacity to experience 'I know'. Atman is only to be experienced. But the individuality in one makes him think that he is the knower and the seer. A person who mistakes a rope for a snake is overcome by fear. Similarly, a person who thinks of himself as the ego or *jeeva* is overcome by fear. Once a person realizes that he is the supreme self, the *Atman*, the fear vanishes. All material objects are inert and cannot shine by themselves. Atman is all pervading. It is the witness. It is not the body, senses, mind or intellect that constitutes matter. Atman is Absolute. The nature of Atman is that it is eternal, pure, real, consciousness, bliss and so on. Through negation and through discrimination one will know that he is Brahman and not the body. Atman is knowledge itself and it does not require any other knowledge to know it. The identity of the individual and supreme soul can be known by the *Mahavakyas* of the Upanishads and by means of negation of everything as 'Not this, not this'. Everything else like body and so on is perishable. One should obtain the knowledge that he is not the body, not the senses, not the mind, not the intellect, not actions, and so on but only is Brahman that is eternal, without desire, without any impurity, ever liberated, ever pure, changeless, unattached, stainless, motionless, indivisible, free, non-dual, infinite and so on. Such an impression removes ignorance just as medicines destroy disease. The spiritual aspirant should sit in a solitary place, should free his mind from desires, control his senses, and meditate with unwavering concentration on Atman that is one without a second. The one who has realized the supreme truth rejects his identification with worldly objects and forms and dwells as the infinite consciousness and Bliss. He becomes the self or Atman. Actually there is no distinction between the knower, known and the object that is known. Just as darkness disappears as soon as the sun rises, similarly, as soon as the sun of knowledge or the divine consciousness emerges all ignorance disappears. Atman is an ever-present reality. But it is not recognized due to ignorance. Due to ignorance Atman appears to be *Jeeva*. Once the real nature of *jeeva* as the self is realized, then, the ego filled individuality disappears and the notions of 'I' and 'mine' also will disappear. The *yogi* of perfect understanding knows that the entire universe is his own self. The universe is Atman just as all earthen pots are made of clay. A liberated person becomes Brahman itself, the *Sat-Chit-Ananda*. The yogi who dwells in the self or Atman becomes a Jivan muktha. He has no attachment or bondage. He is always in Bliss. Though he lives in the midst of upadhis, still he remains aloof and detached from everything. He moves like a wind with total freedom and with perfect detachment. Such a one dwells in 'Vishnu' like water in water or light in light. The ultimate knowledge is realization of Brahman that is non- dual, infinite, eternal, omnipresent, omnipotent, omniscient, indivible, and that is existence- knowledge- bliss or *Sat-Chit-Ananda*. This is referred to as 'Substratum' in Vedanta. Even deities like Brahma enjoy only a particle of this unlimited bliss of Brahman. Just as butter permeates milk, Brahman pervades everything. Brahman is not gross or subtle; not long or short. It is changeless, without qualities, without colour, and so on. Brahman pervades and illumines the universe. There is nothing that is other than Brahman. He who attains this knowledge will discard his identification with his body and objects of name and form. For a *yogi*, the entire universe is his own self. There is nothing that is separate from him. He moves like a wind perfectly detached. He gets totally absorbed in Vishnu, the all-pervading spirit. The one who attains this knowledge becomes all knowing, all pervading and finally attains immortality and liberation.

Atma Panchakam

In this Shankara the devotee identifies himself with Lord Shiva the all pervading one. These six verses also explain the Advaita philosophy of Shankara. In these verses Shankara says, "I am neither the body, nor the senses nor the mind. Pride, soul or intellect but I am Shiva who is the eternal, unattached, far away from worldly attachments, and is the witness of everything. Due to ignorance and absence of knowledge or *gnana*, I mistake a rope to be a snake, and life-to-lifeless thing. When the realized ones point out my ignorance I wake up from this dream of illusion and understand that it is only a rope but not a snake. Similarly, I am not the soul but I am Lord Shiva. Due to *Maya* or ignorance I see the world as real and eternal truth and joy. This notion is similar to a dream in sleep that is not real. I am that pure, complete, eternal and single Shiva. The world is not different from me. It is like a reflection in a mirror. The entire world is within me. So I am Shiva, which is only one and not two. I am never born, never grew and never die, because birth, growth and death are for the body only. The nature of *Karma* is pride; it is not for the soul that is eternal. I am the unattached Shiva. When birth and death come to me I was never born. When there is hunger and thirst I am not the soul. When passion and sorrows come I am not the mind. When there is attachment and detachment I am not the doer."

Brahma Jnanavali Mala

In these 21 verses the characteristic of the one who has realized Brahman are described. Shankara says that by hearing this poem once, one achieves liberation. The one who has realized Brahman, is unattached from attachments of all kinds, is of the nature of *Sat-chit-Ananda*, that is, existence consciousness and bliss. He becomes the very self that is indestructible, ever unchanging, eternal, pure, not caught in *Maya*, ever liberated, formless, infinite bliss, formless, pure consciousness, ever revels in his own self, inactive, indivisible, concentrated bliss, the indwelling consciousness, free from all agitations of mind, beyond *Prakruti* or *Maya*, is of the nature of eternal bliss, the supreme self, beyond everything, supreme light, beyond all different forms, of the nature of pure consciousness, not subject to deterioration, of the nature of bliss, self luminous, beyond the three gunas of *Sattva, Rajas* and *Tamas*, infinite bliss, the inner controller, immutable, all pervading, the superior self, devoid of parts, actionless, the self of all, the primordial one, ancient, eternal and unlimited self, witness of all pairs of opposites, immovable, eternal, witness of all and everything, a mass of awareness, the experiencer without any support but that supports everything, without desires, free from afflictions of body, afflictins caused by other beings and those caused by higher powers, different from gross, subtle and causal bodies, and the witness of the three states of consciousness, auspicious, the inner, outer and the indwelling light, higher than the highest, light of all lights, self luminous light that is the self. Vedanta states that there are two things that are different from each other namely, the seer that is Brahman and the seen that is Maya. He who realizes that he is mere witness only would be liberated. He is the enlightened one says Vedanta. The pot, wall and so on are only clay. So also the entire universe is only Brahman. This is what Vedanta says. Brahman alone is real. The universe is only Mithya that is neither real nor unreal. The Jeeva is only Brahman and not different from it. Vedanta proclaims this.

Dakshinamoorthy Ashtakam

This hymn has 11 stanzas that includes introductory and Phalasthuthi shlokas and gives the summary of Shankara's philosophy of Advaita Vedanta. Since this shloka was very difficult to understand one of the disciples of Shankara by name Sureshwaracharya wrote a commentary called Manasollosa to this. It was later followed by a number of sub commentaries on his commentary.

It is a prayer to the young looking Dakshinamoorthy who taught to his aged disciples the true nature of the supreme Brahman through silence. He taught the Supreme truth through *Chin Mudra*, where the edge of the thumb and the first finger are joined. It shows the unification of *jeevatma* with *Paramatma*. It is said that the chin Mudra represents the union of Shiva, the supreme principle - Brahman and *Shakti* that represents *Maya* or *Prakruti*. These verses point out that just as the image of a thing is seen in a mirror, similarly, the image of the world, that is the soul is seen within one's mind as soul, and outside as world. This is due to Avidya or illusion. During sleep the same truth appears as different but when one wakes up from dream he realizes that all that he saw in dream are false and he is the only one that is the soul that is real. After observing that which exists as real light of truth he understands the meaning of 'TAT TVAM ASI' that is, 'THOU ART THAT' (*Mahavakya* from the *chandogya Upanishad* of *Sama Veda*) and he gets freedom from the cycle of birth and death. Shankara says, 'Salutations to that God who faces the south'. Just as the light kept in a pot with many holes goes out in all directions, similarly, when a person becomes enlightened, wisdom spreads through his ear, mouth, eye, thought senses and so on. With the knowledge that he is Brahman, the pure consciousness, but not the body, mind, senses and so on, he becomes consciousness of itself. Those who think that they are the body, or soul, or intellect or the concept of emptiness, (May be Shankara is referring to the *Shoonya vada* of the Buddhists), are all, ignorant. It is only He, the knowledge represented by Lord Dakshinamoorthy, who can destroy the veil of ignorance and wake up one from the state of *maya*. Just as Rahu covers the Sun during eclipse, shines as before when the eclipse is over, man also gets suppressed when he is under the veil of ignorance due to illusion.

When the veil of ignorance disappears and he wakes up with knowledge he comes to know that even during sleep (This also negates the Buddhist notion that during sleep there is nothing) He, the Brahman exists in all states, waking, dreaming or during deep sleep. All distinctions of the teacher and taught, the father and son, cause and effect and so on are due to illusion. Actually there is only Brahman and nothing else. One must know that the universe consists of God who pervades everything and nothing else. The individual soul can attain the state of Godliness, self-realization, and occult powers easily. Dakshina moorthy is the meaning of Pranava Mantra 'OM'. He is the personification of the supreme wisdom, having extreme clarity of thought. He is the epitome of peace, He is the panacea for all disease of birth and death and He is the treasure house of all knowledge.

Dhanyashtakam

This is a Stotra of 10 stanzas. It tells about the blessed one. It points out, that which maintains senses at peace are wisdom and the understanding of Upanishads is knowledge. He is blessed who wins enemies with in namely, passion, desire, hatred and all extremes of emotions. These emotions are for the downfall of man. The one who drinks the essence of Upanishads that lead to a desire to know about Atman, the one who becomes detached from all worldly things and who wanders in solitude, forsakes the notions of 'me' and 'mine', who views insult and praise in an equal manner, who dedicates all actions and their results to the creator, and is one with the creator, who forsakes the desire of wealth, family and recognition, who walks on the path of salvation, who lives on alms, who always enquires in his heart about the eternal light of the eternal soul, who is neither good nor bad, or great, who with concentration enquires about the eternal truth, who is not entangled in worldly bondages, who gets out of ignorance, sorrow, death, aging, who understands the philosophy of life that all worldly bondages are temporary, who is with the eternal, who forsakes passion, and who gets the company of peaceful, intelligent, and good natured people who live in the forest meditating and analysing the significance of the soul, such a one is blessed. He is victorious who avoids crowd, who is not attracted by women, who has no bad thoughts, and who realises Para Brahman. Such a person's actions are pure and blessed. The entire world is a holy city of Kashi for him and all his actions are totally enveloped by Parabrahman, the eternal truth.

Kaupeena Panchakam

This stotra glorifies the life of a *Sanyasin*. There are 5 stanzas in this. The monk is one who always ponders over the words of philosophy, gets alms for appeasing hunger, is without any trace of sorrow, always thinks of the inner self, and possesses only the loin cloth as his possession. He lives on fruits and plants and nothing else. He controls all senses and is always in the Bliss of Brahman, knows that he is the soul but not the body, and he thinks about nothing else. He always reflects the name of Brahman with devotion and thinks that he is Brahman itself. He wanders alone depending upon alms. Shankara in these verses says that such a one is indeed lucky.

Manisha Panchakam

One can see the essence of Advaita Vedanta in these five verses of this poem. Manisha means conviction. It is in the form of dialogue between two forms of Lord Shiva. In this the out caste who came on the way of Shankara in Kashi questions Shankara's disciples who commanded the out caste to move away from Shankara's path. The outcaste puts a few questions to Shankara that is pregnant with the highest philosophy of ultimate truth. After hearing the questions Shankara realized that the outcaste was none other than Lord Shiva Himself who appeared in the form of an untouchable. In the five verses Shankara also gives the answers. The two questions that were put by the out caste are; "whom are you asking to get away? Is it the physical body made up of food, or is it the consciousness that is asked to move away from your path? Secondly, is there any difference in the reflection of the sun that is seen in the waters of Ganga or a ditch and in the space in a gold pot or a mud pot? Actually where is the difference found in the self which is supreme, whose nature is eternal bliss, which itself is an ocean of Bliss and pure consciousness?"

Shankara himself gives the answers to these questions through these verses. Firstly he says, when a person attains the knowledge that he is not an object of perception but is pure consciousness that shines in all the three states of waking, dreaming and in sleeping deeply, that is the witness of the entire universe, that dwells in the core of all beings from that of the creator Brahma to that of an ant, then he is my *Guru*, irrespective of the fact whether he is a Brahmana or an outcaste. "I am Brahman, the pure consciousness" appears as universe to the ignorant because of *Maya* or *Avidya* or ignorance or nescience that contains the three gunas namely, *Sattva, Rajas* and *Thamas*. The one who has realized this knowledge about Brahman that is Bliss, eternal, supreme, and pure is my *Guru*, irrespective of the fact that whether he is a chandala or an out caste or a Brahmana. The one who knows by the teachings of his *Guru* or the teacher that the entire universe is perishable and then meditates upon Brahman calmly and constantly, has burnt all his past sins, that is the *Sanchita Karmas* that are the accumulated results of Karmas of past lives and those sins of the future, the *Agami Karmas* that are the results of the actions performed in the present birth, submits his body to the *Prarabda Karma*, the allotted results of past actions that are to be borne by the present body and that has given rise to the present body. When knowledge dawns the *Sanchita* and *Agami Karmas* cease to exist as they get destroyed in the fire of knowledge. But *Prarabda* has to be experienced. When Prarabda gets exhausted the *Jeevan Mukta* becomes *Videha Mukta* as the body of the enlightened person falls off. The feeling of 'I' is the reflection of pure consciousness that makes one believe that the mind, senses and body that are insentient appear to be sentient. Because of this notion the external objects are perceived. Just as clouds conceal the sun, the mind, senses and body conceal the self, which are illumined by the Self itself. The *Yogi* who meditates upon on the self only is my '*Guru*'. *The* self that is Brahman is eternal, is ocean of supreme Bliss. By meditating upon the self with a calm mind, the sages experienced fulfillment. The one who gets identified with this Brahman becomes Brahman itself. Who ever such a person may be, he is fit to be worshipped even by the Lord of the Devas, Indra himself.

Maya Panchakam

In the 5 verses of Maya Panchakam Shankara brings out his *Maya Vada*. *Maya* makes even the opposites appear together and brings about what is logically impossible. *Maya* gets superimposed on Atman that is pure consciousness, uncomparable, eternal, partless, and unlimited by space and time, without difference among Gods, world and individual soul. *Maya* makes even those who have masterted Vedas and Upanishads behave like animals by tempting them with wealth and possessions. It makes the Atman that is of the nature of bliss, pure and infinite consciousness the one without a second, identify itself with the physical body, made up of the five elements and get entangled in the whirlpool of maya that is worldly life. It creates notions like caste, creed and the like in the pure bliss-consciousness and also the notion of 'I' ness and also bondage with kith and kin. It creates in Brahman that is homogenous distinctions such as Brahma, Vishnu and Shiva that is really all in one but looks different and in this way creates confusion even for the learned.

Nirguna Manasa Pooja

This is worship to the attributeless spirit. Here the disciple puts five questions and the *Guru* gives the answers in 25 verses. It contains a total of 33 verses. The disciple asks, how is the worship of the indivisible, the Sat- Chit- Ananda that is unconditional and is non-dual state prescribed? Where are the invocation of the fullness and the seat of the all pervading one? How to perform worship, in the form of washing of feet of the supreme that is the pure one? How to perform Abhishekam and so on and how is there the sacred thread for the one who is casteless and who does not know his lineage and so on? What about the application of sandal paste for the unattached and flowers for the odourless? What is the jewel for the undifferentiated one? What about the ornaments for the formless? What is the use of incense for the spotless or of lamps for the one who is the witness of everything? What is the food offering for the one who is always in its own bliss? How to prepare *tamboola* or the betel leaves for the one who rejoices the entire universe, who is self-luminous and illumines everything including the suns and stars and who is praised by the Vedas? How to perform the light ceremony, the *Deeparadhana*? What is the *Pradakshina* or circumambulation that is prescribed for the infinite? How to prostrate before the non-dual reality? What is the hymn or Stotra prescribed for the one who is unknowable even by the Vedas? How can there be ceremony for the one who pervades everywhere?

In answer the *Guru* replies, "Worship *Atmalinga* that shines within the Lotus of your heart that is within the city of illusion that is called the body, by performing *Abhishekam* or ablutions with your mind the water of which is brought from the river of faith, with the flowers of *Samadhi* for the sake of non birth. Lord Shiva is to be invoked with the conviction that 'I am the one, the ultimate. The thought of the self, established in the self is its seat or *Asana*. Washing of the feet of that one is performed by the conviction that

'I have no contact with virtue or sin'. This thought destroys all sins. One should pour the root of ignorance held by the time without beginning as the final water offering. The *Archamana* or sipping is to be performed with the meditation upon that supreme truth. The meditation is to be with the thought that 'all the worlds are blessed by the water of Bliss of Brahman'. This is Abhishekam of the self. The thought that 'I am the light of consciousness without any veil' should form the holy dress of the self. The sacred thread is the conviction that 'I am the thread of garland of all worlds that have the nature of three gunas'. The sandal paste or chandana of the self is the meditation that 'this manifold world with numerous impressions is only supporting me'. For attaining liberation while living, one should always worship the symbol of self with flowers in the form of renunciation of all the three gunas of Sattva, Rajas and Tamas. One should worship the Lord of the Self with the non-dual betal leaves of non-distinction between the Lord, *Guru* and the self. The giving up of all impressions is the *dhoop* or incense, *archana* or worship.

The *Dheeparadhana* or worship with light is the realization of the self that is luminous. The food offering or Naivedya to the self is the rice pudding, the Universe, the Brahmanda of Brahman. The delightful bewerage or *Upasechana* is the drinking of sweet nector of Bliss. Washing of the hands is performed by cleansing the remnants of ignorance with the water of knowledge. The *Tamboola* or chewing of the betal leaves of Lord Shiva is the giving up of the use of all objects of passion. The waving of lights or Niranjana is the knowledge of one's own nature as Brahman, that is most shining, that burns the darkness of ignorance. The ornament of garland and the *Pushpanjali* or the worship with flowers is the remembering vision of the manifold Brahman and the vision of the all-blissful nature of the Self. The circumambulation or *Pradakshina* is the meditation that 'thousands of Brahma's mundane eggs are revolving in me, while the Lord is immovable and steady'. The salutation is the meditation that 'Apart from me none is worthy of salutation'. The saintly act of the self is the idea of the unreality of duties. The *Nama Keertan* or singing the praise of the self is the thought that the self is beyond all names and forms. The reflection or *manana* is the thought of the unreality of things to be reflected upon and the hearing or *Sravana*, the unreality of the things to be heard of. Deep meditation is the knowledge of the unreality of things to be contemplated upon. Perfect steadiness or Samadhi is devotion to the self by the absence of all delusion and distractions in which the mind merges with Brahman. This worship of one's own self that is performed till death or even for a moment is expounded in the Vedas. The one who gives up the illusion of all impressions, as dust from the feet shakes off all ignorance and pain and attains the everlasting bliss or Liberation.

Nirvana Dasakam or Dasa Shloki

It is said that Shankara composed these 10 verses when he met Govindapada at the bank of Narmada River with a request to accept him as Govidapada's disciple. When Govindapada asked Shankara who he was, Shankara replied in these ten verses. These ten verses sum up the essence of Vedanta. These verses point out that Only Atman is there while the world of names, forms and manifestations are Maya and are due to ignorance of man. Atman is the same as supreme Brahman. The one who realizes the self in him only can transcend the world of sorrow. In these verses Shankara expounds the nature of Atman, the ultimate truth that is indestructible and also indescribable. Through these verses Shankara says:

> "I am Pure Atma devoid of the notions of body and mind or senses. I am also not the combination of the elements or individual sense organs. I am that self that exists in deep dreamless sleep state, that is auspicious that is non-dual entity that alone remains and nothing else. The distinctions of caste, creed, or stages of life or rules of conduct or duties do not affect me in any way because I am essentially the self or Atman only. I am also not one with attributes and therefore, for me there is no need of *Dharaṇa, Dhyana* or *Yoga* and so on as I have no notions of 'I' and 'Mine'. I do not identify myself with the body, mind or organs that constitute the non-self. As the Sruti says, in deep sleep state I exist as the one auspicious self that is free from all attributes. The views of other sects like *Sankhya* and other religions like Jaina are not correct because of

the realization that Brahman is only the one that is absolutely pure and whole that remains free from all attributes. There are no outside or inside, upper or lower, middle or across, or any direction for me, the Brahman because it is all pervading like space. I remain, as that one that is auspicious and self, free from all attributes and that has no colour. Brahman is neither big nor tiny, neither short nor long. It is pure effulgence. So it is not knowable. I, the Brahman remain that auspicious self, free from all attributes. There is neither *Guru* nor scriptures nor disciple and learning, neither you nor I, nor this world. Everything is one. Once that Brahman knowledge is attained there is no differentiation. I remain that Brahman. The three states of waking, dreaming and sleeping are only the result of ignorance. I am beyond these and am the fourth state, the transcendental that is beyond the three states. I am that Atman that is everywhere. It is the ultimate. It is self-existent; it does not depend on anything. But the phenomenal world is different from Atman and it is unreal. I remain as that auspicious Atman or self. Brahman or Atman has neither absoluteness nor non-Absoluteness, is neither void nor non void, as it has no duality. It is impossible for me to describe the essence of the entire Vedanta".

Nirvanamanjari

In the 12 verses given in this, Shankara explains who he is. He identifies himself with Lord Shiva that supreme *Yogi*, who is all pervading, beyond the senses, the cause of everything, the ever blissful. He says,

"I am neither good nor bad, neither a *Gandharva* nor *Yaksha*, neither a ghost nor omen, neither a man nor a woman or eunuch. My nature is the effulgent entity, Lord Shiva. I am not a child, a youth, or old man. I do not belong to any class, or a bachelor or a family man. I do not sit in the forest or follow the rules of *Sanyasa* because I am that Shiva who is the Lord of destruction, a supreme yogi who has renounced everything. I am immeasurable, beyond the concept of illusion. Though I may look different, I am the one who brings everything together. Even though I am attached to the trinity of Gods I am that self which has no second, because I am that Shiva who is all pervading and beyond the senses. I am not a thinker, or a wanderer or one who speaks or does or one who consumes or free from abodes, I am that one that plays different roles according to the thought of the mind. I am Shiva, who is the cause of everything. I am not action, or wrong selfish thoughts with attachments. But I am that thought which is at the end of action because I am that Shiva who is thought personified after the end of the body. Those who want to get rid of ignorant action and ignorance without truth do not shine. They are trapped between end, middle, and middle of middle. I am that Shiva. I am not wisdom or completion of tasks or organs or the reproductive seed. I live in the sky of heart and I am beyond the agony of senses because I am that Shiva who is personification of ever-blissful true joy. I am that Shiva who is responsible for creating differences in this world, who is the abode of different forms, the one who cannot be seen as two, who is personification of mind, wisdom, senses, and intelligence, the only source from where everything emerged. I am that Shiva who is crystal clear and pervades everywhere, who is eternal bliss, who created the big universe with its minute parts and is also its source. I am that Shiva who gives power to His devotees, who is like the waves of lightning, and the shine of sun and moon, who playfully creates the differences of 'I' and 'You', and has the entire world at His feet. I am that Shiva who is the source of God of death, who is the reason for the glory of mind, knowledge and senses and who is the reason, and also for the shine of Gods like Brahma, Shiva, Indra, Chandra and so on. I am that Shiva who cannot be classified with in himself, who is infinite like the sky, who has a peaceful form, who is extremely effulgent, who chooses to be nothing, who neither has beginning nor end and who is called Shankara".

Nirvana Shatakam or Atma Shatakam

These verses state that the identification with body, mind, and senses is the fundamental cause of all sorrows. There are 6 verses in this. One has to give up the false notion and realize one's real nature as the supreme Brahman. This is what is known as Liberation. The knowledge, Shankara says is "I am not the mind or the intellect, or ego, or mind stuff, or body, or the changes in the body, or senses, or elements or the life breathe. I am absolute extreme knowledge, Bliss. I am He, I am not Prana, or three five vital airs, (The five vital airs are; *Prana, Vyana, Apana, Samana* and *Udana*) or materials of the body or the Dhathus (marrow, fat, flesh, blood, lymph, skin and cuticle) or the five sheaths of the body-mind complex (*Annamaya Kosha*, or the physical body, *Pranamaya Kosha* or the sheath of vital air, and organs of action like Speech, hands and so on, *Manonmaya Kosha* or the sheath of the mind made up of mind and five organs of perception and *Vignanamaya Kosha* or the sheath of the intellect and *Ananda Maya Kosha* or the sheath of bliss) or the organs of action, or object of senses. I am absolute knowledge, Bliss, *Sat-Chit-Ananda.* I have no aversion or attachment, or greed or delusion, or egotism, or envy, or Dharma or *Moksha*, or desire or objects of desire because all likes and dislikes belong to the mind and not to *Atma.* I am the *Sat-Chit-Ananda.* I am not sin or virtue, or pleasure or pain, temple or worship, pilgrimage or scriptures, the act of enjoying or enjoyable or the enjoyer. I am Sat-Chit- Ananda. I have no death or fear of death or caste, or was I ever born, or had parents, friends or relations. I am not a *Guru* or a disciple. I am *Sat-Chit-Ananda.* I am not affected by the senses. I am not *Mukti* or the knowable. I am without form, without limit. I am beyond space and time. I am everything. I am formless, all pervading, and changeless, without bondage or liberation; I am the basis of the Universe. I am present everywhere. I am that Sat-Chit- Ananda"- the supreme consciousness, the auspiciousness.

Panchikaranam

This is a treatise on Vedanta. The Virat is said to be the sum total effects of all the five elements formed together to form grosser entities forming the Universe, that is the gross body of the soul or Atman. In the waking state, the senses give rise to the knowledge of objects and the Atman that identifies itself with the waking state and gross body is known as 'Vishva' or the world. In the syllable 'AUM', the first letter 'A' represents the combination of gross body, waking state and 'Viswa'. Hiranyagarbha is the combination of the rudimentary elements and their effects, the subtle body. The material subtle body has got 17 parts, namely the five vital forces, ten organs of perception and action, mind and intellect. This is the subtle body of the Atman or soul. When the sense organs are withdrawn, the knowledge of the waking state and the imaginary objects perceived in that state form the dream state. In this state, Taijasa is the Atman that identifies itself with both the dream state and subtle body. The second letter 'U' in 'AUM' represents the subtle body, the dream state and Taijasa. Avyakrta or undifferentiated is the causal body of the Atman. It is the nescience that hides the Atman, is the cause of both gross and subtle bodies. It is bound by the reflection of pure consciousness. It is Avyakrta, is neither existent nor non existent or both. It is neither identical with nor different from Atman. It is neither composite nor non composite. But it is removable with the identity of Atman with Brahman. When all thoughts stop and the intellect also get lost in the causal condition, then the state of deep sleep comes.

The causal body and the deep sleep state are described as Prajna. The letter 'M' in 'AUM' represents the causal body, Nescience, deep sleep state and Prajna. 'A', the waking personality should be resolved in 'U' the dream personality and 'U' should be resolved in to 'M' the deep sleep personality and 'M', should be resolved in to 'AUM' and 'AUM' in to 'I', Then comes 'Samadhi' or the super conscious state that is remaining in a state of Absolute identification. When the identification that ' I am the Atman' the witness of all, the absolute pure consciousness, I am only Brahman, eternally pure, ever enlightened, eternally free and existence absolute, absolute Bliss, one without a second, the inner most consciousness comes, the *Mahavakyas* of Upanishads namely, 'Thou art that',' I am Brahman', 'Consciousness is Brahman', 'This self is Brahman', become the evidences of the identity of Atman, the individual soul and Brahman, the Universal soul. 'Panchakarani' means the five processes by which the five elementary constituents or elements of the Universe are said to combine with one another for forming gross entities that form as units in the composition of physical bodies".

Prathasmarana Stotram

In this Stotra of 4 stanzas, Shankara explains the essence of Advaita Vedanta. He says, "I meditate every morning on the self that shines in the heart, that is, Existence-Consciousness-Bliss, which is the goal of Paramahansas, which is called the fourth state, since it is beyond the three states of waking, dreaming and sleeping and that witnesses these three states. I am that Brahman that is indivisible, and not the physical body, composed of the combination of the five elements. I bow to that supreme self who the Vedas declare is unborn, changeless, the highest inaccessible to the mind, whom words cannot describe, but by whose blessing the faculty of speech functions and who is termed in the Upanishads as 'Neti- Neti', 'Not this- Not this'. My salutations to that supreme self that is infinite, eternal, who is known as supreme *Purusha*, who is beyond the darkness of ignorance, who is effulgent like the sun, who is everything, in whom the entire universe appears just as a rope appears as a snake. One who reads these verses every morning would attain liberation".

Sadana Panchakam

In these verses Shankara gives the essence of spiritual practice. There are 5 verses in this. It is said that at the time of Shankara's Samadhi, a few disciples were sitting around him. One of them requested Shankara to give in a nutshell, what one should do to realize Brahman since all his works is about Advaita Vedanta that may not be understood by all after his time. In reply Shankara is believed to have replied in these verses that contain the essence of spiritual practice. The first verse deals with instructions of what a spiritual aspirant should do while leading his normal life for preparing himself for the spiritual path. In these verses Shankara says, let the spiritual aspirant study the scriptures daily. Let him perform the *Karmas* or duties to him as told in the scriptures. Let God be worshipped through the performance of *Karmas* that is *Vedic yagnas* and sacrifices. Let the mind be alienated from actions born out of desires. Let all sins be destroyed either by performing rites as prescribed in scriptures or by going through the fruits of sinful actions. Further accumulation of sins is to be avoided by performing actions without any attachment to their results and also by dedicating such action to the Lord. The spiritual aspirant should have a firm resolve to realize *Atman* even when he is alive. With this aim he should leave his house and should go to a place where there is less distraction and which is conducive to his spiritual *sadhana*. After leaving the house he should always remain in the company of the wise. He must also have an unflinching devotion to God. He should practice qualities like tranquility of mind, control of senses, detachment from all worldly activities, power of endurance, faith in God, *Guru* and scriptures and single pointedness towards Atman. He has to renounce all *Karmas* and approach a *Guru* for initiation into spiritual path and seek the knowledge of the imperishable Brahman while serving him constantly. He should also learn the *Mahavakyas* contained in the Vedas from the *Guru*. He should continue with his spiritual *sadhana* until the notion 'I am the body' gets eliminated and in its place he gets the firm conviction that 'I am Brahman'. He should ponder over the great *Mahavakyas* of the Upanishads for realization. He should refrain himself from unnecessary arguments and turn his attention to the investigation as stated in Sruti by having only the feeling that 'I am Brahman' by giving up all pride, arrogance, arguing with the learned and so on. He should never allow himself to relax from his spiritual *Sadhana*. First of all he should control his hunger and live on alms alone. He should only take the absolute minimum of food to keep him alive. He should always be satisfied with what he gets and should bear all opposites like heat and cold and so on in an equal manner. He should speak only minimum words that are necessary. He should be indifferent towards all worldly things and give up the feeling of either harshness or kindness to others.

Shankara also gives a description of a liberated sage or a *jeevan muktha* in these verses. He says, such a one should live in seclusion with his mind merged in Supreme *Atman- Brahman*, the one non-dual consciousness. In the fire of Brahman knowledge he should burn away all his *sanchita Karmas*, that is accumulated *Karmas* of his past lives. With the strength of the knowledge of Brahman he should also prevent further accumulation of any *Karma* that is known as *Agami Karmas*. While he lives he should exhaust all his *Prarabda Karmas* that is the allotted *Karmas* by experiencing their results. After that he should fix mind firmly in the supreme Brahman-the Satchidanada Swaroopa, in the non-dual Brahman and then become a *Videha Muktha*, a liberated one without body. In the final verse Shankara says that the one who studies and follows these verses and ponder over them and follows these verses daily will be saved from the cycle of birth and death and would be liberated.

Sata Shloki

The essence of *Prasthana Traya* is given in the 101 verses of this poem. It starts with the glory of *Guru* and ends with a salutation to Vasudeva, the Supreme Being. The *Karma kanda* of the Vedas describe the yagas to be performed for attaining wealth, fame, and progeny and so on for the gross body. The *jeevatma* is the performer and enjoyer of these Karmas. But this *jeevatma* or *Atman* is not the gross body. The pure self is neither the doer nor the enjoyer of the actions. Brahman is considered as associated with the limiting adjunct or Upadhi in the form of subtle body. This is stated to be the jeevatma in the *Karma Kanda*. In the *jnana Kanda* or in the Upanishads the pure Brahman, without any limitations is described. Upanishads teach that one is not the physical body or mind but pure Brahman and everything is Brahman in this Universe. The Self or Atman is experienced in all the three states of waking, drumming and deep sleep. It makes all the organs of body and mind to function. Due to ignorance man identifies the self with the physical body that is composed of perishable things.

The external objects are perceived with senses in the waking state and with mind in dream state. In deep sleep the mind exists but in dormant state. Both the sense organs and mind are insentient because they are composed of the five elements. Man gets attached to his body that is the result of his past Karmas, and that brings bondage resulting in sorrow and misery. It is like the silk worm building a case for protection with the thread coming out of its mouth without realising that the case itself is going to be the cause of its destruction. The physical body is a garb of the soul. *Atma* is different from the body. It is the witness of everything. The body does not affect it. That is what the Upanishads says. The wise ones should meditate on the self. An object is loved only as long as it gives happiness. The two paths that are open to a man are either fulfillment of worldly desires that ultimately lead to sorrow and misery or the attainment of Brahman that is liberation- the infinite bliss. The wise ones choose liberation. The spiritual seeker sees all worldly objects as Brahman. Once a person attains the knowledge of Brahman from a *Guru*, he looks upon the world as the gross body of Atman. The doubts if any are removed through *Manana* or reflection. By Nidhidhyasana or constant contemplation, or meditation he realizes that he is not the body-mind complex but only the self. Dispassion is the pre condition for this self-knowledge. The one who knows that the notions of 'I' and 'My' leads to sorrow, does not seek happiness from material objects. As he knows that all worldly things are temporary, he is unattached to everything. Even when he lives in his house, he lives like a guest. This state is called Vidvat Sanyasin and he is the one who has attained the knowledge of the self.

The spiritual aspirant lives only on fruits that fall from the tree to maintain his life. Usúally when the objects of desire are not got anger arises. On the other hand, if the object of desire is got, then greed arises to protect it. The three causes for the spiritual fall of man are, namely, desire, anger and greed. So the wise should not crave for sense objects. The four main obstacles in spiritual path are, greed, anger, lack of faith and the notion that the world is real. On the other hand, charity, forbearance, The man who eats without offering food to God and feeding the guest incurs sin. The noblest gift is feeding a deserving person. Such a one will never suffer due to lack of food in his house. The Brahman remains hidden and the world is projected as long as one is ignorant. Once the supreme knowledge dawns only Brahman will remain and the universe will have no existence at all. Before creation there was neither existence nor non-existence. It was indescribable. Bondage and liberation also do not exist actually, because bondage exists due to ignorance and liberation does not exist because Liberation is from bondage that does not exist. There is no day or night for the sun. When we see the sun it is day and when we cannot see it, it is night. Similarly, Brahman exists always. The universe that is *Maya*, before creation, merged in Brahman. When creation began *Maya* got transformed as the world. Maya covers the knowledge of Brahman. Ishwara and *jeeva* are like two birds sitting on the tree of *Maya. Jeeva* eats the fruits of the tree that experiences the material objects of the world through sense organs and this leads to misery and happiness. It gets immersed in worldly life forgetting its own real nature as Brahman but Ishwara remains as a mere witness unaffected and unattached sitting on the tree. When the intellect gets purified from desire, anger, and greed and so on it realizes its true nature as Brahman. He then gets freed from *Maya* and ignorance. Sages call this one self or Brahman with various names and forms of Gods. This indwelling self is Brahman or supreme self, is infinite and all pervading. Self does not enter the womb to be born. The subtle body with the mind and sense organs enters the womb as the physical body to be born. At death the subtle body leaves the gross body and goes to a higher or lower worlds according to its *Karma*. After a sojourn it returns to the world and takes a new physical body. When the subtle body consisting of five organs of perception the *jnanendriyas*, the five organs of action the *Karmendriyas*, the five vital airs, the mind and intellect leaves the physical body, it carries with itself the knowledge that one acquired, the effects of his *Karmas* and the impressions of his past actions.

The pure *Atma* has no birth or death. In *Rig Veda* it is stated that the subtle body of the priest Subandu was brought back to the earth by chanting Vedic mantras. The wordly man yearns for wife and then children and then strains every nerve of his body for his family that he considers as the superior most. When he loses them he becomes wretched. The cloud of ignorance conceals the self from the intellect of man. The one who attains knowledge of the actions of the waking state will not bind him. It is a pity that although the actions performed both in the waking and dreaming state are false, the deluded man clings to them ignorant of the self that is the basis of these states. A person considers the happenings in the waking state as real because it lasts longer than the happenings of the dream state. *Maya* or ignorance makes this universe that we experience as real. No one sees the self that makes him capable of functioning in waking or dream state. Even though dream is unreal, when a pleasant dream is seen, then one becomes very happy in the morning. So the unreal dream gives rise to real result in the person. The Upanishads provide the knowledge of Brahman that is real. In dreamless sleep, the organs merge in *Prana* or the vital air that is the source of their manifestation in the waking state. So the Upanishads says that one should meditate on *Prana* for the realization of the self. Fire will burn only a dry wood. Similarly, the fire of knowledge can enter only into a person who has detached himself from worldly bondages.

Everything in the world appears real because of the substratum of Brahman on which they are super imposed. Only by renunciation one will know this Brahman. A spiritual aspirant first becomes a *Jeevan Muktha.* Then he continues to live in his body till his Prarabda gets exhausted and when the body falls he becomes *Videha Muktha.* Both these stages can be achieved only by *Guru*'s mercy, by means of repeated *Asanas, Pranayama* and so on and by constant meditation on the self. One becomes free fróm all identification with the body and desires, after he attains purity of mind and performs duties in a self less manner. His mind gets fixed in Atman and he becomes a *Jeevan Muktha.* When he dies he becomes a *Videha Muktha.* A *Jeevan Muktha* goes beyond all miseries of life and delusion. He is the one who has attained the fourth state that is 'Turia' that is beyond the three earlier states. The body envelops Jeevatma. But it is the reflection of Brahman and is Satvic. It is associated with Prana or the vital force that has *Kriya* Shakti or the power of action. The features of the physical body do not affect it. It has the power to liberate from its apparent bondage that is wrongly attributed to it. Liberation is the unity of *Jeevatma* and Brahman by removing the false identity of the physical body- mind complex and when the mind takes on the form of Brahman. A person who has realized that he is self or Brahman becomes one with Brahman that is imperishable, pure bliss, and shines in the cavity of the intellect. A cloth is nothing but threads woven together. Similarly, the Hiranyagarbha pervades all forms. Brahman, the one Supreme Being takes several forms or beings. Just as a face is not affected by the reflecting medium, Brahman too is not affected by the reflecting medium, that is, the mind and remains the same forever. But Brahman appears to have taken on the characteristics of the beings when it gets reflected. But in reality they do not affect Brahman. Just as the sunrays that fall on the moon remove darkness of the night, similarly, the rays of consciousness fall on the intellect and illumine all objects through sense organs and make the sense organs experience them. When the all-pervading sky is reflected in water, it appears as the sky is limited by water. Similarly, when the all-pervading Brahman is reflected in the intellect, it appears as limited by the intellect. When one realizes that Brahman that is limited by the intellect is the same as the all pervading Brahman and they are the one and the same, nescience that makes the Jeeva and Brahman appear differently will get destroyed and at that time all sorrows would vanish.

It is similar to the puppet dance where one single person behind a screen controls many of the puppets. Similarly, this universe is activated by Hiranya *garbha* that makes all beings experience the consequences of their past Karma. The supreme reality is Brahman that is unchanged in all the three periods of time. Anything appears as real due to its substratum. Similarly, the universe that is unreal appears on the substratum of Brahman that is nothing but truth. Space that accommodate, the self takes different forms and qualities of beings in which it resides. The wise man should realize that it is his own *Atma* that dwells in all beings and everything in this universe is not different from *Atma*, just as waves are not different from the ocean. The one who does not realize this is born and dies again and again. Although the same space exists before and after the pot is made and broken, it is wrongly thought that the space takes the shape and size of the pot and it exists when the pot is there and gets destroyed when the pot is broken to pieces. Similarly, although this self is eternal, and all pervasive, it is wrongly perceived that it comes in to existence with the creation of the universe and it ceases to exist when the universe is dissolved. The world is seen as existing and sentient. It is because the world is pervaded by the substratum that is the self, the pure consciousness. World exists and is experienced along with Brahman but not separately. Even when it is experienced the world has no reality. When this knowledge dawns to one, then, one will realize that only Brahman exists really and nothing else. The one, who has this knowledge of Brahman, always gets established in Brahman. In deep sleep the *Jeeva* experiences supreme bliss that cannot be described in words. No experience of objects will be there in that state. In deep sleep everything merges in Brahman and is in a state of supreme bliss. A person who identifies himself with Brahman enjoys the bliss always. The one who is engaged in selfish worldly activities forgetting this fact will, in the end gets sufferings and misery.

The *Jeevatma* that becomes one with Brahman in that state of deep sleep has no sorrow or misery. Instead it enjoys bliss and remains aloof from all worldly activities. In the state of *Jeevan Muktha*, in deep sleep, there is dissolution of gross and subtle objects. All senses and mind are in dormant state and happiness is experienced. The one who is liberated will not go back to the state of bondage again. The pleasure derived from sense objects is very limited and form infinitesimally small part of the infinite Bliss of Brahman. In this infinite Bliss, the world dissolves in to nothingness. The happiness that comes from sense objects is short lived. It lasts only until some other desire disturbs the mind. This happiness is only a reflection of the Bliss of the self in the mind. The happiness derived from physical body is temporary but the happiness of the state of liberation lasts forever because the mind is in a state of calmness at this stage. So it is to be understood that happiness is only a manifestation of the eternal Bliss of Brahman. When the mind in deep sleep becomes united with the self, it does not go through the experiences of waking or the dream state, but it gets absolute rest in the self. In the dream state, all things that are experienced are the creations of the mind of the impressions of the objects that are experienced in the waking state. At this dream stage, the *Jeeva* withdraws all sense organs and it remains self-effulgent and is a witness of all experiences of the dream. In the dream state *Prana* or the vital force that performs the act of breathing alone safeguards the body. In this state one sees both pleasant as well as unpleasant things and happenings. Just as a rope is mistaken as a snake, the innumerable names and forms appear because the self that is the substratum is not seen then. This creates fear, joy and sorrow and so on. But these have no real existence. They appear only due to *Maya* or illusion.

The *Vedas* state that if Vedic rites are performed as an offering to Brahman, in a selfless manner, without any expectation of results, then it will result in purity of mind that helps one to realize the self. The one who gains *punya*, the good effects after studying *Vedas* and performing Vedic rites dies without knowing the self, then he would enjoy the merits of these good deeds in heaven only for some time but he will have to be reborn again on earth and experience all worldly sufferings. But the one who has acquired the knowledge of the self through the study of Vedas and tries for self-realisation will enjoy happiness in heaven for a longer duration even before the subjective realization of the self. One should therefore meditate on the self. It is only with the light of the self or consciousness objects like sun, moon, and so on become visible. *Prana* is the vital force that governs all organs. They are five namely, *Prana*, *Apana*, *Vyana*, *Samana*, and *Udana* according to their five different functions. This *Prana* is able to perform its activities only because of the presence of Brahman or the self or pure consciousness. So it is the *Prana* of the *Prana*. Similarly, the organs of sense and action are also able to perform their functions only because of the presence of the self. At the same time, Self is only a witness of all activities. Because of the light of this pure consciousness everything else exists and shines. But it is not illumined by anything. The one who gets the realization that 'I am Brahman', due to the grace and compassion of a '*Sadguru*', who is a realized soul, would become a *Jeevan Muktha*, who is free from all doubts and illusions and after his death he would attain the supreme, eternal, abode of bliss and would become *Videha Muktha*. In reality, we are not the body, the sense organs, or action, or the perishable mind, intellect, inert objects, or ego, and attachment and so on. The Being is only a witness that is pure consciousness, the most auspicious, and the innermost self that is the substratum of the entire universe. All the different things in this world with different forms and colours are objects that are looked at by the eyes. The eyes are the 'seer' and the objects are the 'seen'. But the eye that is the 'seer' becomes the 'seen', that is the object that is perceived for the 'seer' that is the mind. But then, the mind also becomes the 'seen' for the self that is the 'seer'. The self is always the subject that sees or is the 'seer'. It is not an object that is 'seen'. Just as a rope appears as a snake, due to ignorance, similarly, self also appears as the miserable Jeeva due to ignorance. When the darkness is removed due to the entry of light then one realizes that it is only a rope but not a snake. Similarly when the light of knowledge dawns due to the grace of *Guru* then one realizes that he is not a mere Jeeva, but Brahaman or self itself.

During daytime the natural light is from sun and at night it is from moon and stars. The eye enables one to see the light. But when the eyes are closed then intellect becomes the light. The 'I' illumines the intellect and that 'I' is the self that illumines all beings and is therefore the supreme light. Although the *Jeevan Muktha* lives in this world until his Prarabdha lasts, he never identifies himself with his body- mind complex. He is also not affected by the pairs of opposites like pleasure and pain, happiness and sorrow, heat and cold, success and failure and so on. He is pure, ever contented, free from illusion of the feeling of 'I' and 'Mine', his mind is firmly fixed in the self, is free from all delusions of life, attachment and fear and is the very incarnation of the supreme Bliss. When one identifies oneself with Brahman, then for him, the difference between the *Jeevatman* and Brahman also gets destroyed along with *Maya* or ignorance. Thereafter even if Maya exists, it will not affect him at all. After sucking the juice of the mango the peel or the outer cover is thrown off. Similarly, the *Jeevan Muktha* who realizes Brahman looks at the world as unreal and gets absorbed totally in Brahman, that is the very existence, pure consciousness, non-dual, immortal, and Bliss. He becomes self-effulgent and goes beyond all attachments. When one realizes that Brahman, which is pure consciousness, untainted by the three gunas of *Sattva, Rajas* and *Tamas*, and that is indicated by the *Maha Vakya* 'Thou art that', that cannot be thought of even by the mind, that is the indwelling self of all, the supreme Lord and the ruler, then the accumulated results of all his past Karmas or actions get destroyed. The knot of the heart that binds the body- mind complex is cut and all the doubts that are the causes of repeated births and deaths get resolved. The transmigration is on account of past *Karmas.* It is like a tree with roots, branches, leaves, fruits that are the emotions and birds that are bondages living in the tree. Knowing all parts of such a tree, all of which are perishable, the wise one cuts this tree with his sword of detachment by meditating upon Lord Vishnu who is the indweller of all beings. The entire universe is born and sustained by the self and finally merge with the self, that is Brahman.

Siddhantha Tattva Vindu

It is a song with 10 verses explaining 'Who am I'. "The self is not the five elements of earth or water or fire or air or ether, or powers, but an undifferentiated dreamless perfect rest and "I am that. I am not the castes or their divisions, rites or rules, mind, thought, and moods, not desire things or have the notion of 'I' and 'Mine'. I am only 'that', that is final and the ultimate. I am not any relationship, Gods, worlds, scriptures, offerings, or shrine. I am the self. I am pure, final and the ultimate. I am not above, below, within, without, in the middle, in front or at the back, east or west. But I am that, that is present everywhere as a unified whole. I am without colours. I am not tall or short, long or small. I am formless and am the effulgence. I am not the teachings, teacher, the student or 'You' or 'I', I am pure consciousness that is ever free. I am not waking, dreaming or sleeping or life or soul. But I am that".

Tattva Bodha (Awakening to Reality)

This work of Adishankara contains lessons on Advaita Vedanta that are very difficult to understand. It is in the form of prose. According to this, the four perfections of knowing reality are—*firstly*, discrimination between lasting and perishable things of the world that is the knowledge that only the real lasts whereas all the others are perishable, *secondly*, lack of craving for material worldly enjoyments while living and the desire for heaven thereafter, *thirdly*, six graces like (a) peace, that is a firm hold on emotions, (b) self control, that is firm hold on passions and lust, (c) steadiness, that is firm hold on the intellect, (d) sturdiness that is willingness to withstand the opposites like heat and cold, sorrow and happiness and so on, (e) confidence, that is firm faith on the teachings of the teacher and the final wisdom and (f) intentness that is, one pointedness and *fourthly*, the craving for freedom. Through these four perfections men can attain reality that is the knowledge that only the self that stands aloof from all is real and all the others are mere fanciful notions.

The self is that, that stands aloof from the three vestures like physical, emotional and causal that is beyond the five veils and is the witness of the three modes. Its nature is (a) being, that is, that which stands through past, present and future, (b) consciousness, with its nature of perceiving and remaining as a witness and (c) Bliss that is its nature of pure eternal joy. The three vestures are;

(A) The physical vesture is the body that enjoys the opposites having birth, growth, turning the corners, decline and decay. It has birth, growth; it turns the corner, declines and perishes.

(B) The emotional vesture enjoys the opposing forces of sorrow and happiness, praise and insults and so on. It has 17 phases namely. Five powers of knowing that includes the power of hearing that captures sounds, touch that seizes contacts, sight that seizes different forms, taste that seizes the power of the tongue in tasting, and smell that captures the odours, the radiation of which are space, air, sun, and the two physicians. Five powers of doing that includes voice that speaks, hands that grasp, feet that walks, putting forth that are throwing off the wastes, generation that is physical enjoyment or procreation. The Five lives are the upward life, the forward life, the uniting life, the distributing life and the downward life. One emotion and One soul.

(C) The Causal vesture is the self that does not know its own nature yet in its true nature it is unerring. It is the substance and cause of the above-mentioned two vestures. The five veils are:

(a) The food formed veil that is the physical vesture.

(b) The life formed veil that is life and the four other lives, voice and four other powers of doing.

(c) Emotion formed veil that is emotion joining itself with five powers of knowing. This is emotion formed veil.

(d) Knowledge formed veil, that is the soul, that joins with the five powers of knowing and.

(e) Bliss formed veil that is the substance that is not pure.

The three modes of self- the waking, dreaming and dreamless sleep states The self in waking state attributes itself to the physical vesture and is called the pervading. The self in the dreaming state attributes itself to the emotional vesture and is called the Radiant. The self in the dreamless deep sleep state attributes itself to the causal vesture and is called the institutional.

How the 24 natures are formed. The primitive five are formed by the three potencies of the evolver, the substance, the force and space. From His glamour ether came, from ether breath came, from breath fire came, from fire water came and finally from water the earth came. From Ether the power of hearing came, from breath the power of touch came, from fire the power of seeing came, from waters the power of taste came and from earth the power of smell came. From the above five natures the inner powers like mind, soul, self assertion and imagination were formed. From the forceful parts of the element ether the power of voice came, from breath the power of handling came, from fire the power of moving came, from water the power of engendering came and from earth the power of extruding came. From the combined forceful parts of these natures the five lives were formed, namely, the upward life, the forward life, the uniting life, the distributing life and the downward life. From the spatial parts of these five natures the five folded elements came by their division. From this five fold primitive nature, the physical vesture was formed.

Life and Lord

The eternal when attributed itself to vestures it is called as life. This life because of the power of nature imagines the Lord to be different from itself. Due to ignorance or lack of wisdom life is called as self. Due to glamour the self is called Lord. Because of the difference in their disguise life and lord are seen differently. As long as this difference continues the cycle of birth and death also will continue. So to go beyond this cycle one should overcome this difference. Actually, life that is equated with the emotional and physical vestures is only the literary meaning of 'THOU'. The real meaning of 'THOU' is, PURE CONSCIOUSNESS that is without any disguises as in dreamless sleep. Both are consciousness. The difference between life and Lord is only apparent but not real. Both are actually one and the same. He who has a firm conviction that he is the stainless being, consciousness, Bliss, the shining, and the inner master, shining wisdom and knows this by direct self-knowledge is free. He is free from all bonds. Such a one enjoys the everlasting bliss.

Upadesa Sahasri

Upadesa Sahasri means thousand teachings. It is in the form of doubts expressed and questions put by the student to the teacher and the teacher's explanation to enlighten the disciple. It contains 1000 teachings. There are two parts in this. The first part is in prose and contains three chapters and the second part that is in verse contains 19 chapters. It gives the substance of all Upanishads. The first 44 verses are mostly in the form of doubts expressed by the student to the teacher that is in the form of questions put and the answers to these questions by the teacher.

Part-1 (Prose)

Chapter—1

According to Sruti, all Vedic actions do not result in reaching the eternal truth. So a spiritual aspirant should seek a teacher to learn about the eternal and the teacher should teach that truth to the disciple. This transmission of knowledge is like a boat that helps in crossing a river. First the teacher should remove the cause for non-understanding of his teaching by the student. He should impart knowledge about good qualities and should also teach the need to avoid bad qualities.

The treatise then tells about the teacher. The teacher starts his teaching by teaching the Sruti text by establishing oneness with the self and then tells about the definition of Brahman. Later he should explain what Brahman is.

Then the teacher explains about creation, life self and liberation. In the beginning ether got formed from the self like foam from water. Then air appeared, from that fire came and from fire, water came and from water earth came, from earth vegetation came. When vegetation was eaten blood formed and then the seed of beings were born from the womb of the mother. Then one enters in to different stages of like Brahmacharya, Grahasthasrama, Vanaprastha and finally Sanyasa. Then, the self that created the body entered into it. Liberation happens when one realizes this self, that is partless and hence whole, pure consciousness. The body exists because of the self. The difference that one perceives between the self and body is because of ignorance. When this ignorance is removed knowledge dawns.

Chapter—2

In this chapter, the knowledge of the changeless and non-dual self is explained. For the question put by the student about the cause of this ignorance, the teacher replies that the cause is delusion and illusion and knowledge liberates one from ignorance and the cycle of birth and death.

The waking and dream states are transitory. Pure consciousness exists in deep sleep and it persists. For an ignorant person, a snake appears in a rope and water appears in a mirage. But with knowledge he realizes that they are non-existent. Similarly, the duality experienced during waking and dreaming states has no existence whatsoever except the knowledge by which it is known. The self, the pure consciousness is therefore eternal and changeless and never ceases to exist in any mental modifications. The experience of this transmigratory existence in waking and in dreaming states is because of ignorance. With knowledge this ignorance comes to an end.

Chapter—3

The Self: A method is given in this chapter for the cessation of all activities of the body, mind and speech that give rise to desirable, undesirable and mixed results. The self is untouched by anything. It is pure. It is not affected by pleasant or unpleasant sound, touch, sight, taste, and smell, because the self is not with in the reach of the opposites like pain and pleasure. The self is also not changeable because it is not of an objective nature. The self is unattached because there is nothing that really exists apart from it.

Part—2 (verse)

Chapter—1

All actions that are accepted and prohibited connect one to the body that brings pain or pleasure and that ultimately ends in either attraction or repulsion. This generates actions again and again that goes on continuously like a wheel forever. The knowledge of Brahman will make one remove his ignorance. This knowledge of Brahman will bring about liberation. But one should perform obligatory duties as long as life lasts because only these along with knowledge will liberate a person. Knowledge is the awareness that the self is changeless. But it would be difficult for a man of knowledge to have knowledge and perform actions simultaneously as they do not go together. So the one who aspires liberation should renounce actions, because at this stage, the notion that one is a doer of actions and experiencer of the results of actions cannot exist. So it is stated in Sruti that renunciation of actions of the body and mind is superior to their performance. Only the one who has egoism would incur sin by the non-performance of duties. A man of knowledge has neither egoism nor the desire for the results of actions.

Chapter—2

Self is known by negation, that is by knowing that Brahman is 'NETI- NETI' or 'NOT THIS, NOT THIS'. Only by negating the previous knowledge a new knowledge will arise.

Chapter—3

The knowledge that the self is Brahman destroys ignorance.

Chapter—4

The fire of knowledge burns the results of actions born of egoism. The knowledge of one's own identity with pure self removes ignorance of identification of self with the body and makes a man free.

Chapter—5

While one is in a moving boat, trees appear to move in opposite direction. Similarly, the transmigratory existence is wrongly thought to belong to the self due to the identification of oneself with the intellect.

Chapter—6

The superimposition of body on the self is ignorance. When the self is known, ignorance will vanish. Self has an independent existence.

Chapter—7

The supreme Brahman is all knowing, all pervading and illuminates all. It is the witness, the supreme that is changeless, pure and non-material. Intellect functions due to the presence of self. The objects of knowledge exist in the intellect only in the waking and dream state. But in deep sleep they do not exist, only self exists. Therefore duality has no real existence. Once knowledge comes self is not seen different from Brahman or intellect.

Chapter—8

The supreme Brahman is free from bondage. It has no birth or duality. It is the same in all beings. It is free from all attributes. It is all pervading. Like ether it is imperishable. It is auspicious, homogenous, whole and actionless. Every being is part of the self but the self is not a part of anything.

Chapter— 9

When we go on negating the previous knowledge, we reach new knowledge and finally we reach the innermost self that is most subtle and all pervasive, that is nothing but existence and consciousness that illumines the intellect. The knowledge of objects in waking and dream states is not real. Brahman is always there but not the object of knowledge.

Chapter—10

Brahman is unborn. It is only one but not many. It is imperishable, unattached, all pervading, and non-dual, pure and without any change, deathless, without old age, immortal, self-effulgent, without cause and everlasting Bliss. Objects appear due to illusion. The states of waking, dreaming and deep sleep states have no independent existence apart from the self. The self is the fourth state that is Turiya or the transcendental state. It is the seer of all the other three states. The body, intellect and sense are not the self or that of the self. They are unreal like dream objects. Self has no body. So it has neither sin nor virtue, neither bondage nor liberation, neither actions nor results. Self is supreme without a second. Though self is in the body, it is not attached to the body. For the one who has the firm conviction that he is Brahman, there is no birth or death. Brahman is auspicious. It has no feeling of 'I', 'mine' and so on. When the pure knowledge of the self comes then there is no pain or grief, delusion or illusion, neither birth nor death.

Chapter—11

All beings are pure consciousness. But due to ignorance, they appear as different. The self is the witness of mind and its functions in the waking and dream state. In deep sleep both mind and its functions are absent. What is present then is only the self, the pure consciousness. As long as there is ignorance, there is that identification of oneself with his body. The self that is the witness exists in all beings. When all superimpositions of the gross and subtle body are negated self becomes very clear.

Chapter—12

The self gets identified with all objects that are seen in the world. Hence man is unable to know himself. Due to ignorance, the intellect that is only the reflection of self is mistaken for self like that of a reflection of a face in a mirror is mistaken to be the person who is in front of the mirror. One should realize that the ego that causes indiscrimination and other mental modifications has no connection whatsoever with the self. 'Thou' in Sruti refers to the one who knows the self. Self has no knowledge or ignorance. It is the supreme power in all beings. He, who has no egoism that he is the knower of Brahman, is the real knower of self or Brahman. The doership while performing actions is false since in this the self is superimposed on the body.

Chapter—13

Self has no vision, hearing, speech, no action, no knowledge, is ever free, pure, changeless and so on. Self has no hunger, thirst, grief, delusion, old age, death and so on. It has no sensation, taste and so on. Self is also devoid of mind and its modifications. It has no concentration or distraction because the self is all comprehensive principle. All beings owe their consciousness to self-only. The self is all and everything. When one knows that the self resides in His body, then he becomes all knowing. Such a person attains the goal of his life. He becomes knower of Brahman-the very Brahman itself.

Chapter—14

The impressions of the objects that are seen in the waking state appear in dream. The objects of dream therefore are not real. Similar is the case with the objects seen in the waking state as well. They too are not real. It is the intellect that is seen in the form of objects in dream state. It is the case in the waking state as well. Actually, the self is the cause of their appearance. The supreme self is not an object of knowledge of the knower. If it is so, then it is only superimposition of the self on the knower. The individual who is the seer, hearer, and thinker is not different from self or Brahman. He is the knower of the self who has no notions of 'me' or 'mine' or 'mine'. For the realized soul, there cannot be any such thought because he has no mind or actions as he has no senses. The self or pure consciousness only illumines all objects of knowledge or ego and so on. The self is the same in all beings, just as the pure, unlimited ether is the same everywhere. The body, mind and their impressions are different from the self as they are only objects of perception.

Chapter—15

Brahman is not different from oneself. The object of knowledge or the object that is seen is different from the seer of the object. The cause of its connection with body is action. So the spiritual aspirant should renounce all actions. Self is free from sin and value. So it is free from all impressions of pain and pleasure. Ego is an object of perception. So also is the case with other functions and impressions of mind. The self is called *Taijasa* in dream state because at this stage, the self is a witness of the modification of mind. In deep sleep self is known as *Prajna* because in this state there are neither objects nor their impressions. The self illumines all and is all knowing. It is the cause of all actions. The self does not require knowledge in order to be known. To reveal one light another light is not required.

Chapter—16

The self is different from the body, senses, mind and intellect. Self assumes the forms while revealing them. The pain and pleasure are for the body only but not for the self. The self is only a witness. It is the seer but not the seen. It is always the subject but not the object. The self is the cause of everything. One should go beyond all the three states of waking, dreaming and deep sleep because they are all unreal. In short all modifications of the primeval cause are unreal. To know the real self to be oneself is the greatest achievement. Illumined by the light of the self that is pure consciousness. The intellect wrongly believes that it is itself consciousness and that there is nothing behind it. This is nothing but delusion. With pure, non-dual knowledge the one who is perfectly convinced of the truth of the self becomes free from ignorance and gets peace forever. He becomes free from the notion of 'I' and 'mine'.

Chapter—17

The self is to be known. That is right knowledge. The notion of the existence of the non-self is ignorance. The destruction of that notion is liberation. The destruction of this ignorance is possible by means of knowledge. Actions cannot destroy the ignorance. Everything else other than the self is not real. The very existence of the universe is in that sense unreal. Pure consciousness or self assumes different forms due to various adjuncts that are superimposed on it. Only in a mind that is purified by *Yama*, *Niyama*, sacrifice, and religious duties, knowledge is revealed. Concentration and one-pointedness of mind and senses is the best and it is superior to all austerities including religious austerities. Self is the substratum of *Maya* or ignorance. Due to *Maya* that which is really one appear to be many. There is no birth or death for the knower of Brahman. The one who has renounced all worldly things is not bound by anything. Self should be meditated upon as '*AUM*'.

Chapter—18

Brahman is self. Ignorance vanishes with the attainment of this knowledge. Sruti teaches that 'I AM EXISTNCE'. The impressions from sense perceptions negate the knowledge 'I AM BRAHMAN'. On account of constant proximity of the conscious self, ego also appears to be conscious and therefore the notion of 'I' and 'MINE' originate. Self cannot be described directly. It can be described only indirectly. The reflection of self in the ego is like that of a face reflected in a mirror. The reflection cannot be the actual face. So also ego cannot be the self. In another sense the reflected face is because of the real face. When the real face is removed the reflection also disappears. So the reflection is not the face but it belongs to the face and is because of the face. However they are not one and the same. People without discrimination think that they both are one and the same. Similarly, intellect is wrongly thought to be the knower because of the superimposition of consciousness on it. Eternal knowledge is that of the self. It is not created by the intellect. The intellect that is illumined by the self becomes the knower. 'Mine' and 'I' are ideas of non-self and the idea of 'I' is that of ego. They are all because of ego. In the knowledge, that 'I AM BRAHMAN'; 'I' stands for Brahman or soul and not the body. Pervaded by consciousness, mental modifications arise in the form of objects. Pain arises due to non-identification of body with soul. One comes to know oneself with the knowledge of the *Mahavakya*, 'THOU ART THAT'. The knowledge of the innermost self becomes possible when ego vanishes. Pain belongs to intellect but not to the self.

Chapter—19

The mind indulges in ideas like 'me' and 'mind'. But the self has no such ideas. Self has no desires and is always contented. The wrong notions disappear as soon as one is free from the perception of differences. Everything that is created by the mind is unreal therefore nonexistent. Mind itself does not exist. Mind superimposes the notion, the seer, seeing and seen. All these are one that is the self. Nothing belongs to self nor does the self belong to anything. The world that is also superimposed does not exist in reality. The duality is unreal as the self is not different from anything. The substratum of all that are superimposed is real and it is the self. Due to ignorance one superimposes the ideas of existence, non-existence and so on the self that is not superimposed on anything. This results in repeated births and deaths. Only with the knowledge of the self and by knowing the self, ignorance and the resultant false knowledge can be negated. The one thousand teachings contained in this form the substance of Upanishads.

Vakya Sudha or Balabodini

This treatise is also known as Bala Bodhani. It contains 46 verses. It gives the essence of the teachings of Advaita Vedanta. It explains the seer and the seen, the power of glamour, the ordinary and the witnessing self, the eternal and imaginary perishable world, and about soul vision. Form or object is the 'seen', the eye is the 'seer'. The mind is both the seer and seen. But self that is witness is never seen. The self shines on all projections of mind like desire, fear and so on. It illumines everything else as well.

When the ray of consciousness enters the thinking mind it gets illumined. The nature of Mind is two fold. One part of it is personal idea and the other part is mental action. The personal idea identifies the ray of consciousness with body. This personal idea disappears in deep sleep and the body loses its consciousness. In dream state this personal idea is half expanded and in the waking state it is complete. When the rays of consciousness enter in to the power of mental action, it builds up mental images and external objects in the dream and in the waking states. The personal form is the result of personal idea as well as mental action. In the three states of consciousness it appears and also vanishes.

There are two powers for glamour. They are extension and enveloping. The power of extension manifests the whole world with attributes of name and form to reality. The enveloping power conceals the inner division between the *seer* and seen and the outer division between the eternal and non-eternal world. This is the cause of birth and death. Ordinary life comes in to being because of the penetration of the ray of consciousness. The ordinary self appears to belong to the witnessing self because the ordinary self is attributed to the witnessing self. But when this power of enveloping vanishes the difference also disappears. The same power conceals the difference between the eternal and the visible world. By its power, the actual or the real appears to be changing. But when this power of enveloping is destroyed, the difference between the real and the visible world becomes clear. Real or eternal is changeless. Change is there only for the visible world. Being, shining, enjoying, form and name are the five elements of existence. The first three elements belong to the eternal or real and the last two belongs to the visible world. Further the first three elements are whole. They are undivided. The division belongs to the last two elements namely, name and form.

One should forget about the divisions of name and form and concentrate on being, consciousness and Bliss that are undivided. One should firstly follow the soul vision inwardly in the heart and then in outward things. Soul vision can be either fluctuating or seady. The fluctuating soul vision is again are twofold. It may consist either in things seen or heard. The fluctuating soul vision that consists of things that are heard is the constant thought that 'I am the self', that is unattached, being, consciousness, Bliss, self-shining and one without a second. Uwavering or steady soul vision is the forgetting of all images and words through direct experience. It is like a lamp steadily burning in a windless place. The soul vision in the heart is without name and form. This is accomplished in the heart. The soul vision that is outward consists of unbroken thought that the real is the single supreme essence, consciousness and bliss. Then one tastes the essence. When the false notion that the body is self disappears, the supreme self will be known. At that stage, wherever mind is directed, soul vision will arise. At this stage all doubts and bondages get removed.

The individual self appears in three degrees, as a limitation of the self, as a ray of conscious self and thirdly as the self, imagined in dream. In these the first alone is real. The *Mahavakya* 'THAT THOU ART' reveals that. The whole world and all the elements and beings are only objects of experience. The imaginary self believes that imaginary world is real. But the real self knows that the world is only imaginary like the imaginary self. The real self knows its real oneness with the eternal.

All features of water like flowing, coldness and so on can be seen in its foam as well. Similarly, the being or consciousness and bliss of the self enter into habitual self that is bound with it and through this it enters in to the imaginary self as well. When the foam melts it merges in the wave and the waves become restful and they merge in to the sea. Similarly, when the being, consciousness, bliss of the imaginary self melt they merge with the habitual self and when the habitual self comes to rest they merge with the supreme self that is the witness of everything.

Vakyavrithi

This treatise explains the Mahavakya 'THAT THOU ART' or 'TAT TVAM ASI' and contains 53 verses. In this the teacher teaches the student who earnestly seeks the means of liberation from the sorrows of bondage. The immediate means to liberation is the direct knowledge of the total identity between the individual self and the universal self. One should give up the intellectual misconception that the body is the self. Instead one should meditate upon the eternal knowledge-bliss-the witness of the intellect-that is pure knowledge. The body is only a modification of elements with a form. The perceiver of the body is different from the body. It is also different from the senses, or mind or intellect or the vital air or *prana*. The seer is not the gross and subtle body. The self is the *seer* that is different from the seen. It is by the self that the body, senses, intellect, mind prana, and ego, all these function. They appear to be dynamic although inert because of the self. The self also illumines the three states of waking, dreaming and deep sleep, the intellect and body. One should realize the Maha vakyas namely, 'I AM Brahman', 'THOU ART THAT' and so on. 'THOU' refers to the self that is witness. 'THAT' refers to the all-pervading Brahman. 'THOU ART THAT' means you; the self is the witness, and the all-pervading one. Until direct personal experience of 'I AM BRAHMAN' is gained one must have self-control and so on, listen to the teacher, read scriptures, reflect and meditate upon them. After following all these, with the grace of a *Guru*, when one's ignorance, that is the basis of the world of plurality is removed then he realizes that he is Brahman. Although such a person is liberated, he will have to go through Prarabda Karmas until he exhauts them. But they do not affect him in any way. The liberated person gains the state of absolute oneness with Brahman, Bliss, and the supreme abode of Lord Vishnu from where there is no going back.

Viveka Choodamani

Viveka Choodamani means crest jewel of wisdom. It contains 580 verses that are in the form of dialogue between the teacher and the disciple. The teacher explains what bondage is, how it exists, how to get free from it, the nature of *Atman*, how to discriminate between self and not self, and how to realize Atman and so on. He points out that selfless actions or *Karmas* remove bondage and they purify the heart, but reality is to be attained by right knowledge and that knowledge comes from perception, investigation through meditation and self analysis but not by bathing in sacred waters or giving alms or breath control. This treatise is supposed to be a masterpiece of Shankara. It provides the cream of Upanishads and *Bhagavad Gita*.

It begins with Shankara's prayer to Govinda Bhagavadpada who was Shankara's *Guru*. It says that the three things that are rare are human birth as male, longing for liberation and the protecting care of the *Guru*. A man kills himself if he does not try for self-realization and liberation.

Then the verses explain about realization that is realizing one's identity with Atman, the significance of self-realization, the means to attain self-realization and the features of a *Guru*. It critically examines the attachment to the physical body and says that one should renounce the desires for worldly pleasures from worldly objects and fix his mind on truth. It also explains the various *Sareeras, Kosas, Gunas, senses, Prana*, methods of *Dhyana* and analysis of Atman. It concludes with the denial of pluralism and describes the state of self-realization. There are various commentaries on this treatise.

Shankara starts by saying, "I bow to that Govinda who is *Sadguru*, who can be understood only through Vedanta, who is beyond the reach of words and also mind, who has attained realization and who is one with Brahman. The three things namely, human birth particularly a male birth, the longing for liberation, and the protective care of a *Sad Guru*, one is able to get only with the blessings of God".

Liberation is obtained not by quoting scriptures or by performing Vedic sacrifices to the various Deities or by performing the rituals of worship. It can be achieved only by the realizing one's identity with Atman. Riches or wealth cannot bring immortality or *Mukti*.

So the wise should try to obtain liberation by not desiring worldly objects of desires. He should instead, approach a good and generous *Guru* for getting the ultimate knowledge.

Karma or actions lead to purification of mind but even ten million actions cannot perceive the reality. Truth can be realized only by discriminating real from non-real, by reasoning, advice of the wise and by reflection. It cannot be realized by bathing in sacred waters or by acts of charity or by doing hundred *Pranayamas*.

The success of the spiritual aspirant in knowing the ultimate truth depends upon the fitness of the seeker of truth. All other factors like circumstances, place or method at best can only be aids in this. The one who is seeking the ultimate truth should be in a position to discriminate real from unreal and then discard the unreal; he should possess all qualities or virtues like calmness. Only such a person is fit to enquire about Brahman and seek that knowledge. The seeker according to Sruti should possess faith or *shraddha*, devotion and *yoga*.

The four means of attainment of truth or the supreme knowledge according to the sages are; firstly, discrimination between the real and the unreal, secondly, renunciation to the enjoyment of results of one's actions or Karmas, thirdly, possessing tranquility of mind and the five virtues like discrimination, that is to have the firm conviction that Brahman alone is the eternal reality and not the transient world, Vairagya or non-attachment and rejection and renunciation of all pleasures of senses and desire for objects that have physical or other forms that are transient. One should also possess *Shama* or calmness that is resting and directing the mind calmly and steadily on Brahman, *Dana* or self-control that is turning away sense organs from sense objects, Thitiksha or forbearance that is bearing all difficulties without brooding over and without anxiety without any reaction or complaint, *shraddha* or faith in the teachings of the scriptures and that of the *Guru*, Samadhana or self-composure that is constantly concentrating on the ever pure Brahman, or fixing thought on Brahman alone and Mumukshutha or eagerness for liberation. Among all factors that are required for obtaining liberation, devotion or *Bhakti* that is the intense longing to know one's real self is the most important. Devotion is nothing but seeking divinity that is one's own inherent nature.

With all these qualities one should approach a *Guru*, who is highly knowledgeable in Vedas, who is sinless, who has no desires, who is the best knower of Brahman, who has identified himself with Brahman, who is calm, an embodiment of mercy, and who is a friend of all beings in helping them to cross over the ocean of the material non real phenomenal existence. Such a *Guru* takes in to his fold the disciple who is worthy enough. He showers his grace and imparts the greatest knowledge.

The *Guru* then asks the disciple to analyze the meaning of Vedanta that leads one to that knowledge that results in the destruction of all misery that is on account of the relative existence in the phenomenal world. According to Sruti, faith, devotion, and yoga or meditation remove all miseries of life and leads to liberation immediately. Due to delusion or *Maya* one thinks himself as the nonself that brings about repeated births and deaths. The fire of knowledge that is kindled by *Viveka* or discrimination burns up the effects of ignorance completely from its very roots and results in self-realization.

The *Guru* clears all doubts of the disciple by providing the necessary answers. The disciple asks about origin, its nature and so on. After providing the necessary replies, the *Guru* tells the disciple that one's bondage can be removed only by himself not by any other whom he considers as his own like sons and so on. Only the patient can cure a disease by taking proper medicines for its cure. One will be able to discern reality only with his spiritual awakening. Yogic practices, philosophical speculations, good works, learning, clear exposition and so on cannot bring about liberation to one. Liberation can be obtained only by realizing one's identity with Brahman. No amount of chanting the mantras or the study of scriptures, or offerings to the Gods or rituals and worship can lead one to liberation, not even in the life time of a hundred Brahmas as they are not the means for obtaining liberation. Liberation can be obtained only by realizing one's identity with the eternal Brahman. Uttering the word 'Brahman' cannot bring about realization. Liberation comes when the apparent universe is removed from consciousness. The *Guru* teaches the truth or knowledge of self that is a treasure hidden and buried in *Maya* and its effects. To obtain that treasure of knowledge one has to dig the earth in the correct place where it is hidden. Similarly, the knowledge of Brahman can also be obtained only through meditation and other spiritual disciplines and by reflecting upon the teachings of the *Guru*.

The first step to liberation is extreme aversion and detachment to all perishable things of the world that are transitory. Then one should practice tranquility, self-control, and forbearance and renunciation. Then as stated in the scriptures, he should give up all Karmas or actions that arise from selfish interests. Thereafter comes attentive listening of the teachings of the *Guru*, then, reflection on that, and finally long and constant and unbroken meditation on the truth. After that the seeker attains the supreme Nirvikalpa state and realizes the bliss of *Nirvana* even in his life, reaches a stage where the subject- object differences disappear and only a single infinite consciousness exists. This is Bliss.

The physical body is gross. It is the abode of illusion like 'I' and 'mine. The elements combine with the parts of another and form the gross body. The sense objects are the subtle essence of these elements giving happiness to the experiencer that is the individual soul. Beings get attached to these sense objects. The sense objects are more poisonous than the poison of cobra. One has to kill this cobra with the sword of detachment. The one who can free himself from the sense objects is only fit for liberation. However the apparent and temporary detachment from the sense objects of the seeker, who want to liberate himself and free himself from the cycle of birth and death, will drown him when he is half way in this journey. But the one who is able to kill the shark of sense objects with the sword of total dispassion crosses the ocean of *Samsara* easily. Therefore one who seeks liberation should refrain himself from all sense objects and should cultivate virtues like contentment, compassion, forgiveness, honesty, peace, straight forwardness, calmness and self control and he is the one who is fit for liberation. Sages reach this state, the supreme through non-attachment to worldly things and all relationships.

The gross body is the great object of delusion. One should conquer it to attain liberation. This gross body is the result of past actions that arise due to a combination of gross elements and subtle elements. The body is composed of waste and filth like skin, flesh, blood vessels, marrow and bones. These are to be ignored. For the *Jeevatma*, gross body is the medium of experience through the three states of *Jagrat* that is the waking state, *Swapna* that is the dream state and Sushupti that is the dreamless deep sleep state. In the waking state or Jagrat, gross objects are enjoyed by the individual soul through gross body. In this state the individual identifies himself with his body totally and enjoys senses objects. The gross body is the location of *Purusha* and is full of gross enjoyments. The various features like birth, growth, change, decay and death are the various features of the gross body. The different colours, built, and conditions like childhood, youth and old age belong to the gross body only. The physical body is also associated with social restrictions like caste and so on and it is also subject to ailments. The gross body consists of five senses like sight, hearing, taste, smell, and touch, five organs of action like tongue, legs, hands, organs of secretion and generation, four external organs like *Buddhi*, or the discriminating faculty, the *Ahamkara* or ego, the mind and the *Chittha* that takes the impressions, and five Pranas like *Prana, Apana, Vyana, Udana* and *Samana*.

The sense organs perceive the objects and the organs of action work with it. The inner organ or *Antha karana* is called *Manas* that analyses the pros and cons, *Buddhi* that deter mines the validity of the objects, and ego with which one identifies oneself with the body and chittha that is remembering things in which it is interested. The same Prana or the vital force becomes five, namely, *Prana, Apana, Vyana, Udana*, and *Samana* according to their functions.

The subtle body or the *Linga Sareera* is made up of eight cities consisting of five organs of action like speech and so on, five organs of knowledge such as ear, the five pranas, the five elements, *Buddhi*, Nescience or *Avidya, Kama* or desire and *Karma* or action. The subtle body is made out of elements before they are subdivided and combined with each other. It has the latent impressions and causes the soul to experience the results of its past actions. However the body is not aware of its real nature.

Dream state is different from the waking state. It belongs to the subtle body. The experiences of the waking state get transformed in to subtle objects and that is what is experienced in the dream state. In this state the supreme Atman shines in its own glory with Buddhi or intellect as its superimposition. The past latent impressions of the waking state are carried over in the dream state. Buddhi or intellect is only a reflection of the supreme Atman. It is like an instrument, chistle to the carpenter. *Atman* affects *Buddhi* but *Bhuddhi* cannot affect *Atman* because Atman is self-luminous, totally detached, and the witness of everything. Qualities are for the organs but not for the Atman- who is the knower.

The mind that is the inner organ is seated in the sense organs and it identifies with them. It has the reflection of Atman. By identification with the body it becomes the doer or experiencer. The three qualities namely, *Sattva, Rajas* and *Tamas* belong to *Ahamkara*. They do not belong to *Atman*. But pure Sattva has the nature of peace, bliss, and cheerfulness. It helps in liberation. Rajas is the source of all desires and disturbances of mind like sorrow, pain and so on and the resulting bondage. It creates qualities like lust, anger, greed, envy and so on. Due to the mixing of qualities like *Sattva* and *Rajas* the positive qualities like faith, devotion, contentment, desire for liberation, truthfulness, and absence of greed appear in different degrees. *Tamas* creates qualities like veiling, wrong judgement, constant disbelief, and doubt and it results in restlessness for the individual. *Tamas* takes *Maya* to be the *Atman* even by the most intelligent person. The one who is in *Tamas* always remains in ignorance. When the sense objects are favourable to ego it becomes happy and *vice versa*. The sense objects have no independent power. It gains its power because the ever-blissful *Atman* that manifests through them. *Atman* that is ever blissful is not affected by anything. It manifests through ego.

In Sushupti or in deep sleep one does not experience pleasure or pain. In this state the mind remains dormant. That is the reason why a man after waking up from deep sleep comments that he slept without being aware of anything. Only the Bliss of Atman is experienced in this state. This has been proved by scriptures as well as by direct experience. In this stage mind and all other organs stop functioning and there is no perception.

Maya or ignorance is only an illusion. It is like water in a mirage. It is the source of all ignorance of man. *Maya* or illusion is the undivided, undifferentiated power of God. Only by the realization of Brahman, Maya can be destroyed. The non-self is the body, senses, mind, ego, objects, feelings, the five elements and the universe. The everlasting substratum of ego is the self. It illumines the intellect. It is self-luminous. That pervades the whole universe. The body, the organs, mind and intellect perform their functions on account of its presence. The innermost self is the primeval *Purusha* or being that is the absolute, infinite bliss.

Inside the gross body, in the *Satvic* mind, in the secret chamber of the intellect it shines. It has no birth or death, no growth or decay. It is changelss and eternal. It is not destroyed when the body is destroyed. It is the essence of pure knowledge and is Absolute. One can realize pure self by means of a controlled mind and purified intellect. One who has that understanding crosses the ocean of life and he does not undergo any more births and deaths. When one identifies oneself with the non-self, then, bondage is the result. This is due to ignorance and the cause for repeated birth and death. Bondage is due to transitory things that are mistaken as real. Just as clouds that are generated by the sunrays cover the sunrays, egoism that is generated by the self covers the reality of the self. The bondage can be destroyed by the sword of knowledge that comes out of discrimination coupled with divine grace. Body cannot be the Atman because it is ever changing, perishable, composed of skin, flesh, blood and bone and therefore is impure. The Atman is the witness of the body, its fe^tures, its activities, its different states and so on. When one removes the identification of self with the body, then he will be free from the cycle of birth and death.

The vital sheath formed by *Prana* coupled with the five organs of action cannot be the self, because it is only a modification of *Vayu* or air that is dependent on the self. The organs of knowledge and mind form the mental sheath. It generates the feeling of 'I' and 'Mine'. The cause of ignorance and bondage is mind. When that is destroyed, all ignorance too gets destroyed. In dreamless sleep the mind is in its causal state and nothing exists there. Both bondage that is due to attachment and liberation that is freeing oneself from bondage are caused by mind alone. Mind helps in liberation through discrimination and renunciation. So it is necessary to purify the mind. However the mental sheath cannot be the pure self because it has a beginning and an end, it has modifications; it is charecterised by pain, pleasure and so on.

Buddhi or intellect along with its modifications and the organs of knowledge forms the *Vignanamaya Kosha* or the knowledge sheath. This knowledge sheath is a modification of *Prakruti*. It is charecterised by egoism and is called Jeeva. It carries out all activities at the relative level. Through previous desires it performs good and bad actions and experiences the corresponding results, the three states of experience, joy and grief. It mistakes the duties, functions, and attributes of life that belongs to the body as its own. This knowledge is effulgent as it is very close the supreme self. By identification of the supreme self with it and by superimposing self on it, it suffers transmigration.

The self luminous Atman is pure knowledge. It shines in the midst of *Pranas* within the heart. Due to superimposition, the supreme self that is eternally unchanging assumes the qualities of that, which is superimposed on it. The *Jeeva* hood that is imposed upon on Atman is due to ignorance or illusion and it is not real. So when the delusion vanishes it ceases to exist. Though the effects of *Avidya* have no beginning, they are destroyed when one realizes the real through perfect knowledge, by discriminating the self from the non-self.

The knowledge sheath or *Vignanamaya Kosha* cannot be the supreme self because it is subject to change, it is limited, and it is an object of the senses and is not everlasting. The blissful sheath or the *Anandamaya Kosha* is fully present during deep sleep. In waking and dreaming states it manifests only partially. However this blissful sheath is also changing, as it is a modification of *Prakruti*. It is also the effects of past good deeds. When all the five sheaths are eliminated by reasoning on Sruti, the witness of the three states, the supreme knowledge, that is absolute, real, changeless, untainted, everlasting bliss, the Atman is revealed. At that state there is no perceiver. So the Atman is understood only by itself. At this stage, the individual soul is the supreme Brahman. Those by which all modifications like egoism and its absence during deep sleep is perceived, that is Atman, the knower.

The self is the cause of all manifestations. The self exists for all the three states of consciousness. It is different from the five sheaths with which the body is made of. It sees everything as a witness but it cannot be seen. It illumines the intellect but it cannot be illuminated. It pervades the entire universe; it illumines everything in the universe. It directs the body, mind and intellect. The Atman is indivisible, eternal, blissful, all knowing, and non-changing. It shines like a sun in the core of the heart. Realising this, one becomes free from birth and death and becomes an embodiment of Bliss. Once the knowledge of Brahman is got there is no return to the transmigratory existence. The self is not different from individual soul. The whole universe is an effect of Brahman and is Brahman. The universe is not real, as it does not exist in deep sleep. So whatever is manifested, including this universe, is the supreme Brahman. There is no differenciation of knower, knowledge and known. This is beyond the reach of mind and speech.

Ishwara and *Jeeva* are one and the same. One should meditate upon this Brahman only. As the mind gradually gets absorbed in the inner most self, the desires for external objects will vanish and Atman will be realized. *Sattvic* and *Rajasic* qualities will destroy the quality of *Tamas*. *Sattva* will destroy *Rajas*. Finally when one gets purified, Sattva also will die. When one gets freed from egoism, he attains his real nature and becomes pure, infinite, ever blissful, and self-luminous. When the desire for realization of Brahman is intense, the egoistic desires would get destroyed. When the Self that is Atman, Bliss, is realised, then there will be neither bondage nor misery. The mind that deviates from the constant meditation of the self, even for a moment, declines very fast. Such fallen men are ruined and it would become very difficult to elevate the mind again. So one should shut the door of the mind to the external world and open it up to the interior to know the self. A perfect *Sanyasin* always reflects on his own self that is the self of the whole universe. He then lives in Brahman blissfully, free from all waverings of the mind. The man, who is attached to the real, becomes real. Through meditation the mind is able to give up all the three qualities and attain Brahman. Dispassion and discrimination are the two wings with which the spiritual aspirant reaches the destination of liberation. The self is Brahma, Vishnu, Shiva or Indra. The self is the universe. Nothing exists except the self.

Prarabda Karma is like a released arrow. Neither its force nor its target can be changed. So even a realized *jnani* will have to undergo its effects. But the fire of knowledge will destroy the fruits of accumulated actions as well as future actions. But only with reference to the physical body *Prarabdha* will have its effects. It has nothing to do with Atman. The knower of Atman does not identify himself with the body. He is a wanderer in this world even without being aware of his own body. He is ever happy and in supreme bliss. Though he is active, yet he is inactive. He is untouched by the experiences of past actions. He is not touched by pleasure or pain, good or evil. He lives with body with the idea of no body. He merely lives like a witness, free from all mental waverings. He lives like an unconcerned spectator of all objects that are perceived by sense organs. He lives as the Absolute Atman. He is Shiva himself. He is the one who has merged with Brahman. Thus liberation consists in the destruction of *Avidya.* The liberated souls become one with Brahman. They do not undergo transmigration. The notions of bondage and liberation are attributes of *Buddhi* or the intellect. It does not belong to the eternal reality, the Brahman. *Maya* creates them. They are not Brahman or Atman. The ultimate truth is that there is neither birth nor death, neither a bound nor a struggling soul, neither a seeker of liberation nor a liberated one.

7

Doctrine of Advaita Vedanta

The doctrine of Advaita Vedanta is the most popular doctrine of Vedanta that is based upon the Vedas particularly that of the Upanishads that is considered as the crown of Vedas. It is a matter of great pride for the Indians that recently; The United Nation's cultural organization recognised the Vedas as a part of world's heritage of oral history. It has stated that Vedic chantings are an intangible heritage of humanity. The Upanishads themselves are collectively termed as Vedanta. The Vedas that is the eternal knowledge was the result of the prolonged and continuous meditation of the ancient seers of India. The ancient Rishis obtained this wisdom in their supra conscious state as vibrations from space. The Vedas are the most ancient knowledge revealed in the world the date of origin of which is not known correctly as well as precisely. They are considered as Anadi or eternal and *Aparusha* or superhuman and therefore has no single founder or author. Advaita Vedanta is born out of the Vedas particularly that of the Upanishads that forms the final part of the Vedas.

From Upanishads that are also called as Shruti Prasthana or revealed scriptures, the knowledge of Brahman is obtained. It is also termed as Shruti Siras that means the head or crown of the Vedas that are Anadi or eternal, Aparushaya or super human, Amnaya, the root texts of tradition, Nigama, the traditional wisdom and Trayi consisting of *mantras*, prose and poetry. Upanishads contain the teachings of the philosophical contents of the Vedas and this forms the fourth and the final section of the Vedas that are the earliest documents of the human mind in the world. 'Upa' means 'under and near or very close' and 'shad' means 'to sit'. The *Guru* or the teacher imparted the Upanishadic teachings to those disciples who were made to sit close to the teacher. They were imparted only to those disciples who were very eager to know the wisdom contained in the Upanishads. According to Shankara the term 'upanishad' is derived from the word 'Shad' that means 'destroy' because Upanishads destroyed ignorance.

The Upanishads do not have a single author. Several sages composed them over a period of time. It is believed in the beginning there were a 1081 Upanishads. But many of them are extinct now. According to *Mukthikopanishad* there are 108 Upanishads. The older Upanishads like *Brahad Aranyaka* and *Chandogya Upanishads* date back to the later Brahmana period, that is, around the middle of the first millennium BCE, while the later ones were composed during the medieval and early modern period. Some of the Upanishads were composed roughly around the 6th century B C that is approximately during the time of Buddha while some of the other Upanishads belong to the period after Buddha. The main figure in the Upanishads is sage Yajnavalkya who taught the great doctrine of 'Neti Neti' that means 'Not this, Not this'. It means that truth can beunderstood only through negation of all thoughts about it. Some of the other important sages whose names are associated with the Upanishads are, *Uddalaka Aruni, Shvetaketu, Shandilya, Aitareya, Pippalada, Sanat Kumara* and so on. We also find many earlier Vedic teachers like Manu, Brihaspathi, Ayasya, and Narada in the Upanishads.

Upanishads have Vedas that has the Samhita, Brahmana and the Aranyaka sections as the basis. Upanishads are referred to as Vedanta meaning the end portion or the culmination of the four Vedas. The spiritual and mystic meaning of the Vedas are brought forth and established in the Upanishads that is collectively called as Vedanta, that has given rise to many Vedantic doctrines the chief and the most popular of all being Advaita Vedanta.

The *Rishi Parampara* of the doctrine of Advaita Vedanta up to Adi Shankara includes Vedic and Upanishadic seers like Vashishta, Sakti, Parasara, Vyasa, Sukha, Uddalaka Aruni of the *Chandogya Upanishad*, and Yajnavalkya of the *Brahad Aranyaka Upanishad* and so on. The supreme teaching of non-duality is also explained in *Vishnu Purana* in the dialogue between sages Ribhu with Nidagha. The *Astavakra Gita* of sage *Ashtavakra* and the Yoga Vashishta of the *Ramayana* give the essence of Advaita in its purest form. In the Manava Parampara are the gurus like *Gaudapada*, the author of Mandukya Karika, attached to *Mandukya Upanishads*. His desciple Govinda was the *Guru* of Shankara and was considered as an incarnation of Adi Sesha, the cosmic serpant. Adi Shankara is regarded as an incarnation of Lord Shiva. Adi Shankara himself quoted the names of a few pre Shankara Vedantins in his works like Bhagavan Upavarsha, the author of Vrittis to Brahma Sutras and *Bhagavad Gita*, *Sundara Pandya*, author of Varttikas to Upavarsha's Vritthi, Brahmanandin who wrote Chandigya Upanishad Vakya and Dravidacharya who wrote Bhashya on Brahmanandin's Vakya, Kasakrtsna, Bhratruhari, the great grammarian and so on.

Although the philosophy of Advaita Vedanta goes back to Upanishads, Gaudapada is considered as the first systematic exponent of Advaita Vedanta. He gave the central teaching of Advaita Vedanta in his *Mandukya Karika*. He was the first historical proponent and the first one to establish Advaita Vedanta on a rational level. But it was Adi Shankara who consolidated the doctrine and gave perfection to it and he is considered as the most important teacher of Advaita Vedanta. It was he who gave the final and beautiful form of Advaita philosophy. Adi Shankara's philosophy of Advaita Vedanta can be summed up in half a verse 'Brahma Satyam Jagan Mithya Jivo Brahmaiva Aparah' that means Brahman that is the Absolute alone is real. This world is unreal. The *Jeeva* or the individual soul is the same as Brahman.

Basis of Advaita Vedanta

Advaita is based upon Shastra or scriptures, Yukta or reason and *Anubhava* or experience. It has no single founder. It is aided by spiritual practices, devotion and *Karma* ending in jnana or knowledge.

It says ultimately there is no difference between the experiencer; experienced that is the world and the universal spirit. Shankara's philosophy of Advaita Vedanta that is one of the Vedantic doctrines is based upon the Upanishad, particularly on the four Mahavakyas of the Upanishads namely, 'Prajnanam Brahma' that is Brahman is consciousness that is found in the Atraeya Upanishad of *Rig Veda*, 'Aham Brahmasmi' or I am Brahman as found in the Brihad Aranyaka Upanishad of *Yajur Veda*, 'Tattvamasi' or that thou art found in the Chandogya Upanishad of *Sama Veda* and 'Ayam Atma Brahma' or This Atman is Brahman found in Mandukya Upanishad of *Atharva Veda*. The Upanishads ascribe all reality or truth to a single supreme ultimate principle or source- Shankara's explanation of Advaita Vedanta philosophy is known as the Kevala Advaita Vedanta or simple non-dualism or uncompromising Monism or Absolute Monism.

Advaita Vedanta, which is a sub school of Vedanta, is also known as non-dualism or monistic system of thought. The word Advaita refers to the merger of the individual self or Atman with the whole or Brahman. Monism means the view that all is one. Monistic philosophy also therefore refers to the identity or oneness or non-duality of the Atman or the individual self and the *Paramatman* or the universal self. Adi Shankara quoted mainly from the Upanishads to explain his doctrine of *Kevala Advaita Vedanta.*

Advaita Vedanta Passages in Upanishads

Aitareya Upanishad

All beings are impelled by consciousness. Consciousness is the beginning and end of the universe. Consciousness is Brahman.

Atma Bodha Upanishad

Brahman exists In the middle of the heart-lotus.

Only Brahman exists as the basis of this world.

The sun that makes the pot shine is not destroyed along with the pot. So also the spirit is not destroyed with the body.

To an owl sun is dark. Similarly, for an ignorant person Brahman also is dark. (He cannot know Brahman)

When clouds block the vision, one thinks that there is no sun. (Similarly when one is engulfed by ignorance he becomes incapable to discern Brahman)

Just as there is no serpent in the rope so also there is no world either.

Nadabidu Upanishad

Even after obtaining *Atma Jnana, Prarbda* does not leave a person. But he does not feel *Prarabda* once he gets the *Tattva Gnana* or the knowledge of truth, because to him body and other things are *Asat* or unreal like the things seen in a dream to one who wakes up after that dream in sleep. So *Prarabda*, that is that portion of past Karma alloted for the present birth, will not affect the Tattva Gnani.

As the clay is the material cause of the pot so also, *Ajnana* or ignorance is the material cause of the universe. So, when *Ajnana* or ignorance ceases to exist then, there is no world or universe or cosmos.

Due to illusion one mistakes the rope for a snake. Similarly, the ignorant not knowing the eternal truth sees the world to be true. When he knows that it is only a rope, his illusory idea of serpent vanishes.

The mind exists so long as there is sound, but with its cessation, there is the state called *Unmani* of Manas that is the state of being above mind. The sound at this state gets absorbed in the *Akshara* or the indescribable and there is that soundless state.

Nirvana Upanishad

The bliss of Brahman is free from the three qualities of *Sattva*, *Rajas* and *Tamas*.

Brahman is realized by discrimination of the real from the unreal and it is beyond the reach of mind and speech.

The phenomenal world is not permanent. It is similar to a world seen in a dream or an elephant seen in the sky that is illusory. Similarly, the body and other things also are perceived by multitude of delusion and it is wrongly believed to exist as a serpent in a rope.

Saubhagyalakshmi Upanishad

Through ceaseless concentrated sight, when one ceases to have the thought of the body, then the self is realized.

SHUKLA YAJURVEDA

Adyatma Upanishad

The one that is unborn resides everywhere. But one does not recognise it. He is the inner self of all beings, sinless and luminous.

Superimposition is the thought that 'I' and 'mine' are the body, senses and so on, that are all other than the self.

Know oneself to be the subject, the witness of the intellect and its operations.

Dissolve the self in the supreme self as the pot space gets dissolved in infinite space.

Just as pulled up water reed stays not still even for a moment, so also *Maya* or ignorance envelops even a Wiseman if he averts his face from truth.

With the vision of the non-dual self, through unwavering concentration, the knots of ignorance in the heart get dissolved without any residue.

Other than the self there is nothing.

After removing all objective appearances super imposed on one's self, one remains alone as the supreme Brahman that is full, non-dual and stirless.

The world is a postulation that is as good as non-existent.

The perception of difference is rooted in the mind. In the absence of mind there are no differences. So one should concentrate one's mind on the supreme self as the subject.

Upon realizing the self as one's own essence one enjoys that timeless bliss, the self, both externally and internally.

Detachment brings knowledge; knowledge results in detachment; Peace is the result of withdrawl and the experience of the self as Bliss leads to peace.

The highest pitch of awareness is seen in the non-occurrence of the sense of egoism.

Wisdom or Prajna is the unwavering spiritual mode in which there is unity of Brahman and Atman.

The one in his wisdom perceives no difference between the subject and Brahman, the creator and his creation is liberated in life.

Just as space is unaffected by the smell of liquor though it touches the pot, that contains liquor, similarly, the self is unaffected by the attributes of its adjuncts. One only is non-dual Brahman. There is no plurality at all.

Advaya Taraka

The notion that the living beings and God are separate entities is due to illusion. Examine and understand the differences, which exist in the world by the method of 'Nethi Nethi', that is 'not this', 'not this' and at last what remains is the Advaya Brahman, that is, that which does not possess two forms.

Brihad Aranyaka Upanishad

Only the self is to be realized because, one knows all through it, just as one may spot an animal through its footprints.

This self is the dearest of all and is the innermost.

As a spider moves along the thread that it produces and as tiny sparks of fire emanated from fire fly in all directions, so also, from this self emanate all organs, all words, all Gods and all beings.

A lump of salt dropped in water dissolves in water and loses its form but it tastes salt. Similarly the self comes out from the elements of this great endless, infinite reality that is, pure intelligence and this separateness gets destroyed with them.

After attaining oneness the self has no more consciousness, because one sees, smells, hears etc., only when there is duality. When once everything becomes self there is none other who sees, hears, and smells and so on.

The knowledge of self is the means to immortality. The underlying unity in all is Brahman. This knowledge of Brahman is the means of becoming all.

The self is the ruler of all beings and king of all beings. Just as the spokes are fixed in the chariot wheel, so also all beings, all Gods, all worlds, all organs and all individual selves are fixed in the self.

Self or Brahman is that which you cannot see but that is the witness of vision, you cannot hear but which is the hearer of hearing, you cannot think but which is the thinker of thought. You cannot know that which is, the knower of knowledge. This self is within all. Everything else other than this is perishable.

Brahman is that which transcends hunger, grief, delusion, decay and death.

The immortal self is never seen but is the witness; never heard but is the hearer; never the thought but the thinker. Everything is mortal while He, your own self is immortal.

The one God is the vital force or Hiranya Garbha. It is called 'Tyat' or 'That'.

The self is imperceptible, undecaying, unattached and unfettered.

Just as a great fish swims alternatively to both the banks of a river, eastern and western, similarly, the self, the infinite being move towards both dream and the waking state and just as a hawk or a falcon flying in the sky becomes tired and stretches its wings and goes towards its nest, so also the infinite being run for the dreamless sleep state. At this stage one is untouched by good and bad.

Just as a leech supported on a straw goes to the end of it and then takes hold of another support, similarly, the self throws this body aside and takes hold of another support. Those who are desireless and hence do not transmigrate get merged in Brahman.

Just as the lifeless slough of a snake is cast off and lies in the anthill, so also the body is cast off.

Brahman has to be reached through mind alone.

Brahman is eternal, taintless, beyond ether, birthless, infinite and constant.

Isavasya Upanishad

The self is unmoving, the only one, faster than the wind. The senses cannot reach it. It remains static yet it overtakes others who run.

The self moves, yet it moves not. It is far yet near. It is within all and also without all.

The self is all pervading, radiant, bodiless, sorrowless, pure, untainted by sin, the all seer, and the lord of mind, transcendent and self-existent.

Jabala Upanishad

The self that is infinite and unmanifest is established and is non different from Avimuktha, that is, Lord Shiva, that is *Saguna Brahman*, the Brahman with attributes.

Mandala Brahmana Upanishad

One enjoys the Bliss of Brahman in the lotus of his heart. *Taraka* is Brahman that is located in the middle of the two eyebrows. It is of the nature of spiritual effulgence of Sachidananda.

Seeing Para Brahman in his own Atman as the Lord of all, that is immeasurable, the birthless, the auspicious, the supreme *Akasa*, the supportless, the secondless, the only goal of Brahma, Vishnu and Rudra and the cause of all and assuming oneself that he who plays in the cave of the heart is such a one, one should rise above dualities of existence and non existence and knowing the experience of Unmani of his Manas he attains the state of *Para Brahman* that is motionless as a lamp in a place devoid of wind.

The destruction of *Manas* comes after the destruction of the collective senses.

Mantrika Upanishad

Those who see with the eye of wisdom perceive the unmanifest as consisting of everything as the only one, purest and all pervading.

That in which all the moving and unmoving is woven, in that very thing they merge as the rivers in the sea.

Mukthika Upanishad

Absolute liberation is attainable only through wisdom but not through *Karma*, rituals, *Sankhya Yoga* or worship.

The unsteady mind is the cause of birth, old age and death. It is generated by desire for objects in excess.

When impressions die out, mind becomes like a lamp that is put out.

Mind becomes non-mind by giving up *Vasanas* or impressions.

Niralamba Upanishad

Brahman is the ineffable spirit. It is non-dual and free from all adjuncts. It is great with all powers and is without beginning and end. It is pure, good, quiescent and unqualified.

The supreme self is Brahman and it is totally different from body and so on.

Ignorance is the illusory knowledge like that of a snake in a rope.

Brahman is everything, all pervasive and non-dual.

Paingala Upanishad

For the knower of the self what use is the Vedas? No duty remains for such a one who is full of wisdom of the ultimate.

As there is no difference when water is poured in water, milk in milk, and ghee in ghee, so is the case with the individual self with the supreme self.

The knower gets dissolved in Brahman that is like the all-pervading sky.

The dissolution in truth is like the pot space in the infinite space.

All actions like purification, mutterings of holy names, sacrifices, pilgrimage to holy places, all are valid only till truth is realized.

The two words determing bondage and liberation are 'mine' and 'not mine'.

When the mind is dementalised there is no more duality.

Satyayaniya Upaishad

Mind alone is the cause of bondage and liberation. The mind attached to objects leads to bondage and the mind freed from objects lead to liberation.

When all desires that cling to the heart are shed, then a man becomes immortal and he enjoys the bliss of Brahman.

Subala Upanishad

In this body of fat, flesh, moisture is placed the pure self of all, within the cave.

The self is immortal, fearless, painless, infinite and seedless. All things are resolved in that self. He who knows this seedless Brahman himself becomes seedless.

The self is not got by hundreds of expositions, or by great learning, or by reliance on intellectual knowledge or through memory power, Vedas, sacrifices, austerities, Sankhya or Yoga, Ashramas, exercises and so on. The Vedic sages achieved it by becoming calm, restrained, withdrawn, tolerant and concentrating.

Trisikhi Brahmana Upanishad

The realization of the universal truth of the unity of Jeevatma and Paramatma that is 'I am Brahman', and 'Brahman is in me', is the real state of Samadhi. The man in this state becomes Brahman and he does not take another birth.

The one who examines the Maha Vakyas with detachment becomes like fire without wood and becomes one with himself. His mind and soul have nothing to get attached to, he becomes stable in the form of wisdom and his soul melts like a piece of salt and he merges in to the sea of pure consciousness. He sees the world that is a thing of passion and magic as a dream.

Yajnavalkya Upanishad

There is consciousness here; everything is consciousness alone, and is pervaded by consciousness and you and I are consciousness and all these worlds are of consciousness.

KRISHNA YAJUR VEDA

Akshi Upanishad

All is one, unborn, tranquil, endless, certain, and immutable.

When non-duality is established and duality gets dissolved, then the phenomenal world becomes merely a dream.

Amritha Bindu Upanishad

When the mind with its attachment for sense objects is annihilated and fully controlled within the heart and if it realises its own essence then the supreme state is obtained.

The supreme state is to be meditated upon, so that Brahman is attained.

That alone is Brahman that is without parts, without doubt or taint. The one who realizes 'I am that Brahman' becomes the immutable Brahman.

Brahman is without doubt, endless, beyond reason, and analogy; beyond all proofs and causeless. Knowing this the wise becomes liberated.

Atman is the same in all the three states of waking, dreaming and dreamless sleep state. For the one who transcends these three states there is no more birth.

The universal soul is present in all beings. Although it is one, it is seen as many, like the moon that appears as many in its reflection in water.

Just as the jar that is shifted from one place to other changes its place but not the space or *Akasa* enclosed in the *jar*, so also, is the *Jeeva* or *Atman* that resembles space or *Akasa*.

Due to *Maya* or illusion and *Avidya* or ignorance one is unable to know the space or that blessed one. But when ignorance vanishes, then the unity will be seen.

After studying the Vedas the intelligent one who aspires for knowledge and realization should discard the Vedas totally, just as a man who wants to get rice discards the husk covering it.

The many-branched Vedas are like cows that are diverse in their colour. But *Jnana* or wisdom is like the milk that is obtained from the cows possessing the same colour.

Just as butter permeates the milk, pure consciousness resides in every being. By using the churning rod of mind one should constantly churn out the butter of pure consciousness.

Taking the support of the rope of knowledge, one should like fire realize the supreme Brahman.

The Amritha Nada Upanishad

The wise after studying all shastras should reflect upon them again and again and then realize Brahman. Finally they should discard all shastras like the firebrand.

Brahma Upanishad

That Brahman who shines within the divine Brahmapura that is His abode, as the faultless one, devoid of manifested effects, self effulgent, all pervading; it is He who controls the jeeva like a spider controlling the king of bees.

In dreamless sleep one goes to one's own abode, like a falcon that goes to its nest and enjoys happiness. So also He, the self, returns by the same way to the dream state like a leech that carries itself to the next point. That state which one does not give up for the next one is the waking state.

This being or self is fully extended to world forms. He is the indwelling controller of things and beings; He is the bird, the crab, and the lotus. He is the *Purusha*, the *Prana*, the destroyer, the cause and the effect, the Brahman and the *Atman*. He is the *Devata* making everything known. Whosoever knows this attains the transcendent Brahman, the underlying support, and the subjective principle.

Within the recess of the heart is the *Akasa* or space of consciousness in which the universe evolves and moves about. The one who knows it knows creation fully.

The one Lord that is in all beings remains hidden and is all pervading. It is the self of all beings. It controls and watches over all good and bad Karmas, lives in all creatures and is the witness, the supreme intelligence, and the one without a second and has no attributes.

As the oil is inside the seasum seed, butter in the curd, water in the flowing waves, fire in the wood, so also Atman that is in one's self is to be discarded by one who seeks for it through truth and austere practices.

Ekakashara Upanishad

The one who knows that the eternal dweller is in the cave of the heart, who is the ancient Lord, who has become all, stays, transcending all wisdom.

Kaivalya Upanishad

The knowledge of Brahman is to be known by means of faith, devotion and meditation.

He (the Brahman) alone is all that was, and all that will be, and the eternal. Knowing Him, one transcends death. There is no other way to freedom from the cycle of birth and death.

Seeing the Atman in all beings, and all beings in Atman, one attains the highest Brahman-not by any other means.

With the self, deluded in *Maya* or ignorance, one identifies himself with the body and does all sorts of things. In the waking state, he, the Jeeva attains satisfaction through different objects of enjoyment like women, food, and drink and so on. In the dream state the *Jeeva* feels pleasure and pain in the sphere of existence created by his own ignorance or *Maya*. During the state of profound sleep, everything gets dissolved in to their causal state and the Jeeva is overpowered by the non- manifestation and exists in the form of bliss. Through past *Karmas*, the very *Jeeva* then returns to the dream or waking state. The being sports in these three cities or states of consciousness. It is from Him that all diversity got sprung up. He is the substratum, the bliss, and the indivisible consciousness, in whom these three cities or states get dissolved. From this *Prana* or vitality, mind, all organs, sky, air, fire, water and earth come forth.

That which is the supreme Brahman, the soul of all, the greatest support of the universe is subtler than the subtle and is eternal and that is yourself and 'Thou art that'.

With the realization that 'I am that Brahman', that manifests the phenomenon of the three states of consciousness, one is liberated from all bondage.

Brahman is the witness, the pure consciousness and the eternal good.

In Brahman everything is born, everything rests and everything is dissolved. It is minuter than the minute, the greatest of the greatest, the manifold universe, the ancient one, the *Purusha* and the ruler, the effulgent one and all good. Brahman has no arms and legs. It is the unthinkable power that sees without eyes, and hears without ears. It knows all and different from all. None can know Brahman. He is ever the intelligence. Brahman alone is taught in the Vedas, He is the revealer of Vedanta or Upanishads and also the knower of Veda. He has no merit or demerit, no distinction, no birth, no self-identity with the body and organs. For Brahman there is neither earth nor water, nor fire, nor air nor ether.

The one who realizes the *Paramatman* who resides in the cavity of the heart, who is without parts and without a second, who is the witness of all, who is beyond both existence and non-existence, attains *Paramatman*.

Katha Upanishad

The intelligent self is unborn, eternal, everlasting and ancient and is not slain even when the body is slain.

The self that is subtler than the subtlest and greater than the greatest is seated in the heart of all beings. One who is free from desire sees the glory of the self through the tranquility of mind and senses and becomes free from all grief.

Brahman is bodiless in all beings, is firmly seated in all perishable things and is great and all pervading.

The self cannot be known by the study of Vedas or by intelligence or by much hearing. It has to be sought after then only it can be attained.

Self cannot be realized by one who has not refrained from bad conduct, whose senses are uncontrollable, who has a wavering mind. One, who is devoid of discriminating intellect and has an unrestrained mind and is ever impure, cannot attain the truth but goes to *Samsara*. But the one who has a discriminating intellect and restrained mind and is ever pure is freed from the cycle of birth and death.

The *Purusha* that is of the size of the thumb resides in the body.

Just as fire, wind and sun though one, assumes separate forms with respect to each form, so also, the indwelling self of all beings, though one, assumes a form with respect to each form.

None can see Brahman with the eye. He is revealed only by the intellect, by restraining the mind and through meditation.

When all the longings of the heart vanish, then a mortal becomes immortal and attains Brahman.

Katha Rudra Upanishad

The self-effulgent light that illumines the universe shines forever. It is the witness of the world, the self of all that is pure, the basis of all beings and whose nature is pure consciousness.

Man attains Brahman not by action, not by begetting children, not by anything else but by knowing Brahman.

That Brahman that is without a second and that is truth, knowledge and happiness is the ultimate object of all knowing.

He who realizes his own self, that is the witness of the power that is called *Maya* and ignorance knows 'I am Brahman alone' and he becomes Brahman itself.

When the oneness is realized then that is the ultimate good, supreme immortality, absolute existence, transcendent Brahman that is beyond the three divisions. When individual experiences even a slight difference in this, then he will have fear.

Consciousness devoid of *Maya* is pure Brahman. When related to the cosmic nescience it is God. Under the influence of the individual ignorance, it is the individual self. When related to the internal organ, it is the knower.

The true essence of Vedantic teaching is, 'Dying one self, becoming one self, one yet remains one Self'.

Maha Narayana Upanishad

The infinite self that is minuter than the minute and greater than the great is set in the heart of all beings.

In the citadel of the body, there is the small sinless and pure lotus of the heart that is the residence of the supreme.

In the interior of this small area there is the sorrowless ether. This is to be meditated upon continuously.

One should meditate upon the supreme-the limitless, unchanging, all knowing causes of happiness of the world that dwells in the sea of one's heart; the heart that is compared with an inverted lotus bud.

In the middle of that narrow space of the heart, Sushumna is the undecaying, all knowing, omnipresent, great fire that has flames on all directions. In the centre of that fire that permeates the whole body, there is that tongue of fire, of shining gold colour, dazzling like the flash of lightening. Paramatman dwells in the middle of that flame. He is also Brahma the creator, Shiva, Vishnu, Indra, the material and the efficient cause of the universe and the supreme self that is self-luminous and pure consciousness.

Rudra Hridaya Upanishad

Paramatman assumes the form of Jeeva through His Maya, just as space inside the pot seems to be different from the space outside the pot. In reality, there is no difference.

When all is understood to be one Omkara, the Absolute, then there is no sorrow and no Maya. Then the attainment of Advaita, the non-charecteristic Paramananda or the everlasting Bliss becomes very easy.

Think that you are the basis of this entire universe, the one, the Kevala Sat- Chit- Ananda. Those who are devoid of Maya alone can understand this great secret. One who understands this becomes Para Brahman itself. He becomes Satchidananda. He attains everlasting peace.

Saraswati-Rahasya Upanishad

The difference that is seen between Brahman and the universe does not exist once Maya's power falls off. Their difference is in creation but not in Brahman.

When the conceit of the body vanishes, the supreme self is realized. All modes of action disappear when the supreme self is seen.

Sarva Sara Upanishad

One looks upon the body other than itself as the self. The cessation of that ignorance is *Moksha* or liberation. *Avidya* or nescience causes this ignorance. That by which this egoism is destroyed is *Vidya* or knowledge.

When the Atman manifests itself as interwoven in all bodies like the thread running through a string of jewels, then it is called the *Antaryamin* or the internal ruler. When the Atman shines forth absolutely free from all limiting adjuncts, brilliantly as a homogenous mass of consciousness in its nature of pure intelligence, independent, then it is known as *Pratyagatman*, the inner self.

That which is permanent in all space, time, substance and causation is Paramatman or the supreme self and *Para Brahman* or the highest Brahman.

That which is Satya, the reality, *Jnana* or knowledge and Anantha the infinite and Ananda or Bliss is Brahman.

Jnana is the essence of intelligence that has no beginning or end.

Brahman is neither the body nor the ten senses, or *Buddhi*, or mind or ego, is without *Prana* and mind, is pure, the witness, pure consciousness, neither the doer nor the enjoyer but a witness to

Prakruti. He is still, eternal, ever joyful and pure. Due to its presence, body, mind and so on function. He is unknowable like sky and air. He is neither form nor action but only Brahman.

Brahman is not body, or birth or death, or *Prana* or mind. It has no hunger or thirst, grief or delusion. It is not the doer and has no bondage or release.

Sukha Rahasya Upanishad

For the wise man who meditates upon Brahman: holy spots, Vedic rites and Mantras are useless.

The four Vakyas are; 1. Consciousness is Brahman; 2. I am Brahman, 3. That thou art and 4. This self is Brahman.

Svetasvatara Upanishad

The conscious subject and the unconscious object, the master and the dependent, the enjoyer and the enjoyed are all unborn. When all these three are realized as Brahman, the self becomes infinite, universal and free from the sense of agentship.

The enjoyer, the enjoyed and the power that brings about enjoyment are the three aspects of Brahman.

Fire is not perceived in the firestick until percussion ignites it although the subtle essence of fire remains in the firestick in a latent manner already. Similarly, by meditating, Atman is perceived as manifested in the body although it was there already.

The self is perceived in self as oil in seasum seed, butter in curd, water in underground spring and fire in wood.

He who by means of truthfulness, self control and concentration looks again and again for this self that is all pervading like butter in milk, and which is rooted in self knowledge and meditation, becomes that supreme Brahman-the destroyer of ignorance.

Just as the same metal disc that was stained by dust before shines brilliantly when cleaned, similarly, the embodied being seeing the truth of Atman realizes oneness, attains the goal and becomes sorrowless.

It is the self; the only one who exists alone at the time of creation and dissolution of the universe that assumes manifold powers and appears as the divine Lord by virtue of His inscrutable power of

Maya. He is that protector of all the worlds and controls all the various forces working in there. The one who realizes this Being becomes immortal.

Higher than the personal Brahman manifested with form is the infinite supreme Brahman who is concealed in all beings according to their bodies and who although remaining single, envelops the entire universe. Knowing Him to be the Lord one becomes immortal.

One passes beyond death only on realizing Him, the Brahman. There is no other way of escape from the cycle of birth and death. There is nothing higher or different from Him, greater or minuter. Rooted in His own glory, He stands like a tree. He is one without a second and immovable. By that being the whole universe is filled.

That being is formless and free from misery. Those who know this become immortal. All others have to suffer misery alone.

This self is the mighty Lord. He is the imperishable, internal light that controls everything. He guides the intellect of all beings to enable them to achieve that extremely pure state of liberation.

Assuming the form of the size of the thumb, by virtue of intellect, emotion, imagination and will, the infinite Being dwells in the hearts of beings as their inner self.

That which is, that which was and that which is yet to be-all these is nothing but this infinite Being.

Without hands and feet, He goes fast and grasps. Without eyes He sees, without ears He hears. He knows whatever is to be known; yet there is none who knows Him. He is the foremost, the great infinite Being.

Subtler than the subtlest, and greater than the greatest, the Atman is concealed in the hearts of all beings.

The Lord of *Maya* projects the Vedas, sacrifices, and spiritual practices, past and future, religious observances, all that the Vedas declare and the whole world including ourselves. That is the nature of Maya - The great God is the Lord of *Maya*.

One is released from all fetters on realizing the Blissful one who engulfs the world and who hides Himself in all beings in an extremely subtle form as the essence finer than ghee.

When ignorance is dispelled, there is neither day nor night, being or non-being. There is only that one auspicious one who is imperishable.

No one can grasp Him above or across or in the middle.

Those who know Him through the faculty of intuition as seated in their heart become immortal.

Supreme Brahman is the imperishable, infinite, secret, and in whom both wisdom and ignorance exist and He governs both of them.

He the Brahman is neither female nor male nor neutral. Whatever body He, the Brahman assumes, He becomes identified with that body.

He, the Brahman is the soul of the universe. He is immortal and His is the rulership. He is all knowing, all pervading, the protector of the universe and the eternal ruler.

Taittiriya Upanishad

In the space of the heart is this person, the Brahman, who is realizable through knowledge and who is immortal and effulgent.

Brahman is truth, knowledge and infinite. He who knows Brahman to be the intellect, located in the space in the heart, identifies with the all-knowing Brahman and enjoys all desirable things simultaneously.

If any one thinks that Brahman is non-existing, then he becomes non-existent. But if any one knows that Brahman exists, then he exists by virtue of that knowledge.

Crave to know that from which all beings are born, by which they live and that towards which they move and into which they merge- that is Brahman.

Tejo Bindu Upanishad

This universe and everything in it-whether the seer or seen are illusory as they resemble the horns of a Hare.

Brahman alone is everything and there is nothing else.

If there is any that is other than Brahman then it is as unreal as the mirage in an oasis.

Know for certain, 'I am Brahman' by giving up the sense of 'I'- Everything then disappears like the flower from the hands of a sleeping person.

Varaha Upanishad

That man who sees his Atman that is all-knowing and is the witness and is beyond all caste and orders of life as of the nature of Brahman becomes Brahman itself.

One who knows his own Atman, as Brahman, that is Bliss and without duality and gunas that is truth and absolute consciousness is not afraid of anything.

That which is consciousness alone, that is all pervading, eternal, all full, and a form of Bliss and indestructible is the true Brahman.

This mundane existence is an ocean of sorrow and is nothing but a long-lived dream or an illusion of the mind.

If the non-dual Brahman is discerned, then all desires for objects would vanish.

Para Brahman is eternal, immutable, free, the one undivided bliss, non-dual, the truth, the wisdom and the endless. •

Para Brahman is truth and absolute consciousness, is invisible, stainless, pure, secondless, not subject to birth and death, caste, law, family and *Gotra*.

When the mind is firmly fixed on the one non-dual and the notion of duality disappears, then, one sees the universe as a dream.

Yoga Sikha Upanishad

Similar to belief that pot is mixed with mud and water is mixed with mirage, is the belief that body is mixed up with the soul and this is because of taking recourse to ignorance.

Yoga Tattva Upanishad

The cycle of births and deaths come only through Ajnana or ignorance and it perishes through Gnana or wisdom only. So Jnana is the only means to liberation.

Just as the smell is contained in the flower, as ghee is contained in milk, as oil is contained in gingly seed and as gold is in the quartz, so also, Brahman is in the lotus located in the heart. Its face is downwards and its stalk is upwards. Manas is located at its centre.

THE SAMA VEDA

Chandogya Upanishad

That which is Brahman is the *Akasa* or space outside the body. That which is the *Akasa* outside the body is the *Akasa* inside the body. That *Akasa* that is inside the body is the *Akasa* within the lotus of the heart. This Brahman is all filling and unchanging. He who knows thus gets all filling and unchanging prosperity.

The entire universe is Brahman. From Him all things originate and unto Him they dissolve and by Him they are sustained.

He who is permeating the mind, who has *Prana* for His body, whose nature is consciousness, whose resolve is faultless, who is formless like *Akasa*, whose creation is everything that exists, who has purity, who possesses all the agreeable odours and all that is of pleasant taste, who pervades all, who is without senses, is free from agitation and eagerness is Atman residing in the lotus of the heart. It is smaller than the grain of paddy, than a barleycorn, than a matured seed, than a grain of millet, and than a kernel of a grain of millet. This Atman is also greater than the earth, sky, heaven and all the worlds. He is Brahman.

In the city of Brahman there is a mansion in the shape of a small lotus. In it is a small inner *Akasa*. What is within that, that should be sought, that alone one should crave to know. This *Akasa* is also large and in it are heaven, earth, fire, air, sun, moon, lightning and stars. Whatever is there in the world, whatever is not; all are contained with in that space.

The inner *Akasa*, the Brahman does not age with the aging body, not killed by killing this body. This *Akasa* is the real city of Brahman. In the real city of Brahman is Atman that is free from evil, old age, death, sorrow, hunger, thirst, and who desires truth.

Jabala Darshana Upanishad

Samadhi is that state in which all the ills of birth and death are destroyed. In this state, there is knowledge that Jeevatma and Paramatma are one.

When one sees all objects within himself and himself as a part of all objects he attains Brahman.

When one sees only the true soul then the entire world appears as an illusion to him and he is cured of all sorrows.

Kena Upanishad

He knows Brahman who thinks it is unknown and he who thinks it is known does not know it.

When Brahman is known as the inner self, in every state of consciousness, it is known in reality.

Brahman is similar to that which is like a flash of lightning or like the twinkling of an eye. This is Brahman in its divine aspect.

Maha Upanishad

Samadhi is freedom of the mind from agency. That itself is oneness and that is the highest and auspicious joy.

One should look only at pure consciousness avoiding the body, bone, flesh and blood that are inauspicious.

Consciousness is the string that holds together all beings like a necklace.

The world- delusion goes away and destroyed by knowledge.

The perceived being inside the visible world is called bondage. In the absence of the visible He is realiszed. Visible is the projection, for example, 'The universe is you and I'. As long as this illusion of the world, that is because of the mind remains, there is no liberation. When the excitement of the visible, like, 'you and I are the cosmos' vanishes, then, only soul remains. With this great dissolution, all visible creation etc., become non-existent and only tranquility remains. There exists the unborn, divine, non-ailing; shining being, and the unsetting sun forever, and the maker of all the supreme self. When there is realization of the falseness of the visible world, then that is wisdom-the only state-everything else is false.

The world is an illusion. Only the mind that is made impure by involvement and so on is worldly life. The same mind is said to be the end of worldly existence when freed from them.

One has no fear on knowing the nature of the self as Bliss unequalled, attributeless and one mass of truth and consciousness, that is beyond all that is beyond, greater than the greatest, lustrous and eternal in nature, wise, ancient being worshipped by all Gods.

A mortal becomes immortal by the vision of Brahman. When the great beyond is seen, the knot of the heart snaps, all doubts vanish and all worldly actions die away.

In a desert mirage is an illusion. Only the desert is real. Similarly, on reflection all the three worlds are nothing more than Chit.

When the weapon of non-projection cuts the mind, then, Brahman that is omnipresent and tranquil, will be obtained. Only the mind can control mind firmly.

When the body exists, there is separation of perceiver, the perceived and the vision connecting them. When the perceiver, perception and the object become one then it is liberation.

When the net of deep rooted impression of empirical life is cut like a fowler's net by a rat, and when due to the power of dispassion, the knots of the heart are loosened, then, one's nature as Brahman becomes crystal clear owing to the experiential knowledge of Brahman, like muddy water treated with the Kataka powder.

Maitrayani Upanishad

This self is like a drop of water in the lotus leaf. Prakruti overwhelms this. Being overcome, one is in a state of delusion and does not see the Lord in himself making him act. He is confused, unsteady, smitten by desire, yearning, conceited, thinking that 'I am that', 'This is mine'; he binds himself by himself as in a net and roams about.

The agent is the elemental self. The inner spirit causes actions by means of instruments. Just as iron pervaded by fire and beaten is split in to many, so also the elemental self pervaded by the inner spirit and pressed by *Prakruti*, becomes many. It assumes the forms of 84 lakhs of living beings that constitute the mass of elemental beings. This is the form of plurality. The spirit, just as a wheel by its driver, impels the constituents. As the fire is not beaten but only the iron is, so also the elemental self is over powered but not the spirit.

Rebirth is unavoidable and is bound by good and bad results of actions performed.

He who is maddened by worldly pleasures is like one intoxicated. He is in the grip of sins and he roams like one who is bitten by a snake, he is in the jaws of danger. Due to passion, one is blinded as in darkness. As one is caught in a magic show, he becomes one in the midst of Maya. He sees everything as in a dream wrongly, that is essenceless like the pith of a plantain, like an actor dressed up for a moment, falsely attractive like a painted wall. Sense objects are the sources of trouble. Attached to them self forgets its supreme place.

The remedy is the winning of knowledge-following one's own Dharma.

By penance Sattva is achieved and by Sattva guna refined mind is got, by the mind spirit is got and when the spirit is attained transmigration stops.

Just as fire without fuel dries in its own source, similarly, the mind calms down with the dying modes of mind.

When a person makes his mind free from dissolution and restlessness and reaches the mindless state, then it is the high place.

The mind is the only cause of bondage and liberation. Attached to objects it gives bondage; without them it gives liberation.

Maitreya Upanishad

The sense objects are clearly the source of danger because the individual self that is encased in the five elements may not remember the highest goal when attached to them.

Just as fire when fuel is exhausted calms down in itself, so also the mind when its activity gets exhausted becomes quiescent in its own source, the self. At that state, the results dependent on activities become unreal. The actions of such a person henceforth do not affect him as he is without attachment and desire.

One should feel the supreme Lord to be present in the midst of the lotus of one's heart, as the spectator of the dance of the intellect, as the abode of supreme love, as beyond speech and mind, as a rescue ship for those sinking in the sea of worldly life, that removes all worries, as of the nature of effulgent existences alone, as beyond thought, as the indispensable, as incapable of being grasped by the active mind, that is immobile, steady and deep, neither light nor darkness, free from all doubts and semblance and is consciousness.

True knowledge consists in seeing no difference in all; deep meditation consists in freeing the mind from thinking sensory objects; bathing is the removal of impurity in the mind and cleansing consists of controlling the senses.

Cleansing of mind is the destruction of three inborn tendencies like *Loka Vasana* or worldly attachment, *Shastra Vasana* or attachment to scriptures and *Deha Vasana* or attachment to the body. Cleansing of the mind is obtaining true knowledge or *Jnana* and dispassion or *Vairagya.*

There is liberation for those who are free from doubts about the non-duality of the Atman.

Renunciation is the oneness of the individual self or *Jeevatma* and the universal self or *Paramatma.*

The wisest take to contemplation on the reality of Brahman; the middle ones contemplate on sacrifices; low people think of the mantras; the lowest are deluded by visit to holy places.

THE ATHARVA VEDA

Annapurna Upanishad

Once it is realized that Brahman is all, man becomes Brahman. One experiences the omnipresent spirit that is peace.

When the mind is rejected, all duality get dissolved.

For achieving liberation, one should meditate upon the bodiless self that is Brahman, being, consciousness and bliss continuously as 'I am that'.

The self is eternal, omnipresent, immutable and flawless.

Being is only one. Through Maya it splits up. So the non-dual alone is, no manifold, no empirical life.

When one beholds all beings in one's self, and one's self in all beings, one becomes Brahman.

The cause of bondage is mental construction. Liberation comes through the absence of it.

Atma Upanishad

Atman is pure, one and non-dual and is always in the form of Brahman. Brahman alone shines.

Just as the whole world is illumined by sun, the splendour of knowledge of Brahman illumines everything.

Just as space becomes space when the pot that encloses the space perishes, similarly, when particular cognitions are dissolved, the Brahman knower himself becomes nothing but Brahman, as milk poured in to milk, oil in to oil, and water in to water.

Ideas such as 'It is', and 'It is not', regarding reality are only notions of the intellect. They do not pertain to eternal reality. Bondage and liberation are set up by Maya and do not pertain to the self.

Bhasma Jabala Upanishad

When Absolute Brahman is realized in its true aspect, as one with Atman, then all ignorance or illusion of considering this universe to be real and separate from one's own self will be burnt in to ashes by the destructive fire of supreme knowledge.

Dattareya Upanishad

Brahman, that is the infinite and peerless alone remains as the residum after negation of everything else.

Mandukya Upanishad

Self is Brahman.

The fourth stage Turiya, after waking, dreaming and dreamless sleep state is that which is not conscious of the internal world or external world or of both the worlds or dense with consciousness or simple consciousness or unconsciousness that is unseen, actionless, incomprehensible, uninferable, unthinkable, and indescribable. When there is identity of self in which all phenomena comes to an end, that is unchanging, auspicious, and non-dual, then that is the self that is to be known.

He who knows the self enters the self by the self.

Mundaka Upanishad

By higher knowledge, the wise realize that which cannot be grasped, that is without source, features, eyes, ears, has neither hands nor feet, but is eternal, multi formed, all pervasive, extremely subtle, undiminishing and is the source of all.

As from a fire that is fully ablaze fly off innumerable sparks that are similar to fire, likewise, from the imperishable originate different kinds of beings and in to it they merge again.

He who knows the supreme immortal Bliss existing in the heart destroys the knot of ignorance.

Brahman is effulgent; near at hand and well known as moving in the heart and it is the great goal. On it are fixed all these that move, breath and wink and do not wink. It consists of the gross and the subtle that is beyond the ordinary knowledge of beings and which is the most desirable and the highest of all.

The self is one without a second, on which are strung heaven, earth and the inter space, the mind and the vital force together with all other organs.

Within the heart in the body where the vital force has entered in five forms is this subtle self to be realized through that intelligence by which is pervaded the mind, the motor and sensory organs of all. It is to be known in the mind, that is pure and in which the self reveals itself clearly.

This self is not attained by study, or by intellect or through much learning. Only through seeking, the self that is sought is attainable and reveals its true nature.

As rivers flowing down become indistinguishable on reaching the sea by giving up their names and forms, so also, the illumined soul when freed from name and form reaches the self effulgent Purusha that is higher than Maya.

The one, who knows the supreme Brahman, becomes Brahman itself.

Narada Parivarjaka Upanishad

Atman is bodiless, transcendent, and all pervading and is present in all bodies that are impermanent.

Advaita Vedanta in Gaudapada's Mandukya Karika

Gaudapada was the *Paramaguru* that is Guru's *Guru* of Adi Shankara. His writings have influenced Shankara immensely and this is clear when we see the interpretation of Advaita Philosophy both by Gaudapada and Adi Shankara. Gaudapad's interpretation of Advaita Vedanta can be seen in his Mandukya Karika that is an expository text on *Mandukya Upanishad* belonging to *Atharva Veda*. Probably this text provided the basic impetus for Shankara's writings. A few points of Advaita Vedanta found in this text are:

If the phenomenal world were to exist, it should also have an end. However this duality is only an illusion. In reality it is non-dual.

When truth is realized, duality disappears.

The wise declare the unreality of all objects in a dream as they are located inside the body and also because they are confined within a limited space only.

Just as the objects seen in the dream state are unreal, so also, they are unreal even in the waking state.

The objects although they bear the mark of unreal appear as though they are real. They have a beginning and end and therefore they are unreal.

The self-luminous self by its own Maya imagines itself by itself and it alone cognizes all objects. This is the fact revealed in Vedanta.

Just as a rope, the nature of which is not seen in darkness is imagined as snake; so also, the self is imagined differently as various things.

When the rope is known as rope only but not a snake then the illusion ceases to exist. This is similar to the knowledge of the self.

The self is imagined as infinite objects due to the Maya of the luminous one.

This world that is viewed on the basis of self is not different. It does not exist independently. There is nothing that is different or non-different from the self.

The aspirant resorting himself to devotion remains in the conditioned Brahman.

The self exists in the form of Jivas. It is similar to ether that exists in a pot.

When the pot breaks, the ether confined in that pot gets merged with the infinite ether; so also, the individual souls gets merged in the self alone.

Although the names and forms and functions of different pots differ, yet the ether contained in them is the same. Similar is the case with the individual souls.

The ether in the jar is neither a modification nor a part of the infinite ether. Similarly, the individual soul is also not a modification or a part of the supreme self.

Since the non-difference of Jiva and the supreme self is proved on the basis of their identity, non-duality alone is reasonable.

The moving and the unmoving that bring about duality is perceived by the mind. But in the absence of mind duality is not perceived.

With the knowing of truth, mind attains a state of non-mind and becomes a non-perceiver and there are also no objects, at that stage, to perceive.

The mind that is dissolved becomes Brahman, the fearless, endowed with the light of consciousness.

Brahman is birthless, sleepless, dreamless, nameless, formless, ever resplendent and omniscient.

The self is devoid of all external organs and is above all internal organs. It is highly serene, always resplendent, divinely absorbed. It is unchanging and fearless.

The highest Brahman exists in one's own self. It is calm and identical with the liberator. It is indescribable and unborn. It is also omniscient.

Just as a fire brand set in motion appears as straight, crooked and so on, similarly, the vibrations of consciousness appear as perceiver and the perceived. These appearances do not come from outside and when the firebrand is not in motion, this appearance do not go elsewhere. So also is the case with appearances when consciousness is in motion or otherwise.

From the relative point of view everything seems to be born and hence they are not immortal. From the absolute plane of perception, everything is unborn self and hence there is no destruction.

In reality none is born. Their birth is due to *Maya*, which again is non-existent.

In dream and waking state consciousness vibrate through illusions as though possessed of duality. But it is the non-dual consciousness that appears as dual.

Just as in dream or magic beings are born and die.

When consciousness becomes free from attachment and does not engage itself in unreal things, then, there comes a state of stillness. This is the supreme state of non-distinction that is birthless, sleepless, dreamless, self-luminous and non-dual.

All souls are by nature similar to ether and eternal. There is no diversity among them.

All souls are by nature illumined, tranquil, unborn, detached, equal, non-different, unique and pure.

Kevala Advaita Vedanta of Adi Shankara

Vivartha Vada of Shankara

Adi Shankara's view is called *Vivartha Vada*-the theory of super imposition or appearance. Just as a rope that is seen in darkness is mistaken to be a snake due to darkness, similarly due to Avidya or ignorance or *Maya*, this world and the physical body and all the worldly objects are believed to be real. When the light comes and when the darkness is removed one realizes that what is believed to be a snake is only a rope, and then the illusion of snake will vanish. But the rope that is mistaken for a snake in darkness remains only a rope. Similarly, the illusion of body and world would disappear once the knowledge of Brahman is obtained. It was a rope in the beginning, when it was mistaken for a snake and also when it is known that it is only a rope. Brahman remains the absolute always. It is due to ignorance that it is mistaken for the physical body, mind, intellect, objects and the world. Brahman becomes the cause of the illusion of the world though there is no world in reality. The unchanging Brahman appears as the changing world due to superimposition of objects that is non- self on Self or Brahman. Due to ignorance, or *Maya*, that is the mysterious power of Brahman, the *Jeeva* or the individual soul is identified with the physical body, mind and senses. The root cause of all sufferings in this world is the lack of knowledge of the reality. Once the knowledge of Brahman dawns, the world disappears and only Brahman that was there before, and also when it was mistaken for the physical body and the world, remains, and *Jeeva* or the empirical self becomes one with Brahman, the universal or cosmic soul- that is Bliss, and the ignorance vanishes instantaneously. When one realizes Brahman, the names and forms of the world will not affect him or influence him in any way. When the darkness or the veil of ignorance that is also called as *Avidya, Maya* or *Mithya* or the unreal is removed by the light of knowledge then the everlasting knowledge that Brahman alone is real will shine and then, the latent, essential, true, and the divine glory of man comes to light. At that stage one becomes fully aware of the four *Mahavakyas* of the Upanishads namely, 'Prajnam Brahma'- that means 'consciousness is Brahman', found in Aitareya Upanishad of Rig Veda 'Aham Brahmasmi' which means, 'I am Brahman' that is found in Brihad Aranyaka Upanishad of *Shukla Yajur Veda*, 'Tatvam Asi' or 'That thou art' found in Chandogya Upanishad of *Sama Veda* and 'Ayamatma Brahma' or 'This Atman is Brahman' found in Mandukya Upanishad of *Atharva Veda* that show the unity of Atman and Brahman.

Due to *Avidya*, the individual soul identifies itself with the gross body, senses, and mind intelligent and so on. *Avidya* or nescience is indescribable and beginingless. Once the knowledge dawns the superimpositions disappear and the individual, the world, the *jeeva*, and also Ishwara get identified with Brahman. The false knowledge then will be replaced by the true and real knowledge. This ignorance is also similar of an oyster that is taken for a piece of silver, the stump of a tree mistaken for a human form, a mirage for water. Similarly, the Atman also is mistaken to be the body by an ignorant. What is ignorance is explained in chapter-2 in Shankara's 'Tattva Bodha'. Knowledge destroys this ignorance, like light that destroyes darkness. The self also due to ignorance appears finite. But once the ignorance vanishes the self truly reveals itself by itself like the Sun when the cloud passes away. Ignorance produces perishable results that rise with the dawn and die with the dusk. Ignorance gets destroyed by the awareness that 'I am Brahman' that is the result of uninterrupted, continuous reflection about oneself. Shankara says that just as medicines cure diseases reflection of the self destroys ignorance. Again he says that for an ignorant person the transmigratory existence appears to belong to the self, just as the trees appear moving in the opposite direction when a person sits in a moving boat. So ignorance is only superimposition of non-self on the self. Once ignorance is destroyed there is light, there is liberation.

Way to Gain Ultimate Jnana or Wisdom

Shankara says that wisdom or *jnana* resulting from self-study or experience alone will result in experiencing the true self. Yogas help man to become pure and help in removing *Avidya. Karma* and *Bhakti* are, to Shankara, the means to *jnana* that leads to *Mukti*. This *Brahma jnana* is not obtaining any new knowledge but removing *Avidya*. It is like the entry of light that removes darkness anywhere. To obtain the ultimate wisdom study of scriptures with the help of *Guru*, performance of Vedic rituals, real *Bhakti*, and selfless service are the means. On the basis of what one had learnt from scriptures and practiced as per scriptures, (from the performance of Vedic rituals), one should ponder over by means of self study and he would gain the ultimate knowledge through Swayanubhava or self experience. Devotion or *Bhakti* and selfless service or Karma is necessary in the phenomenal world. When the Bhakta sees the picture of God he sees the Almighty in that. It makes the Bhakta to think about the qualities and form of God. When the Bhakta gets immersed in the worship he sees only the love, compassion, and the protective qualities of the Lord. When the Bhakta gets immersed in God he forgets the qualities of his Lord and sees only the universal power that the picture represents. When he goes still deeper he forgets himself, loses all his personality, ego and so on and he merges with his Lord. It is common in Hinduism for the Bhakta to address God as 'Mahamaya' or 'paramatma' and so on. It clearly shows that *Bhakti* leads to wisdom or Jnana of the ultimate truth. At its final stage *Bhakti* culminates in Jnana. Similarly, a Karma Yogi may in the beginning have the notion of duality. He may think that he is the doer although the Karma that he performs has no selfish aim. But when he continues to perform *Karma* as an offering to God then he becomes purer and purer and he becomes one with God. At this stage *Karma Yoga* results in Wisdom or *Jnana*. *Karma* in the sense of Vedic rituals is valid in the early stages of spirituality. But when the seeker attains a certain stage all *Karmas* become unnecessary because then the senses of doership vanishes from that person and also he goes beyond all carvings of material pleasures of the world. That is why Shankara said that *Bhakti* and *Karma* are paths to *Jnana* of the ultimate truth. By Jnana he would have meant only wisdom but not material knowledge that is the result of worldly intelligence or accumulation of information. Once one goes beyond the phenomenal world that is only relatively real, and the sense of doership, and becomes totally free from all senses, emotion and mind, and then when one engages oneself in total meditation or self study, on the basis of the knowledge that he has obtained by the various methods and paths that he had followed hithert to, then the necessary jnana or self realization or the knowledge of Absolute Brahman will dawn on him from Swayanubhava or self experience. Knowing about a fruit that is declared to be very tasty by those who have tasted it will not give the necessary knowledge or satisfaction to another who has not tasted it. A look at the pictures of the fruit, theoretical knowledge of the fruit or hearing about the taste of the fruit, or thinking constantly of the fruit all these also will not help one to know the sweet taste of the fruit. If one wants to know how tasty it is, then one has to taste it by himself because no one else can give him the experience of the sweet taste of the fruit except the one who experiences it by consuming the fruit. It is the case with self-knowledge as well. When the true knowledge dawns through self study or Swayanubhava or self experience then one will realize that there is no difference between the experiencer and the thing experienced, and the act of experiencing because all merge in to one single reality namely the Absolute Brahman, the Universal spirit. Shankara says, the sons and his relatives can clear a father's debt. But he alone can remove his bondage. To get rid of any disease the patient alone has to take the medicines. If those close to the patient take the medicines it will not cure the patient who is suffering. So also the bondage caused by ignorance, desire, actions and so on can be overcome only by oneself. The first step of liberation is extreme aversion to all perishable things of the world. Then one has to practice calmness, self-control, forbearance and so on. Finally wisdom through the path of *Vichara* dissolves everything that is created by ignorance. The flame of wisdom has to be kindled by constant meditation on the self. However wisdom dawns or is revealed only in a purified mind. The yogi through the eye of wisdom sees the entire universe as his own self and regards everything as the self and nothing but the self.

The nature of true wisdom is such that it cuts the very root of egoism and burns all actions to ashes. Then there is neither the doer of actions nor the experiencer of the fruits of the actions. With wisdom one becomes completely free from the bondage of the transmigratory existence with the awareness that self is Brahman. In his 'Viveka Chudamani' Shankara says that reality is attained by right *Jnana* or wisdom that comes from perception, investigation, meditation and self-analysis. In his 'Viveka Chudamani, Shankara says, truth can be realized by discriminating the real from the unreal, by means of reasoning, advice of the wise and through reflection. Again he says the fire of wisdom that is kindled by *Viveka* or discrimination would burn up all effects of ignorance totally and would result in self-realisation.

Maya Vada of Shankara

To Shankara, all plurality seen and experienced in the world are unreal; and are due to illusion or *Maya*, on account of *Avidya* or ignorance. *Maya* is an instrument of Brahman. His argument is therefore called as *Maya Vada*. *Avidya* or *Maya* is the power of the Lord. It has no beginning. It is made up of the three gunas. Only with a clear intellect it can be understood from the effect it produces. The whole universe is its creation. *Maya* or *Avidya* is neither existent nor non-existent nor does it partake the characteristics of both. It is also not different from both or not both. It is neither with nor without parts or both. *Maya* is stated to be the most wonderful that cannot be described. Maya is the illusionary power of Brahman. It causes Brahman to be seen as the world and objects. But Brahman however is untouched by Maya. The reality is only Brahman. Brahman is the material cause for the cosmos. The limited mind cannot grasp it. Only with the realization of Brahman Maya can be overcome or destroyed, just as the mistaken notion of a snake that is actually only a rope can be destroyed by discrimination and the light of knowledge. Atman alone has real existence but not the objective world with all its names and forms. The world is only phenomenal or Vyavaharika. It is only relatively real or is only *Vyavaharika Satta.* So from the point of view of real, the world is unreal. But Brahman is *Paramarthika Satta* or the real. The objective world has no real and independent existence. The reality that is Brahman is the constant witness and the substratum in all the three states of waking, dreaming and the deep sleep state of consciousness and that is the real self of man. It pervades the entire universe. The Universe shines with its reflected light. It illuminates everything in the Universe but is not illuminated by anything. It is self-shining. There is no duality between the individual soul and the universal soul. Immature people due to ignorance or Maya view the supreme self that is conditioned by the body, sense organs, mind and intellect as the soul. When once this illusion or Maya disappears and the oneness is known then the distinctions of the doer and the deed will be negated. In a similar manner, once the identity of Jeeva or the individual soul and the universal soul is experienced, there is liberation. He also stressed that all empirical activities are relevant only until that stage when the non-dual is experienced. It is like the experience of dream that becomes an illusion once a person wakes up from the dream. But it is real in the dreaming state. In the same way, once Brahman is experienced, all worldly material activities become irrelevant. One has to transcend the mind to understand and become one with Brahman. When discrimination is developed, to differentiate the true from the false, then true knowledge dawns with the removal of ignorance or Avidya. The only purpose in human life according to Shankara is to know the self through self-effort, that is through knowledge and self-experience with the help of intelligence and intuition. So he says, one will obtain the ultimate knowledge only through self-experience and the study of scriptures. Rituals and so on are only means, which will pave the way for attaining the supreme. It is the mind that is the cause of bondage, transmigration and *Avidya*. When the mind gets destroyed all false notions also get destroyed. An account of Shankara's *Maya Vada* can be found in his work entitled 'Maya Panchakam'.

The World

Shankara developed the comprehension of the world at two levls. At a higher level of understanding, he says, it is possible to comprehend the ultimate oneness of the *jeevatma* or the individual soul with the *Paramatman* or the Universal soul. At the lower level of everyday experience reality is thought of as multiplicity of individuals and objects and as world (That is only due to *Maya* or illusion) that leads to repeated cycles of birth and death. *Moksha* or liberation is possible when there is experiential realization or Vijnana of oneness at the higher level of understanding or comprehension. So according to Shankara, the world is neither real nor unreal. It is only an incorrect perception of the reality.

The Brahman

According to Shankara's doctrine, Atman or soul or Brahman is real. Brahman is existence, knowledge and bliss that is, *Sat-Chit - Ananda*. It is non-dual and infinite, eternal and one. It encompasses the entire universe. Everything is Brahman. It is homogenous. It is one without second. It is non-dual, indivisible. Brahman is *Adrishya.* It cannot be seen with eyes. It is whole, infinite, changeless, the essence, self-luminous, Bliss and so on. It is the seer. It is the silent witness. The supreme Brahman is impersonal and *Nirguna* that is without qualities and *Nirakara* that is formless and *Nirvishesha* that is without any special charecteristic features. It is immutable and eternal. It is *Akarta* or non-agent. It is the witness not the object. It cannot be described. Brahman cannot be distinguished from any other except Brahman itself. The very essence of Brahman is Sat-Chit- Ananda. Through its association with *Maya* it becomes *Saguna* Brahman or Ishwara or God.

To Shankara the higher Brahman is *Nirguna Brahman* and one is able to grasp it only when one transcends the notion of 'I' and 'Mine' and the feeling that the world is real. However as long as one believes that there is world and as long as one has the sense of doership and the feeling 'I' and 'Mine' then he sees only the projection of the higher Brahman that is the Saguna Brahman, that is Ishwara. Adi Shankara knew that the phenomenal world consists of such people mainly. To devotees the supreme *Nirguna Brahman* appears as God. *Bhakti* or devotion however takes one to *Jnana* or the real knowledge or wisdom because it is the path that paves the way for the understanding of the ultimate truth that is Brahman. When one is unable to see the person dear to him one satisfies himself with the photograph of that person that is only the reflection of the actual person. But once he is able to see that one in person the photograpgh of that person has no more importantance and relevance. The higher Brahman is from the transcendental viewpoint or Paramarthika. *Saguna Brahman* is the lower Brahman, the Brahman from a relative point of view or *Vyavaharika*. Absolute or the Higher Brahman is indicated by the Vedas as the irreducible substratum after the negation of all tangible objects. Brahman is the Antaryamin, the Lord who resides in the innermost of all beings. It is the substratum on which all phenomenons are experienced. All actions are possible because of Brahman. Brahman permeates everything as butter permeates milk. It is neither subtle nor gross, neither short nor long; it is without birth and changes. It is without form, qualities or colour. It is that by which everything shines. But it is not illuminated by anything else, as it is self-luminous. It is all pervading and is the witness of everything. But it cannot be described, explained or established by proof; it cannot be compared with anything else. None can deny Atman that is Brahman because it is the essence of the one who denies it. It is the substratum of all wisdom. It is non-dual, one without a second and hence cannot be compared and known that way, it is imperishable and therefore eternal, its presence is felt everywhere within, without, before, behind, above, below and so on, it is *Adrishya* or cannot be seen, it is infinite, full, changeless, self existent, bliss, knowledge, smaller than the smallest and greater than the greatest, the essence, the silent witness, formless and *Nirguna* that is, without attributes and qualities, *Nirakara* that is formless and *Nirvisesha*, that is without attributes and Akarta, that is non-agent, beyond the reach of senses, mind and intellect, beyond space, time and causation, the material cause of the universe, beyond all opposites, the unseen power, that is impersonal, a mere witness, is the subject or perceiver but not the object or the perceived and so on. It can be known only by declaring 'Nethi- Nethi' that means 'not this, not this' as stated in the Upanishads that it can be known.

This *Atma Gnana* or the wisdom of the self could be obtained only through self-knowledge that leads to self-experience. To a devotee Brahman appears as God, and is with form, name and attributes and qualities and is therefore Saguna. Brahman can be indirectly experienced as personal God or Ishwara that is, *Saguna Brahman* possessing qualities. Nirguna Brahman is beyond time and space and transcendental. It is existence, knowledge, absolute and the very Bliss. It is the ultimate. It is beyond the three gunas and the three statres of consciousness. It permeates everything just as butter permeates milk. It is the cause of the universe but it itself is not limited by its self-projection. Due to Avidya one is unable to turn inward and recognize the real self, residing within himself as Brahman. It is like one who is unable to recognize his own face. It is because all his experiences are outward or external and physical. He believes the sense experiences and the impressions of the mind. Once he is able to turn his gaze inward he is bound to experience the Brahman within him. This experience he can gain only when he steps in to another dimension of experience that is beyond the gross and physical.

To comprehend Brahman one has to go beyond the ordinary mind to a superconscious state. Just as a lump of salt melted in water cannot be perceived by the eye, but only can be tasted by the tongue, similarly, the ever-existent Brahman that shines in the core of one's heart cannot be realized by external senses but by the light of divine grace of wisdom. Shankara says that the very essence of Brahman which he calls as the supreme Brahman is Satyam or truth, - Jnanam or knowledge, – Anatam or limitless and *Anandam* or Bliss. It is *Sachidanada- Sat- chit –Ananda*, that is existence-knowledge- Bliss or infinite truth- infinite consciousness- Infinite Bliss. One can see a clear account of what is Brahman in 'Nirvana Dasakam' and in 'Pratha Smarana Stotram' composed by Shankara. Chapters 8, 10 and 13 in 'Tattva Bodha', Shankara tells about Supreme Brahman that is the *Nirguna Brahman*, Jeevatma and the self.

Three Levels of Reality in Advaita Vedanta

We find three layers of reality in Advaita Vedanta. One is the transcendental or Paramartika level in which Brahman alone is real. It is *Amarthika Satta*, the unchanging reality in the midst of all changes. One has to experience this to realize. This is termed as pure existence, *Sat* or Brahman in Upanishads. It is the self in every human being and is the unchanging witness. It is self-luminous and exists by itself without any external support. Secondly, the Pragmatic or Vyavaharika level, in which, *Jeeva* or the individual soul, world, and God or Ishwara are real. This is the reality in the phenomenal world. It is termed as the *Vyavaharika Satta* or the empirical reality. It is from this relative world point of view the souls or Jivas which are the reflections of the Absolute Brahman experience bondage and liberation. This is different from the real inner self in all beings, the Brahman, the existence that is ever free, pure and perfect. When compared to the Absolute existence or Brahman, this is unreal. From the phenomenal point of view Brahman is Ishwara, Jiva and *Jagat*. To operate at this level it is necessary to have devotion, *Karma* and so on. The relative existence can be transcended only through self-realization. The changing universe of names and forms derive their reality from the Absolute, unchanging Brahman. They have no separate existence apart from Brahman. Thirdly, in the apparent or the *Pratibhasika* level, the material world is unreal as the illusion of snake over a rope in darkness. The apparent reality is termed as the *Pratibhasika Satta*. It is like a mirage that is mistaken for water.

Maya or Illusion

The universe is the product of the creative power of Brahman that is known as *Maya*. *Maya* is the indescribable power of Brahman. Due to this the universe is perceived in its plurality. It is experienced in sense- mind and is within time and space. *Maya* hides Brahman. Just as a cloud hinders the sun similarly *Maya* also hides the Absolute reality that is Brahman. *Maya* is the material cause of *Jagat* or the world. Just as the burning property of fire cannot be separated from fire, similarly, *Maya* also cannot be separated from Brahman. Burning is due to fire. But fire is not the product of burning. So is the case with *Maya* and Brahman. All dualities are due to the play of *Maya*. Brahman appears as Ishwara, *Jeeva* and *Jagat* due to the power of *Maya*. *Maya* is the power of Brahman. She is without beginning, and is made up of the three gunas namely, *Sattva, Rajas* and *Tamas*. She creates the whole universe. She cannot be described and is most wonderful. She is neither existent nor non existent or both, neither same nor different nor both. It is neither with parts nor without parts.

Due to *Maya* what is unreal appears as real. It is real at the time of experience. But it has no ultimate existence. It is also dependent on pure consciousness or Brahman. Only through self-realization one will be able to transcend these illusions. All these ignorance is due to mind. Mind alone is *Avidya* or ignorance that is the cause of bondage and transmigration. When the mind is destroyed all illusions disappear. Once it is transcended the waves merge back in to the ocean. Then they are no more waves but the vast expansive ocean. So to be identified with Paramatman or Brahman *Jeeva* has to transcend time, space and causation that are *Maya*. At that stage the *Jeeva*, Ishwara and Jagat are not different from Brahman. It is like one appearing as many. The jewels may be innumerable but their content the gold with which the jewels are made of is the same.

World Both Real and Unreal

To Shankara, *Maya* is the illusionary power of Brahman. Due to *Maya* or ignorance Brahman is seen as the world and objects.

But Brahman itself is untouched by *Maya* or illusion. World is neither real nor unreal. It is a superimposition on Brahman. It is real because it is experienced. Since it vanishes with knowledge it is unreal. *Avidya* or ignorance conceals Brahman and projects the world. But world is relatively real or *Vyavaharika Satta* whereas Brahman is absolutely real or *Paramartika Satta.*

The world is not actually real says Shankara, because, the world is not eternal but gets repeatedly created and destroyed, and it changes. If the world is real or true there should be no change to the world, and also because any super imposition cannot be false. The world is only a superimposition and hence it is false. However the world is not absolutely false either says Shankara. It is false only when compared to Brahman that is only true. In the pragmatic sense world is real, as long as *Maya,* illusion or ignorance remains. It is relatively real because, the world continues to exist even after one obtains liberation, and secondly, *Karma* or good actions are a feature of the world. So it must be true and thirdly, world is a reflection of Brahman that is real. So the world must also be real and finally, logically also the world exists because it is perceived by the senses. So according to Shankara, world is relatively real or is *Vyavaharika Satta* whereas, Brahman is Absolutly real that is *Paramartika satta.* So the world appears real as long as there is ignorance. It becomes unreal when one gets the real knowledge.

Ishwara in Advaita Vedanta

Ishwara or God according to Shankara is Brahman with *Maya.* Ishwara is the reflection of Brahman. Ishwara is the manifested form of Brahman. To a devotee Brahman that is Nirguna appears as God or Brahman that is *saguna.* God or Ishwara is true at the pragmatic level. God according to Shankara is in the level of duality. The same God or Ishwara is understood as Brahman at the state of transcendental consciousness. Actually God is only a reflection of Brahman. A clear mirror reflects the original without any distortions. But it cannot be equated with the original. The original gives rise to the image through mirror. But the image cannot give rise to the original. The image is because of the original, without the original, there is no image but even in the absence of the image the original exists. When the object is far away, one is able to have complete view of the object through its reflection. But when the object comes nearer, one can turn to the very object itself for knowing it. Similaly as and when one advances spiritually, all illusions will vanish and one will realize the unreality of all superimpositions also and with the knowledge gained (due to the disappearance of *Avidya*) he would then turn towards the reality or truth itself. From the relative point of view or *Vyavaharika*, Brahman is with attributes or *Saguna* and from a higher transcendental point of view it is *Paramartika* – the *Nirguna Brahman*. At the transcendental level God is the cosmic spirit or Brahman. While Brahman is *Nirguna*, Ishwara is Saguna. Shankara himself was a true devotee or *Bhakta*. He believed that worship, Vedic internal sacrifices, and rituals are paths that lead one to *jnana* and knowledge and help in attaining *Moksha*.

Jeevatman or the Individual Soul

Shankara says that Atman is *Svatah Siddtha* or self-evident. It needs no external proof. It is not possible to deny the existence of Atman because it is the very essence of the one who denies it. It is the basis of all knowledge. In his *Shloka* 'Aparokshanubhuti' Shankara clearly explains about *Atman*, the physical body and Brahman. What is *Atman* is clearly stated by Shankara in his Slokas 'Nirvana Dasakam' or 'Dasa Shloki and 'Viveka Chudamani'. Due to ignorance *Jeeva* identifies itself with body, mind and senses. But in reality it is the same as Brahman or the Absolute. Atman or the individual soul or the self is identical with Brahman. It is neither separate nor a part of Brahman. It is only one not many. It is absolute. Atman is the real self. Just as the moon appears as many moons, in its reflection, in the numerous bubbles of water, similarly, *jeeva* also appears as many, in the reflection of Brahman. But when once the bubbles burst, then the appearance of the individual moons also will disappear and there will be only one moon. In a similar manner due to Avidya or ignorance due to Maya, *jeeva* appears as many individual *jeevas*. But in reality there is only one *Jeevatma* that is *Paramatma*.

Atman is the ruler of the body. It is internal while the body is external and the body is ruled by Atman. Atman is all consciousness, the holiest while the body is mere flesh and impure. Atman is one and without parts but the body consists of many parts. Atman is existence itself. The body is transient. The world appears to be real as long as the self is identified with the body consciousness. Again, Atman is eternal. It is free from all bondage-merit, demerit, past or future, cause or effect and so on. It is existence itself. For a person suffering from jaundice everything appears yellow. Similarly for an ignorant person Atman appears to be the body. The body, mind and sun are all illumined by the Atman that resides in the core of one's heart. A lighted lamp does not require another lamp to show its light. Similarly, Atman that is consciousness itself does not need any other instrument to illumine itself. It illumines everything. The mind, the sense organs and so on are illumined by Atman. It is not illuminated by anything else. It is pure consciousness and is devoid of all ignorance. Just as there is no darkness in the sun as the sun itself is light, so also the self has no ignorance as it is of the nature of eternal knowledge itself. Due to ignorance, the movement that really belongs to water is attributed to the moon that is reflected in the water. Similarly, enjoyment and other limitations of mind are falsely attributed to Atman. Atman is really the witness that is beyond all sins and merit. It does not experience happiness, misery, and so on because it is beyond the triad- the experiencer, the experienced and experiencing.

The concept of individual *Jeeva* is also therefore true only at the pragmatic level because *Jeeva* feels unique in individuals. But at the transcendental level, there is only one Atman and that is Brahman. Just as pots and earthern jars are only clay, the tangible universe also is nothing but Atman. However this cannot be grasped by intellectual understanding but only through personal experience. With the knowledge of Brahman the veil of *Maya* is torn off, and the jeeva or the empirical self becomes one with Brahman. At that moment, the river, jiva joins with Brahman, the ocean, with the realization of its essential nature of Sat- chit and Ananda. It is like the bubble becoming one with the ocean when it bursts or the salt in a bag that is immersed in an ocean getting mixed with the salt of the water of the ocean. The pure and unlimited ether does not get attached to objects although it takes the shapes of the objects. It is also not tainted by the objects. Similarly, the self is always is the same in all beings.

Liberation or Moksha or Mukti

The cycle of birth and death are caused by *Karma.* All actions good or bad result in certain *karmic* residues or vasanas and these exhibit the results over a period of time. Liberation is the way out of this endless cycle of birth and death. A *Jeevanmukta* is one who is liberated even while alive. He continues to live because of the momentum of *Prarabda Karma* that started operating already. But even these *Prarabda Karmas* do not affect him as he does not identify himself with his body or mind. He also, does not accumulate any new *Karma* as he performs *Karmas* without the sense of doership, and without any desire for the fruits of actions performed by him and his past accumulated *Karmas* are burnt in *Brahma jnana* or the knowledge of Brahman. When he leaves his physical body he attains *Videhamukti* by obtaining freedom from the cycle of birth and death. In his commentary on *Brahma Sutra Shankara* says that the four fold mental and physical practices would help in liberation. They are *Viveka* or discrimination between the permanent and impermanent, Dispassion towards the results of actions, developing qualities like calmness, mental control and so on and the longing for liberation.

He stressed that reason and abstract philosophizing alone cannot lead to Liberation or *Mukti*. A devotee can understand his inner self that is the ultimate only through selflessness and love governed by discrimination that he calls as Viveka. To Shankara, the devotee who worships *Saguna Brahman* or the Brahman with form gets final release or Liberation and attains *Nirguna Brahman* at the end of the cycle of birth and death. But those who know and understand Nirguna Brahman attain immediate final release or *Moksha*, or *Sayo Mukti*.

Though Shankara was not against *Karma* he said that *Karma* alone cannot destroy ignorance, as it is not in conflict with ignorance.

The ignorant long for results and engages in action with the idea of doership and enjoyment. They in their ignorance think, "I act", "I enjoy" and so on. The ignorant man longing for results engages in action. Shankara said that wisdom alone destroys ignorance as light destroys darkness. Wisdom again is not brought about by any means other than *Vichara* or enquiry. Fire is the direct cause to cooking, similarly, wisdom but not any other form of discipline is the direct cause for liberation. Wisdom or *Jnana* purifies the embodied soul stained by ignorance and it then disappears as the *Kataka* nut powder disappears after cleansing the muddy water.

Constant meditation, like the rubbing of two pieces of firewood kindles the flame of knowledge that completely burns up the fuel of ignorance and destroys the ignorance charecterised by the notions of "I" and "Mine". The yogi, who is endowed with complete enlightenment, sees through the eye of wisdom everything as the self and nothing but the self. Perfect knowledge or wisdom alone can remove the superimposition. According to Vedas perfect knowledge or wisdom consists in the realization of the *Jeevatma* and *Paramatma*. The nature of true knowledge is such that it cuts the very root of egoism and burns all actions to ashes. Then there is neither the doer of actions nor the experiencer of actions. Only with constant practice Atman and true knowledge or wisdom can be realized. So, the one who seeks true knowledge should meditate upon Brahman for attaining the desired goal.

The first step to liberation is extreme aversion to all perishable things. Then come calmness, self-control, forbearance and the utter relinquishment of all Karmas as enjoined by the scriptures. Then comes, hearing, reflection on that, and long constant and unbroken meditation on the Truth.

Creation According to Shankara

About creation, Shankara says that at the pragmatic or *Vyavaharika* level, world is a creation of Ishwara with the divine magic of Maya. But just as his own magic does not fool the magician, Ishwara also is not carried away by His creation. It is His sport. Just as from a conscious being, lifeless objects like hair, nails are formed, and similarly, Ishwara also forms the unreal world. He creates the world by combining the five subtle elements of ether, air, fire, water and earth. Ishwara first created Ether through Maya. Air is created from Ether. From air came free, from firewater came and from water earth was born. From the subtle elements gross elements were created. From the gross elements like gross Space, gross fire and so on were created and finally from the gross elements universe and beings were created. During destruction the trend gets reversed. In part –I chapter-1, in his work titled 'Tattva Bodha', Shankara tells about creation.

Shankara: the Reformist

Shankara denounced the caste system and the unnecessary and meaningless rituals. He did not advocate dogmas. He advocated analysis and reason. He asked the true devotee to meditate upon God the Saguna and to offer his wandering mind to God and Brahman who is only the manifestation of the unmanifest Brahman in form and qualities and attributes, to understand the ultimate truth, that is, obtain Jnana or wisdom through his divine love towards his chosen deity and all His creations and selfless Karmas that have neither the sense of doership nor the craving for their results. In this manner when the mind becomes purified like a mirror then wisdom dawns.

Shankara and Buddhism

Some view that Buddhism has influened Shankara's philosophy. Some even go the extent of stating that his philosophy is nothing but Buddhism in disguise and he himself is a Buddhist in disguise. This is because of some similarities found between his teachings and those of Buddhism. Both the religions accept the view that Reality is beyond name and form although there are differences between these two systems. There are also similar views. For example, the theory of *Maya*, is similar to the Buddhist concept of unreality of Samsara. This criticism may also be due to the fact that the *Mandukya Karika* written by Shankara's *Parama Guru*, (Guru's *Guru*) who was the *Guru* of *Govinda Bhagavad Pada* who was Shakara's *Guru*, shows some familiarity with the Madhyamaka and

Yogacara schools of Buddhism. It is because Gaudapada's Karika was written in the context of Vedantic dialogues with various schools of Mahayana Buddhism particularly the Yogachara and Madhyamaka schools. Both Gaudapada and *Mahayana* Buddhism make use of the metaphor of *Alatacakra-* that is, a burning firebrand waved in a circle, creating an impression of a continuous circle of fire. But the Buddhists use this metaphor to point out that the impression of a continuous circle of fire is an illusion created by the momentary spatial positions of the burning brand. So from a Buddhist's point of view, it is an error to see the burning circle, as having any nature of its own as it is not the nature of firebrand. *Gaudapada* on the other hand stresses that the burning brand of fire is the substratum of its momentary, or temporary spatial positions and the waving of the brand causes the illusion of a burning circle. Even if the burning circle is an illusion, its nature is that of a burning brand.

According to Shankara's commentary of the Karika, Gaudapada used this metaphor and terminology only to arrive at Advaita Vedanthic conclusion about Atman, the substratum of which is Brahman. Gaudapada made use of this terminology of Buddhism like any other classical Indian philosopher just to bring about the similarities and dissimilarities between Buddhism and Advaita Vedanta about the notions around the same concepts used by both. It is also a fact that both Vedanta containing the principles of Advaita Vedanta and Buddhism developed more or less simultaneously and it is only but natural that there might have been some interaction between these two. After all the goal of all doctrines is the same. However, Shankara's Advaita Vedanta differs from Buddhism in very many important details although in both the Yogic practices find a place as in any other school of ancient Indian Philosophy.

One must understand that Shankara explained the theory of *Maya* in the background of the real and ultimate Brahman. According to Advaita *Maya* or ignorance emerges from Brahman. But Buddhism arrived at the changeless deathless Absolute truth after understanding the unreality of *Samsara*. Buddhism questions the eternity of the self. Again Buddhism describes the universe as mere illusion. But Shankara stated that there is phenomenal universe that is experienced although it is not the reality. He did not negate the existence of the universe. But he said that the reality of the universe is only relatively real while Brahman is absolutely real. In Advaita Vedanta Brahman that is the self is eternal, ultimate and non-dual reality. Again, Shankara did not accept many of the views of Bhuddhism. For example he was opposed to the negation of being or *Shoonya Vada*. Shoonyata of Buddhism is also not equivalent to Atman or Brahman of Advaita Vedanta. He categorically opposed the negation of being, void or Shoonyata and pointed out that the unmanifest Brahman manifested itself as Ishwara or God or *Saguna Brahman*. He also firmly believed that the unmanifest Brahman manifested as Ishwara or God, the loving perfect being, who is seen by the devotees in the form of Lord Shiva, Vishnu and so on.

The Madhyamikas who belonged to Mahayana Buddhism developed the theory of Shoonya vada. While the shoonya vada is neither real nor false, Brahman is infinite truth, infinite consciousness and supreme Bliss. Agin Soul is believed to be false in Buddhism but in Advaita soul is taken to be real. Further if Shoonya is interpreted as void then it leads to the conclusion that the world also evolved from void. But according to Advaita, the manifest world evolved from Brahman the unmanifest. The Madhyamikas also do not believe in personal God whereas in Advaita, Ishwara or personal God is a manifestation of the unmanifest Brahman. To Madyamaka non-duality is in terms of emptiness or Shoonyata. But according to Advaita Vedanta view of non-duality, phenomenon arises due to *Atma*, the pure consciousness that is Absolute. Shankara says, that the shoonya vada "being contradictory to all valid means of knowledge, we have not thought it worth while to refute".

Misconceptions about Shankara's Interpretations

About Upanishads, it is said, that they give contradictory statements that may give rise to confusion but then, these contradictory statements refer to the different levels of consciousness. It is true in the case of Shankara's interpretation of the philosophy of Advaita vedanta as well. For example in his treatise 'Aparokshanubhuti or self realization Shankara says that the means to obtain wisdom are got by praying to Hari, through austerities and performance of duties as per one's social order and stage of life. In the same treatise he also says that *Vichara* is the only means to attain knowledge and the way to *Vichara* is through self-enquiry. These statements may look contradictory to an ordinary person. But these contradictory statements as in the case of Upanishads relate to different levels of consciousness.

Again in one of his philosophical treatises 'Sadhana Panchaka', Shankara gives the various spiritual practices that a Sadhaka should go through in that, the first step is studying the spiritual scriptures, then, performing all *karmas* as prescribed in the scriptures, then, worship of God through *karmas*, then, making mind detached from actions born out of desires, then, dedication of all actions to God, then, have a firm resolve to attain knowledge, then, leaving the house and going to a place where there is a conducive atmosphere for spiritual *Sadhana*, then, seek *Satsang*, then, have an unwavering faith in God, then, practice qualities like tranquility of mind, control of senses, cessation from all worldly activities, power of faith in God, *Guru* and scriptures, and Atman and one pointedness of mind on Atman, and gain knowledge about the imperishable Brahman and the Mahavakyas of the Upanishads from the *Guru*, one should then continue with the *Sadhana* until he gets over the idea of ' I am the body' and gets the firm conviction that 'I am Brahman'. Then he should refrain himself from all unnecessary arguments and he should lean upon the Upanishads and engage himself in self-enquiry on the lines of Sruti. From this it is clear that the different practices are to be followed at different levels of spirituality attained by the spiritual aspirants.

Further it must be understood that many of the ancient Indian-Hindu scriptures were written either in Vedic or classical Sanskrit. In modern times only very few know to read and write and also understand the writings in this language. So translations have become a necessity in modern times to spread the contents of these ancient Srutis and Smritis of India. So, the confusion and misunderstandings are also due to lack of proper accurate and correct equivalent words in different languages that can convey the correct and exact meanings conveyed in the original writings in Sanskrit language or may also due to lack of proper knowledge on the part of those who translate the original works about the words in other languages that can convey the exact meanings. For example, usually the Sanskrit words 'Jnana' and 'Manas' are translated as knowledge, and mind. How far these translations are accurate and correct is questionable. More than anything, no translated version can ever become equal to the original work as translations have limitations.

It is said that Shankara's philosophy is dry and lacks human touch because he gives importance only to wisdom or *Jnana* but not to *Bhakti* or *Karma.* This notion is because Shankara stresses on *Paramatman* or *Parabrahman*, the supreme Brahman that is devoid of form, name, and qualities or attributes that could be understood ultimately through *Jnana*. But one must understand that Shankara never underestimated the role of *Bhakti* or *karma* in obtaining the ultimate knowledge through self-experience. He only stated that studying and understanding scriptures and performing Vedic rites and rituals alone would not pave the way for the realization of Truth. Shankara himself was a staunch devotee. He composed several hymns in praise of his chosen Deities. He composed hymns on Lord Shiva, Vishnu, Ganesha, Skanda, Lakshmi Narasimha, Godesses like Parvati, Saraswati, Sharada, Bhavani, Tripura Sundari and so on. In all the hymns he saw Brahman through Ishwara.

Shankara's verses are the poetic expressions of deep emotion and love that Shankara experienced towards various Gods, particularly Lord Shiva. Shankara also visited several temples and worshipped the Deities there. It is said that he installed Sri Chakras in several temples including Sri Venkateshwara temple in Tirupati, Kamakshi temple at Kancheepuram, Sri Ranganatha temple at Sri Rangam, Nara Narayan temple at Bhadri and Guhyeshwar temple in Nepal and so on. He also resumed worship in several temples where the rituals were discontinued due to their dilapidated conditions. He could take the masses along with him mainly through *Bhakti* that was suitable to them. *Bhakti* is supposed to be the easiest path in spirituality because it could be followed by any one irrespective of the fact whether one is endowed with the necessary intelligence to understand the spiritual terms and terminology and also the abstract ideas inherent in them. For *Bhakti*, it is enough if one possesses a loving, humble, compassionate heart with love towards the divine. At the level of transcendental consciousness there is no dualism and there is only Brahman, the absolute supreme self. But at the level of dual consciousness there is *Saguna Brahman*, God with form and attributes. This is what Shankara said. When one attains the peak of *Bhakti*, even if he is an illiterate person, the divine grace will make him gain Jnana or wisdom in understanding the eternal truth through intuition. The study of Scriptures teaches the performance of rites and rituals and the greatness of *Bhakti*. Through practice of *Bhakti*, one's mind gets purified and ego less. Similarly Shankara also did not overlook the path of *Karma*, as he himself was a great Karmayogi.

Shankara spent almost his whole life in fulfilling the divine mission for which he was born, and that was to revive Hinduism based on the upanishadic teachings of the Vedas. He traveled to the nook and corner of India on foot with a view to wipe out all misconceptions about the great religion of Hinduism particularly that of the doctrine of Advaita Vedanta. He proved himself not only a great Bhakta or devotee but a *Karma Yogi* as well. Shankara said that *Bhakti* and *Karma* are paths or ways that lead to *Mukti* that is obtained ultimately through *Jnana* or higher level of knowledge that is wisdom. A real *Bhakta* and a real *karma yogi* see one in all. He sees himself in all. He becomes one with all and everything in the universe and through his love he becomes one with all creation and the creator who is none else than Brahman ultimately. Thus Shankara was a *Bhakta* and a *Karma Yogi* in the relative sense. In practical plane of existences, in the phenomenal world Shankara was both a *Bhakta* who believed in *Bhakti* and a Karma yogi both of the highest order that would take one to liberation, It is said that the enlightened ones, for all practical purposes, carry on for a time with dualism. But then it is only for the welfare of mankind.

It is said that once one of the disciples of Shankara was repeatedly saying 'Shivoham', without understanding its real significance. To make his desciple realize, Shankara went to a blacksmith and he drank the molten iron found there. He then asked his desciple to do the same. But the desciple was not able to do that. Then Shankara told him that as far as he is concerned, the molten iron or the icecold water made no difference to him, as he has understood his identity with Shiva. Until the desciple attains that state of knowledge, it is futile on his part to merely repeat Shivoham that means 'I am Shiva'. Shankara emphasized that reason and abstract philosophy would not lead to *Moksha* or liberation.

It is also pointed out that Shankara confuses the common man by saying that the world is both real as well as unreal. The truth is that, Shankara did not deny the material existence of the world that is the world from the relative point of view. To him the phenomenal world does exist but it is not real. A picture that is projected from the projector appears on the screen. Similarly Brahman projects the world. But as soon as the projector stops, the picture also stops and there remains only the white screen. Similarly, as soon as *Maya* that gives rise to ignorance stops the vision of the world also stops and what remains is only Brahman.

The Terms, Gnana, Intelligence, Chit and Chitta, Karma, Bhakti, Desire, Mind and Manas, Gnana and Vijnana in Spirituality

The English translations of many of the Sanskrit terms used in Hindu philosophy and spirituality are confusing many a time, as the English translations do not convey the exact meanings of the terms especially when those Sanskrit terms are used to convey different meanings at different occasions in the scriptures. Especially for an ordinary person the terms that are translated in to English are highly confusing because in most cases only one English meaning is given for any single Sanskrit term while actually the term conveys different meanings at different occasions. Some of such terms that are connected to Advaita philosophy and their possible meanings are taken up here simply to share the views of the author with the readers of this book.

Jnana, Jnana Marga and Vignana: The term *Jnana* is translated as knowledge in English. But in the spiritual context it is more than that. The *Jnana* that we speak in spirituality is *Atma Jnana* that is knowledge of the self or wisdom. Jnana in spirituality does not mean knowledge for worldly things or relating to the phenomenal world that can be termed as lower level of knowledge that makes a person wordly wise. It refers to wisdom, the knowing of the higher level of knowledge that is the knowledge of the ultimate reality. It refers to wisdom or discernment. Wisdom regarding the material things of the world makes a man egoistic, worldly wise and smart enough to be successful in the world, in the ordinary day-to-day life even at the expense of another at times. Such wisdom is not permanent but is only temporary. But Jnana the higher level of knowledge is wisdom born out of the realization of the ultimate, imperishable, supreme Truth as a result of listening to the teachings of a spiritual *Guru*, following the scriptural teachings that are imparted by the *Guru*, contemplating the scriptural teachings of the *Guru* and finally meditating upon them and then understanding them or realizing them by subjective experience. But mere intellectual understanding will not lead to Jnana.

Intelligence or Buddhi helps one to understand the scriptures and the teachings of the *Guru*. But after that the spiritual aspirant ponders over what he has acquired through self-study, then meditating upon that helps him in knowing the real content of the acquired information or knowledge. According to *Sarvasara Upanishad*, *Jnana* is the essence of intelligence that has no beginning or end. Shankara in his 'Tattva Bodha' says that *Jnana* means awareness that the self is changeless. Finally Viveka or discrimination results in Jnana or wisdom. In his work 'Aparokshanubhuti' Shankara says that *Vichara* or self-enquiry is the only means to obtain *Jnana* and he also high lights meditation that is intense and constant and continuous for realizing the supreme truth. Once a person attains wisdom or *Jnana* then scriptural study becomes unnecessary for him because he becomes one who has digested, assimilated, understood the real content of the scriptures and realized experientially, the teachings contained in them.

Jnana Marga is not merely becoming knowledgeable or acquiring and collecting information and becoming a storehouse of information with the aid of *Buddhi* or intelligence. It is a direct Yogic path. It includes study of scriptures, reflection, analysis, meditation, and self-enquiry. It is the path of knowledge of supreme reality or Brahman arrived finally through the process of reasoning and discrimination.

Vijnana refers to the realization of the knowledge that is acquired. It is the spiritual or divine intelligence, the super mind. In ordinary material sense, although the term *Jnana* is referred to as wisdom, the usage *Vijnana* is taken to mean as the result of information given by the lower mind that is bound by senses, that is worldly knowledge. In *Bhagavad Gita* in the chapter on *Jnana- Vijnana* Yoga, Lord Krishna speaks about *Jnana* as Spiritual wisdom and *Vijnana* as understanding or cognition of the ultimate truth and applying it to life. So *Vijnana* refers to the realized or experienced *Jnana* or wisdom. According to some *Jnana* is scriptural knowledge and *Vijnana* is realized, experiential spiritual knowledge. According to Shankara *Jnana* is spiritual knowledge and *Vijnana* is spiritual experience. Sri Ramakrishna Paramahamsa stated that he who has seen milk has *Jnana* where as he who has drunk milk and has been nourished by it has attained *Vijnana.* Again he says that one who has seen fire has *Jnana* but the one who has actually built a fire and cooked on it has *Vijnana.* So understanding the knowledge gathered at the level of the intellect is *Jnana.* The realization of the acquired knowledge at the level of consciousness is *Vignana.* Probably, in the spiritual sense by gaining *Jnana* one becomes a *Jnani* through *Vijnana.*

Intelligence or Buddhi: When Shankara used the term Intelligence or *Buddhi*, he must have denoted, similarly, the higher level of *Buddhi* or intelligence but not the lower level of intelligence. In the material sense, *Buddhi* or intelligence refers to that capacity of an individual to grasp or understand the material knowledge. If a person is worldly wise and safeguards his material interests, and becomes successful in life we categorize that person as intelligent and his success as the result of his intelligence mainly although we also consider him lucky. But then it amounts to lower level of intelligence only. Intelligence or Buddhi, in spiritual sense refers to higher intelligence, the capacity of the brain to understand the real content of the scriptural teachings of the *Guru* and the two fold capacity of the brain namely, Viveka or discrimination and Sad Vidya, that is looking in to the real nature of things. A man who through his Viveka or the capacity to discriminate differentiates between what is really necessary and what is not, and looks in to the real nature of things only can be termed as intelligent from the spiritual point of view. Knowledge that is acquired with the help of intelligence and the capacity to discriminate through Sadhana becomes jnana or wisdom, that is, the knowledge of the ultimate. Vijnana or realisation is experiencing that ultimate. In his 'Viveka Chudamani' Shankara says that Buddhi or intellect is only a reflection of Atman. It is like a chistle to the carpenter. Again he says that bondage or entanglement can be destroyed by the sword of *Jnana* or wisdom that comes out of discrimination coupled with divine grace.

Chit And Chitta: The term chit and chitta also do not convey the same meaning. Brahman is said to be SAT-CHIT- ANANDA. The term Chit here stands for thought free consciousness, which is consciousness beyond thought. It refers to the higher self. It is the universal consciousness. Chitta refers to the lower mind that controls perception, movement, ordinary thought, movement, emotion and so on, the conditioned mind, with deep field of thought. It is the individual consciousness with the unconscious, conscious and sub conscious mind. It belongs to *Manonmaya Kosha.* It has the faculties of memory.

Karma: Karma means external Vedic rituals like Yagas and Yagnas mentioned in the Samhita portion of the Vedas. *Karma* also means the good and bad results of past actions, or it can also mean the performance of actions in the present. When it is said that the *Jnani* performs no *Karmas* it means that there is no need for him to perform external forms of Vedic *Karmas* and also he does not go through or have or bothers about the results of past *Karmas.* External Vedic *Karmas* are intended for the fulfillment of material benefits only and they are of no importance or use for a *Jnani.* As far as *Karma* that refers to the results of past actions are concerned. It is said that the *Jnani* goes beyond all past *Karmas*, because as far as his *Sanchita* or past accumulated *Karmas* are concerned, they are burnt away by his *Jnana* or wisdom, as far as the Agami or future Karmas are concerned, the question of such Karmas does not arise for a *Jnani* because Karmas that are the results of impressions of the mind, for him, are like writings on water that do not leave any marking, and as far as the *Prarabda Karmas*, that are the allotted portion of the past Karmas that are to be gone through even by the *Jnani* in the present birth are concerned, they become immaterial to the *Jnani* because, he, the Jnani goes beyond his attachment to the physical body and mind and therefore nothing affects him physically or mentally because the *Jnani* is one who has disassociated himself from his body and mind. However, as far as Karmas that refer to actions in the present are concerned, even the Jnani has to perform atleast the bare minimum of actions to maintain his life breath as long as he is alive and also actions that are performed by him in the present are meant for the welfare of all beings but not with a view to reap any selfish ends and even such *Karmas* he does without the sense of doership. So even when he performs actions or *Karmas* in this sense, he is not bound by *Karmas*, that is the effect of such actions because he does not even bother about the results of his actions. He performs all *Karmas* in a detached manner. He performs actions as per the demands or requirements of a particular situation. This is what Nishkama Karma means stated by Lord Krishna in Bhagavad Gita.

Shankara in his work 'Tattva Bodha' stresses that one should perform obligatory duties as long as life lasts because only these along with knowledge of the ultimate, that is wisdom, liberates a person. In the same work he also says that in Sruti it is said that renunciation of action is superior to their performance because, to one who is in the spiritual path and who aspires liberation or freedom from the cycle of birth and death, there is no notion that he is the doer of actions and the experiencer of their results. In his 'Viveka Chudamani' Shankara says that selfless actions remove bondage and purify the heart.

Bhakti: Bhakti or devotion in spirituality refers to higher form of devotion in which the devotee has intense, unselfish pure love towards God, the Almighty. The *Bhakta* does not seek for any material comforts or fulfilling any of his desires from God, but in all humility, without any trace of egoism, craves for intense devotion culminating in his merging with the divine, his Deity. Once that stage is attained he gets the *Jnana* that 'All is in him and he is in all' and he sees every one as his own reflection. Thus *Bhakti* paves the way for wisdom or *Jnana*.

Desire: In spirituality it is always said that one should give up desires. But in this sense the term desire refers mainly to the desires for worldly things and comforts and achievements and so on. When one desires for these things then it is only natural that he would not be able to fulfill all his desires. So the unfulfilled desires make him unhappy, frustrated, angry and discontented in life. Such an out come is a great hindrance to spiritual growth, as these would generate great amount of negative energy in one that would hamper spiritual growth. Mind is the origin of desires. The mind that is uncontrolled gives rise to uncontrollable desires. In this the mind becomes the master. But the one who seeks spiritual growth tries to sujugate the mind. He makes his mind his servant that will obey him but not the master that rules over him.

But desires as such are neither good nor bad. Actually, if there is no desire to know the ultimate reality, then there cannot be any spiritual growth. When it is said that the spiritual aspirant should become desireless, it means that the aspirant should become detached or should not be attached or identified with the desires. When one is not identified with the desires he does not get entangled with the desires and hence such desires would not bind him in any way. Desires won't bind a *Jnani* or entangle him in any way. Further his desires are not for selfish ends but for the welfare of all beings. Any unfulfilled desire also will not show their negative results like anger frustration and so on in him because his mind is totally under his control and he knows that he is not the one who desires or fulfills the desires but it is the supreme power that resides in every being.

Mind and Manas: Usually, the term 'Manas' in Sanskrit language is translated as Mind or the faculty of mind in English. However, whether these two terms convey the same meaning or not is questionable. The ordinary meaning of mind refers to the action of the brain involving thought or the thought process. Mind is also stated to be the bundle of thoughts. It is also stated to be the co-ordinating organ of intelligence, thought, understanding, perception and will. It is further defined as that faculty of logical deduction and reasoning and of rational activity and also memory and also remembrance.

The term *Manas* has got different meanings. *Manas* is sometimes stated to be the immortal being. According to one interpretation, the term *Manas* refers to lower mind, the instinctive mind, the sense mind or the empirical mind that is the seat of desire and that governs the sensory and motor organs whereas mind refers to higher *Manas*. According to our ancient seers, *Manas* has four components namely *Manas* that controls the organs of senses and perceptions, that is, the Karmendriyas and *Jnanendriyas*, *Buddhi* that is intellect, *Chitta* that is the discretionary power and *Ahamkara*, that is the ego sense. Probably the four heads of Brahma is symbolic of these four components of *Manas*. These four components in its totality is referred to as *Manas*, that is subtle, and that resides inside one's gross physical body and this *Manas* is activated by that supreme Energy that resides within each and every person. With death only the physical body perishes. The Physical body that is formed with the five elements goes back to the five elements after death whereas the *Manas* continues even after taking a new body until it merges with that supreme energy which the Advaitins call as Paramatma or Para Brahman. *Manas* in Vedic times probably meant individual spirit and basis of speech. In Upanishads *Manas* is associated with speech, breath, and is said to be the intermediate link between the Self and senses. In Darshanas, Manas means a special additional sense organ by which thoughts and sensations have access to Atman.

As per Sankhya philosophy Manas together with intellect or Buddhi and Ahamakara or the ego sense make up the three-fold instrument of Anthakarana. In Buddhist philosophy Manas is the rational or intellectual faculty of the mind. In Pali canon, Manas is synonymous with Vijnana that knows the ultimate, and Manas is also stated to be synonymous with Chitta that is consciousness in Hinduism. Manas in Sanskrit also refers to abstract or higher mind, that is, the principle of creative intelligence. Thus the term Manas conveys different meanings so, probably, it cannot be equated with mind alone. Finally, if Manas in Sanskrit refers to the term Mind in English, then why do Hindus, when they refer to Manas keep their hand pointing towards the heart instead of pointing towards the head, as is the case when we refer to mind. Perhaps, similar to the concepts of higher and lower knowledge, there is also higher and lower *Manas* as well. It is possible that when we say that one should control one's *Manas* and transcend *Manas* to know the ultimate truth, it is meant that one should go beyond the lower, the sensory *Manas* that contains thoughts and emotions relating to the phenomenal world and reach the higher *Manas* that can be equated with Consciousness and then go even beyond consciousness to reach the state of no *Manas* (usually stated as no mind), that is, go beyond consciousness and enter in to pure conscience that is Paramatma or Para Brahman itself.

Bhakti and Karma in Advaita Vedanta

Advaita Vedanta does not deny or belittle *Bhakti* or devotion and *Karma* or action. These are considered as means towards *Jnana* or wisdom. It is proved by the fact that Shankara who is considered as the champion of Advaita Vedanta, besides being a *Jnani* was also a Bhakta as well as a *karma yogi* at the same time.

Bhakti: If Shankara had denied *Bhakti* then he would not have composed so many hymns in praise of the Gods and Goddesses who are considered as Brahman with qualities. He knew that the realization of the ultimate Parabrahman is possible in a direct manner, only for those few who are on the spiritual path, the *jnanis* or people with wisdom, who have gone beyond mind that creates the world, the objects, the relationships, the desires and disappointments, the pleasures and miseries and so on and for whom the world is only an illusion. But the majority belongs to the category of those for whom the world is real and have the notions of 'I', 'mine', 'me', 'you' and 'yours' and so on and who experience the resultant sorrows and miseries of life. As long as one considers the phenominal world to be real, he follows Saguna Aradhana or the worship of Brahman with qualities, in the forms of Gods and Goddesses who are viewed as different from him.

Shankara while composing the Stotras represented the ordinary human being with all his miseries and struggles of life and who approaches his chosen deities for blessings and protection from all sorrows of life. Through his prayers he unburdens all his tensions, worries and so on at the feet of the Lord and feels relieved as he has the firm faith that his chosen Deity will not let him down at any time and will always come as his saviour. As *Bhakti* becomes intense, the devotee's love and devotion reach a peak and become selfless and the *Bhakta* asks from his Deity nothing except total devotion and selfless love that seeks nothing in return. At this stage he becomes a real *Bhakta*, and he gets the necessary *Jnana* that he and his Deity are not different from each other and that they are one and the same and at this stage he sees everything and every one in him and himself in every being and in everything and he becomes a Jnani or a realized being. In this manner, *Bhakti* becomes a path towards jnana or wisdom. Shankara himself through his stotra 'Bhaja Govindam' stressed the need for *Bhakti* to attain enlightenment. In that hymn he asks not to merely repeat the words 'everything is Brahman' or 'I am Brahman' without understanding and realization but instead seek divine protection from God. In his work entitled '*Viveka Chudamani*' Shankara says, among all factors that are required for obtaining liberation, devotion or *Bhakti* that is intense longing to know one's real self is the most important. He further says that devotion is seeking divinity that is one's own inherent nature.

Karma: Karma or action that is physical, mental and emotional has a significant place in Advaita Vedanta. *Karma* also refers to outward forms of Vedic sacrifices and yagnas that are performed with a view to gain some material benefits. But the *jnani* is one who aspires for no material things or pleasures of life. So it becomes unnecessary for him to perform such actions. But even a *Jnani*, for whom the world is not real but only has relative existence, has to perform atleast a certain amount of *Karmas* that refer to actions to maintain his life breath and for the welfare of all beings in the world. Shankara was a *Karma Yogi* in this sense. His life as a wandering monk proved this fact. He went from place to place during his *Dig Vijaya*, entered in to debates and discussions, won over the scholars belonging to other religions and sects, unified all theistic sects, condemned blind superstions and inhuman practices in the guise of Hindu religion, educated people about true Vedic Dharma, established Mutts to spread the philosophy of Advaita Vedanta, visited many temples and performed worship, revived rituals as per Vedic Dharma in many temples where worship and rituals were discontinued, reconstructed the dilapilated temples, composed Stotras in praise of Deities, composed *Prakarana Grantha* that are the philosophical treatises that explained the great philosophy of Advaita Vedanta, wrote *Bhashyas* or commentaries on *Prasathana Traya* and some of the other great Hindu scriptures and so on. He performed all these *Karmas* or actions only for the welfare of all.

When it is said that *Karmas* will not lead to enlightenment or liberation it only means that one cannot liberate himself from the cycle of birth and death by merely performing actions with selfish motive, with a desire for their results and also with a sense of doership. But an enlightened being performs actions in an unselfish manner for the welfare of all beings, without the sense of doership and without aspiring for any selfish ends. He does all actions with great involvement but without any entanglement. He performs actions like an actor who enacts a role in a drama on the stage. He knows that he only acts in a play that lasts only for a short period of time. But he does his act in total involvement so that he can give his best and the spectators can get the best out of him. He lives that moment without bothering about the results of his performance. At the same time he does not get entagled in the role. He never bothers about the results of his performance. He is only bothered about the present, the moments when he is on the stage acting. Since he has no future expectations for his acts, he becomes totally free without any binding or entaglement and so he is able to perform his role without any tension or worry and in this process he is able to bring forth the best in him. When even an ordinary person performs actions in this manner then gradually he becomes a pure being because to him all are one. He devotes his very life for the performance of actions that will promote human welfare as a whole and in the process he becomes a *Jnani* or a realized soul for whom everything and everyone is the same but not different. In short he becomes the one who understands that everything is Brahman or the universal consciousness. Thus Karma becomes a means to Jnana or wisdom.

Advaita Vedanta and Modern Science

The philosophy of Advaita Vedanta can also be explained scientifically showing where modern science and spirituality meet. According to modern science everything in this universe comes out from energy and ultimately goes back to energy. The *Rishis* of yore stated the same fact in another way. They said that the universe is nothing but the manifestation in form of the formless Chaitanya that the Advaitins termed as *Para Brahman* or Paramatma that is the universal soul.

In modern Science, the relationship among mass, frequency, and energy is formulized as equations by Plank and Einstein and the equations suggest that the whole universe blend in to a one that exhibits itself as many, namely, mass, energy, waves and so on. This is similar to Advaita Vedanta that everything in the universe is only a manifestation of that one 'Brahman'.

The great modern scientist Einstein established that E== MC2 where E = energy, M=mass of a particle and C== Speed of light. This means that mass and energy are different manifestations of the same energy. According to the Plancks equation,

$$E == hv,$$

where E== energy of a wave, h== Planck's constant and v=frequency of the wave length.

When the two equations are combined, we get.

$$Mc2=hv$$

It relates the mass of a particle to frequency, that is, anything that is material has an associated wavelength called DeBrogile waves. That means matter is another form of waves and waves another form of energy and so on. It also means that the whole universe merges in to that one that exhibits itself as many such as mass, energy, wave and so on. Ultimately everything in this universe is only one single energy. Advaita Vedanta also points out that everything is the manifestation of one single reality or single absolute energy, or the ultimate truth called Brahman- that is omnipotent, omnipresent and omniscient.

The unified field theory in Physics also attempts to develop a theory that is grounded in the belief that all physical phenomenons should ultimately be explained by some underlying unity. This is the view of Advaita Vedanta as propounded in the Upanishads. Einstein wrote, " He (referring to humans), experiences himself, his thoughts and feelings as something separated from the rest, a kind of optical delusion of his consciousness. The delusion is a kind of prison for us, restricting us to our personal desires and to affection for a few persons nearest to us. Our task must be to free ourselves from this prison by widening our circle of compassion to embrace all living creatures and the whole of nature in its beauty". The delusion mentioned here is what is termed as Avidya in Advaita Vedanta. Once the delusion vanishes knowledge dawns says Advaita Vedanta. Again Einstein the greatest scientist of the 20th century said, "Try and penetrate with our limited means the secrets of nature and you will find that, behind all the discernible concatenations there remains something subtle, intangible and inexplicable". The 'subtle', 'intangible' and 'inexplicable' mentioned here correspond to Brahman the ultimate truth of Advaita Vedanta.

Relevance of Shankara's Philosophy in Modern Times

Shankara's philosophy of Advaita Vedanta can be summed up in one of his famous sentences found in the Prakarana Grantha of Viveka Chudamini. It says, "Brahmam Satyam Jagat Mithya, Jeevo Brahmaiva Na Aparah". It means Brahman alone is real. This world is Maya or unreal. The individual soul is not different from Brahman. World is *Maya* and therefore is not real. It is unreal also because *Maya* or ignorance is not eternal. Once, the knowledge of the real dawns, then *Maya* disappears. But it is relatively real in the sense that it exists for one one until the knowledge about Brahman dawns. Similarly is with *Jeeva*. It appears independent due to *Avidya*. Once the ultimate and real knowledge dawns *Jeeva* gets merged with Brahman without any separate identity. It is like the bubble becoming one with the ocean when it bursts or the space inside the pot merging with the infinite space outside, with the universal ether once the pot is broken into pieces. Thibaut said, "The doctrine advocated by Shankara is from a purely philosophical point of view, and apart from all theological considerations, the most important and interesting one which has arisen on Indian soil; neither those forms of the Vedanta which diverge from the view represented by Shankara nor any of the non vedantic systems can be compared with the so called orthodox Vedanta in boldness, depth and subtlety of speculation".

About what Advaitin calls as Brahman, Vivekananda said, "Brethern, we can no more think about anything without a mental image than we can live without breathing." He added, "by the law of association, the material image calls up the mental idea and *vice versa*— That is why the Hindu uses an external symbol when he worships. He will tell you, it helps to keep his mind fixed on the being to which he prays. He knows as well as you do that the image is not God, is not omnipresent". He further says, "But the Hindu does not stop with this. His ultimate aim is realization of the divine. So he cannot stop with worshipping of images, he must progress further". External worship is not the highest stage. It is the childhood stage in spiritual progress. Mental prayer is the next stage. Then the highest stage is of realization of the ultimate truth, which the Advaitin calls as Brahman. It is like one growing up to become a man after passing through the stage of childhood. But for some it may not be necessary as they go straight to the higher level.

Vivekananda said, 'Inspite of people's curious notions about Advaitism, people's fright about Advaitism, it is the salvation of the world because there in alone is to be found the reason of things. Again he said, 'If a man wants to be rational and religious at the same time, Advaita is the one system in the world for him". He also said that Advaita is the most scientific philosophy. Both science and spirituality are a quest to find out truth but science uses material things of the physical world to find out the truth whereas spirituality makes use of intuition. While science proves its results objectively, spirituality can prove anything through subjective analysis that is beyond reason and is totally based upon intuition. Vivekananda also described Shankara's Advaita as the fairest flower of philosophy that any country in any age has ever produced. He said, "The greatest teacher of the Vedanta philosophy was Shankaracharya. By solid reasoning he extracted from the Vedas the truths of Vedanta, and on them built up the wonderful system of jnana that is taught in his commentaries. He unified all the conflicting descriptions of Brahman and showed that there is only one infinite reality. He showed too that as man can only travel slowly on the upward road all the varied presentations are needed to suit his varying capacity".

Mahatma Gandhi said, "I believe in Advaita. I believe in the essential unity of man and for that matter, all that lives". Pandit Jawaharlal Nehru in his 'Discovery of India', referring to Adi Shankara stated, "He synthesized diverse currents troubling the mind of India and built a unity of outlook. In his life of only 32 years he did the work of many long lives and left such an impression of his powerful mind and rich personality on India that it is very evident right up to this day. He was a curious mixture of philosopher and scholar, agnostic and mystic, poet and saint; practical reformer and able organizer. On the popular plane he destroyed many a dogma and opened the door of his philosophical sanctuary to everyone who was capable of entering it irrespective of caste and creed ". Dr Radha Krishnan in his book on 'Indian Philosophy' says, "It is impossible to read Shankara's writings, packed as they are with serious and subtle thinking without being conscious that one is in contact with a mind of a very fine penetration and profound spirituality. With his acute feeling of the immeasurable world, his stirring gaze in to the abysmal mysteries of spirit, his unswerving resolve to say neither more not less than what could be proved; Shankara stands out as a heroic figure of the first rank in the somewhat motley crowd of the religious thinkers of medieval India. His philosophy stands out complete, needing neither a before nor an after. It expounds its own presuppositions, is ruled by its own end and holds all its elements, in a stable, reasoned equipoise". Bhagavan Ramana Maharshi said that Shiva appeared in the form of Shankara for leading the people to ultimate bliss and oneness with Brahman that is the ultimate truth of the Universe.

Bibliography

Aiyar, R. Krishnaswami (1978). *Outlines of Vedanta*, Bombay: Chetana.

Arapura, J.G. (1986). *Hermeneutical Essays on Vedaantic Topics*, Delhi: Motilal Banarsidass.

Atmananda, Swami (1960). *Sri Shankaracharya's Teachings in His Own Words*, *Byavan's Book Library*, ed. K.M. Munshi and R.R. Diwakar, Vol. 52. Bombay: Baratya Vidhya Bhawan.

Bahadur, K.P. (1983). *The Wisdom of Vedanta*, New Delhi: Sterling Publishers Private Limited.

Bhattacharya, Krishnachandra (1958). *Studies in Philosophy*, Vol. II. Calcutta: Progressive Publishers.

Central Chinmaya Mission Trust (1990). *Shankara, the Missionary*, Bombay.

Chakravarti, Sures Chandra (1947). *Human Life and Beyond*. Calcutta: University of Calcutta Press.

— (1953). *The Philosophy of the Upanishads*, Calcutta: University of Calcutta Press.

Chattopadhyaya, Debiprasad (1959). *Lokata: A Study in Indian Materialism*, New Delhi: Peoples Publishing House.

Chaudhari, Sures Chandra (1955). *Self and Falsity in Advaita Vedanta*, Calcutta: Progressive Publishers.

Das, Saroj Kumar (1937). *A Study of Vedanta (Sree Gopal Basumalik Fellowship Lectures for 1921)*, 2nd ed. Calcutta: University of Calcutta Press.

Dasgupta, S. (1932). *A History of Indian Philosophy*, 2 Vols. Cambridge: Cambridge University Press.

Datta, D.M. (1963). A Some Realistic aspects of the Philosophy of Shankara@, *Recent Indian Philosophy (Papers Selected from the Proceedings of Indian Philosophical Congress 1925-1934)*, ed. Kalidas Bhattacharyya, Vol. I. Calcutta: Progressive Publishers.

— (1972). *The Six Way of Knowing: A Critical Study of the Advaita Theory of Knowledge*, Calcutta: The University of Calcutta.

Deussen, Paul (1912). *The System of Vedanta*, trans. by Charles Johnson, Chicago: Open Court Publishing Co.

Deutsch Eliot (1962). *Advaita Vedanta: A Philosophical Reconstruction*, 2nd ed. Honolulu: The University Press of Hawaii.

Devaraja, N.K. (1962). *An Introduction to Shankara=s Theory of Knowledge*. Delhi: Motilal Banarsi Dass.

Gambhirananda, Swami (trans.) (1977). *Brahma-Sutra Bhashya*, 3rd edn., Calcutta: Advaita Ashrama.

Geaves, Ron (2002). *From Totapuri to Maharaji: Reflections on a Lineage (Parampara)*. 27th Spalding Symposium on Indian Religions, Oxford.

George, Vensus A. (1998). *Authentic Human Destiny: The Paths of Shankara and Heidegger, Cultural Heritage and Contemporary Change*, ed. George F. McLean, Series III B, South Asia, Vol. I. Washington D.C.: The Council for Research in Values and Philosophy.

Gonda, J.A. (1959). The Original Sense and Etymology of Sanskrit Maya, *Four Studies in the Language of the Vedas*. The Hague: Mouton.

Granthavali, Sri Shankara (1998). *Complete Works of Sri Shankaracharya in the original Sanskrit*, v. 1-10, revised ed., Samata Books, Madras.

Greaves, Ron (2002). *From Totapuri to Maharaji: Reflections on a Lineage (Parampara)*. 27th Spalding Symposium on Indian Religions, Oxford.

Guenon, Rene (1981). *Man and His Becoming According to Vedanta*, trans. Richard C. Nicholson. New Delhi: Oriental Book Reprint Corporation.

Hacker, Paul (1949). *Unterweisung in der All-Einheits-Lehre der Inder: Gadyaprabandha*, L. Röhrscheid, Bonn.

Indich, William M. (1995). *Consciousness in Advaita Vedanta*. Delhi: Motilal Banarsidass Private Ltd.

Ingalls, Daniel H. H. (1954). Shankara's Arguments Against the Buddhists. *Philosophy East and West,* Hawaii: University of Hawaii Press, 3(4), 291-306.

Isayeva, Natalia (1993). *Shankara and Indian Philosophy.* Albany: State University of New York Press (SUNY).

Iyar, K.A. Krishnaswami (1930). *Vedanta: The Science of Reality.* Mardás: Ganesh and Co.

Jagadananda, Swami (trans.) (1979). *Aatmajnaanoopedsha of Shankaracharya.* Madras: Sri Ramakrishna Math.

Keay, John (2000). *India: A History.* New York: Grove Press.

Kottackal, Jacob (1982). *Religion and Ethics in Advaita.* Kottayam: C.M.S. Press.

Leggett, Trevor (1995). *Realization of the Supreme Self: the Bhagavad Gita Yogas,* (translation of Shankara's commentary), Kegan Paul International, London.

Levy, John (1956). *The Nature of Man According to Vedanta.* London: Routledge & Kegan Paul.

— (1970). *Immediate Knowledge and Happiness.* London: Thorsons Publishers Ltd.

Madhava, Vidyaranya (1986). *Shankar Dig-Vijaya,* trans. Swami Japasyananda, 3rd ed. Madras: Sir Ramakrishna Math.

Mahadevan, T.M.P. (1938). *Philosophy of Advaita.* London: Luzac & Company.

— (1954). *Gaudapaada: A Study of Early Advaita.* Madras: University of Madras.

— (1985). *Superimposition in Advaita Vedanta.* New Delhi: Sterling Publishers Private Ltd.

Mahavananda, Swami (trans.) (1975). *Brihadaranyaka Upanishad Bhashya,* 5th ed. Calcutta: Advaita Ashrama.

Malkani, G.R. (1927). *A Study of Reality.* Bombay: The Modern Book Stall.

— (1961). *Metaphysics of Advaita Vedanta.* Amalner: The Indian Institute of Philosophy.

McGlynn, James V. and Paul Mary Farley (1966). *The Metaphysics of Being and God,* New Jersey: Prentice-Hall, Inc. Englewood Cliffs.

Merlin, G.R. (1953). *Vedanta Epistemology*. Lamar: The Indian Institute of Philosophy.

Mudgal, S.G. (1975). *Advaita of Shankara: A Reappraisal*, New Delhi: Motilal Banarasidass.

Mueller, Max (1967). *Three Lectures on the Vedanta Philosophy, The Chowkhamba Sanskrit Studies*, Vol. LVII. Varanasi: The Chowkhamba Sanskrit Series Office.

Murthi, K. Satchidananda (1959). *Revelation and Reason in Advaita Vedanta*. Waltair: Andhra University Press.

Nakamura, Hajime (1983). *History of Early Vedanta Philosophy*, trans. Trevor Leggett, et al., Part I. *Religions of Asia Series*, ed. Lewis R. Lancaster and J.L. Shastri, No. I. Delhi: Motilal Banarsidass.

Nihilananda, Swami (trans.) (1955). *Gaudapadakarika Bhashya and Manduukya Upanishad Bhashya*, Mysore: Sri Ramakrishna Ashrama.

O=Neil, L. Thomas (1980). *Maya in Shankara: Measuring the Immeasurable*. Delhi: Motilal Banarsidass.

Organ, Troy Wilson (1964). *The Self in Indian Philosophy*. London: Mounton & Co.

Pandey, Sangam Lal (1983). *Pre-Samkara Advaita Philosophy*, 2nd ed. Allahabad: Darsan Peeth.

Parthasarathy, A. (1989). *Vedanta Treatise*, 3rd ed. Bombay: Vedanta Life Institute.

— (trans.) (1990). *Aatmaboodha* (Knowledge of the Self), 3rd edn. Bombay: Vedanta Life Institute.

Phadke, Sitarama Mahadeva (1911). *Shankaracharyakrta Upadesashasri, Rasikaranjana Grantha Prasaraka Mandali*, Pune.

Prabhavananda, Swami (1962). *The Spiritual Heritage of India*. London: George Allen & Unwin Ltd.

Prabhavananda, Swami and Christopher Isherwood (trans.) (1970). *Crest Jewel of Discrimination (Viveka-Chudaamani)*, New York: New American Library.

Radhakrishnan S. and Moore C.A., (eds.) (1973). *Source Book in Indian Philosophy*, 5th printing. New Jersey: Princeton University Press.

Radhakrishnan, S. (1928). *Vedanta*. London: Allen and Unwin.

— (1941). *Indian Philosophy*, 2 Vols. London: George Allen & Unwin Ltd.

Ramamurthi A. (1974). *Advaitic Mysticism of Shankara.* West Bengal: The Center of Advanced Study in Philosophy, Vishnu Bharati, Shanti Niketan.

Rambachan, Anantanand (1994). *The limits of scripture: Vivekananda's reinterpretation of the Vedas.* University of Hawaii Press, 125, 124.

Roy, S.S. (1982). *The Heritage of Shankara*, 2nd ed. Delhi: Munshiram Manoharlal Publishers Pvt. Ltd.

Sastri, (Mahadeva). (1961). *Bagavat Gita Bhashaya*, trans. Madras: V. Ramamurthi Sastrulu & Sons.

Sastri, A. Mahadeva (1986). *The Vedanta Doctrine of Sri Shankaracharya*, Delhi: Sri Satgun Publication.

— (1977). *The Bhagavad Gita : with the commentary of Sri Shankaracharya*, Samata Books, Madras.

Sastri, Kokileswar (1926). *An Introduction to Advaita Philosophy.* Calcutta: University of Calcutta Press.

Sastry, K. A. Nilakantha (1976). *A History of South India*, 4th ed., Oxford University Press, Madras.

Sharma, Chandradhar (1962). Chronological Summary of History of Indian Philosophy. *Indian Philosophy: A Critical Survey*, New York: Barnes & Noble. p. vi.

Shastri, P.D. (1911). *The Doctrine of Maya.* London: Luzac and Co.

Sinari, Ramkant A. (1970). *The Structure of Indian Thought.* Illinois: Charles C. Thomas Publisher.

Singh, Ram Pratab (1949). *The Vedanta of Shankara: A Metaphysics of Value*, Vol. I. Jaipur: Bharat Publishing House.

Sinha, Jadunath (1971). *Problems of Post-Samkara Advaita Vedanta.* Calcutta: Sinha Publishing House Pvt. Ltd.

Sircar Mahendranath (1934). *Hindu Mysticism According to the Upanishads.* London: Kegan Paul.

Sircar, Mahendranath (1927). *Comparative Studies in Vedantism.* Bombay: Humphrey Milford.

— (1987). *The System of Vedantic Thought and Culture.* New Delhi: Anmol Publications.

Smart, Ninian (1964). *Doctrine and Argumentation in Indian Philosophy*. London: George Allen & Unwin.

Smet, De R.V. (1953). *The Theological Method of Shankara*, An Unpublished Dissertation Submitted to the Faculty of the Pontifical Gregorian University, Rome, for the Degree of Doctor of Philosophy.

Swami, Tapasyananda (2002). *Shankara-Dig-Vijaya: The Traditional Life of Sri Shankaracharya by Madhava-Vidyaranya*. India: Sri Ramakrishna Math.

Taibaut, George (trans.). (1890). *Sacred Books of the East* [SBE], Vols. XXXIV & XXXVIII, ed. Max Mueller. F. Oxford: The Clarendon Press.

Tapasyananda, Swami (2002). *Shankara-Dig-Vijaya*.

Vidyasankar, S. (2006). *Determining Shankara's Date - An overview of ancient sources and modern literature*.

Vimuktananda, Swami (trans.). (1977). *Aparoksanubhuti (Self-realization)*, Swami Vimuktananda, 5th Impression, Calcutta: Advaita Ashrama.

Warrier, A.G. Krishna (1983). *Shrimad Bhagavad Gita Bhashya of Sri Shankaracharya*, Ramakrishna Math, Madras.

Warrier, E.I. (1990). *Aurobindo=s Integral Yoga and Shankara=s Advaita*. India: Vohra Publishers.

Zimmer, Heinrich (1972). *Myths and Symbols in Indian Art and Civilization*, ed. J. Campbell. New Jersey: Princeton University Press.

Index

V

W

Y

●●●